Service-Learning at the American Community College

COMMUNITY ENGAGEMENT IN HIGHER EDUCATION
Edited by Dan Butin

This series examines the limits and possibilities of the theory and practice of community engagement in higher education. It is grounded in the desire to critically, thoughtfully, and thoroughly examine how to support efforts in higher education such that community engagement—a wide, yet interrelated set of practices and philosophies such as service-learning, civic engagement, experiential education, public scholarship, participatory action research, and community-based research—is meaningful, sustainable, and impactful to its multiple constituencies. The series is by its nature cross-disciplinary and sees its readership across the breadth of higher education, both within student and academic affairs.

Dan Butin is an associate professor and founding dean of the School of Education at Merrimack College and the executive director of the Center for Engaged Democracy. He is the author and editor of more than seventy academic publications, including the books *Service-Learning in Theory and Practice: The Future of Community Engagement in Higher Education* (2010), which won the 2010 Critics Choice Book Award of the American Educational Studies Association; *Service-Learning and Social Justice Education* (2008); *Teaching Social Foundations of Education* (2005); and, most recently with Scott Seider, *The Engaged Campus: Majors and Minors as the New Community Engagement* (2012). Dr. Butin's research focuses on issues of educator preparation and policy, and community engagement. Prior to working in higher education, Dr. Butin was a middle-school math and science teacher and the chief financial officer of Teach For America. More about Dr. Butin's work can be found at http://danbutin.org/.

The Engaged Campus: Certificates, Minors, and Majors as the New Community Engagement
    Edited by Dan Butin and Scott Seider

Engaged Learning in the Academy: Challenges and Possibilities
    By David Thornton Moore

Deepening Community Engagement in Higher Education: Forging New Pathways
    Edited by Ariane Hoy and Mathew Johnson

Turning Teaching Inside Out: A Pedagogy of Transformation for Community-Based Education
    Edited by Simone Weil Davis and Barbara Sherr Roswell

Service-Learning at the American Community College: Theoretical and Empirical Perspectives
    Edited by Amy E. Traver and Zivah Perel Katz

Service-Learning at the American Community College

Theoretical and Empirical Perspectives

Edited by
Amy E. Traver and Zivah Perel Katz

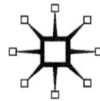

SERVICE-LEARNING AT THE AMERICAN COMMUNITY COLLEGE
Copyright © Amy E. Traver and Zivah Perel Katz, 2014.

All rights reserved.

First published in 2014 by
PALGRAVE MACMILLAN®
in the United States—a division of St. Martin's Press LLC,
175 Fifth Avenue, New York, NY 10010.

Where this book is distributed in the UK, Europe and the rest of the world, this is by Palgrave Macmillan, a division of Macmillan Publishers Limited, registered in England, company number 785998, of Houndmills, Basingstoke, Hampshire RG21 6XS.

Palgrave Macmillan is the global academic imprint of the above companies and has companies and representatives throughout the world.

Palgrave® and Macmillan® are registered trademarks in the United States, the United Kingdom, Europe and other countries.

ISBN: 978–1–137–36170–7

Library of Congress Cataloging-in-Publication Data is available from the Library of Congress.

A catalogue record of the book is available from the British Library.

Design by Newgen Knowledge Works (P) Ltd., Chennai, India.

First edition: October 2014

10 9 8 7 6 5 4 3 2 1

For our students, who deserve the attention

Contents

List of Figure and Tables   xi

Acknowledgments   xiii

Introduction   Service-Learning at the American Community College   1
Amy E. Traver and Zivah Perel Katz

Part I   Service-Learning and Community Colleges

Chapter 1   The Roots of Service-Learning as a Basis for Advancing the Civic Mission of Community Colleges   13
Robert G. Bringle, Kathleen E. Edwards, and Patti H. Clayton

Chapter 2   The Community's College: Contextualizing Service-Learning in the Mission and Development of Community Colleges   37
Vanessa Smith Morest

Part II   Service-Learning in Diverse Community College Contexts

Chapter 3   Hitting Close to Home: When Service-Learners Serve Their Own   53
Heather B. Wylie

Chapter 4   Service-Learning and Immigrant-Origin Community College Students: How and Why Project Design Matters   67
Amy E. Traver, Zivah Perel Katz, and Michael Bradley

Chapter 5   Connecting Past and Present: Nontraditional Learner and Practitioner Experiences through Service-Learning   81
Suzanne M. Buglione and Amanda Wittman

Chapter 6   Race, Ethnicity, and Service-Learning: Understanding Access and Equity Using a Critical Quantitative Approach   95
Drew Allen, Diana Strumbos, and Janelle Clay

Part III Service-Learning and Student Success in Community Colleges

Chapter 7   Service-Learning: A Vehicle for Enhancing Academic Performance and Retention among Community College Developmental Reading and Writing Students   113
Regina A. Rochford

Chapter 8   Connect2Complete: Combining Service-Learning and Peer Advocates to Increase Student Success in Developmental Education   125
Shana Berger and Donna Duffy

Chapter 9   Promoting Community College Student Transfer: The Role of Service-Learning   139
Jaime Lester and Carrie Klein

Chapter 10 The Prism Effect of Service-Learning   155
Mary Prentice and Gail Robinson

Chapter 11 Service-Learning's Role in Achieving Institutional Outcomes: Engagement, Learning, and Achievement   169
Yao Zhang Hill, Tanya Renner, Francisco Acoba, Krista Hiser, and Robert W. Franco

Part IV Service-Learning as Community and Community College Nexus

Chapter 12 Community College Service-Learning Programs: The Well-Traveled Path to Civic Engagement   185
Mary Prentice

Chapter 13 Service-Learning and the Acquisition of Social Capital in the Community College Setting   199
Amy Pucino and Thomas Penniston

Chapter 14 Service-Learning as a Pedagogical Tool for Career Development and Vocational Training   211
Sharon Ellerton, Cristina Di Meo, Arlene Kemmerer, Josephine Pantaleo, Mary Bandziukas, Michael Bradley, and Victor Fichera

Chapter 15 Mapping Routes to Our Roots: Student Civic Engagement in Transportation Planning   225
Rebecca M. Townsend

Part V Future Directions and Considerations in Service-Learning and Service-Learning Research at Community Colleges

Chapter 16 Overcoming Obstacles for Involving Part-Time Faculty in Service-Learning   241
Daniel Maxey and Adrianna Kezar

Chapter 17 Service-Learning among "Nontraditional" College Students:
            Contexts, Trends, and Implications   257
            Shannon S. Fleishman, Kristina Brezicha, and Travis York

Chapter 18 Best Practices in Researching Service-Learning at Community
            Colleges   273
            Amanda Taggart and Gloria Crisp

Part VI Concluding Reflections on Service-Learning and Community Colleges

Chapter 19 The Idea of Place   287
            Scott Evenbeck, Paulette Dalpes, and Linda E. Merians

Chapter 20 There Is a Reason Community Is in Our Name: Thoughts
            on How Service-Learning Expands Community in
            Community College   297
            Robert Exley

Chapter 21 Expanding Faculty Participation and Research in Academic
            Service-Learning at a Community College   305
            Diane B. Call

Chapter 22 Sustaining Momentum   311
            Maria Hesse

Notes on Contributors   319

Index   329

Figure and Tables

Figure

5.1	A Representation of the Characteristics of Nontraditional Students (Buglione 2007)	83

Tables

6.1	Select Characteristics of CUNY Service Corps Applicants and Members	102
8.1	All Possible Combinations of Student Experience with C2C	132
11.1	Seven Principles for Effective Pedagogy and KSLP Aligned Practices	171
11.2	SLO Results for Fall 2012 and Spring 2013 Cohorts ($n = 60$)	177
14.1	Fall 2013 Impact of Service-Learning on CTE Students' Increased Confidence in Workplace Skills	217
14.2	Retention Rates of CTE Students, Service-Learning, and Non-Service-Learning	220
17.1	Inter-Rater Reliability Scores for Coded Nontraditional Student Characteristics ($n = 14$)	261
17.2	Nontraditional Student Characteristics Present in Literature: 2003–2013 ($n = 57$)	263
17.3	Articles That Focus on Nontraditional Students and/or Service-Learning by Sector	264

Acknowledgments

Consistent with its subject, this book was a true community effort. It began with our partnership, forged in 2008 when both of us, faculty members at Queensborough Community College (QCC) of the City University of New York (CUNY), decided to teach a learning community together. Enjoying the experience, we came to adopt service-learning, a pedagogy that was gaining momentum at QCC because of the hard work and advocacy of Jo Pantaleo. We became interested in the study of service-learning through our participation in QCC's service-learning assessment protocol, which was spearheaded by the terrific efforts of Sharon Ellerton and Arlene Kemmerer and supported by a QCC Pedagogical Research Challenge Award. The data that we then gathered led us to a number of presentation opportunities (many funded by QCC's Office of Academic Affairs, Learn and Serve America, and the American Association of Community Colleges), including those to the QCC Fund Board, at an Annual Meeting of the American Association of Community Colleges, and at the annual conference of the International Association for Research on Service-Learning and Civic Engagement, which put us in dialogue with a number of other QCC faculty and staff engaged in and supportive of service-learning, like Nidhi Gadura, Regina Rochford, and Cristina Di Meo. One such presentation, which Amy gave at the inaugural meeting of the mini-conference on community colleges at the Eastern Sociological Society—an effort organized by the always inspiring Lisa Handler, Robin Isserles, and Rifat Salam—led to our meeting Burke Gertenschlager of Palgrave, who initially conceived of and invited this book. Similar acknowledgment is due Dan Butin, whose Palgrave series, 2013 Annual Summer Research Institute on the Future of Community Engagement, and encouragement provided space for this book, and Mara Berkoff and Sarah Nathan at Palgrave, whose patient administrative and editorial guidance helped us to fill this space. Along the way, we also received general support for this book at QCC and across CUNY from: our department chairs Joseph Culkin and David Humphries; our college president Diane B. Call; CUNY's Office of the Vice Chancellor for Research; and two rounds of Professional Staff Congress-CUNY Research Award Program funding support. Finally, we must recognize Gail Robinson and Edward Zlotkowski, whose help led to our meeting many of the book's contributors, and, of course, our contributors (and their students), who put their hearts and words on the page. Thank you all.

From Amy's perspective, this book would not have been possible without the professional mentoring, pedagogical partnership, and friendship of Zivah, who committed much of her research sabbatical and first year of parenthood to this effort. Her poise and cleverness never cease to amaze, and her cooperative spirit and good humor make just about anything possible. Equally central to this project were my students, whose lives, lessons, and good work made their absence from the literature both glaring and frustrating. In them resides the potential and inspiration for significant, necessary social change. Also important was the support of my parents, brother, friends, and colleagues, who knew when to ask about the book—and when not to ask about the book. At the heart of it all, however, were Raenen and Darrin, who evidenced and deserve only the best aspects of community: safety, support, connectedness, trust. And, of course, love.

From Zivah's perspective, Amy was an irreplaceable partner in this project. It was my learning community with her that introduced me to service-learning and gave me the confidence to embrace a new pedagogy. Amy works passionately and tirelessly on all that she takes on, and her energy, insight, and skill as an editor were essential to this book. I have the utmost admiration of her as a scholar, colleague, parent, and friend. The members of the QCC English Department have made the college a second home for me, and I appreciate their kindness, generosity, and collegiality. Every day my students remind me why our first responsibility as academics is to them. They trust us with their education and they give us so much of themselves in their work. What we share over the course of the semester is rewarding, challenging, thought-provoking, and beautiful. My father and sister provide more support than either of them know. Every day they show me how to do better. And to Seth and Ezra—thank you. Our family is my most important work and I love you both.

INTRODUCTION

Service-Learning at the American Community College

Amy E. Traver and Zivah Perel Katz

The American community college (also known as the junior college, the people's college, or democracy's college) is an open-enrollment, regionally accredited institution of higher education that offers terminal vocational programs and college preparatory programs culminating in an associate degree (Cohen and Brawer 2008; Brint and Karabel 1989). A modern American educational innovation, the community college serves as a primary, but often overlooked, gateway to higher education for Americans and students from across the world. In fact, at the time of writing, America's community college system consists of more than 1,100 institutions that provide educational access to nearly one out of every two undergraduates in the United States (American Association of Community Colleges 2014).

Although more than 12 million people are enrolled in the nation's community college system (American Association of Community Colleges 2014), these students—as a group—challenge many of the commonly held assumptions about undergraduates.[1] For example, when compared to their baccalaureate-seeking counterparts, who are frequently considered the norm in higher education, community college students are more likely to be older, working, parenting, low-income, female, of color, and of first-generation college and/or American status (Cohen and Brawer 2008; Bragg 2001; Baker and Velez 1996). These students turn to community colleges for a variety of reasons: an affordable, local college education; help in achieving immediate and/or long-term career goals; access to developmental (or remedial) assistance and coursework; and professional or technical training. They find, in return, the institutional fluidity and flexibility, small class sizes, college-community connections, experiential and/or vocational learning opportunities, and constructivist pedagogies that make these institutions unique (Bragg 2001).

Service-learning is one constructivist pedagogy that is increasingly employed at community colleges. Data from three national surveys conducted by the American Association of Community Colleges (AACC) indicate that "nearly 60 percent of all [American] community colleges offer service-learning in their curricular programs" and that "another 30 percent of [American community] colleges are interested in starting service-learning initiatives" (American Association of Community Colleges 2012a). While defined in a variety of ways, service-learning is broadly characterized as a pedagogical technique that combines organized service meeting a community need with reflective class-based learning. These two foci—*community* and *learning*—make specific sense in the community college context.

From its founding in 1901, the American community college has been defined by its placement in and relationships to the college's surrounding community (Prentice 2000). For example, as open-enrollment institutions of higher education, community colleges are community institutions: they tend to enroll students from the community, and they tend to certify and graduate students who return to and settle in that community (Cohen and Brawer 2008). In fact, Robinson and Barnett (1996) found that more than 70 percent of community colleges claim an institutional commitment to community, a commitment that is frequently expressed in the college's mission statement (Prins 2002; see also Berson 1994). As a result, community colleges are often positioned at the forefront of local community development initiatives (Barnett 1996): reskilling community members during periods of economic transition; serving local businesses with customized training programs for new and existing employees; and educating new and traditionally underserved community members toward individual betterment, civic integration, and democratic participation (Bailey and Morest 2003).

Yet, the American community college is also defined by an institutional commitment to student learning (Prentice 2000). Significantly, the nation's first community colleges were created to both divest research-intensive baccalaureate-granting institutions of their responsibilities to first- and second-year students and expand educational access to students who might otherwise be excluded from higher education (Mellow and Heelan 2008; Brint and Karabel 1989). As a result, community colleges have a long history of privileging student learning over other competing concerns in higher education and of innovating curricula and pedagogies for the success of diverse and frequently marginalized undergraduates.

Consistent with the growing number of community colleges that use the pedagogy, research indicates that service-learning can have a profound impact on communities (Simmons 1998) *and* student learning (see, for example, Kuh 2008; Ash, Clayton, and Atkinson 2005). Unfortunately, however, the bulk of this research has focused on baccalaureate-granting institutions, not on community colleges. According to Kozeracki (2000), analyses of service-learning at community colleges are limited, with most conforming to one of two types: "prescriptive" articles or monographs that provide guidelines on how to initiate a service-learning program or project at a community college; and "descriptive" articles or monographs that detail the structure and participation levels of community college service-learning programs (54). Missing, of course, are "critical analys(es)" of service-learning as it unfolds in the community college context (54). Writing more than ten years after

Kozeracki, Taggart and Crisp (2011) confirm this assessment in their own review of the literature on service-learning at community colleges; they, too, find "little formal analysis of service learning programs at the community college level" (26).

The lack of "critical" or "formal" analyses of service-learning at community colleges is a problem for three reasons. The first reason relates to community colleges as responsible community and educational institutions. According to Taggart and Crisp (2011), there is significant evidence that college students' experiences and outcomes differ according to institutional type. As a result, to best deliver on the promises of service-learning, community colleges must draw on comprehensive and contemporary service-learning research that has been conducted at the appropriate institutional level (Marti 2009).[2] The second reason relates to the future of service-learning as a field of inquiry (Butin 2010a) and a pedagogical practice. Service-learning claims lack external validity and theoretical generalizability when left untested in and across diverse institutions and student populations (Taggart and Crisp 2011). Consequently, to move the field and practice forward, scholars and practitioners must evaluate how service-learning unfolds in its many contexts. The third and final reason relates to trends in higher education enrollment. While approximately half of all American undergraduates are currently enrolled in a community college, this percentage is likely to increase with federal efforts to improve college attainment and individual/family efforts to control rising college costs (American Association of Community Colleges 2012b).[3] Yet, even before they reach a numerical majority, community college students personify important contemporary trends in higher education enrollment, specifically the growing number of students who are aged 24 or older, attending college part-time, financially independent and/or caring for others, commuting, in need of developmental coursework, and of diverse socioeconomic and racial-ethnic backgrounds (Deil-Amen 2011; see also Azziz 2014). If the needs and realities of these students are not made central to service-learning practice and research at *all* levels of higher education, then the pedagogy risks irrelevance.

This book represents one effort to speak to the lack of "critical" or "formal" analyses of service-learning at the American community college. In it we present theoretically informed empirical research studies conducted at single and multiple institutions by service-learning practitioners, service-learning program administrators, and experts in service-learning research and evaluation. Whether read individually or together, these studies stand to benefit service-learning efforts across disciplines and institutional types.

Chapter Outlines

The book is split into six parts. Part I, "Service-Learning and Community Colleges," serves as the theoretical and historical foundation for the book. Part II, "Service-Learning in Diverse Community College Contexts," addresses the diverse student population of the community college and how service-learning can uniquely engage these students. Part III, "Service-Learning and Student Success in Community Colleges," demonstrates service-learning's contribution to community college students' academic success. Part IV, "Service-Learning as Community and Community College Nexus," explores how service-learning strengthens the connections between community college students and the communities in which they live, work, and learn. Part V, "Future Directions and Considerations in Service-Learning and Service-Learning Research at Community Colleges," invites new analyses of service-learning given significant changes in the organization and composition of higher education institutions. Part VI, "Concluding Reflections on Service-Learning and Community Colleges," draws on the perspectives of current and former community college presidents (and administrators) to promote the practice, institutionalization, and study of service-learning.

Part I builds on the ideas presented in this introduction to further ground and support the book. In chapter 1, Bringle, Edwards, and Clayton explore service-learning as a pedagogy, delving specifically into its historical development, contemporary analyses of its impacts on student learning, and the ways in which both relate to and play out in the community college context. While their focus on evidence is significant at all levels of higher education, the authors' suggestions for future service-learning research identify community colleges as significant sites of/for study.

In chapter 2, Morest reviews the history and multiple missions of the community college to ground the institution's broad adoption of pedagogies of engagement like service-learning. Morest also describes the community college student body, highlighting students' needs and strengths as well as the institutional initiatives designed for their success. In general, her chapter makes a strong case for viewing service-learning as both a symbol of and a tool in the open-access mission of community colleges.

While Butin (2010b, 31) argues that service-learning research and practice tends to assume that service-learners are "white, sheltered, middle-class, single, without children, unindebted, and between the ages of 18–24," Morest identifies community colleges as higher education institutions that, by virtue of their open-enrollment policies, serve a disproportionate number of racial/ethnic minority, low-income, adult, and/or immigrant students. As a result, Part II of this book considers service-learning in diverse community college contexts.

In chapter 3, Wylie critiques one of the classic assumptions of service-learning theory: that service-learners have little in common with the individuals and communities they "serve." Drawing on qualitative data gathered in her work at Shasta College, a California community college, Wylie demonstrates how the "server/served" binary falls apart in community colleges, and how the absence of this binary actually *enhances* learning, encouraging community college students to integrate their multiple identities, think critically about the structural nature of the problems they confront, and become agents in their own college trajectories and contexts. In light of these findings, her chapter encourages service-learning practitioners and researchers to consider how institutional context and student demographics shape the form and effects of the pedagogy.

In chapter 4, Traver, Katz, and Bradley build on Wiley to explore how service-learning projects that engage immigrants/immigrant communities unfold at community colleges that enroll a significant percentage of immigrant-origin students. By comparing the results of two different service-learning projects at a community college in the City University of New York, they reveal how project design matters to student outcomes, particularly when that project references students' social positions as immigrants or members of immigrant families/communities. While this finding likely translates to other service-learning projects that blur the "server/served" binary, it also infers the need for careful, comparative design of service-learning projects more generally.

While service-learning is often characterized as a means to bridge the town-gown divide, chapters 3 and 4 show how the pedagogy helps community college students integrate their oft-divided college and community selves. In chapter 5, Buglione and Wittman provide additional evidence for this claim. Using data gathered from two studies of nontraditional students and their faculty, the authors demonstrate how service-learning experiences bolster nontraditional learners' student identities and connect their experiences across multiple worlds. Focusing on the unique strengths and needs that nontraditional students bring to service-learning, and how these strengths and needs are met by faculty, Buglione and Wittman provide insight into the ways in which service-learning can be improved for nontraditional students across institutional types.

Chapter 6 concludes Part II with a call for service-learning program directors and researchers to move beyond considering students' demographic information as simple predictors of their service-learning experiences and outcomes. Instead, Allen, Strumbos, and Clay argue for the use of a critical quantitative approach, where directors and researchers use student information to proactively address issues of equity and access in service-learning program development, implementation, and evaluation. To demonstrate, they show how this approach has informed the rollout of CUNY Service Corps, a new service program at the City University of New York. Yet, in this chapter, the authors do more than complicate and expand the way students' demographic information can be defined/used in service-learning research and practice; they also reveal how an institutional commitment to access and equity in service-learning might require new conceptualizations of "service" and "learning."

In light of this diversity, Part III of the book examines how service-learning might promote the academic success of *all* community college students. Research reveals the many barriers community college students face in their paths to academic success, including academic and financial barriers (Goldrick-Rab 2010). While the goals of the students attending community college differ as widely as their backgrounds—and therefore the term "success" should be thought of in the broadest sense—community colleges must find ways to aid these students in achieving their goals.

In chapter 7, Rochford examines the relationship between service-learning and academic performance and retention among developmental reading and writing students. She studies 15 individual developmental reading and writing courses offered at Queensborough Community College of the City University of New York to reveal higher academic achievement and retention among courses that include a service-learning component. Rochford also shows how service-learning assignments for developmental students must be directly connected to course curricula, include multiple experiences performing tasks, and place students in community-based organizations that are appropriate for their level of literacy. Given the large number of developmental students at community colleges, Rochford's insights stand to benefit a significant section of the population that faces many challenges in terms of academic success.

Berger and Duffy also address the developmental responsibilities of community colleges. In chapter 8, they introduce a new program, Connect2Complete, which pairs peer advocates with service-learners to increase student success in developmental education. In reviewing the theories that ground the Connect2Complete program, describing the program's parts and implementation, and studying how and why the program works, Berger and Duffy identify a number of strategies that community colleges can use to minimize the barriers faced by economically disadvantaged developmental students. They also explore how community colleges might best encourage developmental students' full participation in their various communities.

In chapter 9, Lester and Klein theorize the role of service-learning in promoting community college students' transfer to four-year colleges and universities, as well as their eventual baccalaureate achievement. Acknowledging that rates of student transfer are too low given students' aspirations and the national completion agenda, they integrate the literature on student transfer, engagement, and co-curricular experiential learning to create a model of student transfer success through service-learning. As many students see community colleges as a path to enrollment at and graduation from a baccalaureate-granting institution, Lester and Klein's work addresses a central function of the community college sector.

Chapter 10 explores additional definitions and measures of student success in community colleges. Prentice and Robinson use their research from AACC Learn and Service America grantee colleges to study: (1) the effects of service-learning on student civic engagement; (2) the effects of service-learning on academic learning outcomes; and (3) the effects of service-learning on retention and persistence. Their findings reveal what Prentice and Robinson call the "prism effect" of service-learning: students who participate in service-learning experience a wide range of professional, academic, and personal benefits, including many cited in the research on service-learning *and* many that are unintentional. Their chapter makes a strong argument for service-learning's multifaceted influence on student success.

In chapter 11, Hill, Renner, Acoba, Hiser, and Franco end Part III by describing the cycle of pedagogical innovation, implementation, and evaluation in service-learning that has been in place at Kapi'olani Community College since 1995. The evaluation framework that the Kapi'olani team uses is the "KELA model"—Kapi'olani Engagement, Learning and Achievement model. This model demonstrates how a community college can most effectively organize and utilize internal service-learning research to form a coherent understanding of the relationship between service-learning and various measures of student success. The authors' suggestions for evaluating service-learning programs on community college campuses are sure to be of value to student-success initiatives at all levels of higher education.

Part IV focuses on one specific area of student development through service-learning, community participation and civic engagement. According to the Civic Learning and Democratic Engagement National Task Force (2011), institutions of higher education need to "embrace civic learning and democratic engagement as an undisputed educational priority...where education for democracy and civic responsibility is pervasive, not partial; central, not peripheral" (6). Community colleges, by mission, embrace the promotion of civic engagement among their students, and service-learning is an important contribution to that mission.

In chapter 12, Prentice examines the relationship between service-learning and civic engagement. Drawing on data collected through pre- and post-course civic engagement surveys that were implemented at a number of community colleges during three years of AACC research, she reveals how students develop civic knowledge and commitment through service-learning. By further exploring the impact of multiple service-learning experiences on this development, Prentice also makes a strong case for longitudinal research on and the longitudinal impacts of service-learning pedagogy.

Building on these insights, Pucino and Penniston focus on one effect of students' increased civic engagement: social capital development. In chapter 13, they use data gathered through semistructured interviews with community college students to explore how service-learning facilitates students' acquisition of social capital (i.e., resources that benefit students). This analysis helps to establish the tangible benefits of service-learning to community college students, specifically the formal and informal relationships they develop with faculty and community partners, and the resources—like recommendation letters and information on academic and community programs—they glean therein.

In chapter 14, Ellerton, Di Meo, Kemmerer, Pantaleo, Bandziukas, Bradley, and Fichera examine service-learning's impact on community college students in career and technical education. Analyzing mixed-methods data collected from career and technical courses that incorporated service-learning at Queensborough Community College of the City University of New York, they reveal that service-learning helps students develop the "soft skills" needed to enter the job market. Their results illustrate how service-learning both benefits a significant subset of the community college student population and helps to integrate the multiple missions of the community college.

While chapters 12, 13, and 14 reveal how service-learning experiences can encourage students' civic and professional engagement, chapter 15 concludes part IV by demonstrating how these experiences might also improve public policy. Townsend begins the chapter with an introduction to her "Partnership for Inclusive, Cost-Effective Public Participation" project, which draws on a variety of theoretical frameworks to encourage the participation of marginalized communities in public policy development. Demonstrating how this project, which was financially supported by the Federal Transit Administration, made use of community college students' strengths and networks to improve transportation in the greater Hartford, Connecticut region, Townsend provides a real model for turning the abstract concept of student engagement into unique, practical contributions to local communities.

Part V shifts the book's attention to higher education as a sphere for engagement in its own right. More specifically, it focuses on future considerations in service-learning practice and research given organizational and compositional changes occurring at community colleges and across institutions of higher education. In chapter 16, Maxey and Kezar explore how the growing number of part-time faculty impacts service-learning programs at community colleges. To do so, they provide an important review and contextual analysis of the institution's reliance on part-time faculty, as well as a summary of the strengths of and impediments to part-time faculty participation in service-learning. The authors' case study of Florida's Tallahassee

Community College reveals how institutions can proactively harness these strengths, alleviate or eliminate these impediments, and institutionalize the participation of part-time faculty in service-learning. Their findings serve as a blueprint for engaging part-time faculty in all high-impact practices for student success.

In chapter 17, Fleishman, Brezicha, and York consider the extent to which demographic changes within today's college-going student population are reflected in service-learning practice and research. In their content analysis of the service-learning literature, the authors both employ and deconstruct the umbrella category "nontraditional students," which is frequently used to capture the diversity of American undergraduates today. Revealing the theoretical and empirical limitations of "nontraditional students," they engage four more experientially valid student categories (i.e., nonwhite students, adult students, working students, and students with limited forms of capital) to evidence the dearth of research on diverse students' service-learning experiences. Their recommendations for service-learning practice with and research on these increasingly typical undergraduates will prove valuable at all levels of higher education.

Part V draws to a close with more general information on best practices in service-learning research at community colleges. In chapter 18, Taggart and Crisp explain how to locate and evaluate the limited existing research on service-learning at community colleges. They also outline how this research might direct the implementation and assessment of service-learning programs. The authors close their chapter with clear instructions on how to begin and promote service-learning research at community colleges.

Part VI ends the book with a set of four reflections written by current and/or former community college presidents and administrators. In their positions as leaders of community colleges, these contributors consider the role of service-learning in a holistic way, addressing the pedagogical, institutional, financial, and cultural considerations of implementing service-learning at community colleges.

In chapter 19, Evenbeck, Dalpes, and Merians explore the fundamental importance of engaging with place through service-learning. As Townsend's chapter indicates, engaging with place helps community college students meet the very real needs of their immediate communities. Yet, as revealed in this reflection and evidenced by examples from Holyoke Community College and from Guttman Community College of the City University New York, engagement with place in community college curricula also helps to advance student learning. Evenbeck, Dalpes, and Merians remind readers of the many benefits that come to community colleges when they engage the particular communities of which they are a part.

Building on these reflections, Exley encourages readers to think broadly about their communities of engagement. In chapter 20, he explains how his definition of community evolved and expanded through service-learning and civic engagement. Recounting Snead State Community College's response to others in need during major crises, specifically Hurricane Gustav and the Port au-Prince earthquake, Exley confirms that academically based service can produce—for students, faculty, and staff—the life-changing personal and academic experiences that Prentice and Robinson describe as the "prism effect."

In chapter 21, Call reflects on the need to document and research these effects; describing how faculty scholarship and institutional assessment have been central to service-learning at Queensborough Community College of the City University of New York. Giving voice to many of the recommendations described by Taggart and Crisp and exemplified by Hill, Renner, Acoba, Hiser, and Franco, Call provides important support for the institutionalization and growth of research-based service-learning programs and pedagogy.

Hesse extends this support with advice for helping service-learning programs survive and thrive. In chapter 22, she reflects on the challenges and success of service-learning at Chandler-Gilbert Community College, where a campus-wide service-learning program has grown exponentially during the past 20 years. Hesse's reflections are aimed at faculty, staff, and administrators working on building and sustaining service-learning programs at, in Morest's words, "the community's college."

More than ever, "the community's college" is a crucial educational site, charged with serving the most vulnerable student populations and preparing them for an evermore competitive and fluid global workplace. It is beholden on those working with these students at community colleges, as well as the larger institutions that influence educational policy and funding, to research and explore pedagogies—like service-learning—that may lead to community college student success. We hope that this book is a contribution to that effort.

Notes

1. This figure includes students enrolled in both credit (seven million) and noncredit (five million) courses at community colleges in the United States (American Association of Community Colleges 2014).
2. Unfortunately, given the loss of federal funds to major programs like Learn and Serve America, and the conclusion of AACC's service-learning efforts, the lion's share of this research must also be shouldered by individual scholars and colleges.
3. According to Schaffer (2008), undergraduate enrollment is growing faster at community colleges than it is at baccalaureate-granting institutions in most states.

References

American Association of Community Colleges. 2014. "Fast Facts from Our Fact Sheet." Accessed March 13. http://www.aacc.nche.edu/AboutCC/Pages/fastfactsfactsheet.aspx.
———. 2012a. "Service Learning." Accessed August 16. http://www.aacc.nche.edu/Resources/aaccprograms/horizons/Pages/default.aspx.
———. 2012b. "American Graduation Initiative." Accessed September 19. http://www.aacc.nche.edu/ADVOCACY/AGINITIATIVE/Pages/default.aspx.
Ash, S., P. Clayton, and M. Atkinson. 2005. "Integrating Reflection and Assessment to Capture and Improve Student Learning." *Michigan Journal of Community Service Learning* 11 (2): 49–60.
Azziz, R. 2014. "A Looming Challenge in Higher Education: Our Changing Student." *The Huffington Post*, February 26. Accessed April 1. http://www.huffingtonpost.com/dr-ricardo-azziz/a-looming-challenge-higher-education_b_4855108.html.
Bailey, T. R., and V. S. Morest. 2003. *The Organizational Efficiency of Multiple Missions for Community Colleges*. New York: Columbia University Press.
Baker, T., and W. Velez. 1996. "Access to and Opportunity in Postsecondary Education in the United States." *Sociology of Education* 69 (2): 82–101.

Barnett, L. 1996. "Service Learning: Why Community Colleges?" *New Directions for Community Colleges* 93 (Spring): 7–25.

Berson, J. S. 1994. "A Marriage Made in Heaven: Community Colleges and Service Learning." *Community College Journal* 64 (6): 14–19.

Bragg, D. D. 2001. "Community College Access, Mission, and Outcomes: Considering Intriguing Intersections and Challenges." *Peabody Journal of Education* 76 (1): 93–116.

Brint, S., and J. Karabel. 1989. *The Diverted Dream: Community Colleges and the Promise of Educational Opportunity in America, 1900–1985.* New York: Oxford University Press.

Butin, D. W. 2010a. "'Can I Major in Service-Learning?' An Empirical Analysis of Certificates, Minors, and Majors." *Journal of College and Character* 11 (2): 1–19.

———. 2010b. *Service-Learning in Theory and Practice: The Future of Community Engagement in Higher Education.* New York: Palgrave Macmillan.

The Civic Learning and Democratic Engagement National Task Force. 2011. *A Crucible Moment: College Learning and Democracy's Future, a Report to the Nation.* October 5. http://www2.ed.gov/rschstat/research/pubs/college-learning-democracys-future/crucible-moment.pdf.

Cohen, A. M., and F. B. Brawer. 2008. *The American Community College,* 5th ed. San Francisco, CA: John Wiley & Sons.

Deil-Amen, R. 2011. "The 'Traditional' College Student: A Smaller and Smaller Minority and Its Implications for Diversity and Access Institutions." Paper presented at the Mapping Broad-Access Higher Education Conference at Stanford University. Accessed April 1, 2014. http://cepa.stanford.edu/sites/default/files/2011%20Deil-Amen%2011_11.pdf.

Goldrick-Rab, S. 2010. "Challenges and Opportunities for Improving Community College Student Success." *Review of Educational Research* 80 (3): 437–469.

Kozeracki, C. 2000. "Eric Review: Service Learning in the Community College." *Community College Review* 27 (4): 54–70.

Kuh, G. 2008. *High-Impact Educational Practices: What They Are, Who Has Access to Them, and Why They Matter.* Washington, DC: AAC&U.

Marti, C. N. 2009. "Dimensions of Student Engagement in American Community Colleges: Using the Community College Student Report in Research and Practice." *Community College Journal of Research and Practice* 33 (1): 1–24.

Mellow, G. O., and C. Heelan. 2008. *Minding the Dream: The Process and Practice of the American Community College.* Lanham, MD: Rowman & Littlefield.

Prentice, M. 2000. *Service Learning Programs on Community College Campuses (Report No. EDO-JC-00-10).* Los Angeles, CA: ERIC Clearinghouse for Community Colleges.

Prins, E. S. 2002. "The Relationship between Institutional Mission, Service, and Service-Learning at Community Colleges in New York State." *Michigan Journal of Community Service Learning* 8 (2): 35–49.

Robinson, G., and L. Barnett. 1996. *Service Learning and Community Colleges: Where We Are.* Washington, DC: American Association of Community Colleges.

Schaffer, D. F. 2008. *The States and Their Community Colleges.* New York: Nelson A. Rockefeller Institute of Government, State University of New York.

Simmons, L. 1998. *Tear Down Those Walls/Build a Bridge.* East Lansing, MI: National Center for Research on Teacher Learning.

Taggart, A., and G. Crisp. 2011. "Service Learning at Community Colleges: Synthesis, Critique, and Recommendations for Future Research." *Journal of College Readiness and Writing* 42 (1): 24–44.

PART I

Service-Learning and Community Colleges

CHAPTER 1

The Roots of Service-Learning as a Basis for Advancing the Civic Mission of Community Colleges

Robert G. Bringle, Kathleen E. Edwards, and Patti H. Clayton

Democracy's colleges. Originally referring to land-grant institutions and then claimed by community colleges as well (Ronan 2012), "democracy's colleges" highlight what may be a primary tension facing many institutions of higher education today: how to fulfill—and perhaps integrate—the dual purposes of "doing the work of democracy" (i.e., preparation of students for civic life) and "equalizing opportunity" (i.e., widespread provision of the college education that is a gateway to employment and economic security) (Ronan 2012, 31). This tension may be particularly overt within community colleges, which educate approximately one half of the undergraduates in the United States (including a significant proportion of nonmajority and historically underserved undergraduates) and have a long history of providing widespread access to higher education and vocational training (American Association of Community Colleges n.d., "Community College Trends and Statistics"; Cohen, Brawer, and Kisker 2014). Therefore, both the potential for generating creative and effective approaches to navigating this tension and the stakes of doing so are high within the community college system. This book on service-learning in community colleges is an important step in the ongoing work to leverage service-learning as a strategy for deepening partnerships, nurturing healthy communities, enriching the civic work of faculty, cocreating high-quality civic learning and leadership opportunities with students, and transforming institutions. We provide an overview of service-learning in this context, examining its key role in institutional endeavors to hold fast to their civic mission—within community colleges in particular and higher education more generally—with an eye to what can be learned from community colleges as they use this pedagogy to advance and integrate these dimensions of their identity as democracy's colleges. This chapter seeks to establish service-learning firmly as a viable and effective, albeit complex, strategy for fulfilling the civic mission of higher education institutions—including community colleges—by exploring its conceptual and practice-based roots, the evidence of its contributions to student learning outcomes, and its future evolution.

Tension around Mission in Higher Education

Internal and external pressures are stimulating re-examination of the academy's primary role. Is the core purpose teaching the disciplines, cultivating critical thinking and problem solving, preparing students for careers, promoting economic development, contributing to local communities, generating knowledge, or cultivating the civic capacities needed for a flourishing democracy? The easy, and not inaccurate, answer is that the mission of higher education encompasses all of these possibilities and others. However, these various purposes can and do introduce points of tension and uncertainty regarding priorities, especially in a time of scarce resources and political polarization. One of the foci of the contemporary re-examination of mission is the question of how best to enact the civic purposes of the academy, which have been compromised on many campuses by neoliberalism's corporatizing of the academy and, at some institutions, by the privileging of research over both teaching and engagement with communities (Brackmann 2012; The National Task Force on Civic Learning and Democratic Engagement 2012; Saltmarsh and Hartley 2011). Bringle, Clayton, and Plater (2013) articulate the concern underlying calls for increased attention to civic purposes: "A focus on private gain (credentialing for employment) may displace public good (educating for citizenship) as the primary *raison d'être* of the academy—to the detriment of our students, our communities, and our democracy" (6).

This tension has been raised in several venues in recent years. Prominently, *A Crucible Moment: College Learning and Democracy's Future*, released by the National Task Force on Civic Learning and Democratic Engagement in 2012, calls for a pervasive "civic reform movement" (8) to transform institutions of higher learning so that they "prepare students for careers and citizenship, rather than only the former" (10). The report argues that "the more civic-oriented that colleges and universities become, the greater their overall capacity to spur local and global economic vitality, social and political well-being, and collective action to address public problems" (2). Upon receipt of *A Crucible Moment*, the US Department of Education echoed the report's emphasis on the necessity of producing both employees and citizens: "To fulfill America's promise in our global society, our education system at all levels, from early learning through higher education, must serve our nation *both* as its economic engine and its wellspring for democracy" (Kanter and Ochoa 2012, v, emphasis added).

A Crucible Moment suggests that "it is all the more important that civic learning be integrated into the curriculum, including career training programs" at community colleges (The National Task Force on Civic Learning and Democratic Engagement 2012, 10). These institutions may find it especially challenging to maintain the civic dimension of their mission, however. Community colleges are under pressure to serve as engines of economic development and are "especially vulnerable to the pressures of corporatization" (Jones 2008, 213). Jones offers as one example that community college students "demand education for economic success and quick progress through convenient programs, not education for citizenship" (214). One study of community colleges concludes that "community colleges see academic, economic, and civic concerns as part of their primary purpose" but "place a higher priority... on enabling students to reach their individual goals, providing a quality education, and pursuing economic achievements than they do on democracy, citizenship, and related issues" (Prins 2002, 40).

Although *A Crucible Moment* indicates that "a robust approach to civic learning is provided to only a minority of students" (2) and that civic development is not "yet an expectation for every college student" (6), The Democracy Commitment established a goal that "every graduate of an American community college will have had an education in democracy" (Ronan 2012, 32). Launched in 2011, The Democracy Commitment provides "a platform for the development and expansion of community college programs, projects, and curricula that aim to engage students in civic learning and democratic practice across the country" (The Democracy Commitment n.d., para 5). This project partners with national organizations (e.g., Association of American Colleges and Universities, American Association of State Colleges and Universities, and national civic organizations) to develop programs that integrate civic initiatives more fully on community college campuses. These programs target a broad array of democratic issues such as equal access to education, equal justice, civic skills, and diversity issues. The Democracy Commitment holds great promise for strengthening community college initiatives to sustain the civic dimension of their dual mission; decades of work to develop service-learning as an approach to civic education make clear that it has much to offer in support of this ambitious and necessary community college agenda.

Service-Learning and the Civic Mission of Higher Education

Service-learning has emerged throughout higher education as a leading strategy for reclaiming and centering civic purposes in the work of students, faculty, and staff and is viewed by many practitioners and scholars as a mechanism through which the academy can fulfill its democracy-building mission (Saltmarsh and Zlotkowski 2011; Langseth and Plater 2004; Colby, Ehrlich, Beaumont, and Stephens 2003; Bringle, Games, and Malloy 1999). Sigmon (1979) was one of the first practitioner-scholars to formalize service-learning as a theory-grounded teaching and learning strategy and partnership process designed to advance academic and civic learning as well as address community concerns. Campus Compact, formed in 1985 to support colleges and universities in institutionalizing community-campus engagement and civic learning, now includes over 30 state chapters and more than 1,100 public and private two- and four-year colleges and universities (Campus Compact n.d.). Other national organizations (e.g., National Society for Experiential Education, Association of American Colleges and Universities, American Association of State Colleges and Universities, American Association of Community Colleges [AACC]) have provided venues for professional meetings and disseminated resources to support implementation of high-quality service-learning. The International Association for Research on Service-Learning and Community Engagement and the *Michigan Journal for Community Service Learning*, among others, have enabled the development of a growing base of research, theory, and best practices focused on community-campus engagement. Launched in 2006, the Carnegie Foundation's elective classification for Community Engagement foregrounded service-learning—and related approaches to community engagement and civic learning in the curriculum—as a defining dimension of the engaged campus.

The community college system has both connected with these initiatives and developed its own. For more than 20 years the Community College National Center for Community Engagement (formerly the Campus Compact National Center for Community Engagement) has supported service-learning course design, partnership development, assessment, and the development of best practices, including through the online, peer-reviewed *Journal for Civic Commitment*. As one example of the center's work, in order to capitalize on the applied orientation of two-year institutions and the research emphasis of many four-year institutions, the *2 + 4 = Service on Common Ground* grant, funded from 1997 to 2000, partnered community colleges and universities to develop service-learning courses and other joint projects focused on community issues (Chitgopekar and Swaba 1999, 3). The 2 + 4 program challenged the competitive zero-sum gain assumptions that can often be held by institutions trying to access the same resources by identifying shared areas of interest for all institutions and community organizations involved in these long-term projects.

Similarly, for 18 years the AACC provided leadership and more than $5.5 million in federal funding to community colleges through the Community Colleges Broadening Horizons through Service Learning grant program. Before closing in 2012 with the end of funding from Learn and Serve America, the program helped community colleges build capacity and infrastructure for service-learning, engage in faculty development and training resources, conduct assessment, and enhance the credibility of the pedagogy.

Led not only by these initiatives but also by regional and local organizations and networks and countless individual practitioners and scholars throughout the country and across all institutional types, service-learning has undergone steady growth for the past two decades (Campus Compact 2013). Within the community college system in particular, two-thirds of the institutions' curricula included service-learning in 2012, up from 3 percent in 1995 (Cohen, Brawer, and Kisker 2014, 296). Service-learning is associated with and has contributed to many changes in higher education around mission, assessment, curriculum, promotion and tenure, infrastructure, and community partnerships. However, to paraphrase one of the pioneers, Timothy Stanton, rather than service-learning transforming higher education through prioritizing and leveraging its civic mission, it may be that higher education has instead changed service-learning (personal communication 2001). Many of the early practitioners had hoped that their strong emphasis on students and community members as colleagues, on reciprocal community-campus partnerships, and on civic learning and social change would transform the ways in which the academy functioned internally and partnered externally. However, too often service-learning has been implemented in a manner that neglects these fundamental principles and enacts instead the commodification that is pervasive in contemporary higher education (e.g., positioning students as helpers rather than colleagues; setting up community placements rather than partnerships; counting service hours rather than developing authentic measures of impact). Thus, service-learning has, to a large extent, not yet produced profound systemic change within the academy or, arguably, fulfilled the promise envisioned by its founders (Saltmarsh, Hartley, and Clayton 2009). Tracing the political, sociocultural, philosophical, and pedagogical roots of service-learning may contribute to understanding the possibilities for and constraints on its transformational potential for all types of institutions of higher education, including community colleges.

Roots of Service-Learning: Historical Landscape

The evolution of service-learning has been influenced by several historical forces. Dewey (e.g., 1938) provided a philosophical and intellectual foundation for service-learning by advocating an experiential education that would develop students' democratic skills and capacities toward improving the human condition. Examining his contributions, Benson, Harkavay, and Puckett (2011, 52) explain:

> Dewey theorized that education and society were dynamically interactive and interdependent. It followed, therefore, that if human beings hope to develop and maintain a particular type of society or social order, they must develop and maintain the particular type of education system conducive to it; that is to say, if there is no effective democratic schooling system, there will be no democratic society.

Building on this foundation, the trajectory of service-learning has involved refocusing the ends toward which it is implemented: social justice (phase 1), disciplinary learning (phase 2), student-centered learning (phase 3), and democratic civic engagement (phase 4) (Zlotkowski and Duffy 2010). While not encompassing all extant interpretations of the historical evolution of service-learning, these phases—which have to some extent coexisted and so are not intended as a linear, chronological outline—provide a useful structure for thinking about the philosophical, pedagogical, political, and sociocultural roots of service-learning within higher education. This section briefly reviews the first three phases; the contemporary phase of democratic civic engagement will be examined in more depth in the subsequent section.

Service-Learning as Social Justice Strategy

Service-learning as social justice was the original vision for the pedagogy (Stanton, Giles, and Cruz 1999). In the 1960s and 1970s, individuals from campus and community alike "found themselves drawn to the idea that action in communities and structured learning could be combined to provide stronger service and leadership in communities and deeper, more relevant education for students" (Stanton, Giles, and Cruz 1999, 1). Involved in community organizing, civil rights activism, and progressive initiatives to improve K-12 education, these pioneering students, faculty, staff, and community members brought experience and knowledge from a variety of fields and integrated their commitment to social justice with their vision for higher education (Stanton, Giles, and Cruz 1999).

In addition to harkening back to Dewey's philosophical perspectives on education and democracy, these pioneers also looked to critical pedagogy and popular education for guidance. Freire (1970, 72), a critical pedagogue, warned against the "banking model of education" whereby students are treated as empty receptacles to be filled with regulated knowledge from instructors and called instead for dialogic education that positioned everyone involved as teacher-student and student-teacher. Horton (1998), a popular educator and founding director of the Highlander Research and Education Center, also emphasized the value of co-teaching and co-learning and called for grounding education in people's lived experiences and valuing the knowledge they bring to any educational undertaking. Both individuals saw the purpose of education in terms of social justice: creating spaces where people (oppressed and privileged) can work together to challenge and change the status quo (Horton and Freire 1990).

Today's practitioner-scholars of what is called "critical service-learning" (e.g., Porfilio and Hickman 2011; Mitchell 2007) carry forward the spirit of this phase, distinguishing between service-learning as a teaching strategy only and service-learning as also a means of raising questions about and changing dominant conditions of privilege and oppression (Mitchell 2007; O'Grady 2000). Working within this tradition and anticipating resistance from community college faculty who want to use service-learning as a "neutral" pedagogy through which to teach course content, Lisman (1997) speaks to the unique responsibilities of two-year institutions to the communities with which they characteristically have close relationships and calls for a shift in paradigm from instrumental and atheoretical reasons for service-learning to community engagement in order to fulfill these responsibilities and retain a social justice focus. With service-learning contesting the technocratic orientation of higher education by explicitly incorporating the perspectives of marginalized and oppressed community members, Lisman expects that "we will hear a challenge to our overly simplistic forms of competency-based education that indirectly perpetuate the great gaps between the haves and the have-nots in our society under the false veneer of 'educational equality'" (87).

Service-Learning as Discipline-Specific Teaching and Learning Strategy

According to Zlotkowski and Duffy (2010) the evolution of service-learning has been marked by a division between those who desired it to "remain [a] fringe phenomenon...rather than risk sacrificing its social efficacy to more academic ends" and those who "argued that nothing in the long run could be achieved unless a way was found to lend community-based work the academic legitimacy that would broaden its appeal" (35). While service-learning operates at the periphery on many campuses, much energy has been directed toward positioning it as a pedagogy within the disciplines—partly in response to resistance to service-learning from faculty and others who conceive the purpose of higher education to be teaching disciplinary content and skills and producing disciplinary knowledge. A significant example is the 21-volume series, Service-Learning in the Disciplines, edited by Zlotkowski and originally published by the American Association for Higher Education (now by Stylus Publishing), which assembles examples of integrating service-learning into a wide range of curricula primarily as a means to teach course content.

At professional schools and community colleges, "disciplinary" coursework often translates to "occupational" or "professional" education and to general education courses as preparation for transfer to four-year institutions. Robinson and Barnett (1996) found that at community colleges service-learning was most prevalent in the social sciences and humanities, followed by health, science/math, and technical/vocational courses. Service-learning can be integrated into occupational education and work training courses as well as general education and other interdisciplinary courses through the same process it is incorporated into disciplinary courses—as a means of teaching course content. A key factor in accomplishing such integration is involving faculty and administrators across the community college campus to develop an "understanding of the constitutive features of civic education and a willingness to incorporate goals and pertinent teaching strategies into...instruction" (Higginbottom and Romano 2006, 25). Use of service-learning as a way of teaching course content in this context can provide an opening to consider the role of civic knowledge, skills, and attitudes in career preparation and, more generally, in teaching the public purposes of the professions and in cultivating civic-minded professionals (Hatcher 2008; Sullivan 2005).

Service-Learning as Powerful Pedagogy for Student-Centered Learning

Following from the focus on service-learning as an effective strategy for teaching course content, new inquiries emerged for service-learning educators as they began to question the value of academic knowledge if it cannot be applied in various settings (Zlotkowski and Duffy 2010). These inquiries reflected a larger paradigm shift called for by Barr and Tagg (1995) in how educators think about teaching and learning. Rather than approaching teaching as an instruction-centered practice, Barr and Tagg (1995, 4) encouraged a learning-centered process, suggesting that "a college's purpose is not to transfer knowledge but to create environments and experiences that bring students to discover and construct knowledge...to make students members of communities of learners that...solve problems." With this paradigm shift came enhanced attention to innovative teaching and learning strategies. Because of its critically reflective, experiential, community-engaged nature, service-learning was readily framed as a student- or learning-centered pedagogy: "because there are few 'right' answers in responding to community settings, students have to make inquiries, try multiple solutions, and persevere" (Zlotkowski and Duffy 2010, 37). In accordance with the emphasis on student learning instead of social justice, work such as Kolb's (1984) experiential learning cycle (consisting of the four processes: abstract conceptualization, active experimentation, concrete experience, reflective observation) became central in informing course design and faculty development (Chism, Palmer, and Price 2013).

Adult education models (e.g., Cranton 2006; Mezirow 1991) inform service-learning in particular and education more generally in community colleges, centering—similar to critical pedagogy and popular education—relationality and critical reflection on the learners' lived experiences. Transformative learning theory (Mezirow 1991) relies on critical self-reflection and dialogue with others as ways in which new cognitive meaning is made within individuals, as opposed to external factors such as textbooks or lectures. Cranton (2006) incorporates the importance of authenticity in relationships to transformative learning theory, developing a five-faceted model of authenticity in relationships, one point of which is developing genuine and open relationships between individual teachers and students. When expanded to incorporate educational spaces outside of the classroom and to integrate students, faculty, and community members as teachers and learners, developing authentic relationships for transformative learning requires critical questioning of status quo expectations of how individuals behave. This represents a paradigm shift away from teacher-centered instruction toward transforming "their perspective on [students, faculty, community members] until it becomes multifaceted and open to the differences among the human beings" who are partners in this educational relationship (8). For the purpose of democratic civic education, service-learning then becomes an ideal avenue for meaning making by adult learners because it is already designed to include critical reflection (initiated via course-reflection assignments or other more organic developments), dialogue (among all partners), and authentic relationality (fostered through the processes of cocreation and partnerships).

Roots of Service-Learning: Contemporary Landscape

Service-learning is increasingly framed in the fourth phase as democratic civic engagement and, as such, is situated within multiple tension points related to, for our purposes here, conceptions of citizenship, the role of academic expertise, and market-based ideology. One of service-learning's most significant contributions to higher education is its focus on civic learning, and it has catalyzed considerable discussion regarding the meaning and substance of such learning. Battistoni (2002), for example, describes multiple ways in which disciplines and professions define civic learning. Westheimer and Kahne (2004, 238) identify three conceptualizations of citizenship in higher education—personally responsible, participatory, and justice-oriented—and explain that "the decisions educators make when designing... programs often influence politically important outcomes regarding the ways that students understand the strengths and weaknesses of our society and the ways that they should act as citizens in a democracy." Such work highlights the influence of epistemology and value commitments on the design of civic education, which in turn shapes what students (and faculty and community partners) learn.

Saltmarsh, Hartley, and Clayton (2009) in the *Democratic Engagement White Paper* explore the incongruence between the dominant technocratic epistemology and the flourishing of democracy. The technocratic approach to education and to community-campus engagement—the model that underlies far too much service-learning—enacts and encompasses hierarchical power dynamics between faculty and students and between campus and community: experts transfer knowledge to students and apply knowledge to solve problems *for* communities—in both cases acting on and reinforcing deficit-based assumptions that disempower students and community members and deny their legitimacy as sources of knowledge. Service-learning framed as technocratic engagement—applying academic expertise and resources to those in need—limits possibilities for shared voice, decision making, and responsibility and, therefore, feeds the "general crisis of democracy" in our society (Boyte in Saltmarsh et al. 2009, 8). Service-learning conceptualized and practiced as democratic civic engagement, on the other hand, "seeks the public good *with* the public and not merely *for* the public as a means to facilitating a more active and engaged democracy" (Saltmarsh et al. 2009, 9). Jameson, Clayton, and Jaeger (2011, 262) make clear the implications for civic learning and practice:

> Working together in this way means that students, faculty, and community members share power and responsibility and communicate as equals across their various roles... partners navigate their way through disagreements to shared commitments... [and through the] tensions... at the core of democracy (e.g.,... between short-term and long-term,... efficiency and effectiveness,... local and global, and... individual interests and the common good).

Tensions associated with contemporary conceptions of service-learning as democratic civic engagement also occur as a result of the dominant socioeconomic narrative that frames systems in terms of individualism, competition, efficiency, and return on investment. Neoliberal ideologies subtly shape budget allocations, faculty roles and rewards, research agendas, curricular design, learning goals, and community-campus partnerships (Brackmann 2012; Dennis 2010). The "student as customer"/"student as consumer" model (Jones 2008; Levin 2005) that increasingly pervades higher education is in many ways at odds with the historical roots of service-learning. Neoliberalism can introduce considerable confusion among the students, faculty, and community members who the pedagogy invites into personal, collaborative relationships that are not appropriately subject to the norms associated with clients and customers. In this context, service-learning confronts higher education with a choice that is high stakes in light of its civic mission: marketing an image of the student as an institutional citizen regardless of the depth of actual commitments and work (because doing so enhances the reputation of the institution, acquires grant money, and aids recruitment) *or* engaging in authentic democratic actions and the social critique that is needed to advance the public good—even when, perhaps especially when, such a stance puts academics at odds with the systems of power that hold great sway over the public perceptions and funding of higher education. Within this current neoliberal landscape, community colleges experience the push and pull of their varied institutional purposes: general education, occupational education, and community education (Cohen, Brawer, and Kisker 2014). Levin (2005) goes so far as to argue that "the community college has directed its operations toward supporting one of its missions, economic development, at the expense of other missions, in order to maintain legitimacy in the broader political economy" (15).

The current neoliberal ethos of the United States heightens the significance of conceptualizing and enacting service-learning as democratic civic engagement: increasing the likelihood of moving beyond resolving "social problems" to proactively cocreating just and equitable communities, in part through integrating the academic, professional, and civic education of young people and adults. Service-learning's emphasis on the ways in which students—indeed, everyone involved in the educational enterprise—can and do cocreate their communities is paralleled with its positioning of them as cocreators of their own learning processes and outcomes; together, these two underlying convictions highlight the transformational potential of service-learning in each of these four framings but perhaps especially in their integration. They also call attention to the importance and unique challenges of designing, implementing, and assessing the pedagogy in ways that enable this potential to be fulfilled.

Student Learning through Service-Learning

Service-learning as a mechanism for advancing and integrating the civic mission of higher education will only be successful to the extent that it is designed and undertaken as a set of partnerships among all stakeholders—students, faculty, staff/administrators, community organization staff, community residents (Bringle, Clayton, and Price 2009)—and to the degree that it achieves the full range of outcomes mutually established by members of both campus and communities. In this section we provide a brief summary of best practices and evidence with regard to student learning processes and outcomes; we will not review literature on theories related to learning and research on outcomes for other constituencies. Readers interested in theories of change, assessment of outcomes, and future research as they apply to communities, faculty, institutions, and partnerships are referred to the two volumes edited by Clayton, Bringle, and Hatcher, *Research on Service-Learning: Conceptual Frameworks and Assessment* (2013a, 2013b).

Service-Learning as Powerful Pedagogy

As challenging as good teaching is, a strong empirical base exists that establishes the conditions under which learning best occurs—many of which are aligned with well-designed service-learning. Tinto (1993) and Pascarella and Terenzini (1991) highlight the importance of students' academic and social integration, demonstrated by relationships with peers, interaction with faculty, and involvement in active learning. Chickering and Gamson (1987) suggest that good educational practice (a) encourages contact between students and faculty; (b) develops cooperation among students; (c) involves active learning techniques; (d) includes prompt feedback; (e) emphasizes time on task; (f) communicates high expectations; and (g) values diverse ways of learning. Marchese (1997) posits as keys to deep learning: (a) active learning strategies; (b) frequent feedback from others that is provided in nonthreatening ways; (c) collaboration; (d) cognitive apprenticeship (i.e., relationship with a mentor with whom students can learn generalization of principles, transfer of knowledge between theory and practice, and analysis of perplexing circumstances); and (e) practical applications in which students are involved in tasks that have consequences with a safety net for high-stakes mistakes.

Research by Eyler and Giles (1999) demonstrates that well-designed service-learning is characterized by many of these attributes of strong learning environments. Service-learning also brings the added value of students developing rich learning relationships not only on campus but also in communities. In addition to faculty and staff and other students, community members serve as mentors, provide perspective and feedback, and set and maintain accountability around expectations. Particularly at community colleges, which draw students from local communities and educate students who remain in those communities, the capacity for service-learning to broaden and deepen a sense of place is an important outcome (see chapter 19 in this book).

The knowledge, skills, and values that service-learning—when done well—can foster align with what Kuh (2008) calls *high-impact practices*. Using multiple years of data from the National Survey of Student Engagement, high-impact practices are those that "are correlated with positive educational results for students from widely varying backgrounds" (Schneider 2008, 1). Kuh's (2008) research shows that these high-impact practices, while beneficial to everyone, are especially worthwhile to traditionally underserved student populations (especially first-generation students and African American students); in other words, they are especially worthwhile to a large portion of community college students.

Service-learning may be an unfamiliar way for students to learn and as a result has the potential to challenge their identities and roles as learners and to cultivate their capacities for lifelong, interdependent, and independent learning. Its counternormative (Clayton and Ash 2004; Howard 1998) nature, from a student perspective, includes ways in which students are expected to (a) be intensively engaged in the teaching and learning process outside the classroom; (b) connect their experiences in communities with academic material in the course through critical reflection; (c) achieve and provide evidence of learning in civic and personal domains as well as academic domains, including learning that is not always specified in books or by instructors; (d) establish and nurture partnerships with community members; (e) function as co-educators and co-generators of knowledge and as leaders and change agents; and (f) assume responsibility for articulating their own questions, monitoring their own and their peers' progress, and assessing their own and others' outcomes. Well-designed service-learning builds students'—indeed, all partners'—capacities to teach, learn, serve, partner, and generate knowledge in these atypical ways and deliberately leverages this very counternormativity to cultivate a wide range of learning outcomes.

What We Know from the Research at Community Colleges

Although research (i.e., students, faculty, institutions, community impact) is more prevalent on four-year institutions, there is research that has been intentionally focused on service-learning at community colleges. Taggart and Crisp (2011) review 17 empirical studies of student learning in service-learning at community colleges, noting, however, that the pedagogy was operationalized and its outcomes assessed in very different ways across this body of research (with the implication that some of the examples might not constitute service-learning per the AACC definition). Most of the studies reviewed indicated connections between participation in service-learning and some form of positive attitudes toward civic involvement. In addition, Berson and Younkin (1998) found an association between service-learning and higher final course grades, and Hollis (2002) documented that students in a service-learning course earned higher grades on essays and tests than did students in a comparable non-service-learning course. Prentice (2009) reported higher retention to subsequent semesters but lower grades among students in service-learning than non-service-learning developmental reading, writing, and life skills courses.

Prentice and Robinson (2010) used a self-report outcomes scale and focus groups to investigate community college student learning across multiple campus grantees in the 2006–2009 Horizons project. They found that students who had completed one or more service-learning courses reported statistically higher learning than did non-service-learning students on five of six outcomes: critical thinking, communication, career and teamwork, civic responsibility, and academic development and educational success, but not global understanding and citizenship. They find it particularly significant to the goals of community colleges that service-learning seems to "provide students with opportunities to learn information that is important not only in acquiring specific curricular content, but also in developing skills beyond the curriculum that are necessary for their academic development and preparation for professional success" (Prentice and Robinson 2010, 12–13).

In a targeted initiative to identify high-impact educational practices in community colleges, the Center for Community College Student Engagement (CCCSE), in partnership with the Carnegie Foundation for the Advancement of Teaching, has launched a multiyear research agenda. The inaugural report, *A Matter of Degrees: Promising Practices for Community College Student Success: A First Look*, provides initial data on promising practices, explained as: "educational practices for which there is emerging evidence of success: research from the field and from multiple colleges with multiple semesters of data showing improvement on an array of metrics, such as course completion, retention, and graduation" (CCCSE 2012, 3). In this report, CCCSE identifies *experiential learning* as one of five promising practices for sustaining college students' success. The data also shows that 77 percent of students have never been asked to participate in a community-based project for a course (CCCSE 2012, 22).

However, the vast majority of the research on student learning in service-learning, some of which we will review below, has been based on students in four-year institutions. In the most recent edition (6th edition) of *The American Community College*, Cohen, Brawer, and Kisker (2014) point to the paucity of scholars interested in community colleges as well as community colleges' own advocates' inability or disinclination to critically examine student outcomes given the heavy link to future funding.

The priorities of community colleges can certainly guide their engagement with current research, which, insofar as it addresses shared goals, may be suggestive if not directly transferable to community college students. As an example, the AACC definition of service-learning (see chapter 10 in this book) highlights intended student learning outcomes in academic, civic, and personal arenas; and there is a substantial body of research documenting student gains in each of these categories (see, e.g., Jameson, Clayton, and Ash 2013 for a review of research on academic learning; Battistoni 2013 for a review of research on civic learning; and Brandenberger 2013 for a review of research on personal development).

Taggart and Crisp (2011, 26) note, however, that

> research focusing specifically on four-year institutions is problematic as there is a wealth of empirical support for the assertion that a community college setting uniquely impacts student outcomes such as persistence (e.g., Pascarella, 1999; Pierson, Wolniak, Pascarella, and Flowers, 2003). As such, it is not appropriate to assume that a service learning experience will impact students attending two-year colleges and four-year institutions in the same ways. Rather, methodologically sound empirical work done with community college samples is required to establish the relationship between service learning and outcomes for community college students.

We are aware of no empirical evidence that systematically differentiates the impact of service-learning experiences on students in different types of institutions, including community colleges.

The extent to which service-learning has distinct outcomes for community college students and the nature of any such differences may be of interest as an area for future research. How service-learning is related to the community college context with regard to student characteristics (e.g., educational objectives, demographics, conflicting demands on student time), curricular issues, community partnerships, issues related to place, and how these influence the design of optimal service-learning experiences needs further exploration with regard to practice, theory, and research. The chapters in this book provide a significant contribution to anchoring work on service-learning within the community college context. A more nuanced set of questions is being focused on by the CCCSE in which high-impact "experiential learning" can be broken down into more precise practices in order to determine if there are distinctions between service-learning, internships, co-curricular community service, and apprenticeships. Having more precise data about the impact of these various types of practices on learning outcomes, student persistence, subsequent job success, and student progress to four-year degree programs will support community colleges in understanding how they are achieving various aspects of their mission.

What We Know from the Research More Generally

As Steinberg, Bringle, and McGuire (2013) note, service-learning is versatile and has been implemented in a variety of ways, in many types of courses, in different community settings, often with different learning objectives, and based on different underlying theories. Although this versatility results in heterogeneity that complicates systematic assessment and research, evidence of the efficacy of service-learning, particularly on student outcomes, is accumulating—with the caveat that much of the research (both in general and in the community college context) suffers from small sample size and lack of control groups, does not control for self-selection of students into service-learning courses, relies on self-report, uses designs that do not permit clear causal inferences (Steinberg, Bringle, and McGuire 2013), and infrequently includes samples from community colleges. Nevertheless, the quality of research is improving, and practitioner-scholars have a growing body of evidence on which to draw when designing service-learning courses. As Bringle and Clayton (2012, 117–118) conclude as an overall summary:

> Service learning, designed as serious academic work, can result in learning outcomes that enrich and extend traditional pedagogies... engage students in ways that promote academic learning and critical thinking while also contributing to their civic knowledge, skills, and dispositions... [and] promote problem-solving skills, higher-order reasoning, integrative thinking, goal clarification, openness to new ideas, ability to adopt new perspectives, and systemic thinking.

Here we review results of select key studies and summaries of research during the past 15 years.

Taking advantage of a large sample of first-year students and the capacity to collect data from a subsample of the same students four years later, Vogelgesang and Astin (2000) conclude, after controlling for preexisting student characteristics (e.g., participation in community service), that service-learning favorably influences self-reported values and beliefs (e.g., commitment to activism, promoting racial understanding, self-efficacy), academic outcomes (e.g., critical thinking skills, writing skills, grades), and leadership (e.g., interpersonal skills).

Eyler and Giles (1999) used pre- and post-problem-solving interviews to investigate reasoning abilities among service-learning students. This study revealed that "participation in well-integrated and highly reflective service-learning courses was a predictor of increased complexity in analysis of both causes and solutions to social problems" (75).

Eyler, Giles, Stenson, and Gray (2001) provide an annotated summary of early research conducted on service-learning in higher education. Generally, this research found that service-learning was positively related to students' (a) academic learning (e.g., grades, problem analysis, cognitive development); (b) personal development (e.g., self-efficacy, spiritual growth, moral development);(c) interpersonal development (e.g., ability to work with others, communication skills); (d) cultural and racial understanding (e.g., reduction in stereotypes); and (e) social responsibility (e.g., citizenship skills, commitment to service).

Astin and Sax (1998) conducted a large-scale five-year postgraduation survey of college graduates at four-year institutions and, taking into account preexisting differences, found that involvement in service-learning during college produced self-reported gains in civic responsibility (e.g., future plans to volunteer, efficacy to change society, commitment to influence social values), academic development (e.g., aspirations for advanced degree), and life skills (e.g., leadership skills, interpersonal skills, conflict resolution skills).

Novak, Markey, and Allen's (2007) meta-analysis of nine research studies reports an effect size favoring service-learning that translated into over a 50 percent advantage on cognitive outcomes for students in service-learning courses. Other meta-analyses examine student outcomes for service-learning courses in comparison to traditional courses, documenting that service-learning is also positively associated with academic, personal, and civic (social) outcomes, with the effect sizes ranging from small through moderate to large depending on the studies sampled (Yorio and Ye 2012; Celio, Durlak, and Dymnicki 2011; Conway, Amel, and Gerwien 2009). Felten and Clayton (2011) review research that suggests that service-learning, while not enhancing factual knowledge, does produce higher performance on tasks (e.g., essay exams) eliciting higher-order cognitive skills and depth of knowledge. In a qualitative review of research, Eyler (2011) concluded that service-learning produced favorable outcomes on students' political interest and efficacy, their sense of connectedness to community, social responsibility, future interest in community life, and life skills—outcomes that are particularly relevant to both citizenship and employment.

Beyond learning outcomes, there is reason to believe that service-learning—as is the case with all high-impact pedagogies (Kuh 2008)—has a positive effect on students' persistence in higher education. Service-learning has been found to improve student satisfaction with their chosen institution (Berson and Younkin 1998). Bringle, Hatcher, and Muthiah (2010) found a positive relationship between participation in 22 service-learning courses (versus non-service-learning courses) on 11 campuses and the intentions of first-year students to continue at the same institution the following year. Lockeman and Pelco (2013) found that students enrolled in service-learning courses, compared to those who had taken no service-learning courses, earned more credits, had a higher grade point average, and graduated at higher rates. These differences existed even though the service-learning students also had greater financial need while enrolled. Possibly more relevant to community college student populations, Lockeman and Pelco found that minority (71 percent vs. 29 percent) and low-income students (72 percent vs. 28 percent) who took service-learning courses graduated at significantly higher rates than those who did not. CCCSE has acknowledged that experiential education is among the high-impact practices that can contribute to community college student success (e.g., matriculating to a four-year institution, completing a certificate program). It is now time for additional research to consider how service-learning as a high-impact practice for community college students can simultaneously contribute to community colleges' multiple missions and for whom and under what conditions.

Future Directions

As practice and research continue to evolve and as the pedagogy of service-learning increasingly provides an avenue for navigating the tensions between and integration of the dual missions of education for civic health and education for economic growth, community college institutions and individuals (e.g., faculty, staff, students, community members) alike need to remain focused on questions such as the following:

- What among the roots of service-learning do we need to harken back to and reinvigorate in attempts to use it effectively as a means of achieving multiple

institutional and community ends? In particular how can the various community college initiatives—general education (e.g., liberal arts and other courses serving a transfer function), occupational education (e.g., workforce development, certificate programs), and community education (e.g., adult basic learning, ESOL)—be integrated for the shared purpose of democratic civic education, and how might service-learning be a tool for that integration?
- What of the rich legacy of creative responses to social injustice, student activism, local community advocacy, and work to define discipline-contextualized civic learning goals do we risk diminishing or losing altogether if we allow local economic concerns to overshadow or displace civic concerns? How can community colleges provide models for the integration and enhancement of economic outcomes through a focus on civic concerns in their communities?
- What of the current tensions related to the purposes and processes of service-learning, both conceptual and practical, most need to be embraced and leveraged as catalysts for developing innovative approaches to community-engaged teaching, learning, partnerships, and scholarship that are customized to the community college landscape?
- How can assessment and research better inform understanding and practice so that community colleges are better positioned to develop the institutional capacity to integrate and improve all aspects of mission to the benefit of more students and their communities?

In terms of anticipated future developments, the coming years will likely see a vertical integration of civic education that encourages and supports developmentally—and coherently—designed curricular service-learning (Butin and Seider 2012; Jameson, Clayton, and Bringle 2008) and co-curricular service (Hoy and Meisel 2008). Ronan (2011, 3–4) posits a "civic spectrum" that runs across the P-20 educational continuum, in which "students advance along the educational pipeline as efficiently as possible, their knowledge and skills growing as they move along, and eventually resulting in certificates or degrees that empower them to be both effective citizens and productive employees." Noting the key role of community colleges, which "are positioned between K-12 and the university, with a stake in the productivity of both sectors," Ronan (2011, 3) advocates P-20 partnerships that "enable students in the lower division of postsecondary education to begin civic work in their communities that would follow them into their upper division"; to implement such continuity, "faculty would come together as civic colleagues across the arbitrary boundaries of separate institutions, linked by the common experiences of students in their institutions who are engaged in civic work where their schools and colleges reside."

Community colleges can strengthen and guide higher education's commitment to democratic civic engagement, which values the multiple perspectives contributed through a diverse citizenry. But current neoliberal influences on budget allocations, hiring practices, and curriculum decisions "threaten [community colleges'] mission of access, particularly for underserved or marginalized groups" (Levin 2005, 23). As one way to reframe this challenge, Sturm, Eatman, Saltmarsh, and Bush (2012, 4) "invite consideration of…whether and how diversity, public engagement, and student success efforts relate to one another." They point to the significant interdependence of these goals:

> The frameworks and practices needed to change student access and success depend upon making progress on faculty diversity. The conversation about diversity and inclusion has profound implications for the legitimacy and efficacy of community engagement... There is tremendous untapped potential for knowledge and resource sharing and collective impact if these efforts are more effectively connected with each other and built into the core values and practices of higher education. (4)

A second important future direction, then, involves connecting service-learning—structurally and in practice—to these institutional priorities as one compelling way in which community colleges attend to diversity, public engagement, and student success in the context of socioeconomic pressures (Bringle, Clayton, and Plater 2013).

Third, with the increasing numbers of diverse students attending four-year institutions, community colleges can help think about how to simultaneously problematize dominant, deficit-based ideologies while also making visible and valuable the knowledge born from lived experiences that minority students—who may also be personally familiar with community partners—may possess. Community colleges serve a diverse student population. In its 2014 Fact Sheet, AACC reports that 48% of African American, 56% of Hispanic, and 59% of Native American undergraduate students were enrolled in community colleges in Fall 2012; the average student age was 28, with 57% of students falling between 22 and 39 years of age. Additionally, part-time students outnumbered full-time students by as many as three to one (Cohen, Brawer, and Kisker 2014), and 41% of those part-time students were also working full-time (AACC 2014). Much of the current research on service-learning, however, describes students as a monolithic group; authors routinely acknowledge that service-learning participants are most often white, middle-class, and female (Davi 2006; Boyle-Baise 2002; O'Grady 2000). This limitation applies equally to other identities, such as persons of color, persons of lower socioeconomic status, or almost any other marginalized socially constructed identity. Given the diversity of students in community colleges though, service-learning students cannot all be white, middle-class, and female, and because community colleges are so deeply embedded in the local communities and students also come from these communities, service-learning courses have the opportunity to create a space for critical thinking about topics that are relevant to the lived experiences of the students, not distant or impersonal course content.

Conclusion

Parsons and Lisman (1996, 3) call on community colleges to "act as catalysts for a national movement of community renewal." This call has been echoed across institutional types, but community colleges are well positioned to act on it because of their emphasis on teaching, on community, and on place.

Given their dual mission of preparing students for democratic citizenship and for employment and their close relationship with local communities, community colleges are in a unique position to challenge the dialectic to view occupational education and civic education as separate, necessarily oppositional, foci. As democracy's colleges, community colleges can lead all of higher education in this shifting landscape, serving as a model for what it means to integrate two important functions of education in our society and thereby educate civic-minded professionals (Hatcher 2008; Sullivan 2005).

Further, because their students are "local, with strong personal ties to community businesses, organizations, and other residents," community colleges can also contribute in significant ways to how the academy frames students, communities, and the relationship between them (Barnett 1996, 9). Equally if not more fundamental than concerns with employment, community college students and the faculty, staff, and community members with whom they partner in service-learning are truly *of* the communities in which their institutions are located (see chapter 19 in this book). These students and their institutions can teach us all what it is to ground the collaboration between campus and community in a strong sense of place, with the associated honoring of local history and local visions for the health, vibrancy, and sustainability of local relationships. Perhaps the most important aspect of the civic mission of community colleges is to honor and harness, inquire into and inform the rest of the academy about, the role and power of a place-based understanding of ourselves and our communities, which community psychologists refer to as a feeling of belonging, of membership (Chavis, Hogge, McMillan, and Wandersman 1986). That we are *members* of, not simply residents in or contributors to, our communities is the core element of civic identity and civic action in a democracy and, therefore, is at the forefront of service-learning's potential contributions, if the pedagogy is understood and designed accordingly. Community colleges have an important leadership role to play in fully leveraging this pedagogy toward such essential ends and providing an example to the rest of higher education on how to do so.

References

American Association of Community Colleges (AACC). 2014. "2014 Fact Sheet." http://www.aacc.nche.edu/AboutCC/Documents/Facts14_Data_R3.pdf

———. n.d. "Community College Trends and Statistics." http://www.aacc.nche.edu/AboutCC/Trends/Pages/default.aspx.

Astin, Alexander W., and Linda J. Sax. 1998. "How Undergraduates Are Affected by Service Participation." *Journal of College Student Development* 39: 251–263.

Barnett, Lynn. 1996. "Service-Learning: Why Community Colleges?" *New Directions for Community Colleges* 1996 (93): 7–15.

Barr, Robert B., and John Tagg. 1995. "From Teaching to Learning: A New Paradigm for Undergraduate Education." *Change* 27 (6): 12–26.

Battistoni, Richard M. 2002. *Civic Engagement across the Curriculum: A Resource Book for Service-Learning Faculty in All Disciplines*. Providence, RI: Campus Compact.

———. 2013. "Civic Learning through Service Learning: Conceptual Frameworks and Research." In *Research on Service Learning: Conceptual Frameworks and Assessment. Vol. 2A:*

Students and Faculty, edited by Patti H. Clayton, Robert G. Bringle, and Julie A. Hatcher, 111–132. Sterling, VA: Stylus.

Benson, Lee, Ira Harkavay, and John Puckett. 2011. "Democratic Transformation through University-Assisted Community Schools." In *"To Serve a Larger Purpose": Engagement for Democracy and the Transformation of Higher Education*, edited by John Saltmarsh and Matthew Hartley, 49–81. Philadelphia, PA: Temple University Press.

Berson, Judith. S., and William F. Younkin. 1998. "Doing Well by Doing Good: A Study of the Effects of a Service-Learning Experience on Student Success." Paper presented at the American Society of Higher Education, Miami, FL, November.

Boyle-Baise, Marilynne. 2002. *Multicultural Service Learning: Educating Teachers in Diverse Communities*. New York: Teachers College Press.

Brackmann, Sarah. 2012. "Community Engagement and the Public Good: A Case Study of Land-Grant Universities." PhD diss., University of Georgia.

Brandenberger, Jay. 2013. "Investigating Personal Development Outcomes in Service Learning." In *Research on Service Learning: Conceptual Frameworks and Assessment. Vol. 2A: Students and Faculty*, edited by Patti H. Clayton, Robert G. Bringle, and Julie A. Hatcher, 133–156. Sterling, VA: Stylus.

Bringle, Robert G., and Patti H. Clayton. 2012. "Civic Education through Service-Learning: What, How, and Why?" In *Higher Education and Civic Engagement: Comparative Perspectives*, edited by Lorraine McIlrath, Ann Lyons, and Ronaldo Munck, 101–124. New York: Palgrave Macmillan.

Bringle, Robert G., Patti H. Clayton, and William G. Plater. 2013. "Assessing Diversity, Global, and Civic Learning: A Means to Change in Higher Education." *Diversity and Democracy* 16 (3): 4–6.

Bringle, Robert G., Patti H. Clayton, and Mary F. Price. 2009. "Partnerships in Service Learning and Civic Engagement." *Partnerships: A Journal of Service-Learning and Civic Engagement* 1: 1–20.

Bringle, Robert G., Richard Games, and Edwards A. Malloy. 1999. *Colleges and Universities as Citizens*. Needham Heights, MA: Allyn and Bacon.

Bringle, Robert G., Julie A. Hatcher, and Richard N. Muthiah. 2010. "The Role of Service-Learning on the Retention of First-Year Students to Second Year." *Michigan Journal of Community Service Learning* Spring: 38–49.

Butin, Dan, and Scott Seider, eds. 2012. *The Engaged Campus: Certificates, Minors, and Majors as the New Community Engagement*. New York: Palgrave Macmillan.

Campus Compact. n.d. "List of Members by State." Accessed November 23, 2013. http://www.compact.org/membership/list-of-members-by-state/.

———. 2013. *Creating a Culture of Assessment: 2012 Campus Compact Annual Member Survey*. Boston: Campus Compact.

Celio, Christine, I., Joseph Durlak, and Allison Dymnicki. 2011. "A Meta-Analysis of the Impact of Service-Learning on Students." *Journal of Experiential Education* 34: 164–181.

Center for Community College Student Engagement. 2012. *A Matter of Degrees: Promising Practices for Community College Student Success: A Look Forward*. Austin: University of Texas at Austin. http://www.ccsse.org/docs/Matter_of_Degrees.pdf.

Chavis, David M., James H. Hogge, David W. McMillan, and Abraham Wandersman. 1986. "Sense of Community Through Brunswick's Lens: A First Look." *Journal of Community Psychology* 14: 24–40.

Chickering, Arthur W., and Zelda F. Gamson. 1987. "Seven Principles for Good Practice in Undergraduate Education." *AAHE Bulletin* 39 (7): 3–7.

Chism, Nancy Van Note, Megan M. Palmer, and Mary F. Price. 2013. "Investigating Faculty Development for Service Learning." In *Research on Service Learning: Conceptual Frameworks and Assessment. Vol. 2A: Students and Faculty*, edited by Patti H. Clayton, Robert G. Bringle, and Julie A. Hatcher, 187–214. Sterling, VA: Stylus.

Chitgopekar, Anu, S., and Joseph Swaba. 1999. "Finding the Common Ground: An Introduction and Overview." In *Where Is the Common Ground? Insights into Service-Learning Collaborations between Community Colleges and Universities*, edited by Anu S. Chitgopekar and Joseph Swaba, 3–6. Mesa, AZ: Campus Compact National Center for Community Colleges.

Clayton, Patti H., and Sarah L. Ash. 2004. "Shifts in Perspective: Capitalizing on the Counter-Normative Nature of Service-Learning." *Michigan Journal of Community Service Learning* 11: 59–70.

Clayton, Patti. H., Robert G. Bringle, and Julie A. Hatcher, eds. 2013a. *Research on Service Learning: Conceptual Frameworks and Assessment. Vol. 2A: Students and Faculty*. Sterling, VA: Stylus.

———, eds. 2013b. *Research on Service Learning: Conceptual Frameworks and Assessment. Vol. 2B: Communities, Institutions, and Partnerships*. Sterling, VA: Stylus.

Cohen, Arthur, Florence Brawer, and Carrie Kisker. 2014. *The American Community College*, 6th ed. San Francisco, CA: Jossey-Bass.

Colby, Ann, Thomas Ehrlich, Elizabeth Beaumont, and Jason Stephens. 2003. *Educating Citizens: Preparing America's Undergraduates for Lives of Moral and Civic Responsibility*. San Francisco, CA: Jossey-Bass.

Conway, James M., Elise L. Amel, and Daniel P. Gerwien. 2009. "Teaching and Learning in the Social Context: A Meta-Analysis of Service Learning's Effects on Academic, Personal, Social, and Citizenship Outcomes." *Teaching of Psychology* 36: 233–245.

Cranton, Patricia. 2006. "Fostering Authentic Relationships in the Transformative Classroom." *New Directions for Adult and Continuing Education* 109: 5–13.

Davi, Angelique. 2006. "In the Service of Writing and Race." *Journal of Basic Writing* 25: 73–95.

The Democracy Commitment. n.d. "About Us." Accessed July 25, 2013. http://thedemocracycommitment.org/about-us/.

Dennis, Dion. 2010. "The Shepherd, the Marketer, and the Actuary: Education-Based Service Learning and Civic Engagement as Neo-Liberal Governmentalities." In *A Foucault for the 21st Century: Governmentalities, Biopolitics and Discipline in the New Millenium*, edited by Sam Binkley and Jorge Capetillo-Ponce, 154–172. Newcastle upon Tyne: Cambridge Scholars Publishing.

Dewey, John. 1938. *Experience and Education*. New York: Touchstone.

Eyler, Janet. 2011. "What International Service Learning Research Can Learn from Research on Service Learning." In *International Service Learning: Conceptual Frameworks and Research*, edited by Robert G. Bringle, Julie A. Hatcher, and Steven G. Jones, 225–245. Sterling, VA: Stylus.

Eyler, Janet, and Dwight E. Giles Jr. 1999. *Where's the Learning in Service-Learning?* San Francisco, CA: Jossey-Bass.

Eyler, Janet, Dwight E. Giles Jr., Christine M. Stenson, and Charlene J. Gray. 2001. *At a Glance: What We Know about the Effects of Service-Learning on College Students, Faculty, Institutions and Communities, 1993–2000*, 3rd ed. Washington, DC: Learn and Serve America National Service Learning Clearinghouse.

Felten, Peter, and Patti H. Clayton. 2011. "Service-Learning." *New Directions for Teaching and Learning* 2011 (128): 75–84.

Freire, Paulo. 1970/2000. *Pedagogy of the Oppressed*, 30th anniversary edition. New York: Continuum.

Hatcher, Julie A. 2008. "The Public Role of Professionals: Developing and Evaluating the Civic-Minded Professional." PhD diss., Indiana University.

Henry, Sue Ellen. 2005. "'I Can Never Turn My Back on That': Liminality and the Impact of Class on Service-Learning Experiences." In *Service-Learning in Higher Education*, edited by Dan Butin, 45–66. New York: Palgrave Macmillan.

Higginbottom, George H., and Romano, Richard M. 2006. "Appraising the Efficacy of Civic Education at the Community College." *New Directions for Community Colleges* 136: 23–32.

Hollis, Shirley A. 2002. "Capturing the Experience: Transforming Community Service into Service Learning." *Teaching Sociology* 30 (2): 200–213.

Horton, Myles, with Judith Kohl and Herbert Koh. 1998. *The Long Haul: An Autobiography*. New York: Teachers College Press.

Horton, Myles, and Paulo Freire. 1990. *We Make the Road by Walking: Conversations on Education and Social Change*, edited by Brenda Bell, John Gaventa, and John Peters. Philadelphia, PA: Temple University Press.

Howard, Jeff. 1998. "Academic Service Learning: A Counter Normative Pedagogy." *New Directions in Teaching and Learning* 73: 21–29.

Hoy, Ariane, and Wayne Meisel. 2008. *Civic Engagement at the Center: Building Democracy through Integrated Co-Curricular and Curricular Expe*riences. Washington, DC: American Association of Colleges and Universities.

Jameson, Jessica, Patti H. Clayton, and Sarah L. Ash. 2013. "Conceptualizing, Assessing, and Investigating Academic Learning in Service Learning." In *Research on Service Learning: Conceptual Frameworks and Assessment. Vol. 2A: Students and Faculty*, edited by Patti H. Clayton, Robert G. Bringle, and Julie A. Hatcher, 85–110. Sterling, VA: Stylus.

Jameson, Jessica, Patti H. Clayton, and Robert G. Bringle. 2008. "Investigating Student Learning within and across Linked Service Learning Courses." In *Scholarship for Sustaining Service Learning and Civic Engagement*, edited by Melody A. Bowden, Shelley H. Billig, and Barbara A. Holland, 3–27. Charlotte, NC: Information Age.

Jameson, Jessica K., Patti H. Clayton, and Audrey J. Jaeger. 2011. "Community Engaged Scholarship as Mutually Transformative Partnerships." In *Participatory Partnerships for Social Action and Research*, edited by Lynn M. Harter, Jane Hamel-Lambert, and Judith Millesen, 259–277. Dubuque, IA: Kendall Hunt.

Jones, Julie. 2008. "Foundations of Corporatization: Lessons from the Community College." *The History Teacher* 41 (2): 213–217.

Kanter, Martha, and Eduardo Ochoa. 2012. Foreword to *Crucible Moment: College Learning and Democracy's Future*. Washington, DC: Association of American Colleges and Universities.

Kolb, David. 1984. *Experiential Learning: Experience as the Source of Learning and Development*. Upper Saddle, NJ: Prentice-Hall.

Kuh, George D. 2008. *High-Impact Educational Practices: What They Are, Who Has Access to Them, and Why They Matter*. Washington, DC: Association of American Colleges and Universities.

Langseth, Mark, and William M. Plater, eds. 2004. *Public Work and the Academy: An Academic Administrator's Guide to Civic Engagement and Service-Learning*. Bolton: Anker Press.

Levin, John, S. 2005. "The Business Culture of the Community College: Students as Consumers; Students as Commodities." *New Directions for Higher Education* 2005 (129):11–26.

Lisman, C. David. 1997. "The Tension of Theory and Practice in Service-Learning." In *Tensions Inherent in Service-Learning: Achieving a Balance*, edited by Terry Pickeral and Karen Peters, 77–89. Mesa, AZ: Campus Compact National Center for Community Colleges.

Lockeman, Kelly, and Lynn Pelco. 2013. "The Relationship between Service-Learning and Degree Completion." *Michigan Journal of Community Service Learning* 20 (1): 18–30.
Marchese, Theodore. J. 1997. "The New Conversations about Learning: Insights from Neuroscience and Anthropology, Cognitive Studies and Work-Place Studies." In *Assessing Impact: Evidence and Action*, edited by Ellen E. Chaffee, Peter T. Ewell, Sherril. B. Gelman, George Kuh, Theodore J. Marchese, Margaret A. Miller, and Grant Wiggins, 79–95. Washington, DC: American Association for Higher Education.
Mezirow, Jack. 1991. *Transformative Dimensions of Adult Learning.* San Francisco, CA: Jossey-Bass.
Mitchell, Tania D. 2007. "Critical Service Learning as Social Justice Education: A Case Study of the Citizens Scholars Program." *Equity and Excellence in Education* 40 (2): 101–111.
The National Task Force on Civic Learning and Democratic Engagement. 2012. A *Crucible Moment: College Learning and Democracy's Future.* Washington, DC: Association of American Colleges and Universities
Novak, Julie M., Vern Markey, and Mike Allen. 2007. "Evaluating Cognitive Outcomes of Service Learning in Higher Education: A Meta-Analysis." *Communication Research Reports* 24: 149–157.
O'Grady, Carolyn. 2000. *Integrating Service Learning and Multicultural Education in Colleges and Universities.* Mahwah, NJ: Lawrence Erlbaum.
Parsons, Michael, and C. David Lisman. 1996. "Promoting Community Renewal through Civic Literacy and Service Learning." *New Directions for Community Colleges* 93.
Pascarella, Ernest. T., and Patrick T. Terenzini. 1991. *How College Affects Students: Findings and Insights from Twenty Years of Research.* San Francisco, CA: Jossey-Bass.
Porfilio, Bradley, and Heather Hickman, eds. 2011. *Critical Service-Learning as Revolutionary Pedagogy: A Product of Student Agency in Action.* Charlotte, NC: Information Age Publishing.
Prentice, Mary. 2009. "Service-Learning's Impact on Developmental Reading/Writing and Student Life Skills Courses." *Community College Journal of Research and Practice* 33 (3): 270–282.
Prentice, Mary, and Gail Robinson. 2007. *Linking Service Learning and Civic Engagement in Community College Students.* Washington, DC: American Association of Community Colleges.
———. 2010. *Improving Student Learning Outcomes with Service Learning.* Washington, DC: American Association of Community Colleges.
Prins, Esther S. 2002. "The Relationship between Institutional Mission, Service, and Service-Learning at Community Colleges in New York State." *Michigan Journal of Community Service Learning* 8 (2): 35–49.
Robinson, Gail, and Lynn Barnett. 1996. "Service Learning and Community Colleges: Where We Are." Survey Report. Washington, DC: American Association of Community Colleges.
Ronan, Bernie. 2011. *The Civic Spectrum: How Students Become Engaged Citizens.* Dayton: Kettering Foundation. http://kettering.org/wp-content/uploads/The_Civic_Spectrum.pdf.
———. 2012. "Community Colleges and the Work of Democracy." *Connections: The Kettering Foundation's Annual Newsletter* 31-3. http://kettering.org/wp-content/uploads/8_CONNECTIONS2012_Ronan.pdf.
Saltmarsh, John, and Matthew Hartley. 2011. *"To Serve a Larger Purpose": Engagement for Democracy and the Transformation of Higher Education.* Philadelphia, PA: Temple University Press.
Saltmarsh, John, Matthew Hartley, and Patti H. Clayton. 2009. *Democratic Engagement White Paper.* Boston, MA: New England Resource Center for Higher Education.

Saltmarsh, John, and Edward Zlotkowski, eds. 2011. *Higher Education and Democracy: Essays on Service-Learning and Civic Engagement.* Philadelphia, PA: Temple University Press.

Schneider, Carol Geary. 2008. "Liberal Education and High-Impact Practices: Making Excellence—Once and for All—Inclusive." In *High-Impact Educational Practices: What They Are, Who Has Access to Them, and Why They* Matter, written by George Kuh, 1–8. Washington, DC: American Association of Colleges and Universities.

Sigmon, Robert. 1979. "Service-Learning: Three Principles." *Synergist* 8: 9–11.

Stanton, Timothy K., Dwight E. Giles Jr., and Nadinne I. Cruz. 1999. *Service-Learning: A Movement's Pioneers Reflect on Its Origins, Practice, and Future.* San Francisco, CA: Jossey-Bass.

Steinberg, Kathryn, Robert G. Bringle, and Lisa McGuire. 2013. "Attributes of High-Quality Research on Service Learning." *Research on Service Learning: Conceptual Frameworks and Assessment, Vol. 2A,* edited by Patti H. Clayton, Robert G. Bringle, and Julie A. Hatcher, 27–53, VA. Sterling: Stylus.

Sturm, Susan, Tim Eatman, John Saltmarsh, and Adam Bush. 2012. *Full Participation: Building the Architecture for Diversity and Community Engagement in Higher Education*, catalyst paper. http://community-wealth.org/sites/clone.community-wealth.org/files/downloads/paper-strum-et-al.pdf.

Sullivan, William M. 2005. *Work and Integrity: The Crisis and Promise of Professionalism in America*, 2nd ed. San Francisco, CA: Jossey-Bass.

Taggart, Amanda, and Gloria Crisp. 2011. "Service Learning at Community Colleges: Synthesis, Critique, and Recommendations for Future Research." *Journal of College Reading and Learning* 42: 24–44.

Tinto, Vincent. 1993. *Leaving College: Rethinking the Causes and Cures of Student Attrition,* 2nd ed. Chicago, IL: University of Chicago Press.

Vogelgesang, Lori, and Alexander Astin. 2000. "Comparing the Effects of Community Service and Service-Learning." *Michigan Journal of Community Service Learning* 7: 25–34.

Westheimer, Joel, and Joseph Kahne. 2004. "What Kind of Citizen? The Politics of Educating for Democracy." *American Educational Research Journal* 41: 237–269.

Yorio, Patrick L., and Feifei Ye. 2012. "A Meta-Analysis on the Effects of Service-Learning on the Social, Personal, and Cognitive Outcomes of Learning." *Academy of Management Learning and Education* 11: 9–27.

Zlotkowski, Edward, and Donna Duffy. 2010. "Two Decades of Community-Based Learning." *New Directions for Teaching and Learning* 123: 33–43.

CHAPTER 2

The Community's College: Contextualizing Service-Learning in the Mission and Development of Community Colleges

Vanessa Smith Morest

The community college is a uniquely diverse sector of American higher education as students from a wide range of academic and personal backgrounds enroll for a multitude of reasons. This diversity was not necessarily the intention of the founders of community colleges, but it is a condition that has emerged over time as a result of their expansion and has become part of their mission of providing access to postsecondary education. There are currently over 1,000 community colleges in the United States, enrolling more than seven million students nationwide. In the fall of 2012, community colleges enrolled 50 percent of undergraduate students attending public institutions, and 38 percent of all undergraduates (NCES 2013).[1] Today, community colleges enroll students reflecting an infinitely diverse range of ages, races, and nationalities. There is a complexity not only in the background of community college students but also in their educational goals. Individuals are brought together in community college classrooms with seemingly little more in common than the classes they are taking. This diversity is an important asset of community colleges, particularly when the faculty finds ways to incorporate it into their teaching.

The community college classroom creates a unique milieu for learning. The diversity of students' experiences enters into classroom discussions and products of student work, and students often report this diversity in the classroom to be one of the strengths of their college experience. The Community College Survey of Student Engagement (CCSSE), a national survey, reports that 45 percent of students said they "had serious conversations with students of a different race or ethnicity other than (their) own" often or very often at their college. Nearly as many (41 percent) reported having "serious conversations with students who differ [from themselves] in terms of their religious beliefs, political opinions, or personal values."[2]

Besides the demographic diversity of their students, there are other characteristics of community college classrooms that create a rich environment for teaching and learning. Nearly one third of students, according to CCSSE results, are raising children or caring for other dependents in their households. Since the majority of community colleges do not have on-campus housing, most community college students are commuters. Community colleges therefore reflect multiple communities, including that of the college campus and those of the communities where students live.

This chapter explores community colleges as a setting for service-learning. The educational environment of the community college presents both benefits and challenges. There are many strong connections between the values and purposes of service-learning and the community college, starting with the role of the colleges within their local communities. These connections have deep roots, so the chapter begins with a review of the historical development of community colleges, particularly as it pertains to the "open door" policy and the mission of serving the local community. It then looks at some of the challenges shaping teaching and learning in today's community college classrooms and how community colleges are addressing those challenges. The chapter then returns to service-learning as it relates to this context. Finally, it concludes with some recommendations about scaling up service-learning programs, as despite the fact that two-thirds of community colleges offer service-learning, many programs remain relatively small in scale.

Origins and Development of Community Colleges

Throughout their history, community colleges have expanded access to higher education. The first community college, Joliet College, in Illinois, opened in 1901 as a collaboration between Joliet High School and the University of Chicago. The impetus to establish Joliet was driven in part by the growing popularity of higher education that was spurred by urbanization and the emergence of white-collar jobs. As the University of Chicago attracted students with increasingly diverse academic preparation, the university president, William Rainey Harper, sought a new type of institution that would absorb the growing numbers of underprepared students. At the same time, J. Stanley Brown, principal of nearby Joliet High School, sought to solve a different though related problem, as he wished to expand access to college for his students by offering some college-level coursework at his school. Brown eventually collaborated with Harper and together they were able to establish Joliet Junior College in 1901 (Brint and Karabel 1989), as an extension school associated with Joliet Township High School.

Two-year colleges grew in number throughout the 1920s to 1940s, so that by 1950 there were over 300 public junior colleges (Cohen and Brawer 2009). Throughout this period of expansion, community colleges were seeking an identity within higher education. The forces shaping community colleges were many. On the one hand, as the label of junior colleges implies, many colleges were founded by local educational and political leaders who were enthusiastic about expanding access to the baccalaureate degree. On the other, business and industry leaders, with the support of the American Association of Junior Colleges, sought to secure a unique niche for the colleges in vocational education (Dougherty 1994; Brint and Karabel 1989). The one mission all could agree upon was that the colleges should focus on the educational needs of their local communities.

The community focus was institutionalized as early as 1947 with the publication of the findings of President Truman's Commission on Higher Education, which issued a report calling for community colleges to "serve chiefly local community educational needs." The report goes on to say that although the colleges "may have various forms of organization and may have curricula of various lengths, its dominant feature is its intimate relations to the life of the community it serves" (Ratcliff 1994, 14). The mission of serving local educational needs proved to be a broad mandate for community colleges, making it possible for the colleges to offer a wide-ranging curriculum including everything from air-conditioning repair to philosophy. The position expressed by the Truman Commission was a threshold for community colleges since it broadened the mission and formalized the institution's responsibility to serve the local community. Community colleges greatly value the flexibility implied by their service role as each institution's unique blend of programs and services reflects the socioeconomic makeup of the towns and cities it serves.

The 1960s saw another major expansion in community colleges, nearly doubling in number between 1950 and the late 1970s. During this period, community colleges became increasingly involved in offering occupational education. There has been a great deal of debate about the impact of "vocationalization" of the community college curriculum and its consequences for community college students (Dougherty 1994; Brint and Karabel 1989). On the one hand, the critical role of community colleges in local workforce development contributed to stronger ties to the local community. On the other, students were increasingly able to graduate from community colleges while taking fewer liberal arts courses.

Today, academic programs are widely varied, but generally include a blend of transfer degrees for students who plan to attend four-year colleges or universities and occupational degrees and certificates for students seeking to enter the workforce directly. Transfer programs are typically available in the liberal arts, as well as in career fields such as business, health, criminal justice, and education (Cohen and Brawer 2009). These programs of study are popular at community colleges, just as they are at four-year colleges and universities. The definition of community colleges is somewhat more flexible than it sounds, as increasingly community colleges are adopting bachelor's degree programs, making it more difficult to distinguish between community colleges and other sectors of higher education. However, even in states such as Florida, where bachelor's degrees are becoming common at community colleges, two-year degrees and one-year certificates continue to form the primary focus of the institutions.

In addition to offering the associate degree, community colleges typically offer a wide range of educational programs and services intended to meet their community's economic and social needs. For example, most community colleges offer some form of noncredit education, through which the institutions provide courses ranging from classes for children to certification programs (such as those for computer technicians or real estate agents). The types of noncredit offerings provided by community colleges depend on the availability of funding, state-level policy, and community needs. This wide range of educational offerings strengthens ties between the institutions and their communities, making it possible for community colleges to engage with many different groups, from the very young to the elderly and from low- to high-income earners.

The role of community colleges in providing access to higher education is reinforced by the open door admissions policy of the colleges. Admissions to most community college programs are nonselective, requiring only high school completion or evidence of the "ability to benefit" from college. Accessibility is further guaranteed by keeping costs low, as community college tuition and fees for full-time students average $2,790 per academic year, compared with $8,070 for public four-year institutions (NCES 2012).[3] The principle of maintaining an open door policy for admissions creates a symbiotic relationship between the colleges and their communities, ensuring that institutions will prioritize meeting local needs.

Community College Students

Community colleges are the most diverse sector of American higher education, bringing together students with a variety of academic goals. For some, a class or two will suffice, while many others are in it for the long haul as they seek associate degrees and higher. As of 2011, 40 percent of community college students are over the age of 24 (NCES 2013).[4] In recent years, the average age of community college students has been coming down as the colleges enroll increasing numbers of traditionally aged students and high school students who are "dual enrolled" in both high school and college. Community colleges are attractive to many because they are close to home, inexpensive, and offer a great deal of flexibility to students. These colleges have become critically important to students of color: 15 percent of community college students are black and 20 percent are Hispanic. For Hispanic students, these rates are more than double those of public universities (NCES 2013).[5]

For many students who enroll in community colleges, earning an associate degree is not their primary goal. However, among those students for whom it is their primary goal, succeeding in college can be challenging. Community colleges and four-year colleges alike focus on the first-year experience of college students as a time that is particularly critical to successful outcomes. For example, data collected from Achieving the Dream colleges indicate that 14 percent of students earn no credits at all during their first semester at college because they fail and withdraw from all of their classes (JBL 2008). National statistics indicate that only 40 percent of first-time, full-time, degree-seeking students return to the college at which they started after one year (fall-to-fall retention) (NCES 2012).[6] There is currently a national spotlight on degree completion at community colleges, where graduation rates are only 20 percent after three years. Many will argue that graduation does not tell the complete story of community college students, as students enter with wide-ranging goals, but nevertheless the low rates of completion are noteworthy.

Community college students face challenges in three different areas: academic, social, and financial. For many students, the first semester is spent taking college preparatory courses in developmental English and mathematics. Several studies find that the overall percentage of students taking at least one developmental course at community colleges is 40–45 percent (Bailey, Jeong, and Cho 2009; Attewell et al. 2006; Parsad and Lewis 2003). However, these estimates may be low, particularly for community colleges enrolling higher proportions of students of color. Results coming out of Achieving the Dream colleges, which are by definition largely low-income and minority-serving institutions, indicate higher rates of participation. In their database, 59 percent of students enrolled in at least one developmental course (Bailey, Jeong, and Cho 2009).

The social challenges facing students include those related to family background and their current home life. Community college students are more likely to be the first in their families to attend college (Próspero and Vohra-Gupta 2007; Ishitani 2006). This presents challenges to students as they develop academic goals and learn how to navigate the curriculum. Community college students are also more likely to be immigrants or children of immigrants. These students must learn to navigate not only the postsecondary curriculum but also financial aid systems and the college culture. Finally, community college students frequently have multiple responsibilities outside of school. They are significantly more likely to be working and raising a family than students at four-year institutions.

Community colleges cater to their busy, commuter students by making it possible to limit time spent on campus. Many of the structures through which students immerse themselves in college life and develop social ties on campus are either scaled back or altogether absent from community colleges. These include, for example, dormitories, athletics, clubs, and other typical student organizations. The downside of emphasizing efficiency in social relationships on campus is that students have fewer opportunities to become integrated into the college experience, which research indicates is important to student success (Tinto 1975, 1993). The degree to which this impacts community college students is debated in the literature, but it is fair to say that the limited amount of time students have available for college-related activities makes it difficult to engage students outside the classroom.

Financial challenges relate closely to the social challenges faced by community college students. Students choose community colleges because they are conveniently located and affordable. The incentive structure shaping college choice contributes to community colleges enrolling disproportionate numbers of students who do not have adequate resources to pay for college. Estimates indicate that 45.4 percent of full-time students and 71.8 percent of part-time students work while attending community college (NCES 2011).[7] Many students find themselves coping with significant time and financial commitments while in college. Because the majority of community college students enroll part-time, it can take years to earn an associate degree, during which time the burden of family and work commitments can overwhelm them.

Community college instructors respond by seeking out educational reforms that help students to form social and academic ties on campus. Researchers have found that the classroom is the best place to reach students for these supports because it is where students spend the most time on campus. Through interviews with 238 community college students, Deil-Amen (2011) found that connections with peers and faculty occurring at the classroom level were highly important to students.

Approximately three-quarters of the students in her study described the "support and approachability of teachers or other students within the classrooms as fundamental to their feelings of comfort in the college" (Deil-Amen 2011, 63). She found that colleges should proactively create these socially integrative moments for students by focusing on how they can be accomplished in classrooms since they are critical to success but not likely to occur outside the classroom.

The Student Success Movement

Finding ways to help community college students forge connections has proven to be a powerful focus for student-success reforms. These connections may be with other students, faculty and staff, or with the community. Not only do community college instructors seek ways to help their students forge social ties, but they also focus on developing their academic connections. Students can gain a better sense of their own academic futures by connecting with the curriculum and understanding how their early coursework will ultimately lead to more advanced courses, degree completion, and a career. This section describes several trends emerging out of the student-success movement at community colleges.

Learning Communities

Learning communities generally involve linking two or more classes, making it easier for faculty to work in teams and for students to develop relationships with each other and with the faculty. Learning communities typically last only one semester and are often focused on new, first-time students. Community colleges have engaged in a variety of practices with regard to the selection of courses that are linked and how those connections are made. For example, at the City University of New York's (CUNY's) LaGuardia Community College in Queens, New York, learning communities are part of a First-Year Academy. These first-year academies are offered in Business and Technology, Allied Health, and Liberal Arts. Each academy has at least one developmental course (if needed), a seminar for first-year students, an introductory-level course, and a Studio Hour during which students learn how to build an ePortfolio. Kingsborough Community College, also part of the CUNY system, offers a wide range of learning communities, including their Opening Doors Learning Communities, which comprise as many as 33 cohorts of up to 25 students each semester taking block programs of three linked courses: English, the Freshman Seminar, and a General Education Discipline course. Kingsborough also offers learning communities in English as a Second Language and Advanced Learning Communities for students in their second semester.

Some of the best practices associated with teaching in learning communities focus on developing an integrated and holistic learning experience for students based on the belief that "students persist in their studies if the learning they experience is meaningful, deeply engaging, and relevant to their lives" (Lardner and Malnarich 2008, 32). For example, when faculty develop shared assignments, it not only relieves the pressure of competing academic demands on students (i.e., two different papers due on the same day), but demonstrates connections between subject areas so that students can understand developing academic skills and knowledge as a comprehensive process.

When a true community of learners emerges, students and faculty work as a team. Partnered faculty members visit each other's classrooms and work on integrating curriculum. This allows faculty to expand upon the topics and concepts being presented in the learning community from their unique disciplinary perspectives. This kind of coordination also helps students forge connections in their knowledge and understanding of the subjects. Close connections between faculty members also make it easier to identify students who are having difficulty in more than one subject area and for the college to match students having difficulty with the services that will help them.

Applied and Contextualized Learning

Community colleges also seek to engage students in the curriculum by helping them develop connections between their current and future learning. This is particularly relevant for students starting with low skill levels in mathematics, reading, and writing. In developmental courses, the material being taught does not resemble college-level work and students get frustrated as they cannot see the connection between educational and career goals. Community college instructors are experimenting with ways to integrate developmental math and English into an occupational or applied curriculum.

An example of this receiving attention from researchers is the Washington State Integrated Basic Education and Skills Training (I-BEST) program. Through the I-BEST program, students are exposed to a curriculum that contextualizes developmental education within a workforce-training curriculum. Courses are taught by teams of developmental and technical/professional instructors. In one study, I-BEST students had earned more college credits after three years than comparison students, and 8 percent more had earned certificates (Zeidenberg, Cho, and Jenkins 2010).

The Carnegie Foundation for the Advancement of Teaching's Statway project is another large-scale effort at contextualization. Statway is a yearlong pathway that takes students through developmental mathematics and into college level mathematics through statistics, data analysis, and quantitative reasoning. The premise for this program is that statistical skills and perspectives are essential for many occupational and professional fields. One of the central insights of the Statway program is that students use real datasets throughout the curriculum, because

> first, working with real data rewards students with answers to interesting research questions, thereby increasing their motivation to complete the task. Second, real data bring students as close as possible to the actual research experience. Third, real data provide an opportunity to teach students to cope with problems that arise in practice. (Statway™ 2010, 2)

It is still too early to know the results of Statway; however, this demonstrates that the idea of applied learning can be used for a wide range of purposes.

Redistributing the Use of Classroom Time

A third way in which community colleges seek to engage students through active and collaborative learning is by changing the way classroom time is used altogether. This happens in several ways. In developmental mathematics, math "emporiums" are used. In these classes, students obtain instruction through videos and online material. Faculty use classroom time to answer questions and give students opportunities to work on math problems. Sometimes these are also called "flipped classrooms," because faculty members provide lectures to students to review outside of class, while using class-time for workshops and interactive learning. Students can work individually or in groups, solving problems with the support of faculty.

At the Community College of Baltimore County (CCBC), developmental English students are placed in college-level courses, but they must also enroll in smaller workshops taught by the English faculty. This approach has been evaluated at CCBC with positive results (Jenkins et al. 2010). Another variation in the use of classroom time involves adaptive technologies. These are online programs that constantly assess and provide feedback on student learning. When students master the curriculum, they are introduced to more difficult topics. If they are unable to find the correct answers, the online program will continue to provide explanatory videos and practice problems until students can demonstrate an understanding of the material.

These ideas are opening doors to new ways of thinking about community college teaching. It has become clear that increasing the success rates of community college students involves finding new ways to engage students in the process of learning. Opportunities to retain students in college and help them to make progress toward their degrees occur in the classroom, as the classroom experience encompasses the entire college experience for many community college students. One of the most important elements of engaging students through the classroom is to help them discover connections. These may be connections with faculty or other students, connections involving the subject matter, or connections between college and other aspects of their lives (e.g., their career ambitions).

Service-learning fits into this paradigm of reform. Like learning communities, service-learning can cross disciplinary boundaries by challenging students to forge connections between various areas of knowledge. It also has the potential to encourage students to learn together in communities as they engage in teamwork to complete their volunteer tasks. Service-learning also offers many opportunities for applied and contextualized learning. This is particularly helpful in the liberal arts where hands-on learning is less common than in occupational courses. Finally, service-learning reflects a redistribution of students' learning time away from traditional textbooks and lectures. In the next section, I briefly describe some of the important ways in which service-learning dovetails with community college education.

Community Colleges and Service-Learning

Service-learning forms a natural fit with community colleges because it is at the nexus between experiential learning and the community college ethos of democratic education. Since the majority of students entering community colleges lead hectic and challenging lives, it is critical that classroom-based activities are engaging and valued by students. It can be difficult to find this combination in some of the introductory-level community college courses, since so many students enter the freshman year underprepared for college. Students' daily efforts to balance college with their rest of their lives opens up an opportunity for students to both learn from their own communities and contribute to them through their college work.

The American Association of Community Colleges (AACC), the major national association of community colleges, began promoting and supporting service-learning initiatives at community colleges in 1994. They estimate that 60–70 percent of community colleges today are embracing some form of service-learning and community engagement (Jeandron and Robinson 2010). Service-learning helps students to develop an understanding of citizenship in terms of becoming productive members of their local communities. Civic engagement can be an important contribution of community colleges to their local communities, as many students and alumni live and work near their colleges throughout their lives. Through service-learning, community colleges can strengthen their communities in the short-term by committing volunteer hours and in the long term by by developing local citizens. Community college students comprise the parents, workers, employers, and voters in the communities surrounding their colleges, so teaching them about the benefits of service and civic engagement can benefit the whole community.

Higher education is a powerful force in shaping peoples' lives and many community college students are directly engaged in a struggle to overcome the odds of educational stratification. A structured experience that spans the boundaries of college and community can be helpful to students in framing their educational experiences and planning for the future. As Franco (2002, 133) observes, through service, community college students can become civically engaged:

> Through well-structured, school-based service-learning and campus-based reflection and leadership, community college students from across the ethnic and income spectrums will be actively engaged in creating democratic and equitable schools and will learn how to create a democratic and equitable America.

The benefits of service-learning to both community college students and the institutions are clear. In fact, as community colleges undertake efforts to structure the first-year experience through learning communities and new curricular approaches, as I have described, service-learning can be a particularly potent tool for increasing the academic and social integration of students. However, despite more than two decades of experience with service-learning, the number of community college students who have engaged in service-learning remains relatively low. Efforts to establish service-learning programs encounter many of the same challenges that confront the scaling up other programs and initiatives at community colleges. The next section reviews some of these challenges.

Challenges of Scale at Community Colleges

In comparison to four-year colleges and universities, community colleges are relatively flexible and open to change. The past decade, during which many reform efforts along the lines of those described in this chapter have been attempted, provides evidence of the willingness to adopt new ideas. However, research finds that scaling up change is far less common at community colleges than one might expect. This is one finding of the work done through the Developmental Education Initiative, which was funded from 2009 to 2012 by the Bill and Melinda Gates Foundation. Through that initiative, colleges were provided with $743,000 over three years to scale up existing interventions to reach larger numbers of developmental education students. During this time period, the number of developmental education students served by at least one "focal strategy" for increasing student success rose from 18 percent to 41 percent. While this is significant growth, fewer than 50 percent of developmental students were involved, falling well short of the estimates of the colleges themselves (Quint et al. 2013, 31). Research on the Lumina Foundation–funded Achieving the Dream project and on learning communities also describe similar challenges encountered by colleges when they seek to expand programs and initiatives (Rutschow et al. 2011; Visher et al. 2010).

Despite the important benefits to community colleges and their students, service-learning programs confront challenges similar to those faced by other new initiatives at community colleges (Higginbottom and Romano 2006). One of the most often cited challenges to expanding and developing new initiatives at community colleges involves obtaining faculty buy-in (Largent and Horinek 2008). While many community college instructors embrace change and are engaged in innovation in their classrooms, it is often difficult for these early adopters to encourage larger numbers of colleagues to become involved in their activities. Sometimes the infusion of grant funding will help, but the lessons from the Developmental Education Initiative and Achieving the Dream project suggest this is not necessarily the case.

Heavy reliance upon part-time faculty is one of the challenges confronting classroom-based initiatives such as service-learning (see chapter 16 in this book). Adjunct faculty members spend less time at the college and may be juggling teaching assignments at multiple institutions. For all community college instructors, contracts, promotions, and tenure govern the availability of time for meetings and work outside the regular teaching load. The teaching load itself can be quite high, as full-time instructors generally teach four or five courses each semester. The challenge of finding time to work on special projects is even more acute for part-time faculty, many of whom lack not only time but office space on campus as well.

The challenge of scaling up also involves students. Similar to faculty, community college students are also disproportionately part-time. Not only do students spend little time on campus, but the experience of a decade of trying to improve student success consistently finds that it is difficult to motivate students to participate in voluntary activities, even those that they perceive as being helpful to them. In order to be effective, students must be mandated to participate, whether this means enrolling in innovative courses, meeting deadlines, or engaging in college activities. Special curricular constraints also shape efforts at bringing reforms to scale at community colleges. Capturing students during their first year at a college necessitates embedding new initiatives in developmental education, since this is where so many community college students begin their college journey. In the higher-level courses, curriculum is constrained by the need to cover a lot of material in a relatively small number of credits (an associate degree is approximately 20 courses). This is true of occupational programs that often have to meet standards set by industry-based accreditation. It is also true for transfer-oriented courses, as faculty are highly aware of the need to make sure that their curricula articulate with those of four-year institutions so that students can transfer the credits toward the bachelor's degree. These are the common challenges confronting community college faculty nationwide seeking to innovate in their classrooms.

Discussion and Recommendations

Successful service-learning programs appear to have several characteristics in common with other student-success initiatives, including leaders that champion the pedagogy, ample training and recognition for faculty and students, and strong evaluation systems to measure and document success (Jeandron and Robinson 2010; Largent and Horinek 2008). Community colleges are just beginning to gain experience with implementing large-scale curricular changes such as those described in this chapter.

Student-success initiatives require resources and cross-departmental collaboration and communication. Community college administrators therefore have a critical role to play in establishing and bringing to scale service-learning programs. Their support is needed to obtain resources, ensure that professional development of faculty can occur, and create ways to recognize and reward students for participation. There are important benefits not only to students but also to institutions in expanding the use of service-learning, particularly when community colleges serve not just as part of the local community but also as leading organizations in the strengthening of communities.

This obligation to the community is central to the mission of community colleges as open door institutions. The open door of community colleges can be interpreted in a variety of ways. On the one hand it reflects the principle that postsecondary education should be accessible to all students. Family background, financial status, and even weak academic preparation need not present formal barriers to earning a college degree in the United States. Of course, in reality, community colleges battle hard with the challenges of providing access while at the same time maintaining standards and helping students to reach goals that may be unrealistic or ill-informed.

A second interpretation of the open door involves the relationship between community colleges and their communities. It is within the mission of community colleges to serve as a catalyst in their communities—to not just exist in the community but to actually contribute to its development and improvement. Community colleges are highly varied in their efforts to meet this ideal. Some do this through workforce development programs while others collaborate with social service organizations, non-profits, and K-12 school systems. For many community college instructors, the classroom is a place where students can gain important intellectual abilities, such as critical thinking and understanding social justice, which will help them to better the community throughout their lives. Regardless of the focus of community engagement, most community colleges have at least one or more organizational units within the college devoted to establishing and nurturing these ties.

Service-learning unites these interpretations of the open door mission. Evidence suggests that finding ways to integrate students academically and socially into campus life can help to increase the chances of student success, thus helping colleges to deliver on their promise of access. In particular, active and collaborative teaching techniques seem to work best to enhance engagement, and service-learning is certainly one way to accomplish this aim. But, service-learning has the capacity to reach beyond simply engaging students, to help them find ways to impact their local communities. By providing students with opportunities to develop and reflect upon their communities and to connect classroom learning with the realities of work and society, community colleges can better reach the ideal of becoming an engine for change within their communities.

Notes

1. Table 303.70.
2. These results are from the 2013 Community College Survey of Student Engagement (CCSSE), items 4s and 4t. The survey and results from community colleges nationwide can be found on the CCSSE website: http://www.ccsse.org under "standard reports."
3. Table 330.10.
4. Table 303.55.
5. Table 306.5.
6. Table 378.
7. Table A-45–1.

References

Attewell, Paul, David Lavin, Thurston Domina, and Tania Levey. 2006. "New Evidence on College Remediation." *Journal of Higher Education* 77 (5): 886–924.

Bailey, Thomas, Dong Wook Jeong, and Sung-Woo Cho. 2009. *Referral, Enrollment, and Completion in Developmental Education Sequences in Community Colleges*. New York, NY: Community College Research Center, Teachers College, Columbia University.

Brint, Steven, and Jerome Karabel. 1989. *The Diverted Dream: Community Colleges and the Promise of Educational Opportunity in America, 1900–1985*. New York: Oxford University Press.

CCSSE. 2012. Community College Survey of Student Engagement 2012 frequency report.

Cohen, Arthur M., and Florence B. Brawer. 2009. *The American Community College*, 5th ed. San Francisco, CA: Jossey-Bass.

Deil-Amen, Regina. 2011. "Socio-Academic Integrative Moments: Rethinking Academic and Social Integration Among Two-Year College Students in Career-Related Programs." *The Journal of Higher Education* 82 (1): 54–91.

Dougherty, Kevin J. 1994. *The Contradictory College: The Conflicting Origins, Impacts, and Futures of the Community Colleges*. Albany, NY: State University of New York Press.

Franco, Robert W. 2002. "The Civic Role of Community Colleges: Preparing Students for the Work of Democracy." *The Journal of Public Affairs*: 119–138.

Higginbottom, George H., and Richard M. Romano. 2006. "Appraising the Efficacy of Civic Education at the Community College." *New Directions for Community Colleges* 136 (Winter): 23–32.

Ishitani, Terry T. 2006. "Studying Attrition and Degree Completion Behavior among First-Generation College Students in the United States." *Journal of Higher Education* 77 (5): 861–885.

JBL. 2008. "Students Earning Zero Credits." In *Data Notes*. Bethesda, MD: JBL Associates, Inc.

Jeandron, Carol, and Gail Robinson. 2010. *Creating a Climate for Service Learning Success.* Washington, DC: American Association of Community Colleges.

Jenkins, Davis, Cecilia Speroni, Clive Belfield, Shanna Smith Jaggars, and Nikki Edgecombe. 2010. *A Model for Accelerating Academic Success of Community College Remedial English Students: Is the Accelerated Learning Program (ALP) Effective and Affordable?* New York: Community College Research Center, Teachers College, Columbia University.

Lardner, Emily, and Gillies Malnarich. 2008. "A New Era in Learning-Community Work: Why the Pedagogy of Intentional Integration Matters." *Change Magazine* July-August.

Largent, Liz, and Joh B. Horinek. 2008. "Community Colleges and Adult Service Learners: Evaluating a First-Year Program to Improve Implementation." *New Directions for Adult and Continuing Education Summer* 118: 37–47.

NCES. 2011. *Condition of Education.* Washington, DC: National Center for Education Statistics.

———. 2012. *Digest of Education Statistics.* Washington, DC: National Center for Education Statistics.

———. 2013. *Digest of Education Statistics.* Washington, DC: National Center for Education Statistics.

Parsad, Basmat, and Laurie Lewis. November 2003. *Remedial Education at Degree-Granting Postsecondary Institutions in Fall 2000.* Washington, DC: National Center for Education Statistics.

Próspero, Moisés, and Shetal Vohra-Gupta. 2007. "First Generation College Students: Motivation, Integration, and Academic Achievement." *Community College Journal of Research and Practice* 31: 963–975.

Quint, Janet, Shanna S. Jaggars, D. Crystal Byndloss, and Asya Magazinnik. 2013. *Bringing Developmental Education to Scale: Lessons from the Developmental Education Initiative.* New York, NY: MDRC.

Ratcliff, James L. 1994. "Seven Streams in the Historical Development of the Modern American Community College." In A Handbook on the Community College in America, edited by G. A. Baker III. Westport, CT: Greenwood Press.

Rutschow, Elizabeth Zachry, Lashawn Richburg-Hayes, Thomas Brock, Genevieve Orr, Oscar Cerna, Dan Cullinan, Monica Reid Kerrigan, Davis Jenkins, Susan Gooden, and Kasey Martin. 2011. *Turning the Tide: Five Years of Achieving the Dream in Community Colleges.* New York, NY: MDRC.

Statway™. 2010. *Instructional Design Principles for Statway™.* Stanford, CA: The Carnegie Foundation for the Advancement of Teaching.

Tinto, Vincent. 1975. "Dropout from Higher Education: A Theoretical Synthesis of Recent Research." *Review of Educational Research* 45: 89–125.

———. 1993. *Leaving College: Rethinking the Causes and Cures of Student Attrition*, 2nd ed. Chicago, IL: University of Chicago Press.

Visher, Mary G., Emily Schneider, Heather Wathington, and Herbert Collado. 2010. *Scaling Up Learning Communities: The Experience of Six Community Colleges.* New York, NY: National Center for Postsecondary Research.

Zeidenberg, Matt, Sung-Woo Cho, and Davis Jenkins. 2010. *Washington State's Integrated Basic Education and Skills Training Program (I-BEST): New Evidence of Effectiveness.* New York, NY: Community College Research Center, Teachers College, Columbia University.

PART II

Service-Learning in Diverse Community College Contexts

CHAPTER 3

Hitting Close to Home: When Service-Learners Serve Their Own

Heather B. Wylie

"That's me. They are me. It's weird being here and still a part of them." Mike shifted in his seat, a little uncomfortable, as we chatted during office hours. Mike, a white, working-class male in his late 30s recently returned to school seeking a second career in the wake of drastic layoffs in construction jobs in the area. To avoid "all that writing," Mike instead opted for the course's service-learning project. His choice came as somewhat of a surprise, since, as an unemployed veteran, he did not seem to fit the profile of a "service-learner." Neither did Kristen. Standing in the office doorway during the last week of class, she suddenly broke into tears, struggling to speak. "I found my voice, Heather. Doing this [service-learning project], I, for the first time, didn't feel alone. There's a lot of us out there—survivors, you know?"

Comments like these, from a broad spectrum of my sociology students at Shasta College, a California community college, forced me to critically examine a fundamental assumption within the field of service-learning, namely what service-learning students look like. Research assumes and programs are often constructed around the "ideal type" service-learning student: a full-time, white, young, single, childless, economically advantaged college student (Butin 2010). This assumption situates "border-crossing" and "bridging divides" as a primary pedagogical goal of engaged learning. Implied within this paradigm is the construction of those served as outsiders and thus the bearers of difference and "otherness."

This framework proved problematic for me as an instructor, researcher, and civic and community engagement coordinator, since the vast majority of my service-learning students are not "ideal types." Rather, this group of predominantly first-generation college students with families, debt, and jobs often found themselves "serving" populations that looked a lot like them. Class conversations, survey comments, and student assignments were telling a story largely absent in the service-learning literature.

I was therefore left with the question: How does service learning "work" when the students doing the service are interacting with populations that mirror their own racial/ethnic, class, and cultural identities? Or as Butin (2010, 32) posits, "What happens when the postsecondary population *is already* [original emphasis] of those identity categories?"

Drawing on qualitative data from 78 service-learning students enrolled in seven of my sociology courses over a period of two academic years, this chapter suggests two answers to this question. First, service-learning situates identity and identity formation as key components to successful learning in higher education when learners are "serving their own." Students, when encouraged to embrace their social location rather than disregard it (or worse, reject it), can, through service-learning, recognize the structural nature of not only their own experiences but also that of many of today's social problems. In doing so, service-learning can help students recognize what sociologists refer to as "personal troubles" versus "public issues" (Mills 1959). This "critical shift in consciousness" thus poses a direct threat to traditional structures of higher education in general and service-learning in particular, structures that predicate student success on *separation* from one's social location and assimilation into dominate paradigms (Guffey, Shepard, and Tom 2002).

Second, service-learning projects that link personal experience to social structures are essential to the process of institutional reform. Here, service-learning becomes a pedagogy that inspires students to see education as a tool for institutional change. In short, service-learning, when critically reconsidered, creates spaces for more holistic, process-oriented models of teaching and learning that encourage students to become part of, versus simply a product of, the educational system (Guffey et al. 2002).

Community colleges are particularly suited for critical reexaminations of service-learning as a meaningful teaching tool given their mission and increasingly diverse student populations. While the social and economic role of community colleges and institutions of higher education in general remains an ongoing point of contention, the continued mission of all two-year colleges is to extend educational opportunities and encourage civic engagement (Gleazer 1994). Yet, the diversity of community college student populations demands that civic engagement pedagogies, like service-learning, tackle problematic assumptions about college students' identity in order to remain an effective teaching tool. This chapter thus seeks to contribute to the small but growing literature that challenges fundamental assumptions within the field of service-learning theory and practice and, in doing so, expands its value as a pedagogical tool.

Literature Review

In key ways, the field of service-learning continues to be based on often unacknowledged and problematic assumptions, the most obvious being the design and implementation of service-learning projects suited to an "ideal type" student. That is, "one who volunteers her time, has high cultural capital, and gains from contact with the 'other'" (Butin 2010, 31). This is a problem for students in all institutions of higher education who fall outside of this construct, particularly those in community colleges. Assumptions of privilege within the field keep many from taking advantage of traditional service-learning opportunities. Students may avoid taking service-learning designated courses or, when given the choice, opt for more standard course assignments. For those that do participate in service-learning, they are required, in ways both subtle and blatant, to "give up their active roles in vital communities to become recipients of cultural messages" from the dominant paradigm (Guffey et al. 2002, 10). They essentially must take on the characteristics of this privileged "ideal type" in order to succeed.

In addition to creating barriers and dismissing alternative ways of knowing, this assumption can reinforce the very thing service-learning seeks to challenge, namely social injustice (e.g., Cipolle 2010). The field, in its enthusiasm to "build bridges" and "connect communities," often fails to critically examine identity and identity politics as they play out within these relationships. Mitchell (2008, as cited in Mitchell and Donahue 2010, 175) suggests that

> one of the unspoken truths about service-learning is that it is a pedagogy that has traditionally targeted privileged students. The frameworks that guide how we shape and teach service-learning courses have often been about crossing borders and connecting across difference with that "difference" mostly embodied by the community served.

Butin (2010, 32) goes further by highlighting the very real possibility of service-learning turning into the "'whitest of the white' enclave in postsecondary education," assuming this "ideal type" remains unchecked. In short, the field of service-learning has and, to some degree, continues to focus on and construct itself around white, middle-class students serving "underrepresented" populations, thereby reinforcing "otherness," a crucial element in maintaining systems of social inequality.

Similarly, Eby (1998) criticizes traditional service-learning programs for constructing service opportunities where students enter the communities as outsiders. This, he argues, reinforces the idea that communities themselves are deficient and need outside resources to fix their problems. By defining needs as deficiencies, students are able to and, in some ways, expected to separate themselves from the problems they encounter (Eby 1998). Left unexamined, service-learning simply becomes one person "helping" someone less fortunate with little or no recognition of the structural nature of social problems. This early note of caution, however, went unheeded in the enthusiasm for promoting a pedagogy focused on "doing good."

The fact that the race and class of the "ideal type" service-learning student remains invisible also serves to reinforce established social hierarchies. When left unexplored and unexamined, the assumed whiteness and privileged economic status of service-learning students constructs a "normative backdrop" upon which the service-learning literature rests (Smith 2004, 1). This effectively silences competing voices not only within the literature on service-learning but in the experiences of students that do not fit within this narrow stereotype. According to Green (2003, 277), it is only by doing the work of "dismantling" the privilege built into the pedagogy of service-learning that the field can start to tell the "difficult stories" of inequality. This critical and challenging process of deconstructing this "good work" can (1) serve to challenge (rather than reinforce) social stratification, and

(2) expand service-learning beyond "bridge building" between have and have-nots, which, as discussed earlier, simply accentuates the idea of "other." Instead, service-learners serving "their own" provides a more interesting context for the integration of multiple identities (e.g., minority and college student) and the recognition of the structural nature of social inequality.

The historic lack of critical reflection in this field is problematic not only at the level of individual experience but for the institution of higher education as a whole. This built-in binary of server/served ultimately reinforces an educational system that promotes an "abstract, theoretical, top-down perspective," one that seeks to distance students from their "indigenous context" and to replace that context with dominant Western beliefs and values (Guffey et al. 2002, 8). As inherently problematic as this is, the marginalization of lived experience is even more challenging for those students who fail to conform to this hidden curriculum since they can "find themselves in a discontinuous, and in many ways conflicted, setting where the potential for ongoing acquisition of complex cultural knowledge, values and attributes becomes severely limited" (Guffey et al. 2002, 8). Comprehension of course material, and ultimately success in college, can thus prove daunting for those students attempting to maintain and integrate their underrepresented identities in the learning process.

As service-learning matures, however, advocates have become increasingly self-reflective on the use of this pedagogy within diverse student populations. Green (2003, 276), for instance, calls for a closer examination of how service-learning is experienced differently "by those from different groups and [a closer look] at the gaps between our theories of service-learning and our theories of subject position(s), of race, class, gender, and sexuality." In doing so, research suggests that the "difference" that Mitchell (2008) alluded to earlier no longer lies between a privileged service-learning student and an "underserved" community but rather within the lived experiences of students within the classroom. As community college classrooms become more diverse, spaces begin to exist among the students themselves. Numerous studies exploring the relationship between class and the experience of service-learning have recognized the importance of examining how students of different economic backgrounds experience service-learning (Yeh 2010; Henry 2005; Lee 2005). Other studies have examined how service-learning influences students of color (Shadduck-Hernandez 2005; McCollum 2003; Green 2001; Chesler and Scalera 2000; Coles 1999).

With few exceptions, however, the literature has failed to adequately examine a central concept in the field, the idea of "border-crossing." Service-learning has been packaged, for the most part, as an opportunity for students to connect with "other" communities, generally those less privileged than their own. This proves problematic, however, in light of the increased diversity in community college student populations. How does service-learning work when the ones doing the service are essentially "serving" their own? In what way(s) does this complicate fundamental binaries in the service-learning field (e.g., server/served, student/teacher, and classroom/community) (Butin 2010, 32)? Implied here is the notion of identity. Specifically, what role does service-learning play in identity exploration and construction among students with diverse backgrounds? Might service-learning act as a bridge, not necessarily between disparate communities but rather between disparate identities?

Also, as more colleges and universities heed Cruz's (1990) advice to create service-learning programs committed to diversity, ones that "make possible the effective participation of low-income working people, single parents, and others who experience constraints defined by different economic and cultural realities," how might this affect higher education in general and community colleges in particular? Work exploring service-learning and diverse student populations, including Larson-Keagy (2002) and Conley and Hamlin (2009), suggests that teaching that embraces diverse student populations, including service-learning, can shift higher education toward more "holistic, process-oriented learning...where students are brought into direct contact with the socio-cultural and ecological patterns present in their community" (Guffey et al. 2002, 10).

Method

Context

Shasta College, located 160 miles north of Sacramento, California, is a rural community college that serves three counties (over 10,000 square miles) and parts of three others, all of which rank among the poorest in California. Poverty has, since the collapse of the mining and timber industries, persisted as a significant social and economic problem in the area. Median family income is between $43,944 and $38,137 over the three counties compared to $60,883 for the state (US Census Bureau 2010). Allied to this is the relatively low rate of completion at Shasta College. While the high school graduation rate exceeds the state average (27 percent to 31 percent across the three counties versus 22 percent for the state), the college's completion rates are significantly lower than the state average (9 percent to 14 percent compared to 19 percent) (US Census Bureau 2010). Primarily a service-based economy, the region's major employers are the federal and state governments, health care, and tourism. Unemployment in the three counties ranges from 13.1 percent to 15.7 percent in 2012 compared to 7.8 percent for the state (US Census Bureau 2010). Poverty, combined with a proximity to a major interstate highway, is in part responsible for high rates of drug use and drug-related crime in the region. The rate of felony and misdemeanor arrests for drug crimes in Shasta County, the area most directly served by the college, exceeded the state average at 1,181.96 (per 1,000) compared to 961.65 (per 100,000) (Indicators of Alcohol and Other Drug Risks 2010). Reading student autobiographical essays in my introductory courses semester after semester underscores how truly widespread and devastating poverty, unemployment, and drug abuse are not only to individuals but to the region as a whole.

Diversity within the three counties is largely based on class, not race or ethnicity. Containing the largest city in the northernmost part of the state, the region nonetheless remains primarily white, non-Hispanic (82 percent) followed by Hispanic (10 percent), multiracial (3 percent), American Indian (2 percent), Asian (2 percent), black or African American (1 percent), and Native Hawaiian and other Pacific Islander (less than 1 percent) (Shasta College 2013). The region is experiencing a small but growing number of Hispanic immigrants given the agriculture industry just south of the county (Shasta College 2013).

The college's student population reflects the region's demographic profile. About three quarters identify as white with other ethnic/racial groups comprising between 1 percent and 10 percent each. The college serves a higher percentage of white students compared to the community college system statewide, although the number of Hispanic students is steadily increasing. Over half of the students are under the age of 25. The remainder of them are between the ages of 25 and 29 (12 percent), 30 and 39 (13 percent), 40 and 49 (10 percent), and 50 or older (10 percent). As such, students are somewhat younger in comparison to those in the statewide system. The majority of students are working class as reflected by the use of financial aid and college support services (Fact Book 2011).

Participants

Research for this study is based on qualitative data—collected via interviews, course assignments, pre- and post-service surveys, and informal conversations—from 78 service-learning students enrolled in seven study courses over a period of seven semesters, fall 2009 to fall 2012. These were not officially designated as "service-learning" courses as the institution currently has no formal designation process. In four of the seven courses (two Sociology of Gender courses [fall 2009 and 2010] and two Sociology of Minorities courses [spring 2010 and 2011]), students were given the option to engage in a semester-long service-learning project or to undertake the standard research-essay assignment. These students self-selected to commit a minimum of 15 hours to a service-learning project with a local community partner.

Service-learning projects were required in the remaining three courses (two Sociology of Gender courses [fall 2012 and 2011] and one Sociology of Minorities course [spring 2012]). In one of these, the Sociology of Minorities spring 2012 course, students self-selected into groups depending on their specific interests and created service-learning projects that met the needs articulated by a particular minority group in the region. The remaining two courses were designed for the student leadership fellows program, which trains college students to serve as service-learning advisors for the area youth. In these courses, students assisted kindergarten through sixth grade students in the design and implementation of service-learning projects that met community needs identified by the youth. Throughout the process, fellows received training in leadership, mentoring, and career exploration. All sociology students and fellows were required to submit reflection assignments and give oral presentations on their projects.

Students in both situations represented a demographically diverse cross-section of the student population, a population in stark contrast to the "ideal type" service-learning student discussed earlier. The majority was female (68 percent women, 32 percent men). This is not surprising as sociology classes tend to attract more female students, and service-learning is often culturally coded as "care work" and thus defined as feminine. The vast majority came from working-class backgrounds (74 percent), based on their eligibility for the Board of Governor's (BOGG) fee waivers, and 42 percent worked at least part-time. The racial/ethnic makeup of the student sample also reflects that of the college population as a whole. The majority was white non-Hispanic (77 percent), followed by Hispanic (10 percent),

Asian (.08 percent), black or African American (.04 percent), and American Indian (.01percent).

Students worked with a variety of community partners, including nonprofit organizations focused on domestic violence, homelessness, primary education, after school programming, reproductive outreach education, and youth with learning disabilities. The majority of the populations served by these agencies was working-class and/or underrepresented minorities. In short, here were service-learning students "serving" their own communities.

Study data were organized and analyzed through a process of open coding. The same conceptual categories were used across the data.

Analysis

According to the data collected, service-learning can be a valuable learning tool for diverse student populations, a tool that honors and connects multiple identities. In doing so, it underscores students' understanding of the structural nature of seemingly individual problems and creates spaces that challenge hierarchical learning models in higher education.

Connecting Multiple Identities

How does service-learning work when students identify with the populations with which they work? What happens when they are not "outside" but rather "part" of the communities served? The research here suggests that shared social locations between students and their communities complicates the notion of "helping," or the server/served binary found in more traditional service-learning projects. "Help" has typically been offered as a mirror image of the individualized definition of need, where the "...answer to need as deficiency is an outside person whose service fills the deficiency...which exaggerates the importance of the person who serves [and] demeans the person served" (McKnight, 1996 as cited in Eby 1998, 4). Service-learning projects that locate the learner within their context of everyday life move us beyond the serious limitations of the "ideal type" student.

Mike's experience with disadvantaged youth, as discussed in the introduction, responds to McKnight's (1996) critique. As an individual with a background very similar to the youth with whom he worked, Mike entered his site not as an outsider offering "help" to someone in need, but rather as someone who, because he could identify with the experiences of these young men and women, offered the possibility of alternative life paths. Like these youths, Mike grew up in a low-income, rural town where few, if any, fellow high school students attended college. Divorce, drug abuse, domestic violence, and unemployment were common growing up. Discussing a reflection journal entry during office hours, Mike commented, "This really brought it all back for me. You know, those times when I was left home for days at a time...a few bucks left on the counter for food." This sense of connection was juxtaposed with his current identity as a college student, one seemingly very separate from his previous social location; however, far from creating tension or confusion about his identity, the service-learning experience seemed to, as Conley and Hamlin (2009) put it, bridge his community of origin with his academic community. It provided a connection between these two seemingly disparate worlds. As Mike wrote in a reflection near the end of service:

> I struggled for the first year or two here [at college] trying to figure out how I fit in. I didn't belong here. People talked differently, acted different, I didn't seem to fit...working with these kids though helped me see the connection between who I am and who I want to be. It [the service-learning project] helped me see how my education connects to something real.

This experience, like those reported by many other students, created a space for Mike to construct and reconstruct an identity that, in the words of Maldonado et al. (2005, 633), "simultaneously promotes the practice of both dominant and transformative forms of cultural and social capital to achieve academic success."

This phenomenon was reported by other students on post-service surveys as well. In response to the question, "Did this experience positively impact how you felt about yourself as a college student?" a majority of students (64 percent) answered in the affirmative. Similarly, 58 percent of students strongly agreed with the following statement: "Service-learning helped me understand connections between my life experiences and future academic and career goals." Among the ten in-depth interviews I was able to conduct, seven interviewees made comments suggesting service-learning helped in the bridging of disparate identities. For example, one student, Esperanza, mentioned that service-learning "helped me connect where I came from and who I am now, you know, as a person in college." This was especially poignant as this same student had expressed a high degree of anxiety about feeling "pulled in two different directions" in terms of her cultural background and academic goals. These data suggest then that shared social location provides an opportunity for the affirmation and integration of identities previously considered contradictory, even incompatible (e.g., racial/ethnic minority and college student), within higher education. As mentioned earlier, this is important since students experiencing a disconnect between who they are and what the institution expects them to be can, and often do, become disillusioned with the promise of higher education.

Understanding the Structural Nature of "Individual" Problems

Service-learning as a means of identity formation also serves to reinforce the development of students' sociological imaginations. While obviously important to the field of sociology, this perspective is arguably key in the formation of an informed citizenry. Generally considered to be the ability to see patterns, structures, and social context in understanding individual and social behavior, the sociological imagination helps differentiate between what Mills (1959, 12) refers to as "personal troubles of milieu" (i.e., problems specific to a particular individual or group) and "public issues of social structure" (i.e., those situations that extend beyond the individual to society itself). Service-learning projects that maintain the server/served binary position students as privileged "outsiders," thus reinforcing their tendency to see public issues as personal troubles. This matters because the failure to recognize the structural nature of many of today's social problems reinforces individualistic explanations so common in popular political and cultural rhetoric. As such, traditional service-learning projects can end up reinforcing, rather than challenging, structural inequality.

However, because this binary breaks down when students share backgrounds similar to those with whom they work, service-learning projects can actually serve to make explicit what is often implicit in how these students understand and experience the social world. More specifically, service-learning projects reframe students' experiences with social inequality as a public issue and not a personal trouble. Kristen, for example, volunteered to work on a project with a local women's shelter. I was struck by this decision as I knew from previous writing assignments that she, herself, was a victim of sexual assault. During our first interview, when we discussed the feasibility of her service-learning project, Kristen expressed the need to "help others" who had been in her situation. Initially I was reluctant to agree to the match, as I was concerned that the experience might prove emotionally overwhelming for her; however, within a month, I was convinced that not only was it a good match, no other experience could have underscored domestic violence as a public issue in quite the same way. No article, text, or course lecture would have convinced this young woman of the social context that contributed to her experience with sexual violence.

For example, Kristen's project-long reflections demonstrated her growing understanding of the structural nature of gender violence. During an informal conversation after class, Kristen mentioned how she felt "weird" about being so "excited" to be around other women who had been through what she had experienced: "I was helping them clean up after a meeting and I just felt…I don't know…like this was bigger than me. This anger, shame, ugliness wasn't really mine." Throughout the semester, Kristen helped with and then eventually facilitated presentations on gender discrimination to various civic groups and organizations. In her reflection journal afterward, she made the connection between her experience and the public issue of sexual violence:

> It was powerful to talk with these young women and explain how this whole thing, sexism, discrimination is so much bigger than them. That it's the system that's broken, not them. Nothing they did or do will ever justify being treated unequally. That really, if we want to deal with domestic and sexual assault, we've got to deal with gender discrimination.

Had this opportunity not been available, it is unlikely that she would have made this connection on her own. Her service-learning project provided a larger context in which to situate her specific experience, allowing her to ultimately shift the blame for this act of violence from herself to a social structure that creates and recreates spaces that promote gender violence.

Recognizing the structural nature of social problems was a key outcome of another student service-learning project. Over the course of the semester, this group identified discrimination against members of the lesbian, gay, bisexual, and transgender (LGBT) community as a public issue versus a personal trouble. A group of four Sociology of Minorities students, one of whom openly identified as lesbian, focused on institutionalizing a campus Safe Zone program, one that trains faculty, staff, and administration to be "safe" resources for LGBT students to turn to with questions, concerns, and/or resources. Their specific goal was the creation of a comprehensive and inclusive advocate training manual.

An analysis of their pre-service surveys and reflection assignments revealed how these four students conceptualized discrimination based on sexual orientation and gender identification as solitary acts of "bad apples." Damian, for instance, noted in an early journal entry that "these idiots that do stuff like call gays names and push them around should be punished. The laws should be changed that put them in prison for a long time." Comments like these reinforce the perception that discrimination against the LGBT community is a personal trouble, that they are isolated acts of social deviants. However, after hosting a focus group composed of members from the LGBT community, there was a noticeable shift in students' comments. This group was convened to solicit feedback on an early draft of the advocate training manual. In a debriefing session afterward, three of the four students mentioned frustration with the systematic nature of discrimination. For example, when asked about her big "take-away" from the meeting, Christine stated: "It surprised me how very few of them mentioned one bad person or one jerk who did something wrong. Their fear and frustrations really seem to be about society as a whole and how things are set up against them."

This shift, and others like it, suggests that service-learning can prove valuable in helping students recognize the role of social structures in maintaining social inequality. This was in large part because of the absence of the traditional server/served binary in service-learning. While obvious in the case of the one self-identified lesbian, this applies to the other students as well. The lack of a clear socioeconomic and cultural hierarchy (e.g., working-class status, racial/ethnic minority status) between these students and the LGBT community provided opportunities for them to situate their own experiences with discrimination within a larger structural context, a context that is currently organized to reinforce and sustain heterosexual and cisgender privilege (the latter referring to individuals that identify with the gender they were assigned at birth).

Challenging Hierarchical Learning Models in Higher Education

Avenues of identify formation that link personal experiences to social structure, like service-learning, are essential to the "work of building institutions that fully realize the promise of diversity" (Ortiz and Santos 2010, 5). Doing so can create spaces that challenge traditional "top-down" approaches to higher education. This is especially important in rural/minority populations, as conventional teaching methods often create distance between the learner and her or his culture, teaching students to see the borderlands of their existence as zones of separation versus transformation (Larson-Keagy 2002, 2). This research, however, suggests that service-learning projects that move beyond the "ideal type" student model and encourage participation by a diverse student population in culturally validating service projects with communities similar to their own, can, as Yeh (2010) suggests, inspire students to engage in their community and use their education as a tool for institutional change.

For example, well over half the students reported on post-service surveys that their service experience made their education "matter" to them in new and significant ways. A majority of respondents (61 percent) answered "yes" when asked: "Did your service-learning project have a positive impact on how you feel about your college experience?" Similarly, 64 percent strongly agreed that their service-learning project made them feel like a more active participant in their educational experience. A project de-brief session with a male Asian American student, Chris, underscored the usefulness of service-learning as a tool in the shift toward more holistic, process-oriented learning, one that incorporates student experiences in, rather than separates student experiences from, the learning process. Chris had spent the semester working on a group service-learning project designed to increase access to reproductive health care in the Latina/o community. After the eight-hour community training session organized by his service-learning group, he stated: "This project made me feel like I matter here. I mean, I felt respected, like I had something to give...because of that, I feel like I actually learned something."

Conclusion

Recognizing the preliminary nature of these findings, this study nonetheless raises questions and creates momentum for future research and reflection on the experience of and interactions with service-learning pedagogy. As this case study shows, service-learning works in many and often overlooked ways, depending not only on the population being served but also on the students doing the service. Minority students experience service-learning in ways distinctly different from their privileged counterparts. Service-learning bridges identities in profound and particular ways for students sharing similar social locations to the populations they work with, and this connection creates opportunities for students to recognize the structural nature of many of today's social problems. Likewise, in moving beyond early and problematic assumptions within the field of service-learning, this teaching tool can ultimately provide grounds for a much needed shift in higher education; one that honors multiple ways of knowing, embraces student experiences, and responds to real cultural, social, and economic changes.

References

American Association of Community Colleges. *Fast Facts from Our Fact Sheet.* Accessed November 18, 2013. http://www.aacc.nche.edu/AboutCC/Pages/fastfactsfactsheet.aspx.

Butin, Dan W. 2010. *Service-Learning in Theory and Practice: The Future of Community Engagement in Higher Learning.* New York: Palgrave Macmillan.

———. 2005. "Service-Learning Is Dangerous." *The National Teaching & Learning Forum* 14 (4).

Chesler, Mark A., and Carolyn V. Scalera. 2000. "Race and Gender Issues Related to Service-Learning Research." *Michigan Journal of Community Service Learning* 7: 18–27.

Cipolle, Susan Benigni. 2010. *Service-Learning and Social Justice: Engaging Students in Social Change.* New York: Rowman and Littlefield.

Coles, Roberta L. 1999. "Race-Focused Service-Learning Courses: Issues and Recommendations." *Michigan Journal of Community Service Learning* 6: 97–105.

Conley, Paige A., and Maria L. Hamlin. 2009 "Justice-Learning: Exploring the Efficacy with Low-Income, First-Generation College Students." *Michigan Journal of Community Service Learning*: 47–58.

Cruz, Nadinne. 1990. "Principles of Good Practice in Combining Service and Learning: A Diversity Perspective." Response to Wingspread Principles of Good Practice in Combining Service and Learning. http://www.servicelearning.org/filemanager/download/Principles_of_Good_Practice_for_Combining_Service_and_Learning.pdf.

Eby, John W. 1998. *Why Service-Learning Is Bad*. Accessed November 1, 2011. http://www.servicelearning.org/library/resource/4703.

Fact Book. 2011. Prepared by the Office of Research and Planning.

Franco, Robert. 2002. "Our Communities' Colleges: Cultivating Civic Roots in a Diverse Democracy." In *Through Whose Eyes: Service-Learning and Civic Engagement from Culturally Diverse Perspectives*, edited by Elizabeth Larson-Keagy. Mesa, AZ: Campus Compact, National Center for Community Colleges.

Gleazer, Edmund J. 1994. "Foreword." In *America's Community Colleges: The First Century*, edited by Allen A. Witt, James Wattnbarger, James Gollattschedk, and Joseph Suppiger. Washington, DC: Community College Press.

Green, Ann E. 2001. "'But You Aren't White': Racial Perceptions and Service-Learning." *Michigan Journal of Community Service Learning* 8 (1): 18–26.

———. 2003. Difficult Stories: Service-Learning, Race, Class, and Whiteness. *College Composition and Communication*. 55 (2).

Guffey, John, Frank Shepard, and Juanita Tom. 2002. "In the Beginning…GEMS: Year One." In *Through Whose Eyes: Service-Learning and Civic Engagement from Culturally Diverse Perspectives*, edited by Elizabeth Larson-Keagy, Mesa, AZ: Campus Compact-National Center for Community Colleges.

Henry, Sue Ellen. 2005. "'I Can Never Turn My Back on That': Liminality and the Impact of Class on the Service-Learning Experience." In *Service-Learning in Higher Education*, edited by Dan W. Butin, 45–66. New York: Palgrave Macmillan.

Indicators of Alcohol and Other Drug Risk and Consequences for California Counties. 2010. Accessed July 26, 2013. http://www.adp.ca.gov/Prevention/pdf/indicators_2010/Shasta.pdf.

Information and Demographics. (n.d.). Accessed November 1, 2011. http://www.ci.redding.ca.us/demographics.html.

Jefferson, Thomas. 1789. Letter to Richard Price, Paris January 8.

Kipp, Samuel M., III, Derek V. Price, and Jill K. Wolford. 2002. "Unequal Opportunity: Disparities in College Access among the 50 States." *Lumina Foundation for Education*. Monograph online. Accessed July 26, 2013. http://www.luminafoundation.org/tag/state_education_systems/page/4/.

Larson-Keagy, Elizabeth. 2002. "Introduction." In *Through Whose Eyes: Service-Learning and Civic Engagement from Culturally Diverse Perspectives*. Mesa, AZ: Campus Compact: National Center for Community Colleges.

Lee, Jenny J. 2005. "Home Away from Home or Foreign Territory?: How Social Class Mediates Service-Learning Experiences." *NASPA Journal* 42 (3): 310–325.

McCollum, K.C. 2003. "Perceptions of College Students of Color about Community Service-Learning through Tutoring." PhD diss., University of Massachusetts Amherst.

McKnight, John. 1996. *The Careless Society: Community and Its Counterfeits*. New York: Basic Books.

Maldonado, David E. Z., Robert Rhoads, and Tracy L. Buenavista. 2005. "The Student-Initiated Retention Project: Theoretical Contributions and the Role of Self-Empowerment." *American Educational Research Journal* 42 (4): 605–638.

Mills, C. Wright. 1959. *The Sociological Imagination*. Oxford: Oxford University Press.
Mitchell, Tania D. 2008. "Traditional vs. Critical Service-Learning: Engaging the Literature to Differentiate Two Models." *Michigan Journal of Community Service Learning* 14 (2): 50–65.
Mitchell, Tania D., and David M. Donahue. 2010. "'I Do More Service in This Class Than I Ever Do at My Site': Paying Attention to the Reflections of Students of Color in Service-Learning." In *The Future of Service-Learning*, edited by Jean R. Strait and Marybeth Lima. Sterling, VA: Stylus Publishing.
Ortiz, Anna M., and Silvia J. Santos. 2010. "Campus Diversity and Ethnic Identity Development." *Association of American Colleges & Universities* 13 (2).
Phillippe, Kent A., and Leila Gonzalez Sullivan. 2005. *National Profile of Community Colleges: Trends and Statistics*, 4th ed. Washington, DC: American Association of Community Colleges.
Shasta College. 2013 *Educational Master Plan 2012–2039*. Accessed July 23, 2013. www.shastacollege.edu.
Shadduck-Hernandez, Janna. 2005. "'Here I Am Now!' Community Service-Learning with Immigrant and Refugee Undergraduate Students and Youth: The Use of Critical Pedagogy, Situated-Learning and Funds of Knowledge." PhD diss., University of Massachusetts Amherst.
Smith, Phil. 2004. "Whiteness, Normal Theory, and Disability Studies." *Disability Studies Quarterly* Spring (24).
US Census Bureau. 2006–2010 American Community Survey. Accessed July 27, 2013. http://factfinder2.census.gov/faces/nav/jsf/pages/index.xhtml.
ServiceLearning.Org "What Is Service Learning?" Accessed November 1, 2011. http://www.servicelearning.org/what-is-service-learning.
Yeh, Theresa Ling. 2010. "Service-Learning and Persistence of Low-Income, First-Generation College Students: An Exploratory Study." *Michigan Journal of Community Service Learning*: 50–65.

CHAPTER 4

Service-Learning and Immigrant-Origin Community College Students: How and Why Project Design Matters

Amy E. Traver, Zivah Perel Katz, and Michael Bradley

Perhaps paradoxically, America's community colleges are global institutions: their vocational orientation is informed by the skills and cultural competencies required in our globalized economy (Malkan and Pisani 2011); their funding structure is tied to what many define as a global neoliberal ideology (Saunders 2010); their doors are open to international students and they increasingly facilitate study-abroad opportunities (Smith 2013); and their example has become a model for the expansion of educational access and opportunity in communities around the world (Redden 2010). Yet, America's community colleges are global institutions for one decidedly *local* reason as well: they are situated in what Logan and Zhang (2011) call "global neighborhoods"; communities that are multiethnic, multiracial, and home to a burgeoning number of immigrants.

Today, as in the past, America's community colleges serve as the primary gateway to higher education for the new Americans, undocumented immigrants, and English Language Learners (ELL) residing in the nation's "global neighborhoods" (Malkan and Pisani 2011). In fact, Connell (2008) estimates that approximately one-quarter of community college students come from an immigrant background. Given the realities of our globalized world, these students, like all community college students and their baccalaureate-seeking peers, are expected to spend a significant portion of their college careers engaging multicultural curricula, advanced technologies, and theories and debates regarding globalization (American Association of Community Colleges 2001). One technique used to engage them in this regard is service-learning. According to Goldstein (2004), service-learning—when married with the aforementioned curricula, theories, and debates—encourages students to understand the bidirectional relationship between local problems and global forces/flows. It also provides students with some of the practical skills or competencies required for success in our globalized world (Annette 2003).

At the time of writing, little is known about how globalization-themed service-learning projects unfold in community colleges, particularly those that enroll a significant percentage of immigrant-origin students, that is, students who are first- or second-generation immigrants. In this chapter, we use three semesters of pre- and post-course survey data and end-of-semester service-learning reflections to speak to this gap. These data and reflections were collected during our implementation of two different service-learning projects in a globalization-themed learning community at Queensborough Community College, The City University of New York. Consistent with course and college objectives, we aim to understand how globalization-themed service-learning projects affect community college students' understanding of global concepts and development of global competencies, and to compare how project design mediates these effects. We begin the chapter with a review of the theoretical literatures relevant to service-learning, globalization, and immigration. We then segue into a discussion of the methods employed in our study. After presenting our study findings, we conclude the chapter with directions for future research.

Service-Learning, Globalization, and Immigration

According to Goldstein (2004), the majority of American undergraduates find the scale and complexity of globalization overwhelming. In fact, when confronted with the supranational forces that structure our ever-changing world, many come to feel powerless in their more local lives. Yet, because globalization's impacts are *experienced* at the local level, globalization can also be *transformed* at the local level. Service-learning, a high-impact pedagogy that integrates course learning and community action, is one tool faculty can use to highlight the linkages between the local and the global while also encouraging student engagement in and around course topics.

To date, few scholars have studied globalization and service-learning (Keith 2005; see Kozma 2010 and Goldstein 2004 for notable exceptions). For Keith (2005), this is surprising, as service-learning practitioners/researchers and globalization theorists share an interest in matters of diversity, multiculturalism, citizenship, and community development. Significantly, most of the scholarship at this intersection focuses on immigrant populations in the United States: reviewing projects that address the rights of day laborers (Calderon 2007), facilitate English-language instruction (d'Arlach, Sánchez, and Feuer 2009), meet the material needs of immigrant families (Tilley-Lubbs 2009), and record oral histories of migration (Huisman 2010).

Immigration serves as a powerful focus for globalization-themed service-learning projects for two reasons. First, immigration highlights the connection between the local and the global in uniquely concrete terms: students come to contextualize personal immigration narratives in their study of the global forces that ground the movement of people (Snarr and McNamarra 2004; see also Huisman 2010). Second, immigration weds matters of global multiculturalism with interpersonal, intergroup contact: students come to understand concepts like cultural diffusion and ethnonationalism as they enact, confront, and cross the very boundaries they study (Jay 2008; Green 2001).

Yet, immigration also serves as a *complicated* focus for globalization-themed service-learning projects. For example, while many civic-engagement scholars and all immigration policies privilege the nation-state, theories of globalization tend to problematize national borders (Snarr and McNamarra 2004). Likewise, while principles of reciprocity and exchange theory inform service-learning project design and national immigration policies respectively, notions of interdependence are central to ideas and acts of globalism (Keith 2005).

What is perhaps most powerful *and* complex about globalization-themed service-learning projects that unfold in colleges and universities across the United States, however, is that a growing number of the students poised to engage in these projects are immigrants and/or the children of immigrants, themselves (i.e., first- or second-generation immigrants) (Erisman and Looney 2007). How do these students make sense of a service-learning project that references their own position in society? How do they situate themselves in relation to the project, the course material, and community members given their proximity to the topic? In what ways, if any, does this proximity mediate their engagement/success in the project and the course? These questions are particularly relevant in the nation's community colleges where students from immigrant backgrounds are disproportionately enrolled (Erisman and Looney 2007).

Also worth questioning is the design of globalization-themed service-learning projects. While many service-learning projects are designed to engage students as writers, Kozma (2010) describes how writing-based service-learning projects are essential to courses that confront globalization theory. Building on Deans' (2000) distinction between the three models—writing *for*, writing *about*, or writing *with* the community—for service-learning writing, Kozma demonstrates how projects that ask students to write *with* the community are most compatible with their understanding global concepts and developing global competencies. Significantly, Kozma's study was conducted during her time as an instructor at Wayne State, an American university with a large percentage of minority and first/second-generation immigrant students. Thus, and in line with Fitch's (2005) efforts to ascertain how service-learning project design mediates students' development of learning outcomes, one must also ask the following: How and why does the design of globalization-themed service-learning projects matter to college students who are touched by immigration?

A small but growing literature on the service-learning experiences of students of color reveals the extent to which service-learning projects are normed to the needs and development of specific students, most typically affluent, white, nonimmigrant service-learners (Seider, Huguley, and Novick 2013). In fact, research indicates that because service-learning projects often unfold in communities of color, service-learners of color confound one of the most traditional features of service-learning project design: the boundary between "service provider" and "other" (Kincaid and Sotiriou 2004). Consequently, service-learning experiences and impacts often diverge by race. While students of color are more likely than white students to *identify* with the service topic and/or the community-members served (Chesler, et al. 2006; Green 2001; Cohen 1995), white students are more likely than students of color to discuss and connect with each other around their service experiences in class (Seider, Huguley, and Novick 2013; Green 2001). Consistent with these findings, new research by Alcantar (in press) and Perez (2011) reveal the extent to which definitions, measures, and models of civic engagement ignore the perspectives and experiences of Latina/o college students and undocumented college students. In recognition of the many first- and second-generation immigrant college students, particularly those studying in America's community colleges, globalization-themed service-learning projects must be designed, implemented, and studied with these ideas in mind.

Research Questions

In this chapter, we examine how globalization-themed service-learning projects unfold at a community college that enrolls a significant percentage of students who are first- or second-generation immigrants. Consistent with the learning and general education objectives of the courses and college in which these projects unfolded, we ask two related questions. First, how does participation in a globalization-themed service-learning project affect community college students' understanding of global concepts and development of global competencies? Second, how and why does the design of globalization-themed service-learning projects matter to, or mediate, these impacts?

Method

Instructional Setting

This study was conducted at Queensborough Community College (QCC), one of the seven community colleges in the City University of New York (CUNY). In the fall of 2012, QCC enrolled 14,092 degree/certificate students and another 1,619 non-degree students. At that time, approximately 66 percent of QCC's degree/certificate students were full-time students, 53 percent of QCC's degree students were female, and the average age of a QCC degree student was 23 (Queensborough Community College Office of Institutional Research and Assessment 2012).

QCC's students reflect the population of the New York City borough of Queens, which has long been regarded as one of the most racially/ethnically diverse urban areas in the world (The City of New York 2014a). In 2012, approximately 28 percent of the degree students attending QCC described themselves as Hispanic, 25 percent as black/non-Hispanic, 22 percent as white/non-Hispanic, and 25 percent as Asian or Pacific Islander (Queensborough Community College Office of Institutional Research and Assessment 2012). Given these student demographics, QCC has been designated a Hispanic-serving institution.

Also reflective of the college's location in Queens, the New York City borough where more than half of residents are foreign-born (Semple 2013), many of QCC's students are first- or second-generation immigrants. In the fall of 2012, approximately 30 percent of QCC's degree/certificate students were born outside of the United States. While these students represent 139 different nations, the majority of QCC's immigrant students hail from China, Jamaica, Guyana, South Korea, Colombia, Ecuador, Haiti, the Dominican Republic, and India. Also in the fall of 2012, QCC's degree/certificate students reported speaking 87 different languages, with 39 percent of students speaking a language other than English at home. At this same time, 7 percent of QCC's degree/certificate were international students (Queensborough Community College Office of Institutional Research and Assessment 2012).

In the fall of 2012, approximately 70 percent of first-time, full-time QCC students needed some form of developmental coursework, with 12 percent requiring triple remediation in reading, writing, and math (Queensborough Community College Office of Institutional Research and Assessment 2012). In an effort to address these fairly typical student needs, as well as to integrate student/academic support services and to improve the college's overall rate of student retention, QCC implemented the Freshman Academies model in 2009. Consistent with this model, all first-time full-time QCC students enroll in one of six Freshman Academies. A hallmark of each of these academies is students' early and consistent exposure to multiple high-impact educational practices (Kuh 2008), including but not limited to learning communities, writing-intensive experiences, and service-learning. At QCC, writing-intensive courses and learning communities are so designated in the college's course catalog; courses that integrate service-learning projects are not. In order to graduate from QCC with an associate degree, students are required to take at least two writing-intensive courses. In contrast, students need not participate in a learning community or service-learning project to graduate from the college.

Participants and Projects

Participants in this study included students enrolled in three different semesters of a QCC learning community titled "Global America," which pairs English 101 (English Composition 1) and Sociology 101 (Introduction to Sociology) in the study of globalization. The pairing together of these two courses works particularly well because of the requirements of the various degree programs on campus. English 101 is required by all but a few of the degrees QCC offers. Sociology 101 is a popular course among first-year first-semester students because it is either a requirement for, or satisfying of the social science elective required by, many degree programs. Moreover, these particular sections of Sociology 101 were writing intensive. This learning community has run at least once a year every year from 2009 to 2012.

One important feature of the "Global America" learning community is a mandatory service-learning project that is assigned in and shared across the two courses. Over the course of the history of "Global America," this service-learning project has addressed a number of global phenomena; however, since the spring of 2010, the project has focused on immigration. This study compares the effectiveness of two service-learning projects of different designs implemented across three different semesters. Although the two projects differed in design, they were both oriented toward the same goals. These common project goals were informed by the course objectives of Sociology 101 and English 101, QCC's general education objectives, and recent writings on future-forward global competencies (see, e.g., National Education Association 2010):

1. to encourage students' interest in topics of globalization and immigration;
2. to increase students' sense of collective responsibility to/for the topics of globalization and immigration;
3. to develop students' writing, research, and group-work skills;
4. to encourage students' deep, critical thinking about topics of globalization and immigration;

5. to encourage students' awareness of social locations and sensitivity to cultural diversity.

Additionally, each of these projects fit into one of Deans' (2000) models of service-learning writing programs.

Project one was implemented during the Spring 2010 and Fall 2010 semesters with two different groups of students (25 students and 25 students, respectively). In each semester, students worked in groups to research and write different sections of an article focused on distinct aspects of contemporary immigration reform in the United States. The article was prepared for the newsletter of a local nonprofit immigrant-rights organization, thus falling within Deans' (2000) "writing for the community" category. The semester culminated in the service-learning project, which was completed during class time over the last three weeks of each term.

Project two was implemented during the Fall 2011 semester with 25 students. In this semester, students worked with ELL on campus to produce videos modeled after the television show *We Are New York*, which was designed to "help immigrant New Yorkers practice English while informing them of the city's resources" (The City of New York 2014b). The ELL were part of an on-campus program that helps new Americans become language ready to gain admission to CUNY. This project fell within Deans' (2000) "writing with the community" category because the students worked with their ELL peers to identify and research topics on the daily struggle of immigrants, and to write, produce, and film their English-language tutorials/video projects. Unlike the first project, the second project unfolded throughout the semester, beginning with students interviewing their ELL peers in September and finishing with the production and viewing of the videos in December.

Of the combined 50 students engaged in project one, 37 students completed a pre-course survey and 26 students completed a post-course survey. Of the 25 students engaged in project two, 19 students completed a pre-course survey and 22 students completed a post-course survey. Approximately 75 percent of survey respondents across the two projects were students of color. Significantly, exactly 40 percent of the respondents in project one self-identified as Hispanic-Latina/o while more than 38 percent of respondents in project two self-identified as Asian/Pacific Islander. Women were overrepresented among survey respondents: 75 percent of respondents to survey one were female and 62 percent of respondents to survey two were female. The average age of survey respondents for project one was 19 years and the average age of survey respondents for project two was 18 years.

Instruments

This study employed a mixed-methods approach, which synthesized pre- and post-course survey data with data collected from students' end-of-semester service-learning reflection essays. The survey instruments were administered as part of a larger college-wide research protocol, directed by QCC's Office of Academic Service-Learning, on students' opinions of and experiences with volunteering, service-learning, and civic engagement. Although the content and concerns of the survey instruments used across projects one and two were the same, there were some differences in how these survey instruments were constructed.

Project one's pre- and post-course survey instruments consisted of 19 statements about volunteerism, service-learning, and students' service-learning experiences during the surveyed semester. Students were asked to score their agreement with these statements on a five-point scale that ranged from "Strongly Disagree" to "Strongly Agree." These statements were matched across pre- and post-course survey instruments. Project one's pre- and post-course survey instruments also included demographic questions. In addition, project one's post-course survey instrument included five open-ended questions that were designed to gather more information about students' service-learning experiences during the surveyed semester.

Project two's pre- and post-course survey instruments consisted of 18 questions about volunteerism, service-learning, and students' service-learning experiences during the surveyed semester. As with project one, students were asked to respond to these statements on a five-point scale, and these responses were also matched across pre- and post-course survey instruments. While each of project two's survey instruments included demographic questions, project two's post-course survey instrument included 15 closed-ended questions about the impact of service-learning on students' achievement of QCC's general education requirements.

As part of their requirements for the learning community, students in project one and students in project two completed end-of-semester service-learning reflection essays. Students completed these take-home essays independently in response to a series of assignment prompts. While the prompts varied according to the design of projects one and two, they were both developed by faculty members and informed by the five common project goals outlined above. While students needed only to complete one end-of-semester service-learning reflection essay to receive credit in each of the paired courses, they received a separate English 101 grade and a separate Sociology 101 grade for the same essay.

Procedure

This study was conducted during the Spring 2010, Fall 2010, and Fall 2011 semesters. Each semester, a staff member from QCC's Office of Academic Service-Learning administered the pre- and post-course surveys to students during meetings of Sociology 101: the pre-course survey was administered during the first or second week of each semester; the post-course survey was administered during the fourteenth or fifteenth week of each semester. Students were advised of their rights as research participants during both points of survey administration and were allowed to opt in or out of the study at either point of survey administration.

The data from each survey were entered and cleaned by the third author. Only students with both pre- and post-course surveys were included in the third author's statistical analyses. Paired samples t-tests were used to assess whether there were any statistically significant changes, at both the .05 and .10 levels of significance, over the course of each service-learning semester. The first and second authors then aligned these statistical results with the five common project goals.

The first and second authors employed content analysis to analyze the end-of-semester service-learning reflection essays of only those students who opted in to the study. After multiple readings of each essay, the first and second authors independently analyzed the essays using conceptual categories or codes that were collaboratively determined, emergent, and related to the five common project goals. Following these independent analyses, the first and second author compared their individual findings to establish agreement.

Results/Discussion

Findings indicate that both project designs were generally successful in encouraging students to reach the five common project goals, but that this success often manifested in different and potentially significant ways. In this section we briefly review the findings related to project design and common project goals one through three; however, as our most interesting and significant findings relate to project design and common project goals four and five, we focus the bulk of our attention in this section there.

Goal One: To Encourage Students' Interest in Topics of Globalization and Immigration

Educational theorists from Dewey (1916) to Ladson-Billings (1992) argue that students find a topic interesting when it is experientially and culturally relevant to their lives. In this way, both project one and project two were successful: 97 percent of respondents from project one and 94 percent of respondents from project two stated that service-learning had made the academic study of globalization and immigration relevant to them.

Goal Two: To Increase Students' Sense of Collective Responsibility to/for the Topics of Globalization and Immigration

As addressed earlier in the chapter, many Americans come to feel disempowered by the overwhelming scale and complexity of globalization (Goldstein 2004). For this reason, it was heartening to see that both project designs encouraged students' sense of collective responsibility: the number of survey respondents from each project who believe that "it is very important to be involved in helping others in the community" increased significantly over the course of the surveyed semesters, regardless of project design.

However, while both projects increased students' sense of collective responsibility, significant differences emerged in how students conceptualized whom they felt responsible to help, how, and when. For example, project one's survey respondents, who were "writing for the community" by way of an article on immigration reform for a local nonprofit immigrant-rights organization's newsletter, seemed to conceptualize this "help" as unfolding in the future and at a policy level (precluding their direct involvement). In contrast, project two's survey respondents, who were "writing with the community" by way of creating English instructional videos with ELL on campus, seemed to conceptualize this action on a more immediate and microlevel. In fact, in contrast to project one's survey respondents, project two's survey respondents characterized their service-learning as a form of "help" and described how it had already led them to act in different ways outside of class. Consistent with this characterization and effect, only project two's survey respondents experienced significant semester gains in both their sense that they can "have a positive effect on the community" and the likelihood they would "volunteer in the next 12 months."

Goal Three: To Develop Students' Writing, Research, and Group-Work Skills

Experts in the field of information studies and education argue that students in today's global world must know how to work in groups (see, e.g., Cogburn 1998). Of goal three's component parts, service-learning project design most directly impacted students' group-work skills, as 72 percent of project one's survey respondents and 78 percent of project two's survey respondents stated that the project helped them to work effectively with others. Yet, project two was much more successful in getting students to work in *diverse* groups, which is a particularly significant global competency: while 66 percent of project one's survey respondents said that service-learning had encouraged them to work with people from backgrounds different from their own, 96 percent of project two's survey respondents claimed the same. Moreover, in their service-learning reflections, project two's respondents, who had worked in collaboration with ELL, were more likely to comment on the group nature of their service-learning work and to describe the project as engaging group members' "collective creativity and intelligence," a topic discussed in Sociology 101.

Goal Four: To Encourage Students' Deep, Critical Thinking about Topics of Globalization and Immigration

While critical thinking is widely heralded as a twenty-first century skill (see, e.g., National Education Association 2014), students must also understand how to direct this skill at the global forces and flows that render it necessary. Significantly, the majority of students in both projects one and two felt that service-learning had encouraged deep critical thinking about the topics of globalization and immigration. However, content analysis of students' service-learning reflection essays revealed that each project did so in very different ways. Consistent with research indicating that service-learning challenges students to move beyond easy or clichéd opinions about controversial topics (Jay 2008), project one seemed best suited to our efforts to complicate students' perspectives on the topics of globalization and immigration. This result was likely a function of the project's requirement that students research the costs and/or benefits of individual immigration reforms and that they engage a balanced, journalistic writing style to convey what they had learned.

For example, when reflecting on her research into Arizona law SB 1070, one student wrote about the dialectic relationship between restrictive immigration policies and national economic growth: "Upon researching this topic, I very quickly came to an understanding that although globalization has allowed the United States to prosper it also presents challenges." This answer is representative of the type of student learning facilitated by the design of project one: a relatively nuanced understanding of the relationship between immigration and global forces/flows on the macrolevel.

Goal Five: To Encourage Students' Awareness of Social Locations and Sensitivity to Cultural Diversity

In his description of the "five minds" necessary for our globalized future, Gardner (2008) includes "respectful minds," which "[respond] sympathetically and constructively to differences among individuals and among groups" (157). While both projects sought to foster "respectful minds" by encouraging students' awareness of social locations and their sensitivity to cultural diversity, project design seemed to matter to how these minds took shape.

Interestingly, very few of project one's respondents conveyed a felt connection to immigrant communities in their service-learning reflection essays. Given the demographics of QCC's student body and students' Queens' neighborhoods, these results suggest that project one's macro-orientation discouraged students' from actively exploring how immigration has enlivened their own social locations, families, and communities. In contrast, students in project two seemed to connect to globalization and immigration on deeply personal levels, often using their service-learning reflection essays to define themselves and their ELL partner(s) as similarly situated individuals and/or members of similarly situated families. For example, a project two respondent, who had immigrated to the United States from Korea ten years prior, wrote: "It was due to this project that I remembered the forgotten experience that I faced when I had struggled due to the process of learning English." Another project two respondent wrote: "This project gave me the opportunity to see what my parents went through when they first came to the United States, having a hard time learning and understanding the English language and transition into American life."

As suggested by these writings, students' personal connections often provided the foundation for their feelings of sympathy—even empathy—toward their immigrant peers and neighbors: more than three-quarters of project two's respondents claimed that they had more positive feelings toward people of different cultures as a result of their service-learning project. Likewise, these personal connections also seemed to reduce the hierarchies that can haunt service-learning relationships (Kincaid and Sotiriou 2004) and to promote the sense of interconnectedness that grounds globalization's best moments (Goldstein 2004). For example, a project two respondent who was himself a child of immigrant parents wrote:

> Had I not participated in this project my knowledge and outlook on globalization would have been minimal; it made me look at the way people interact and how we are all connected even though we are separated. Laughing and learning with people from all over the world made me a much more open-minded person.

Conclusion

In this chapter, we examine how globalization-themed service-learning projects unfold at QCC, a community college that enrolls a significant percentage of students who are first- or second-generation immigrants. In particular, we study how these projects affect community college students' understanding of global concepts and development of global competencies, and how and why service-learning project design might mediate these impacts. To do so, we compare the effectiveness of two different project designs, implemented across three semesters of the "Global America" learning community at QCC, in satisfying the five common project goals mentioned earlier in the chapter. In project one, students were "writing for the community" (Deans 2000): producing an article on immigration reform for a local nonprofit immigrant-rights organization's newsletter. In project two, students were "writing with the community" (Deans 2000): creating English instructional videos with ELL on campus.

Although exploratory and preliminary, this study points to two opportunities in globalization-themed service-learning project design that relate to faculty efforts to encourage students' development of global competencies and their engagement with issues of globalization and immigration. First, while the very nature of globalization requires that students develop these competencies and engage these issues at both the macro- and microlevels, this dual-level orientation might be even more important for community-college students who are first- or second-generation immigrants. After all, these are students whose lives simultaneously reflect and unfold at the global and local levels and whose sense of themselves as learners *and* immigrants/members of immigrant families requires the active integration of both (Walqui 2000). Yet, to achieve this dual orientation, globalization-themed service-learning projects must address both the macro- and the microlevels *explicitly*; it is not enough to point to the global and expect students to connect it to the local and vice versa. In the end, a synthesis of the two project designs described herein may prove most successful in this regard.

Second, this study points to a new model of service-learning writing that amends the three models Deans (2000) identifies: "writing *as* community." Best illustrated by the feelings of empathy and interconnectedness that project two's students' scriptwriting engendered, writing *as* community differs from Deans' writing *with* community in one important way. While writing *with* community seems to integrate community members' voices into students' service-learning writings, writing *as* community blends students' and community members' voices together to produce a shared text. Again, this new model of writing might be most essential for those globalization-themed service-learning projects that engage community-college students who are immigrants and/or the children of immigrants. Studies indicate that global forces of homogenization and universalism have rendered and/or encouraged the mobilization of particular identities (e.g., particular religious and/or ethnic identities) (Turner and Khondker 2010). While often experienced as a source of strength, this particularism—when combined with the trials of pan-ethnic identification/organization (Lopez and Espiritu 1990), the socially structured rationality of racial distancing (McClain, et al. 2006), and the persistence of ethnic enclaves (Logan and Stults 2011) in the United States—can preclude a collective "immigrant-American" identity. Yet, writing *as* community can reinforce a sense of collectivity even among diverse members. In fact, as Jay (2008) argues, when diverse service-learners engage in active problem solving they often forge a sense of solidarity that allows for and even promotes the appreciation of difference. In the end, a project design that encourages students to see themselves/their families both through the concepts of globalization *and* in the experiences of their similarly situated immigrant neighbors might be best aligned with the reflective and action-oriented principles of service-learning.

As with any study, there are limitations to these research findings: as first and second authors we studied our own projects and courses; our students prepared a portion of the data collected for a grade; the surveys we used were part of a larger college-wide research protocol and not of our own design; and we studied two unique project designs using different, small samples and no control group(s). Some of these limitations, like the last in the preceding list, point to interesting directions for future research: for example, to what extent, if any, did the ethnic-racial composition of the project samples (40 percent of the respondents in project one self-identified as Hispanic-Latina/o; about the same number of respondents in project two self-identified as Asian/Pacific Islander) matter to students' reception of their respective projects? To what extent did the samples' majority female and traditionally aged student composition matter as well? Taken together, however, these findings and limitations point to the need for a thoughtful approach to the implementation of service-learning projects and service-learning research, one that accounts for differences across institutions of higher education, between project designs, and within our increasingly diverse student populations. They also point to new areas for theoretical development at the intersection of the globalization and service-learning literatures. For example, future studies might dig more deeply into how globalized service-learning projects complicate the nation-centric and often hierarchical orientations of the pedagogy.

References

Alcantar, Cynthia M. In press. "Civic Engagement Measures for Latina/o College Students." In *New Perspectives on Critical Quantitative Inquiry*, edited by Frances K. Stage and R. Wells. San Francisco, CA: Jossey-Bass.

American Association of Community Colleges. 2001. "AACC Position Statement on International Education." Accessed November 12, 2013. http://www.aacc.nche.edu/About/Positions/Pages/ps11132001.aspx.

Annette, John. 2003. "Service-Learning Internationally: Developing a Global Civil Society." In *Deconstructing Service-Learning: Research Exploring Context, Participation, and Impacts*, edited by Shelley H. Billig and Janet Eyler, 241–249. Greenwich, CT: Information Age Publishing.

Calderon, José. 2007. "The Day Labor Project." In *Race Poverty, and Social Justice: Multidisciplinary Perspectives through Service-Learning*, edited by José Calderon, 57–62. Sterling, VA: Stylus.

Chesler, Mark A, Kristie A. Ford, Joseph A. Galura, and Jessica M. Charbeneau. 2006. "Peer Facilitators as Border Crossers in Community Service Learning." *Teaching Sociology* 34 (4): 341–356.

Cogburn, Derrick L. 1998. "Globalization, Knowledge, Education, and Training in the Information Age." Paper presented at the Second International Congress on Ethical Legal and Societal Challenges of Cyberspace, Monte-Carlo, Principality of Monaco, October 1–3.

Cohen, Lorraine. 1995. "Facilitating the Critique of Racism and Classism: An Experiential Model for Euro-American Middle Class Students." *Teaching Sociology* 23: 87–93.

Connell, Christopher. 2008. *The Vital Role of Community Colleges in the Education and Integration of Immigrants*. Sebastopol, CA: Grantmakers Concerned with Immigrants and Refugees.

d'Arlach, Lucia, Bernadette Sánchez, and Rachel Feuer. 2009. "Voices for the Community: A Case for Reciprocity in Service-Learning." *Michigan Journal of Community Service Learning* Fall: 5–16.

Deans, Thomas. 2000. *Writing Partnerships: Service-Learning in Composition*. Urbana, IL: NCTE.
Dewey, John. 1916. *Democracy and Education: An Introduction to the Philosophy of Education* (1966 Edition). New York: Free Press.
Erisman, Wendy, and Shannon Looney. 2007. *Opening the Door for the American Dream: Increasing Higher Education Access and Success for Immigrants*. Washington, DC: Institute for Higher Education Policy.
Fitch, Peggy. 2005. "In Their Own Voices: A Mixed Methods Approach to Studying Outcomes of Intercultural Service-Learning with College Students." In *Improving Service-Learning Practice: Research on Models to Enhance Impacts*, edited by Susan Root, Susan Jane Callahan, and Shelley H. Billig, 187–211. Greenwich: IAP.
Gardner, Howard. 2008. *Five Minds of the Future*. Boston, MA: Harvard Business Press.
Goldstein, Don. 2004. "Service Learning and Teaching about Globalization." *Review of Radical Political Economics* 36 (3): 307–313.
Green, Ann E. 2001. "'But You Aren't White:' Racial Perceptions and Service-Learning." *Michigan Journal of Community Service Learning* 8 (1): 18–26.
Huisman, Kimberly. 2010. "Developing a Sociological Imagination by Doing Sociology: A Methods-Based Service-Learning Course on Women and Immigration." *Teaching Sociology* 38 (2): 106–118.
Jay, Gregory. 2008. "Service Learning, Multiculturalism, and the Pedagogies of Difference." *Pedagogy: Critical Approaches to Teaching Literature, Language, Composition, and Culture* 8 (2): 255–281.
Keith, Novella Zett. 2005. "Community Service Learning in the Face of Globalization: Rethinking Theory and Practice." *Michigan Journal of Community Service Learning* Spring: 5–24.
Kincaid, Nita Moots, and Peter Sotiriou. 2004. "Service Learning at an Urban Two-Year College." *Teaching English at the Two-Year College* March: 248–259.
Kozma, Cara Lindsey. 2010. "Thinking Globally, Writing Locally: Re-Visioning Critical and Service Learning Pedagogies with Globalization Theory." PhD diss., Wayne State University.
Kuh, George. 2008. *High-Impact Educational Practices: What They Are, Who Has Access to Them, and Why They Matter*. Washington, DC: American Association of Colleges and Universities.
Ladson-Billings, Gloria. 1992. "Culturally Relevant Teaching: The Key to Making Multicultural Education Work." In *Research and Multicultural Education*, edited by Carl A. Grant, 106–121. London: Falmer Press.
Logan, John R., and Brian J. Stults. 2011. "The Persistence of Segregation in the Metropolis: New Findings from the 2010 Census." Providence, RI: US2010 Project.
Logan, John R., and Wenquan Zhang. 2011. "Global Neighborhoods: New Evidence from Census 2010." Providence, RI: US2010 Project.
Lopez, David, and Yen Espiritu. 1990. "Panethnicity in the United States: A Theoretical Framework." *Ethnic and Racial Studies* 13 (2): 198–224.
Malkan, Rajiv, and Michael J. Pisani. 2011. "Internationalizing the Community College Experience." *Community College Journal of Research and Practice* 35: 825–841.
McClain, Paula D., Niambi M. Carter, Victoria M. DeFrancesco Soto, Monique L. Lyle, Jeffrey D. Grynaviski, Shayla C. Nunnally, Thomas J. Scotto, J. Alan Kendrick, Gerald F. Lackey, and Kendra D. Cotton. 2006. "Racial Distancing in a Southern City: Latino Immigrants' Views of Black Americans." *The Journal of Politics* 68 (3): 3571–3584.
National Education Association. 2010. "Global Competence Is a 21st Century Imperative." NEA Education Policy and Practice Department. Accessed March 4, 2014. http://www.nea.org/assets/docs/HE/PB28A_Global_Competence11.pdf.

National Education Association. 2014. "Preparing 21st Century Students for a Global Society." NEA Education Policy and Practice Department. Accessed March 4, 2014. http://www.nea.org/assets/docs/A-Guide-to-Four-Cs.pdf.

Perez, William. 2011. *Americans by Heart: Undocumented Latino Students and the Promise of Higher Education*. New York: Teachers College Press.

Queensborough Community College Office of Institutional Research and Assessment. 2012. *Queensborough Community College factbook*. Accessed September 15, 2013. http://www.qcc.cuny.edu/oira/factbook.html.

Redden, Elizabeth. 2010. "The 'Community' College Internationally." *Inside Higher Education*, June 16. Accessed Feburary 7, 2014. http://www.insidehighered.com/news/2010/06/16/intl.

Saunders, Daniel B. 2010. "Neoliberal Ideology and Public Higher Education in the United States." *Journal for Critical Education Policy Studies* 8 (1): 42–77.

Seider, Scott, James P. Huguley, and Sarah Novick. 2013. "College Students, Diversity, and Community Service Learning." *Teachers College Record* 115 (3). Accessed March 3, 2014. http://scholar.harvard.edu/huguley/publications/college-students-diversity-and-community-service-learning.

Semple, Kirk. 2013. "Immigration Makes and Sustain New York, Study Finds." *The New York Times*, December 18. Accessed March 4, 2013. http://www.nytimes.com/2013/12/19/nyregion/chinese-diaspora-transforms-new-yorks-immigrant-population-report-finds.html?_r=0.

Smith, David J. 2013. "A Framework for Teaching Global Peace." *Community College Times*, July 24. Accessed September 11, 2013. http://www.communitycollegetimes.com/Pages/Campus-Issues/A-framework-for-teaching-global-peace.aspx.

Snarr, Michael T., and Michelle McNamara. 2004. "Going beyond Service Learning: Analyzing Local Effects of Hispanic Immigration." Paper presented at the annual meeting of the International Studies Association, Montreal, Quebec, Canada. Accessed May 26, 2009. http://www.allacademic.com/meta/p72258_index.html.

The City of New York. 2014a. "The NYC Experience: Queens." Accessed March 3, 2014. http://www.nyc.gov/html/ocnyc/html/experience/queens.shtml.

———. 2014b. "We Are New York: Practice English." Accessed March 4, 2014. http://www.nyc.gov/html/weareny/html/home/home.shtml.

Tilley-Lubbs, Gresilda. 2009. "Troubling the Tide: Perils and Paradoxes of Performing Service-Learning in Immigrant Communities." *International Journal of Critical Pedagogy* 2 (1): 67–87.

Turner, Bryan, and Habibul Haque Khondker. 2010. *Globalization East and West*. Thousand Oaks, CA: Sage.

Walqui, Aida. 2000. *Access and Engagement: Program Design and Instructional Approaches for Immigrant Students in Secondary Schools*. McHenry and Washington, DC: Delta Systems and Center for Applied Linguistics.

CHAPTER 5

Connecting Past and Present: Nontraditional Learner and Practitioner Experiences through Service-Learning

Suzanne M. Buglione and Amanda Wittman

The importance of understanding the community college as a vital aspect of the higher education landscape has never been more needed, nor more difficult. The American community college is a unique higher education institution greatly influenced by many internal and external forces. Community colleges are open-access institutions drawing a diversity of students including those who are first-generation and underprepared, face socioeconomic challenges, have personal immigrant histories, seek employment or transfer pathways, and/or are nontraditional learners with complex work and family demands. Many community college faculty members are not doctorally prepared, are part-time faculty, and possess fewer pedagogical tools than university faculty. Externally, community colleges are considered responsible for the health and economic stability of their area and for regional efforts to remediate existing educational achievement gaps. The complex nature of community colleges and their students have a direct impact on the successful persistence and completion of students (Cohen and Brawer 2008). In this chapter, we suggest that service-learning can be leveraged within this dynamic setting and we focus on practices that students and faculty use to help navigate the complexity of the nontraditional student experience specifically.

The Nontraditional Student Universe

To more clearly understand how service-learning can be effectively used with nontraditional students, it is critical to develop a nuanced articulation of the nontraditional student universe. There is no commonly accepted way to define and, thus, count individuals who do not fit the traditional student demographic (generally accepted as 18–22 years old, first-time attendees at college). Without a universal definition, some institutions use age as the primary criteria for defining nontraditional learners, counting those students who are over 25 years of age as adults, and therefore, nontraditional. Others define this population by characteristics that are not limited to age. The definition conversation is complicated further by the dearth of research with this population, the value and relevance of adult-learner literature to the discussion, and the often-used paradigm that separates younger and older students.

We engage with these complications by remaining flexible in terminology and references throughout the chapter. We advocate for the use of characteristics to define these learners as a promising practice, but given the reality of the current dialogue, we intertwine terminology of and research about nontraditional students and adult students as a way to provide a more complete picture of these learners and their experiences.

Even the term "nontraditional" is quickly becoming an outdated concept as many institutions engage a majority of students who are either adult learners as defined by age or nontraditional as defined by characteristic. This shifting tide is reflective of a decrease in the number of traditional-age students in the current populations of many states and places a greater emphasis on the academic success of nontraditional learners (Complete College America 2011). Broadly defined, nontraditional students comprise almost three-quarters of all American undergraduates (National Center for Education Statistics 2011). However, many in higher education continue to promote practices, policies, and normative values based on a traditional student model. While this is problematic at all institutions, those working for community colleges must begin to see nontraditional learners as the new traditional student.

As already discussed, defining the universe of nontraditional learners has been fraught with challenges. An age-based definition limits the ways we account for the diversity of experiences among community college students. Instead, we advocate for a more universal use of the classification system defined by the National Center for Education Statistics (NCES). The NCES defines nontraditional students as having one or more of the following seven characteristics: delayed enrollment in postsecondary education; part-time enrollment; financial independence of parent(s); working full time while enrolled; having dependents other than a spouse; are single parents; and/or lacking a standard high school diploma (NCES 2002). NCES further defines nontraditional students on a continuum of minimally nontraditional (i.e., students who present one nontraditional characteristic), to moderately nontraditional (i.e., students who present two to three characteristics), to highly nontraditional (i.e., students who present four or more characteristics) (NCES 2002). While many campuses will continue to use age as the defining characteristic of nontraditional students, we find greater value in using NCES criteria since they can be applied to students regardless of their age, and thus allow for a broader understanding of students enrolled in community colleges.

In addition to specific characteristics, nontraditional students also have unique experiences in college. Importantly, these students often have a unidimensional experience and location within their colleges: the classroom and the classroom only. While traditional students are often wrapped up in services and support—residence life, health and counseling services, co-curricular activities—nontraditional students are not likewise engaged. Inconvenient hours and the demands of work and family conflict with the resources offered to traditional students. Lack of orientation to college life and on-campus social networks contributes to a sense of isolation (Bowl 2001). In addition, nontraditional students work more, study less, and generally have lower academic achievement (Walpole 2003). These factors encourage nontraditional students to root their collegiate experience solely in the classroom (CCSSE 2006). For example, while 45 percent of American community college students have worked on projects with other students during class, only 21 percent have done so outside of the classroom (CCSSE 2006). The classroom becomes the single opportunity for these students to become part of an academic community.

Nontraditional students also have a unique orientation to learning. As students, they need to find value in learning, have strong intrinsic motivation and readiness to learn, and need choices and engagement (Kasworm 2005; Lundberg 2003; Knowles, Holton, and Swanson 1998). They also bring a formed sense of identity to their learning, drawing from a vast set of prior learning experiences, both positive and negative (Kasworm 2005; Mezirow 1997). The universe of the nontraditional student is complex and diverse from that which is often associated with traditional students. Figure 5.1 reflects the universe of the nontraditional learner, with NCES characteristics represented in oval shapes, learning characteristics represented in the triangles, and other identity characteristics represented in the rectangles. This model emphasizes that recognizing the interconnected nature of these characteristics can give us a clearer picture of the universe of nontraditional students. It provides a basis for conversations on community colleges about this population and

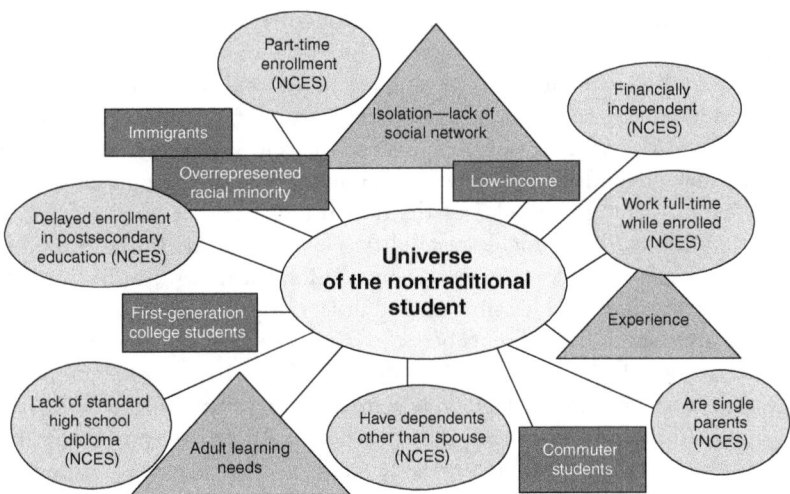

Figure 5.1 A Representation of the Characteristics of Nontraditional Students (Buglione 2007).

can create dialogue about ways to become more responsive to the needs of nontraditional students.

Although nontraditional students have always been in the community college classroom, their population growth on campuses has made them more visible. As a result, faculty have begun wondering how to teach these students in a better manner, administrators are searching for solutions to provide tailored services to these students, and the students themselves are actively participating in the dialogue about their experiences and needs. With this increased visibility comes a need for a better understanding of the experience of nontraditional students—and those who work with them. The problem is clear: "While nontraditional student numbers have increased, our understandings of the unique factors that predict adult student success have not increased likewise" (Lundberg 2003, 665).

Theoretical Connections: Nontraditional Learning and Service-Learning

One area of research and practice that can help increase our understanding of nontraditional student success is that of service-learning. Concurrent to the rise in the number of nontraditional students in higher education generally and at community colleges specifically, there has been a shift on campuses across the country with regard to practices of teaching and learning. Over the past 20 years, pedagogical shifts toward experiential learning have been seen across institutional types, throughout multiple disciplines, as well as within curricular and co-curricular experiences. Today service-learning is a commonly accepted pedagogy in higher education. This shift works well in the community college setting where there is a long tradition of hands-on experience to gain workforce skills.

While there are many types of experiential learning, we focus on service-learning as a pedagogical innovation since the community-based, hands-on, and reflective nature of this pedagogy suggests that it can be an effective teaching and learning practice to use on nontraditional students in the community college context, given what we know about their learning orientation, prior learning experiences, and formed identities. In addition, while adult learning theory only focuses on one characteristic of the nontraditional experience, the move to synthesize the experiential learning and adult learning literatures provides a starting point for theorizing nontraditional learning. The idea of the dimensions of adult learner experiences (Saddington 2000; 1998) provides a solid framework with which to examine this move toward experiential learning with nontraditional learners. Saddington (2000; 1998) connects experiential learning and adult learning theories by suggesting that there are shared philosophical roots between the disciplines, drawing from humanist perspectives, such as the perspective offered by Knowles, Holton, and Swanson (1998), who first defined andragogy as a method of responding to adult learner needs, and radical perspectives such as the perspective offered by Freire (1998; 1993), whose critical pedagogy work highlights the political inequities in education.

In this framework, Saddington examines humanist theories of education that focus on human freedom, dignity, and potential with the central assumption that people act with intentionality and values. This body of work notes that the learner is at the center of a process of discovery and self-actualization, seeking acceptance and wholeness as a central value of knowledge. In this thinking, the learner's life experience is utilized for integration, not only as a source of knowledge but also as the content of the curriculum.

Saddington complements this with an examination of radical theories that focus on societal and individual freedom connected to praxis, a process of reflection and action leading to transformative learning. Praxis results in questioning and reinterpreting cultural assumptions related to experience as a key value. As a process, education is radical in nature because it seeks understanding at a root cause level (Saddington 1998).

Saddington's model concludes that the role of the learner's life experience is basic to not only understanding societal context but also becomes a call to transformative action that serves as a source of student knowledge. In this frame, students broaden their awareness and gain personal meaning related to sociocultural dynamics that are grounded in their life experiences and their ways of reflecting on that experience from a radical perspective (Saddington 1998).

Service-learning, with its dual focus on action and reflection, is a suitable pedagogy in which to enact Saddington's frames for the nontraditional learner experience. Nontraditional students both need and bring a social context to their learning and see their learning as a call to transformative action. Utilizing service-learning methods builds upon many elements of nontraditional students' experiences.

Methodology

Given that service-learning is most often used in traditional undergraduate settings, there is little empirical research connecting the experiences of nontraditional learners to service-learning courses. Even scarcer is empirical research on nontraditional service-learners in the community college setting. We address this gap through two empirical studies focused on nontraditional learners in service-learning courses and those who teach them. While our studies did not focus solely on the community college setting, the findings resonate deeply within the community college context and our discussion allows us to identify powerful practices for community colleges developing service-learning programs, curricula, and pedagogical approaches for nontraditional students on their campuses.

The first study, a phenomenological inquiry, examined the lived experiences of 13 nontraditional students. All 13 students identified with at least four of the NCES characteristics, and thus could be classified as highly nontraditional students. All students were enrolled in credit-bearing, undergraduate higher education courses and engaged in pedagogy related to service and learning, including a few practicum or cooperative education courses. Some of the students in this study were enrolled in community college, some in baccalaureate-degree granting institutions, and some in both simultaneously. Research was conducted through extensive open-ended interviews with each participant. The central question of this study focused on the relationship between the pedagogical intervention of service-learning and the nontraditional learner's identity development: To what extent do experiences of learning and service contribute to the civic and student identities of highly nontraditional students?

The second study, a mixed-methods approach, examined how faculty and practitioners adapt pedagogical and programmatic strategies to engage nontraditional learners in service-learning. A call for participants was sent through established service-learning networks, and the authors were referred to additional faculty and practitioners through snowball sampling. This study began with a web-based survey of practitioners who worked with nontraditional students at community colleges, as well as baccalaureate institutions and graduate universities ($n = 32$). The second stage of the study included follow-up telephone interviews ($n = 10$) with participants who agreed in the original survey to be interviewed. The central questions of this study focused on the particular innovations developed by practitioners and faculty in their work with nontraditional learners: Why do practitioners choose service-learning for their classes with nontraditional students? What do faculty and practitioners learn through the experience?

Data analysis included qualitative approaches related to reading and memoing data, grouping statements in meaning units, and developing textual descriptions and visual maps of themes. Inter-rater reliability (Smith, Flowers, and Larkin 2009) was increased through the intentional engagement of the researchers and the participants acting as co-researchers. Thematic comparisons of findings from the two studies allow us to see both student and practitioner perspectives on the experience of service-learning in classrooms with nontraditional students. These thematic comparisons are contextualized within Saddington's model to give the findings structure and meaning across the two separate studies.

Findings

Understanding Societal Context

In both studies, the application of service-learning as a pedagogical model allowed students to gain a better understanding of their societal context and their place within that context (Saddington 2000). For the students, service-learning provided a true application of what they learned in class. It helped them have a better understanding of their chosen fields of study and allowed them to see themselves as professionals in that field, while also affirming their roles within their communities. This encouraged them and affirmed their choices on their academic paths. Faculty using service-learning articulated its value in allowing nontraditional learners to understand their communities better and explore activism in new ways.

In comparison to the traditional student experiences of service-learning (Eyler, Giles, Stenson, and Gray 2001), faculty reported differences in motivation levels of the learners and suggested that nontraditional students were generally more motivated to succeed in the classroom than traditional students. Faculty noted that nontraditional learners come to class with significant life experiences and are motivated by career success, proving themselves to family and friends, and new learning. One student participant shared, "At first I wasn't really sure—I didn't know if I had the zeal or not [for service-learning]—I felt like I know everything so I was like, what am I going to do, but I am glad I took it because it gave me a different concept on the patients I want to work with." Students reported that they were specifically interested in new learning that had emotional value, was manageable, and that broke down stereotypes. They reported that service-learning helped them gain specific skills and confidence in their chosen fields and that it often reinforced values that they already held.

Transforming Curricula for Personal Meaning

Both nontraditional students and faculty suggested that the content of the curriculum was essential to the learning process, especially in service-learning courses. The student participants highlighted group work as essential to helping them negotiate intergroup relations, especially with traditionally aged students in their classrooms. Group work and discussions became leveling mechanisms that allowed nontraditional learners to share their lived experiences in ways that were understood and appreciated. In addition to in-class assignments, nontraditional learners, given their preexisting community connections, responded well to service-learning assignments that included a choice of service placement. One faculty participant shared,

> In the community, adult students have told us that they are more engaged. They don't just put in hours, they get to know people in the community more, they are more confident in their ability—this is their perception of themselves. We found that adults want to make more choices, decisions about placement.

Faculty agreed that incorporating flexibility into the service experience greatly helped nontraditional learners to be successful.

Both faculty and nontraditional learners were able to articulate course elements that were challenging. Nontraditional learners struggled with the lack of preparation for group work by traditional students and wanted more reflection-based activities. Faculty found that nontraditional learners' competing priorities can be a barrier to enthusiasm for service-learning and suggested that while flexibility and choices are necessary, it helps to make service-learning assignments required: students have less of a chance to opt out or prioritize other areas of their lives. Despite the perceived barriers at the onset, nontraditional learners found great value in service-learning, noting that it was worth the challenges. Almost all student participants noted concerns about engaging in service-learning initially citing multiple life demands; one student participant summed up the experience all students reported at the close of the interviews, "It was a blessing in disguise."

Not only is the content of the curriculum important to nontraditional students, our findings reveal that nontraditional students see themselves as partners with the faculty in creating the curriculum for the classroom and as partners to their service-learning sites. They seek faculty relationships that are peer-like. One student participant happily shared about the faculty, "she treated us as if we were graduate students," noting how impactful this relationship was for her. Faculty members articulated the advantage of utilizing nontraditional learners' experiences and expertise as extra support in the classroom. The partnerships that form between nontraditional students and community partners reflect the students' identity as experienced community members themselves. One faculty participant shared,

> I think they [nontraditional students] need to be involved in the community and there needs to be an important purpose to their work...feel like they are contributing...there has to be a final product and it is important to present back to community partners. They want to describe the process back to the partner and talk about the bits and the scars, not just write a paper as a final outcome...to be honest about the flaws they see at the agencies they are working with. They tend to be more verbal, and are the leaders.

Students' advanced ability to function in the community environment can sustain and support partnerships and their academic paths in new ways.

Convergence of Life Experience: Past, Present, and Future

Nontraditional learners constantly have to negotiate their multifaceted student identity, which often manifests a convergence of their past and present life experiences. Faculty clearly spoke to nontraditional learners' identity negotiations in their service-learning courses. For the students, the real tensions occurred as they attempted to navigate social perceptions from others in their lives, whether they were traditional students, faculty, family, or friends. Nontraditional learners articulated the pressure that arose from having to deal with other people's perceptions. One student participant recalled, "My mom didn't encourage me [to go back to school]; she said I don't want you to be upset when you fail...she was trying to be helpful" and another shared, "There is another guy who is actually older than me in the program and that makes me feel better...sometimes I kind of feel like the dad in the group."

In addition, the students articulated that because they came to the classroom with different experiences, they were often disconnected from traditional college support mechanisms. As they juggled the competing areas of their lives, they were often left without a clear understanding of expectations for the classroom experience or mentors to help them negotiate their experience. These experiences were countered in service-learning as students found value in their nontraditional status, bringing previous knowledge and a sense of the community to the work.

Faculty articulated that nontraditional learners were better able to connect with service assignments when those experiences helped them bring together their life backgrounds and future career development. For example, when learners understood that the service could provide them with direct experiences that translate well to real-world jobs, they were more motivated to participate. Faculty also saw that nontraditional learners were better able to translate their service experiences into their new areas of career focus than traditional students. Faculty reported that service-learning helps nontraditional learners make mental shifts with regards to their career and job focus and brings together converging life experiences. One faculty participant noted the career opportunities inherent in service-learning:

> We see adults in transition there. It's important for us to pay attention to the ways that they learn and get them back into the groove during this transition...an example is one adult student who came to us because he was unemployed and

needed more work experience...The benefits they bring is that they have so much experience and so many skills and knowledge that can be used in service-learning. One example was the student who made a video about the Farmer's Market...they used their professional skills...They've never been to college and now are in with younger students. The personal benefits that all students get from service-learning are really important to these adult students. They are upset and worried about their lives. Service-learning changes their perspective.

Both practitioners and students found that service-learning helps students negotiate their current life situations with their past experiences and future goals in integrated ways.

Reflection

Reflection is the core of successful service-learning and important for praxis. This is true for any student, but these studies clearly show unique ways that nontraditional learners interact with the process of reflection. Faculty agreed that for nontraditional students, the process of self-exploration is deeper and more connected to real-life experiences than it is for traditional students, who sometimes engage with reflections on a more theoretical level. The students agreed and reported that meaning was drawn from their life experiences and their specific histories of challenge, including pressure as first-generation students, past employment and experiences with academic failure, and even challenges with addiction.

Students found that meaning-making specifically occurred through connected readings, written reflections, and clear course materials that they could easily access and understand. For some nontraditional students, reflection helped to resurrect a community identity, which, in turn, supported their student identity development. A student participant reflected on his service-learning experience and how it reinforced his student identity, "The project excited me to push forward—it helped me know that this [his studies] was the right direction, the right thing." Faculty agreed that reflection shifts nontraditional learners' orientation to the world, to the service experience, and to classroom knowledge.

Discussion

Our research reveals that service-learning works for nontraditional learners, but in unique and underexplored ways that have significant impacts on their student and self identities and on their learning and success. The combined results of the studies highlight two important revelations. The first is that service-learning with nontraditional students opens up new spaces to think about partnerships. As service-learning has been embraced under the umbrella idea of civic engagement, there has been a call to understand the role of this specific pedagogy in forming campus-community partnerships that are reciprocal and democratic (Hartley 2010; Bringle and Hatcher 2009). Yet, too often, the narrative of partnerships focuses narrowly on the individuals—faculty, community service professionals, community partner leaders—who envision and build a particular partnership. It is necessary to go beyond these stakeholders and recognize that "service-learning's full academic and social impact will not be achieved until the circle of Service-Learning leadership is further extended to include students" (Zlotkowski, Longo, and Williams 2006, 3).

Our research suggests that focusing on the ways nontraditional students engage as fully actualized partners throughout the service-learning process highlights their unique role in sustaining campus-community partnerships. As nontraditional learners, these individuals develop student identities that are layered and drawn from multiple sources, past and present (Kasworm 2005). These students can help faculty, practitioners, and community partners articulate new paradigms for partnership that are open to the multilayered identities of all involved in service-learning.

The second revelation of these two studies reaffirms the importance of using nontraditional teaching and learning practices with nontraditional learners. The findings reinforce the idea that nontraditional approaches work with nontraditional learners to increase learning and success. Experiential learning—in this case, service-learning—addresses the different needs and motivations that nontraditional students have in the classroom. Faculty and students both agreed that there are benefits to using service-learning. Community engagement activities provide nontraditional learners with direct experiences that translate well to real-world jobs and can help them make mental shifts in regard to their career and job foci. Faculty find that the focus on reflection—a learning tool required in quality service-learning experiences—allows nontraditional learners to engage in a process of self-exploration that is deeper and more connected to real-life experiences. Faculty recognize that reflection shifts students' orientation to the world, and students report that they are able to explore activism and their self-identity as community actors in new ways (Brookfield 2000; Cunningham 2000; Saddington 1998). Service-learning allows nontraditional students to understand "new normals" in regard to their life, community, and—most importantly—classroom experiences.

The findings also shed light on one of the major drawbacks of using service-learning with nontraditional students. Those who teach nontraditional students often suggest that students' multifaceted lives prohibit their use of nontraditional pedagogies. In fact, as evidenced by the students in our studies, many nontraditional students also adopt this narrative. Yet, both the students and faculty in our studies indicated that this "time challenge" was mostly perceived. Students and faculty articulated strategies that they used to overcome this challenge, which are discussed in the next section on powerful practices, and all agreed that the increased satisfaction with the learning experience was worth the time investment.

Powerful Practices

Curriculum Redesign

To improve significantly the service-learning experiences of nontraditional students, faculty and practitioners should consider changes to their course curriculum and project design. First, they should make the service relevant to the lived experience of each student. While this is important for all students, nontraditional students particularly seek an explicit connection between their service experience and their life outside the classroom. Second, it is important to ensure flexibility in assignments by offering students choices in service placement, timing, and reflection modalities. This allows nontraditional students to connect their lives to their service-learning. Yet, both faculty and students agree that while making assignments flexible and offering choices are essential, it is also important to make service-learning mandatory: this holds all parties accountable and offers more gratification to the student for spending the time on the service experience. Third, nontraditional students look for personal connections to course readings and service. Practitioners and faculty should be intentional in choosing readings that connect to the communities in which service is offered and finding creative ways of helping students to incorporate their personal lives, families, and/or professional identities into their service. Last, graded reflections and assignment feedback early and often are critical. Nontraditional students bring intrinsic motivation to their learning and therefore need and want early and regular feedback to aid them in seeing the value of the experience.

Rethink Partnerships

As we have already suggested, these studies encourage us to rethink partnerships in the service-learning context. Nontraditional learners should be seen as partners to faculty, other students, and community members in new ways. The relationships within the classroom and in the community need to tap into nontraditional students' skills and experiences. For faculty, this means adopting a supportive, not dictatorial, attitude in the classroom. As we have suggested, being flexible in assignments is important and this may mean that a faculty member needs to rethink his or her relationship with community partners. For example, working with partners in different parts of town, developing an in-depth project with one partner, or allowing students to pick their own partner can deepen the experience for nontraditional students and temper some of the barriers—like work schedules, family commitments, and transportation challenges—that can preclude their full participation. This may mean finding new partners or allowing nontraditional students to introduce new community partners. Co-locating the class is another powerful practice that allows students more flexibility and requires faculty to rethink their partnerships. This practice has the class meet off-campus or at the service-learning site, allowing all students to learn in a new space that can be meaningful to nontraditional students.

Connect to Career Services

Service-learning experiences can help nontraditional students identify in new ways as professionals and support retention by previewing career possibilities. This is especially true for students who return to school to change or advance their careers. A powerful practice that can help nontraditional students explicitly tie their service-learning experience to class content is storytelling. Storytelling allows nontraditional students to reflect on where they came from and to articulate their identities in new ways, thus cementing their changing perspectives of themselves as professionals (Abrahamson 1998). Additionally, explicitly connecting the service-learning experience and coursework to career helps nontraditional students find meaning in a pathway of courses that can seem long and unattainable. Another method to promote career mindedness is to enable family service, which allows students to bring their families with them on their service experiences. This can allow nontraditional students' families to see them in new, professional ways.

Conclusion

This chapter examines the experiences of nontraditional learners and faculty who are involved with service-learning. We believe that the implications for practice in the community college setting are evident. Specifically, we encourage faculty to become more knowledgeable about the NCES characteristics that define nontraditional students. At the institutional level, we encourage continued efforts to identify and count nontraditional learners, as making these students visible helps faculty, administrators, and staff connect them to resources and opportunities. We also believe these studies show the powerful potential of service-learning for nontraditional learners, so we encourage further institutional commitment to service-learning courses, faculty, practitioners, and partners. To conclude, we offer "powerful practices" for those interested in using and institutionalizing service-learning with nontraditional students in the community college context: curriculum (re)design, rethinking partnerships, and connecting to career services. While these powerful practices will promote nontraditional students' college success, they are also likely to help *all* students be successful in the service-learning classroom. According to McDowell (2011), strategies that sustain and support the students who already feel on the margins will in turn sustain mainstream, traditional students. Our combined studies of faculty and nontraditional students involved in service-learning reinforce the powerful potential of service-learning as a pedagogy and a movement that invigorates student learning and success.

References

Abrahamson, Craig. 1998. "Storytelling as a Pedagogical Tool in Higher Education." *Education* 118 (3): 440–451.

Community College Survey of Student Engagement (CCSSE). 2006. *Act on Fact: Using Data to Improve Student Success.* http://www.ccsse.org/publications/CCSSENationalReport2006.pdf.

Bowl, Marion. 2001. "Experiencing the Barriers: Non-Traditional Students Entering Higher Education." *Research Papers in Education* 16 (2): 141–160.

Bringle, Richard, and Julie Hatcher. 2009. "Innovative Practices in Service-Learning and Curricular Engagement." *New Directions for Higher Education* 147: 37–46.

Brookfield, Stephen. 2000. "The Concept of Critically Reflective Practice." In *Handbook of Adult and Continuing Education,* edited by Arthur Wilson and Elisabeth Rayes, 33–49. San Francisco, CA: Jossey-Bass.

Buglione, Suzanne. 2007. "Nontraditional Approaches with Nontraditional Students: Experiences of Learning, Service and Identity Development." EdD diss., University of Massachusetts-Boston.

Cohen, Arthur M., and Florence B. Brawer. 2008. *The American Community College,* 5th ed. San Francisco, CA: Jossey-Bass.

Complete College America. 2011. *Time Is the Enemy.* www.completecollege.org/docs/Time_Is_the_Enemy.pdf.

Cunningham, Phyllis. 2000. "A Sociology of Adult Education." In *Handbook of Adult and Continuing Education,* edited by Arthur Wilson and Elisabeth Rayes, 573–591. San Francisco, CA: Jossey-Bass.

Eyler, Janet, Dwight Giles, Christine Stenson, and Char Gray. 2001. *At A Glance: What We Know about the Effects of Service-Learning on College Students, Faculty, Institutions and Communities, 1993–2000.* http://www.compact.org/wpcontent/uploads/resources/downloads/aag.pdf.

Freire, Paulo. 1993. *Pedagogy of the Oppressed.* New York: Continuum.

———. 1998. *Pedagogy of Freedom: Ethics, Democracy and Civic Courage.* Lanham, MD: Rowman & Littlefield Publishers.

Hartley, Matthew. 2010. *Universities in Partnership: Strategies for Education, Youth Development and Community Renewal.* San Francisco, CA: Jossey-Bass.

Kasworm, Carol. 2005. "Adult Student Identity in an Intergenerational Community College Classroom." *Adult Education Quarterly* 56 (1): 3–20.

Knowles, Malcom, Elwood Holton, and Richard Swanson. 1998. *The Adult Learner: The Definitive Classic in Adult Education and Human Resource Development,* 5th ed. Houston, TX: Gulf Publishing.

Lundberg, Carol. 2003. "The Influence of Time-Limitations, Faculty, and Peer Relationships on Adult Student Learning." *Journal of Higher Education* 74 (6): 665–688.

McDowell, Cesar. 2011. "Designing for the Margins." Keynote given at the annual meeting for the International Association of Research on Service-Learning and Civic Engagement, Chicago, IL, November 2–4.

Mezirow, Jack. 1997. "Transformative Learning: Theory to Practice." *New Directions for Adult and Continuing Education* 74: 5–9.

National Center for Education Statistics (NCES). 2002. *Special Analysis: Nontraditional Undergraduates.* http://nces.ed.gov/programs/coe/2002/analyses/nontraditional/index.asp.

Saddington, Tony. 1998. "Exploring the Roots and Branches of Experiential Learning." *Lifelong Learning in Europe* 3: 133–138.

———. 2000. "The Roots and Branches of Experiential Learning." *NSEE Quarterly* Fall: 2–6.

Smith, Jonathan, Paul Flowers, and Michael Larkin. 2009. *Interpretative Phenomenological Analysis: Theory Method and Research.* London: Sage.

Walpole, Marybeth. 2003. "Socioeconomic Status and College: How SES Affects College Experiences and Outcome." *The Review of Higher Education* 27 (1): 45–73.

Zlotkowski, Edward, Nicholas Longo, and James Williams, eds. 2006. *Students as Colleagues: Expanding the Circle of Service-Learning Leadership.* Providence, RI: Campus Compact.

CHAPTER 6

Race, Ethnicity, and Service-Learning: Understanding Access and Equity Using a Critical Quantitative Approach

Drew Allen, Diana Strumbos, and Janelle Clay

Across the nation, community colleges serve a diverse population of students representing a tremendous range of races, ethnicities, and ancestries. Service-learning opportunities, however, have historically been available to a somewhat small subset of students in postsecondary institutions. As more community colleges, and departments and faculty members within these colleges, develop service-learning programs, the opportunity to participate in service-learning is becoming available to a much larger and more racially and ethnically varied population than in the past years. This influx of new groups of students in service-learning raises interesting questions about whether and how the experience of service-learning may differ depending on student background. Perhaps, more importantly, it brings to light the question of who has access to service-learning in the first place and, if service-learning is a valuable experience for students, what is being lost by not offering students this opportunity. In our work, we explore these questions using a critical quantitative approach, focusing on the City University of New York (CUNY) Service Corps, a new service program at CUNY, as a case study. As members of the Office of Research, Evaluation, and Program Support, tasked with evaluating the CUNY Service Corps, we are uniquely situated to explore issues of data and research on the program, although we did not play a primary role in the design of the program itself. In this chapter, we focus on how data on program applicants and participants can be used by researchers and practitioners to ask critical questions relating to equity and access in service-learning.

Setting the Stage: Racial/Ethnic Group Differences in Educational Attainment

Community colleges are an important point of entry into postsecondary education for students from underrepresented and diverse backgrounds who might not otherwise have the opportunity to enroll in college, including an increasing number of low-income students, recent immigrants, students of color, and first-generation college enrollees (Teranishi, Suarez-Orozco and Suarez-Orozco 2011; Conway 2009; Bailey and Morest 2006; Bueschel 2004). For many students, community colleges represent the first step onto a path toward economic stability and can provide connections to the workplace and potential employers. In many cases, community colleges are the only postsecondary institutions these students attend. Given the unique mission of community colleges and the nonselective nature of many of these institutions, issues of access and equity play an important role in the development of policies and programs designed to support these students. Numerous studies have documented the correlation between race/ethnicity and measures of community college access and success (Bensimon and Bishop 2012; Perna 2007). Thus, one way to understand access and equity is to look closely at the experiences of students from racial and ethnic groups that are historically underrepresented in higher education. As service-learning opportunities expand to greater numbers of community college students, it is necessary for practitioners, educators, and researchers involved in service-learning activities to understand the nuanced role that race/ethnicity has played in community colleges more broadly.

While educational attainment has increased over the years for students of color, degree attainment among students of color remains low and behind that of their white peers. In 2012, among people 25 and older, only 31 percent of blacks and 21 percent of Hispanics had obtained a postsecondary degree compared to 45 percent of non-Hispanic whites (US Census Bureau 2012). A closer look at graduation rates of two-year public degree granting institutions reveals that in 2011, 22 percent of students had graduated within three years and the graduation rate was even lower for certain groups—15 percent among black students and 17 percent among Hispanic students (Knapp, Kelly-Reid, and Ginder 2012). Over the past several years, many colleges and universities have developed new programs and policies aimed at addressing this significant gap in educational attainment, while at the same time existing strategies and academic initiatives have been expanded to serve a wider population of students. For community colleges, opportunities like service-learning have become key strategies for connecting their diverse student bodies to the surrounding communities, as well as supporting students academically toward their goal of attaining a degree.

As colleges continue to explore options for addressing racial/ethnic gaps in achievement through service-learning, it is important to consider how participation in service-learning impacts students of color. Research has demonstrated the impact of participation on students' academic achievement and their connections with the broader economic, civic, and community issues outside of the four walls of the classroom (Prentice and Robinson 2007; Bringle and Hatcher 1996). Participation in service-learning has been found to increase students' interest in course subjects, develop their problem-solving and academic skills, and provide students with the opportunity to share experiences in group discussions and presentations (Bringle and Hatcher 1996). For community college students specifically, Prentice and Robinson (2010) found service-learning to be a useful tool for building students' skills and for exposing them to potential career pathways. However, very few studies of service-learning have explored differences in outcomes for students of color and those from underserved communities (Novick, Seider, and Huguley 2011). In a recent meta-analysis of the impacts of service-learning on student outcomes, the authors were unable to look at differential effects by race/ethnicity because prior studies did not have sufficient data available (Celio, Durlak, and Dymnicki 2011). With the increase in enrollment rates of students of color at higher education institutions, researchers and practitioners must pay attention to differential rates of participation in service-learning and explore the variation of experience and impact on these various student groups. Over the last several years, researchers have developed new approaches to understanding the educational experiences of underrepresented persons in different types of educational settings such as community colleges. The next section will explore one such framework—the critical quantitative approach—and explain how it can be used by researchers and practitioners to explore issues of access and equity vis-à-vis service-learning in the community college setting.

Critical Quantitative Approach

As many of the chapters in this book illustrate, service-learning can take place in a wide variety of institutional types, contexts, disciplines, and settings. By looking across these contexts using quantitative data, researchers and practitioners can better understand and isolate issues of equity and access. Often, research on service-learning focuses exclusively on the average student experience within the program or institution. Program participation is described based on the number of students served, the number of service projects, or the number of partnerships created. Student outcomes associated with service-learning, such as grades in courses or measured changes in feelings toward civic engagement, are aggregated and averaged across all students. Little attention is paid to the context in which each individual student experiences service-learning.

Over the past few years, quantitative education researchers have begun to approach their analyses through a theoretical framework that explicitly addresses the diverse contexts of educational experiences and the various backgrounds and perspectives of students themselves. Stage (2007) referred to this type of analysis as a *critical quantitative approach* that "focuses on questioning and then modifying models or creating new models that better describe the ever-differentiating individuals who are the focus of educational research" (9). Critical quantitative researchers use data to proactively address defined questions of equity and access by moving past the traditional positivistic and post-positivistic approaches. The *quantitative criticalist*, as Stage and Wells (2014) point out, questions the typical quantitative theoretical frameworks and proposes new quantitative analyses to better address underlying biases, contradictions, or overgeneralizations. The critical quantitative approach not only involves the questioning of assumptions and methods, but also acknowledges that quantitative researchers bring their own biases and assumptions that can affect the types of data, methods, analyses, and interpretations employed in research (Carter and Hurtado 2007).

The critical quantitative approach is informed by critical theory as outlined by Kincheloe and McLaren (1994) and builds upon the assumption that mainstream research methods and practices can often function to reproduce class, race, and gender oppression. The critical quantitative approach centers on the idea that quantitative researchers can use large datasets and decidedly nonqualitative methods to address the central tenants in critical theory that have traditionally only been explored through qualitative means. Quantitative criticalists, according to Stage and Wells (2014), have used this perspective in two primary ways to reveal inequities: (1) through analysis of quantitative data across subgroups, populations, and contexts; and (2) to question existing quantitative methods, models, and theories. The approach is based on the idea that researchers should use data to question and illuminate the traditional theories and methods, rather than to simply confirm them.

Statistics on the racial/ethnic composition of students in community colleges, including many of them cited in this book, often mask the considerable variation within subgroups of students. Researchers and practitioners often compare outcomes across broad racial/ethnic categories, making an assumption that these categories represent the most appropriate groupings. Teranishi (2007) has highlighted the limitations of these groupings by detailing the significant variation among Asian Americans and their experiences in higher education. Using critical race theory as a framework, Teranishi stressed that each racial/ethnic category is composed of unique subgroups, ethnicities, family structures, and challenges that should be taken into account in order to fully understand how educational programs and policies can address students' unique needs. This type of critical quantitative analysis is particularly constructive for the ongoing conversation in higher education about equity and access because it challenges assumptions and raises questions that traditional positivistic and post-positivistic quantitative approaches fail to take into account.

Multiple researchers have used quantitative analyses to examine important issues of access and success (Perna 2007; Perna and Titus 2005). In her research, Perna (2007) highlighted the strengths and weaknesses of using quantitative methods to analyze racial/ethnic group differences in college enrollment. While quantitative analysis allows researchers to address concerns of validity through the inclusion of multiple variables in an analysis, quantitative datasets often suffer from a limited number of cases that would allow researchers to drill down into specific subgroups and compare across them. More relevant to the service-learning context, Alcantar (forthcoming) has used a critical quantitative approach to call into question definitions of civic engagement and has noted that the concept of "civic engagement" might have different meanings for individuals from different cultural/racial backgrounds. Research has documented the relationship between civic engagement and educational attainment; however the definitions and attitudes toward civic engagement in college can be exclusionary of students of color and those from underserved communities because of these students' experiences and backgrounds. Alcantar argues that definitions of civic engagement and traditional service-learning/civic engagement models are developed from the perspective of a white, middle-class, 18–24-year-old, four-year college male student.

Some research has highlighted the issue of varied context while examining the types of placements/work that are a part of service-learning and how they are "marketed" to students. Specifically, many researchers have noted the positioning of this type of experience as an opportunity to engage privileged students in community service experiences that are "foreign" to them. Many service-learning courses and projects are largely based on social and civic issues that exist within disadvantaged or underserved communities. This type of positioning may inhibit students of color from participating in service-learning opportunities. For example, research has shown that students of color at one university were less likely to participate in a service-learning course, a possible result of identifying the course/program as a "white charitable program" because of the university's large, white student population and its location in a city with a high proportion of people of color (Novick, Seider, and Huguley 2011).

Many studies examining the unique experiences of students in higher education from various backgrounds have been qualitative in nature. Indeed, much can be learned from rich qualitative research that highlights nuanced aspects of students' experiences. Palmer and Wood (2013), for instance, examined experiences of underrepresented racial and ethnic minorities in science, technology, engineering, and mathematics (STEM) programs at community colleges. It is our goal, however, to demonstrate that critical quantitative analyses can play a vital role in understanding these experiences as well. It is with this critical quantitative underpinning that we now turn to examples from the CUNY Service Corps, a unique service program in New York City.

Programs Designed to Support Diverse Student Populations: Examples from CUNY

As the largest urban public university in the country and one of the most diverse, CUNY has been well positioned to develop strategies to support students from a wide variety of ethnicities, backgrounds, and perspectives. The demographic makeup of the CUNY student body reflects the population of New York City, one of the nation's most ethnically diverse urban areas. Across CUNY's 18 undergraduate institutions, black, Hispanic, and white students each represent more than a quarter of all undergraduates, with Asian students representing another 19 percent. In the university's seven community colleges, diversity is even more evident, as demographics differ significantly from the overall CUNY numbers. In fall 2012, approximately two-thirds of CUNY's community college students were Hispanic (38 percent) or black (29 percent), with another 17 percent white, and 16 percent Asian. Approximately four in ten CUNY community college students were born outside of the United States—hailing from 199 countries—and over half were the first in their families to attend college (CUNY OIRA 2013a). Like many community colleges around the country, CUNY's associate degree-granting institutions serve a student population whose racial/ethnic composition is driven largely by the colleges' surrounding geographic locales (Goldrick-Rab and Kinsley 2013).

University enrollment statistics, however, do not tell the whole story. Underlying the considerable diversity in student enrollment is the less encouraging story of differential rates of graduation by race/ethnicity. For example, while the three-year graduation rate for white and Asian students at CUNY community colleges is 20 and 21 percent respectively, the rate for other students is considerably lower: 11 percent for black students, and 11 percent for Hispanic students (CUNY OIRA 2013b). Related to this are differential rates of enrollment in noncredit developmental coursework. Among CUNY's entering first-time freshman cohorts, black and Hispanic students are significantly more likely to require developmental/remedial coursework compared to Asian and white students.

In response to these issues, CUNY has developed a host of programs to support student access and success in community colleges, with a specific focus on underserved populations. For example, the university's Central Office of Academic Affairs has designed numerous academic support programs, adult literacy initiatives, workforce development, continuing education, and collaborative programs with the New York City public school system. These programs were designed to specifically target and support students from diverse academic, socioeconomic, and racial/ethnic backgrounds. It is also from this office that the CUNY Service Corps was recently created and implemented.

CUNY Service Corps: Design and Implementation

The CUNY Service Corps was designed in early 2013 to provide opportunities for CUNY students, faculty, and staff to work on projects that improve the short- and long-term civic, economic, and environmental sustainability of New York City and of its residents and communities. From the initial planning phase of the program, the Service Corps model stressed the creation of a unified student cohort that would collectively represent the university by serving the various communities throughout the city. In the spring of 2013, the program accepted applications for its pilot cohort from seven CUNY colleges (including two community colleges). A select group of 719 students meeting certain eligibility criteria ultimately enrolled into the centrally administered program and were assigned service placements that typically last 24 weeks over two semesters. Participants were expected to serve at their placement an average of 12 hours per week. Although students were required to attend an intensive orientation and participate in workshops throughout the academic year that connected service projects to academic disciplines and broad concepts, the Service Corps does not follow a typical service-learning model, nor was it designed to. In the first year of the program, college credit was not explicitly tied to assignments, and service projects were not directly connected to coursework in most cases. Perhaps most notably, the students were paid at a rate of $12 per hour for these assignments.

During the design phase of the Service Corps, existing service-learning models were reviewed and leading experts in the field were consulted. It was quickly acknowledged from the early stages, however, that the Service Corps was a unique approach to both service and learning. The program, while embracing many of service-learning's core notions, represents a notable trend of expansion in the meaning of "service-learning." The Service Corps model differs from traditional service-learning in two main ways: (1) students are paid for their work and (2) participation is not connected to specific coursework or an academic discipline. The paid aspect of the work raises questions about whether projects in which students are paid to work on community projects do, in fact, constitute "service." While offering payment may raise concerns about students' motivations for participating, when viewed through the lens of access, the payments can be a crucial way of supporting students' ability to participate in opportunities that they would not have had otherwise. Financial considerations have been found to affect many students' persistence in college, particularly low-income students and students of color (Swail, Scott, Redd, and Perna, 2003). Paying students for their participation opens the opportunity to a broader range of students who might have otherwise needed to use the time to work a paying job. Likewise, by not connecting participation to coursework or an academic discipline, the program raises the question of whether the Service Corps can really be labeled a "service-learning" initiative. Broadly defined, service-learning involves the intersection—and in most cases integration—of academic content with service projects within the context of a community. Again, this modification allows the Service Corps to reach a more diverse group of students. Specifically, the program model allows for the participation of students from a wide range of disciplines and departments, expanding access to students in academic majors and disciplines that traditionally offer fewer service-learning opportunities to students. However, not being tied to coursework also means that in most cases, students do not earn credit for their work. In future years, the Service Corps plans to work more closely with faculty and academic departments to embed projects within courses and to allow credits to be granted to students who participate. While the model deviates from the traditional notion of service-learning, we feel that, given the program's overall goal of engaging civic-minded college students in service opportunities throughout diverse neighborhoods in the city, the Service Corps can serve as a useful lens for examining service-learning and related service programs. The large and diverse cohort of students also presents a unique case through which to explore issues of race/ethnicity across multiple institutional contexts.

A Focus on Opportunities for a Diverse Population

From the very beginning, conversations about the Service Corps program prioritized the need for diversity among members and the desire for the Service Corps members to represent the overall CUNY population and the populations of each participating college. Throughout the planning phase and launch of the program, emphasis was placed on creating opportunities for students who are often underrepresented in volunteer or service programs. As mentioned above, it was an explicit priority to expand opportunities for lower-income students who often do not have the time available to volunteer because of the need for paid work to help support themselves and their families. The choice to pay Service Corps members for their work at the placement sites was part of a strategy to give lower-income students the opportunity to participate in the program.

While not as overt, racial and ethnic diversity among participants was also a priority, as was inclusion of students who identify as Lesbian, Gay, Bisexual, Transgender, or Queer (LGBTQ). An early planning document about recruitment reflected this focus on diversity, listing a strong recommendation "to recruit from programs serving non-traditional/underserved/underrepresented students" (CUNY Service Corps 2013). The application for students was also designed with this focus on diversity in mind. Students were asked about their racial/ethnic identity, Hispanic/Latino origin, gender identity, household income, and whether they identified as LGBTQ in order to measure rates of application and selection across these groups. During the recruitment and application process, staff monitored the racial/ethnic and gender distribution of applicants so they could shift their recruitment approach if certain populations were applying at a disproportionate rate. As a result, the applicant pool represented the CUNY population remarkably well.

The selection process, on the other hand, did not take these demographic or background factors into account. Each application was read by one or two reviewers with information on race/ethnicity, Hispanic/Latino origin, gender identity, LGBTQ identification, and household income removed so that these factors would not influence the assessment and scoring of the application. After applications and recommendations were scored, students were invited for group interviews; students were selected from this pool based on their performance in the group interviews. As seen in table 6.1, the group of officially enrolled Service Corps members, which

Table 6.1 Select Characteristics of CUNY Service Corps Applicants and Members

	All Applicants	*Service Corps Members*
Race/Ethnicity		
% Hispanic or Latina/o	31.1	31.0
% Black	23.8	26.8
% Asian	17.7	18.1
% White	16.3	13.6
% Other or More Than One Race	11.1	10.4
Gender		
% Female	61.6	63.6
% Male	38.4	36.4
Other Characteristics		
% Lesbian, Gay, Bisexual, Transgender, or Queer (LGBTQ)	5.0	5.8
% Native Language Other Than English	40.8	39.8
% Born Outside of US Mainland	44.3	43.5
Household Income		
% Less than $10,000	20.4	22.8
% $10,000 to $24,999	37.4	33.7
% $25,000 to $39,999	16.9	16.7
% $40,000 or higher	25.3	26.8
TOTAL (*N*)	1,961	719

included 719 students from seven CUNY colleges (including two community colleges), reflected the applicant pool and the overall CUNY population in terms of race/ethnicity and other demographic and background factors.

An analysis of rates of selection and participation by demographic and background factors showed that students were selected into the program at roughly the same rates across racial/ethnic groups. Black students were selected at the highest rate (47 percent of applicants received an offer), while Hispanic students were selected at the lowest rate (42 percent). There were, however, much larger differences in terms of rates of enrollment. Only 87 percent of white students accepted the offer to participate, compared to 93 percent of Asian students, 94 percent of Hispanic students, and 97 percent of black students. Similarly, of those students who accepted the initial offer, rates differed by race/ethnicity in terms of completing the training and ultimately enrolling in the program—78 percent of white students enrolled, compared to 92 percent of Asian students, 92 percent of Hispanic students, and 90 percent of black students. Given the different populations served by the colleges, some of these differences by race/ethnicity may be due in part to differences in acceptance and enrollment rates across colleges. For example, the College of Staten Island, which had the largest percentage of white students, had the lowest rates of acceptance and enrollment in general.

In this chapter, we report aggregate numbers for all seven colleges, because focusing only on the community colleges results in very small sample sizes for certain racial/ethnic groups. Of the 1,961 students who applied, 311 were from the two CUNY community colleges that offered the program. There are, however, some notable differences in applicants between the senior and community colleges. First, community college students reported lower incomes overall, with 28 percent of applicants reporting less than $10,000 in household income versus 19 percent at the senior colleges. Furthermore, 71 percent of community college applicants reported a household income of less than $25,000 versus 55 percent of senior college applicants. Related to this, 84 percent of community college applicants were Pell grant recipients, compared to 65 percent of senior college applicants. Community college applicants were also older, with 21 percent of applicants over 26 years old, compared to 14 percent in the same age range at the senior colleges; and more likely to report a native language other than English (54 vs. 28 percent) and to be born outside of the US mainland (58 vs. 42 percent). Finally, a lower percentage of community college applicants reported that they had volunteer experience at the time of application—74 percent compared to 81 percent of senior college applicants. These differences are not surprising given what is known about the populations who attend community colleges and senior colleges, but are nonetheless important to note.

The critical quantitative approach to understanding the Service Corps starts with the analysis mentioned above—disaggregating rates of application, selection, and enrollment by race/ethnicity and other factors. Instead of assuming that all students have the same access to the program, this approach identifies areas of access and drop-off and ensures that data are analyzed in such a way as to shed light on whether certain groups are more or less subject to exclusion from participation or from the opportunity to apply. However, this analysis is only a very first step. There is still much to learn about how and why students from different backgrounds are interested in participating in service-learning and how these students may view civic engagement and community involvement in varied ways. Additionally, it is necessary to take a critical look at how race/ethnicity is defined and measured in the first place.

With this in mind, we turn to highlighting several important limitations to the race/ethnicity data collected by the Service Corps. As with most social science and education data, the race/ethnicity categories are limited and do not accurately represent the multilayered and complex identities of students. In order to analyze whether the participating students represent CUNY overall, it is necessary to use five limited categories—American Indian/Native Alaskan, Asian, black, Hispanic, and white—to make comparisons to the larger population since these are the categories that are used in CUNY's institutional reporting. Statistics based on these categories are the most readily available and also the most used by university administrators. However, students clearly do not fit neatly into these categories and when given the opportunity to better express their identities, they often do so. As shown in table 6.1, approximately one in ten students selected multiple categories of race/ethnicity. Although students were given the option to select multiple race/ethnicity categories, students who selected more than one category were ultimately placed in one category for analysis of comparisons to the larger population.

Second, the simplistic race/ethnicity categories mask the huge variation of student ancestry and ethnic origin and completely ignore any distinction between recent immigrants and the native born, which are arguably more salient to a student's identity. It is possible to use two other questions from the application to learn more about Service Corps students: "What is your country of origin?" and "Other than English, what language(s) are you most comfortable speaking?" While these questions come with their own limitations, they reveal some of the variation. For example, while the category "Asian" is used as if it represents one large group, the top languages spoken by applicants in this category are Bengali (63), Chinese (50), Cantonese (42), Urdu (34), Korean (16), Hindi (15), and Punjabi (12), demonstrating a sizeable range of ethnic groups. Perhaps more striking, students from the Middle East and North Africa are completely invisible in the race/ethnicity categories, subsumed under the "white" category, despite research showing that many people from the Middle East and North Africa do not identify as white (Majaj 2000). The seventh most frequent language spoken was Arabic (42 applicants), lending support to the idea that a significant proportion of applicants to the Service Corps were of Middle Eastern and North African descent. Similarly, the "black" category includes recent immigrants from many areas of Africa and the Caribbean as well as African Americans who have been in the country for many generations. Likewise, the "Hispanic" category includes students from a large range of countries. Because these race/ethnicity categories are so broad, the question of whether the Service Corps members represent the CUNY population overall is difficult to answer. In the future, we will analyze data separately by language and/or country of origin to further examine whether and how these distinctions matter to their application, enrollment, and success in the program.

These subgroup categories are also important given that students' understanding of what service means and their definition of "community" may be related to their ethnic or cultural identity and the norms and traditions within those cultures, as discussed by other researchers (Alcantar [forthcoming]; Hernandez, et al. 2013). From a practical standpoint, this may be useful to keep in mind when thinking about recruitment strategies and messaging about the program. From a research standpoint, it is critical to consider these distinctions as we attempt to measure students' motivations and to learn about their experiences. For example, much of the existing research on service-learning and other service programs uses surveys to measure levels of civic engagement and responsibility (e.g., see Corporation for National and Community Service 2008). These surveys often use the language of "community," asking questions such as how strongly participants agree with the statement "I have a strong attachment to my community." Survey respondents may have very different understandings of what this means and how their community is defined. Research on the Service Corps also uses the language of "community" without knowing what this means to different students. In the future, focus groups or interviews with students may be used to delve into this issue and add context to the way students answer questions about community. Absent that understanding, we can only look at differences in how students respond to these types of questions. In a pre-program survey of Service Corps members, students were asked to report how strongly they agreed with the statement "Being involved in a program to improve the NYC community is important." This question specifically refers to the NYC community, but still leaves room for ambiguity. Significant differences in responses were found by race/ethnicity, with 82 percent of Hispanic/Latino students strongly agreeing, compared to 66 percent of Asian students. Of black and white students as well as students in the other/more than one race category, 78–79 percent strongly agreed with the statement.

Another survey question asked students to select the most important reason for being in the Service Corps. Differences were found by race/ethnicity, although none were statistically significant. The most popular reason, "It allows me to provide a valuable service to my community," was selected by 36 percent of black students, compared to 25 percent of Asian students, 22 percent of Hispanic/Latino students, 19 percent of white students, and 19 percent of students in the other/more than one race category. Again, this question of what "my community" means to students may depend on cultural context as well as how close personally they feel to the community or communities served by the program. Keeping these issues in mind, we turn to a discussion of how the critical quantitative framework will inform our ongoing evaluation of the Service Corps and its outcomes.

Critical Evaluation: Understanding Program Outcomes

The Service Corps program, much like other service-learning programs, has multiple goals for students. The primary goals are to increase civic engagement/responsibility and to improve transferable skills for the workplace. Other goals are to increase confidence and leadership skills, to develop a stronger connection to CUNY and an identity as a representative of CUNY, to increase awareness of social issues and knowledge of organizations in NYC, and to introduce students to public service careers. With these goals in mind, an evaluation plan was developed for the

Service Corps to measure progress toward these goals as well as to look at how the program was implemented and the general variation across colleges and community partners. The evaluation plan, initially developed by a team of researchers and staff representing various backgrounds and perspectives, uses a combination of surveys, interviews, focus groups, and administrative data.

In future years, evaluation of the Service Corps will use a robust comparison group comprised of current CUNY four-year and community college students and will look at longer-term outcomes such as academic progress and, eventually, employment and labor market outcomes. The critical quantitative approach will be used at all stages—informing how variables are defined and measured, the ways language is used in surveys and interviews, and how researchers analyze data to better understand how the program is experienced by students with different backgrounds and orientations. Just as long-term outcomes of program participation will be compared across colleges and projects, outcomes will also be examined across racial/ethnic categories. Where possible, within-group variation in outcomes will also be examined and critiqued. For instance, the impact of Service Corps participation on academic performance and persistence will be analyzed for different racial/ethnic groups separately using multivariate techniques that will attempt to tease out the unique outcomes based on race/ethnicity. Community college student outcomes will be analyzed separately to better understand the unique impacts of service-learning on students at these types of institutions. Questions about what might be driving any differences will be investigated. Finally, a critical quantitative approach to the evaluation of the Service Corps emphasizes the fact that not all outcomes are easily measured using quantitative data and that researchers and practitioners must recognize these limitations and be more inclusive in terms of methods and about how program success is defined.

Asking Critical Questions to Better Understand Equity and Access

The critical quantitative approach is a useful theoretical framework to help guide analyses of race/ethnicity and other important student subgroups for service-learning. As Bensimon and Bishop (2012) pointed out, research and evaluation are often not designed to take race/ethnicity into account, and researchers often fail to use race/ethnicity as more than simply a predictive demographic variable. A critical quantitative approach can help illuminate issues of access and equity in service-learning. By proactively examining race/ethnicity through a critical quantitative lens, researchers and practitioners can better understand the needs of community college students and of service-learning initiatives themselves. Based on our experience and from the examples taken from CUNY Service Corps, we recommend three major areas in which questions can be addressed using critical quantitative analyses: program management, program evaluation, and research.

Program management: Service-learning program developers, faculty members, and administrators can use existing quantitative data to help inform everyday decision making and program development. Existing frameworks for critically looking at administrative data can be adapted for various service-learning contexts. One example of an existing instrument, the "Equity Scorecard," was developed by Bensimon and colleagues as a tool for higher education institutions, researchers, and practitioners to collaboratively develop an awareness of access and equity issues by examining quantitative data (Bensimon and Chase 2012). This type of tool can be used to facilitate discussions among service-learning stakeholders about the ways in which students from diverse backgrounds can best be served. Such analyses could involve the critical analysis of eligibility criteria for service-learning opportunities. At CUNY, there are significant differences in the racial/ethnic distributions between students who are enrolled in noncredit developmental education and those who are not. If enrollment in developmental education is used as eligibility criteria to participate in service-learning opportunities, what implications might the policy have on students of color?

Another example relates to outreach and recruitment of students. If students from different backgrounds have different understandings of community and of civic engagement, the type of messaging used to describe the program could affect which students apply and participate. Program developers and faculty members should be mindful of the language they use to describe service-learning opportunities so as to ensure that it resonates with a wide range of students.

Program evaluation: Evaluation of service-learning at community colleges should take into account individual student experiences and relate them to specific program goals and outcomes. Quantitative analyses can help illuminate evaluation questions that can be further analyzed using qualitative approaches. A critical approach can also assist evaluators in understanding a specific program's implementation and the variety of forms that service-learning can take. According to Eyler and Giles (1999), weak or modest effects of service-learning may be due, in part, to the considerable variability in implementation of programs. Evaluation plans can include logic models and outcomes that specifically relate to different implementations and diverse student groups. According to Carter (2006), analyzing differences across groups can help identify program and policy factors that expand access and equity.

Research: Some researchers have called into question the prevalence of quantitative analyses being undertaken in the service-learning field. Butin (2006) highlighted the potential of quantitative analyses to undermine the institutionalization of service-learning and argues that it is impossible to quantify the value of service-learning. We acknowledge the limitations of quantitative analyses in the traditional positivistic sense, but maintain that researchers should utilize quantitative methods to challenge these limitations and to develop new models, rather than minimalize the utility of statistical analyses altogether. Research on the impacts of service-learning at community colleges must involve the analyses of outcomes for *all* students. What types of opportunities benefit certain groups of students? Which students tend to benefit and which ones do not? What are the characteristics of community colleges that have successful service-learning initiatives? Does neighborhood context play a stronger role for students from certain backgrounds? Seminal research by Astin and Sax (1998) found that participation in volunteer service positively corresponded with 12 outcomes related to civic responsibility. These outcomes included increased commitment to helping others, serving the community, promoting racial understanding, doing volunteer work, and working for a nonprofit organization. An ideal next step for researchers is to build upon existing research by specifically exploring some of these outcomes for individual groups of students based on common backgrounds and perspectives. Studies documented by Eyler and Giles (1999) are ripe for further exploration using a critical perspective.

Finally, researchers can use a critical quantitative approach to understand the unique context of the community college. Most existing research tends to focus on bachelor's degree-seeking students. Students enrolled at community colleges have unique academic histories, needs, and goals (Bailey et al. 2004). The fact that many community college students attend part-time, transfer to other institutions, and are difficult to track longitudinally via traditional data systems should not dissuade researchers from examining this important student population. These challenges should simply encourage researchers to develop alternative quantitative approaches to better understand these students and their pathways through service-learning. St. John and Musoba (2010) called for expansion of opportunities for underrepresented students in higher education by creating new and diverse educational pathways. Service-learning has the potential to play a critical role in providing such opportunities at community colleges. As service-learning opportunities expand, it is essential that researchers and practitioners critically examine the intersection of race, ethnicity, civic engagement, and service-learning at community colleges to better understand how best to serve students from diverse backgrounds.

References

Alcantar, Cynthia M. Forthcoming. "Civic Engagement Measures for Latina/o College Students." In *New Perspectives on Critical Quantitative Inquiry*, edited by Frances K. Stage and R. Wells. San Francisco, CA: Jossey-Bass.

Astin, Alexander W., and Linda J. Sax. 1998. "How Undergraduates Are Affected by Service Participation." *Journal of College Student Development* 39: 251–263.

Bailey, Thomas, Mariana Alfonso, Juan Carlos Calcagno, Davis Jenkins, Gregory S. Kienzl, and D. Timothy Leinbach. 2004. *Improving Student Attainment in Community Colleges: Institutional Characteristics and Policies*. New York, NY: Community College Research Center, Teachers College, Columbia University.

Bailey, Thomas, and Vanessa Morest. 2006. "The Community College Equity Agenda in the Twenty-First Century: Moving from Access to Achievement." In *Defending the Community College Agenda*, edited by Thomas Bailey and Vanessa Smith Morest. Baltimore, MD: The Johns Hopkins University Press.

Bensimon, Estela M., and Robin Bishop. 2012. "Why 'Critical'? The Need for New Ways of Knowing." *The Review of Higher Education* 36 (1): 1–7.

Bensimon, Estela M., and Megan M. Chase. 2012. "Equity Scorecard for Higher Education." In *Encyclopedia of Diversity in Education*, edited by James A. Banks, 813–817. Thousand Oaks, CA: SAGE Publications, Inc.

Bringle, Robert G., and Julie A. Hatcher. 1996. "Implementing Service-learning in Higher Education." *Journal of Higher Education* 67 (2): 221–239.

Bueschel, Andrea C. 2004. "The Missing Link: The Role of Community Colleges in the Transition between High School and College." In *From High School to College*, edited by Michael. W. Kirst and Andrea Venezia. San Francisco, CA: Jossey-Bass.

Butin, Dan W. 2006. "The Limits of Service-Learning in Higher Education." *Review of Higher Education* 29 (4): 473–498.

Carter, Deborah. F. 2006. "Key Issues in the Persistence of Underrepresented Minority Students." *New Directions for Institutional Research* 130 (Summer): 33–46.

Carter, Deborah F., and Sylvia Hurtado. 2007. "Bridging Key Research Dilemmas: Quantitative Research Using a Critical Eye." *New Directions for Institutional Research* 133 (Spring): 25–35.

Celio, Christine I., Joseph Durlak, and Allison Dymnicki. 2011. "A Meta-Analysis of the Impact of Service-Learning on Students." *Journal of Experiential Education* 34 (2): 164–181.

Conway, Katherine. 2009. "Exploring Persistence of Immigrant and Native Students in an Urban Community College." *Review of Higher Education* 32 (3): 321–352.

Corporation for National and Community Service, Office of Research and Policy Development. 2008. *Still Serving: Measuring the Eight-Year Impact of AmeriCorps on Alumni*. Washington, DC.

CUNY Office of Institutional Research and Assessment. 2013a. *A Profile of Undergraduates at CUNY Senior and Community Colleges: Fall 2012*. The City University of New York.

———. 2013b. *Three-Year Graduation Rates of Full-time, First-time Freshmen in Associate or Certificate Programs, by Race/Ethnicity: Fall 2008 Entering Cohort*. The City University of New York.

CUNY Service Corps. 2013. *Internal Recruitment Planning Document*. The City University of New York.

Eyler, Janet, and Dwight E. Giles Jr. 1999. *Where's the Learning in Service-Learning*. San Francisco, CA: Jossey-Bass.

Goldrick-Rab, Sara, and Peter Kinsley. 2013. *School Integration and the Open Door Philosophy: Rethinking the Economic and Racial Composition of Community Colleges*. New York: Century Foundation.

Hernandez, Ebelia, Michael Mobley, Gayle Coryell, En-Hui Yu, and Gladys Martinez. 2013. "Examining the Cultural Validity of a College Student Engagement Survey for Latinos." *Journal of Hispanic Higher Education* 12 (2): 152–173.

Kincheloe, Joe L., and Peter L. McLaren. 1994. "Rethinking Critical Theory and Qualitative Research." In *Handbook of Qualitative Research*, edited by Norman K. Denzin and Yvonna S. Lincoln. London: Sage Publications.

Knapp, Laura G., Janice E. Kelly-Reid, and Scott A. Ginder. 2012. *Enrollment in Postsecondary Institutions, Fall 2011; Financial Statistics, Fiscal Year 2011; and Graduation Rates, Selected Cohorts, 2003–2008: First Look (Provisional Data) (NCES 2012–174rev)*. US Department of Education. Washington, DC: National Center for Education Statistics. Accessed December 16, 2014. http://nces.ed.gov/pubsearch.

Majaj, Lisa Suhair. 2000. "Arab-Americans and the Meanings of Race." In *Postcolonial Theory and the United States: Race, Ethnicity, and Literature*, edited by Amritjit Singh and Peter Schmidt, 320–337. Jackson: University Press of Mississippi.

Novick, Sarah, Scott C. Seider, and James P. Huguley. 2011. "Engaging College Students from Diverse Backgrounds in Community Service-learning." *Journal of College and Character* 12 (1): 1–8.

Palmer, Robert T., and J. Luke Wood. 2013. *Community Colleges and STEM: Examining Underrepresented Racial and Ethnic Minorities*. New York, NY: Routledge.

Perna, Laura W. 2007. "The Sources of Racial-Ethnic Group Differences in College Enrollment: A Critical Examination." *New Directions for Institutional Research* 133 (Spring): 51–66.

Perna, Laura W., and Marvin A. Titus. 2005. "The Relationship between Parental Involvement as Social Capital and College Enrollment: An Examination of Racial/Ethnic Group Differences." *Journal of Higher Education* 76 (5): 485–518.

Prentice, Mary, and Gail Robinson. 2007. *Linking Service-Learning and Civic Engagement in Community College Students*. American Association of Community Colleges.

Prentice, Mary, and Gail Robinson. 2010. *Improving Student Learning Outcomes with Service Learning*. American Association of Community Colleges.
St. John, Edward P., and Glenda D. Musoba. 2010. *Pathways to Academic Success: Expanding Opportunity for Underrepresented Students*. New York: Routledge.
Stage, Francis K. 2007. "Answering Critical Questions Using Quantitative Data." *New Directions for Institutional Research* 133 (Spring): 5–16.
Stage, Francis K., and Ryan S. Wells. 2014. "Critical Quantitative Inquiry in Context." *New Directions for Institutional Research* 158: 1–7.
Swail, Watson Scott, Kenneth E. Redd, and Laura W. Perna. 2003. "Retaining Minority Students in Higher Education: A Framework for Success." *ASHE-ERIC Higher Education Report* 30 (2).
Teranishi, Robert. 2007. "Race, Ethnicity, and Higher Education Policy: The Use of Critical Quantitative Research." *New Directions for Institutional Research* 133 (Spring): 37–49.
Teranishi, Robert, Carola Suarez-Orozco, and Marcelo Suarez-Orozco. 2011. "Immigrants in Community Colleges." *Future of Children* 21 (1): 153–169.
US Census Bureau, Current Population Survey. 2012. *Annual Social and Economic Supplement*.

PART III

Service-Learning and Student Success in Community Colleges

CHAPTER 7

Service-Learning: A Vehicle for Enhancing Academic Performance and Retention among Community College Developmental Reading and Writing Students*

Regina A. Rochford

In the fall of 2006, Queensborough Community College, the City University of New York (CUNY), was awarded the American Association of Community College's Community Colleges Broadening Horizons through Service Learning grant. The goal of this grant was to support community colleges in developing wide-ranging service-learning programs to address the needs of students and community residents from diverse cultural and ethnic backgrounds (Robinson 2007).

Queensborough Community College resides in one of the most ethnically diverse counties in the country (New York State Comptroller 2006). Approximately 45 years ago, almost 84 percent of its students were white and middle class. Conversely, the present population reflects the diverse cultural mix in this community: (1) 22 percent Caucasian, (2) 24 percent African American, (3) 28 percent Hispanic, (4) 25 percent Asian, and (5) 1 percent Native American. Moreover, many students are adults, parents, and nontraditional learners (Queensborough Community College Office of Institutional Research and Assessment 2013).

When new freshmen enter Queensborough, approximately 70 percent require developmental reading, writing, or mathematics. African American and Hispanic learners are 10 percent more likely to be placed in developmental classes than Asian and Caucasian freshmen, and in contrast to Native Speakers of English (NSE), English Language Learners (ELL) demonstrate a 20 percent lower pass rate in developmental reading and a 10 percent lower pass rate in developmental writing (Queensborough Community College/CUNY Fact Book 2013). Finally, only 24–34 percent of the developmental students graduate after six years (Queensborough Community College Office of Institutional Research and Assessment 2010).

In view of these challenges, several faculty members in the Department of Academic Literacy at Queensborough Community College incorporated service-learning pedagogy into their developmental reading and writing courses to determine if active, reflective learning and community involvement could improve student performance and retention. The purpose of this chapter is to discuss the impact of service-learning on developmental reading and writing students at Queensborough Community College and to compare individual service-learning courses so that developmental service-learning practitioners at the community college level can design more effective programs.

Literature Review

These days most community colleges are under pressure to accelerate students through developmental education, despite the fact these learners are academically underprepared and at risk of failure because of financial instability, a history of academic failure, and low self-esteem (Roueche and Roueche1999). As a consequence, developmental educators are continually seeking new methods to advance their students' academic performance. Thus, when Eyler and Giles (1999) established a connection between service-learning and student learning, developmental educators in community colleges began to incorporate this pedagogy into their classrooms (Prentice 2009).

In 2008, Stavrianopoulos reported that entering community college freshmen who took part in a service-learning program were more engaged in the educational process, and even claimed to be more academically and emotionally empowered because of their involvement. Service-learning has also resulted in enhanced academic outcomes in developmental community college students' reading and writing skills (Rochford 2013; Rochford and Hock 2010). Moreover, Rochford (2013) and Prentice (2009) also reported significantly higher grade point averages (GPAs) and rates of retention among developmental community college reading and writing students who participated in service-learning activities.

Prentice (2009) also determined that developmental students who had participated in service-learning enhanced their academic and interpersonal skills over the course of the semester. In addition, this study revealed that the students had acquired a greater sense of civic responsibility and were more driven to persevere toward their career goals. Likewise, faculty members who participated in this investigation also asserted that developmental students who had completed their service-learning requirements were more motivated to complete their college education.

Hypotheses

To assess the impact of service-learning on this unique developmental community college population, the following research hypotheses were examined:

1. In contrast to non-service-learning developmental reading and writing students, developmental students who participate in service-learning will exhibit

(1) higher GPAs, (2) enhanced scores on the ACT Reading Compass and ACT Writing Sample Assessment exams, (3) increased retention, and (4) completion of more college credits.
2. In contrast to developmental service-learning students who participate in one service-learning activity during a semester, developmental classes that engage in semester-long service-learning activities will evidence (1) higher GPAs, (2) increased ACT Reading Compass and ACT Writing Sample Assessment scores, and (3) improved rates of retention.

Method

Institutional and Instructional Setting

When students enter CUNY, their reading and writing ability is evaluated to determine their readiness for college-level coursework; however, some students are exempt from these assessments if they have achieved adequate scores on the Scholastic Aptitude Test (SAT) or the New York State English Regents exam. When nonexempt freshmen enter CUNY, they must take the ACT Reading Compass and the ACT Writing Sample Assessment exams to determine if they require developmental reading or writing courses. These tests were intended to measure the reading and writing ability of students as they enter and exit two-year colleges (CUNY/ACT Test Administration Manual for the Asset Writing Skills and Reading Skills Assessments and ACT Writing Sample Assessment 2000). If students earn below a 7 on the ACT Writing Sample Assessment or less than a 70 on the ACT Reading Compass, they must register for developmental reading and/or writing courses at a community college in CUNY. After successful completion of the required developmental courses and before they proceed into any of the credit courses such as English composition, psychology, sociology, history, and economics, they must pass the ACT Writing Sample Assessment with at least a score of 7 and the ACT Reading Compass exam with a minimum score of 70.

At CUNY's Queensborough Community College, developmental reading and writing courses are taught in two separate tracks in the Department of Academic Literacy. One track is for NSE; the other is for ELL. The NSE track offers four courses: (1) BE111 Development of Composition Skills, (2) BE112 Advanced Composition Workshop, (3) BE121 Development of Reading Skills, and (4) BE122 Advanced College Reading and Study Skills. The ELL track offers five courses: (1) BE201 Beginning ELL Composition, (2) BE203 Intermediate ELL Composition, (3) BE205 Advanced ELL Composition, (4) BE225 Basic ELL Reading Skills, and (5) BE226 Advanced ELL College Reading and Study Skills. Students' placement in these courses varies according to their scores on the ACT Reading Compass and the ACT Writing Sample Assessment exams.

Service-learning was adopted as a developmental pedagogy at Queensborough in 2007. After the instructors in Academic Literacy became familiar with service-learning research, they were advised to design small, simple programs that they could enhance as they became more comfortable with this pedagogy. Therefore, some of the department's initial service-learning programs revolved around one activity, such as teaching one lesson or doing one presentation; however, as the faculty evolved and became more proficient with the pedagogy, they developed thematic service-learning projects that spanned the entire semester.

In addition, although the Academic Literacy Department requires each course to address specific learning outcomes, each instructor enjoys the freedom to meet these learning outcomes by employing unique pedagogies, books, and materials. Thus, each service-learning project was conceived by individual instructors who desired to connect with specific community-based organizations that piqued their interests. Consequently, some classes read literature and wrote letters. Others researched and designed presentations or brochures, whereas some tutored lower-level students. Accordingly, this analysis investigated the general impact of service-learning on developmental students, and it also compared and contrasted individual programs to identify the characteristics of the most effective curriculums.

Participants

After obtaining approval from the Institutional Review Board, it was determined that during 2008 and 2009, a total of 15 developmental classes had participated in service-learning. These courses included: (1) BE 226 Advanced ELL College Reading and Study Skills, (2) BE201 Beginning ELL Composition, (3) BE203 Intermediate ELL Composition, (4) BE205 Advanced ELL Composition, (5) BE111 Development of Composition Skills, (6) BE112 Advanced Composition Workshop, and (7) BE121 Development of Reading Skills.

Procedures

To create an experimental group, the following de-identified data were collected for each developmental class that participated in service-learning: (1) ACT Reading Compass scores, (2) ACT Writing Sample Assessment scores, (3) GPAs, (4) the number of college credits completed successfully, and (5) whether or not these students were still enrolled in the college. For the control group, the same information was gathered for all of the other non-service-learning developmental classes offered in the Department of Academic Literacy. It should be noted that the data collected reflected students' scores after they completed the most advanced developmental courses.

Both the experimental and control groups were divided by course, section, and semester. Hence, the experimental and control groups consisted of 397 and 3,746 participants, respectively.

Results

Contrast of Service-Learning to Non-Service-Learning Developmental Students

To explore hypothesis one, which stated that in contrast to non-service-learning reading and writing students, developmental students who participated in service-learning would exhibit (1) higher GPAs, (2) enhanced scores on the ACT Reading

Compass and ACT Writing Sample Assessment exams, (3) increased retention, and (4) the completion of more college credits, a t-test of independent means was performed. The results indicated significant differences between the experimental and control groups for the categories of: (1) ACT Reading Compass scores ($p < .01$), (2) the total number of credits completed ($p < .001$), and (3) the GPAs ($p < .001$). An inspection of the mean for the ACT Compass Reading scores indicated that the experimental group's mean score was 67.19 whereas the control group was 69.44. Thus, ACT Compass Reading scores were significantly higher among the control group. Although statistical significance was not achieved for the category of ACT Writing Sample Assessment scores, the experimental group earned slightly higher mean scores of 6.44 in contrast to the control group's 6.41.

An examination of the mean scores for the category of total number of credits completed revealed that the experimental group averaged 19.22 credits, whereas the control group earned 14.93, and these results were statistically significant ($p < .001$). In addition, the mean GPA in the experimental group was 2.11, which was significantly higher ($p < .001$) than the mean GPA of 1.85 in the control group. Therefore, the experimental group that participated in service-learning earned significantly more college credits and higher GPAs than the control group.

To ascertain if service-learning participants, who were enrolled from 2008 through 2009, were more likely to continue to be registered in the college, a chi-square test was conducted, and the results were statistically significant ($p < .05$). An analysis of the experimental and control groups indicated that 72 percent of the experimental group remained enrolled in the college, in contrast to 67 percent of the control group. Therefore, the service-learning students exhibited a higher rate of retention because they continued to be enrolled in the college.

Thus, the first research hypothesis, which stated that participation in service-learning in developmental reading and writing courses would result in (1) higher GPAs, (2) improved scores on the ACT Reading Compass and ACT Writing Sample Assessment exams, (3) improved retention, and (4) the completion of more college credits, was partially supported by these results.

Contrast of Individual Developmental Service-Learning Courses

An Analysis of Variance (ANOVA) was performed to explore the second hypothesis, which stated that in contrast to developmental service-learning students who participated in one service-learning activity during a semester, developmental classes that engaged in semester-long service-learning activities would evidence (1) higher GPAs, (2) increased ACT Reading Compass and ACT Writing Sample Assessment scores, and (3) improved rates of retention. The ANOVA indicated statistical significance among ACT Reading Compass scores, ACT Writing Sample Assessment scores, and GPAs. To determine exactly where the statistically significant differences occurred, a Tukey HSD procedure was performed for each category.

Among the 15 service-learning groups, a Tukey HSD procedure evidenced significant differences in eight groups for ACT Reading Compass scores. Overall, the higher reading scores were exhibited in the advanced NSE and ELL reading and writing courses with the exception of one low-level BE111 NSE writing class. Another

Tukey HSD procedure revealed 30 statistically significant differences among the 15 service-learning groups for ACT Writing Sample Assessment scores. Once again, the subjects in the lower-level writing courses exhibited the most difficulty achieving the minimum passing score of 7. The last Tukey HSD procedure exhibited 20 statistically significant differences for GPAs among the 15 service-learning classes. With the exception of BE122SL6 and BE112SL4, the lower GPAs generally resulted in the lowest-level reading and writing classes probably because many of these students were ELL and were the most underprepared. Thus, the second research hypothesis, which stated that in contrast to service-learning students who participated in one service-learning activity during a semester, developmental classes that engaged in semester-long service-learning activities would evidence (1) higher GPAs, (2) increased ACT Reading Compass and ACT Writing Sample Assessment scores, and (3) improved rates of retention, was partially supported by these findings.

Discussion

Contrasting Service-Learning Students with Non-Service-Learning Developmental Students

It was originally theorized that in contrast to non-service-learning reading and writing students, developmental students who participated in service-learning would exhibit (1) higher GPAs, (2) enhanced scores on the ACT Reading Compass and ACT Writing Sample Assessment exams, (3) increased retention, and (4) completion of more college credits. The statistical analyses revealed that the service-learning participants' evidenced (1) higher GPAs, (2) a greater rate of retention, and (3) completion of more college credits. The increased GPA findings are critical because as students advance through their credit courses, if their GPAs drop below 2.00, they are placed on academic probation. Worse yet, if they are unable to increase their GPAs and maintain the minimum standard, they risk being dismissed from the college. Moreover, when community college students attempt to transfer to four-year colleges in CUNY, if their GPAs are low, they may not be accepted. More generally, these outcomes suggest that students who participated in service-learning developed improved academic skills. Theory indicates that one potential explanation for this progress is the students' recurrent interactions with their classmates, instructors, and community-based organizations, which assisted them in developing a broader understanding of their course content, lectures, and readings (Prentice and Robinson 2010).

Next, an inspection of the mean scores for the category of total number of credits completed also revealed that the service-learning students completed significantly more college credits than the control group. These results suggest that the service-learning experience generated more academically and psychologically competent learners, because they registered for and completed more college-level courses successfully. They also support Prentice (2009) who reported that service-learning experiences enhanced participants' self-confidence by requiring them to take leadership roles and assert themselves in real-life situations so that they matured into self-assured learners.

A chi-square analysis also indicated that service-learning students enrolled in 2008 through 2009 were statistically more likely to persist in college. This is a key finding because according to Bailey, Jeong, and Cho (2012), only 35 percent of developmental community college students complete the entire developmental course sequence. In addition, most drop out at the beginning of their developmental coursework, and almost half fail to complete the first developmental course they take. However, 72 percent of the developmental service-learning participants continued to be enrolled in the college two to three years later. It is believed that the higher rate of retention occurred because frequent, quality contact with faculty, students, and community-based organizations afforded academic, social, and personal support, which according to Tinto (1995) and Tinto and Russo (1994) are crucial predictors of student persistence. Moreover, these results support the findings of Prentice (2009) who demonstrated that students who participated in developmental service-learning classes evidenced a higher rate of retention in future semesters, and they are especially valuable inasmuch as low retention rates are frequently an issue among community college students (Tinto 1993).

Contrasting with Individual Service-Learning Developmental Courses

An ANOVA assessed the second research hypothesis, which contrasted developmental service-learning classes that participated in one service-learning activity to developmental classes that engaged in semester-long service-learning activities to determine if semester-long activities resulted in (1) higher GPAs, (2) increased ACT Reading Compass and ACT Writing Sample Assessment scores, and (3) improved rates of retention. These analyses demonstrated that the service-learning projects, which required students to engage in a series of activities throughout the term so that they frequently participated in thematic reading, writing, analysis, and synthesis, produced the best overall results because these tasks directly connected to their course content and provided recurrent hands-on experiences. However, it should also be noted that these positive results were evidenced in the more advanced NSE and ELL reading and writing courses. It is theorized that the lower-level ELL did not benefit as much as the advanced learners because they were the recipients of the service in their classes and hence were never challenged to convey their new skills. In contrast, when the advanced ELL imparted their knowledge to others, they had to master new material and demonstrate their ability to communicate it successfully.

A Tukey HSD procedure also confirmed that the highest mean reading score (76.68) occurred among the BE112SL4 NSE students. Since BE112 is a writing course, the focus of the semester was on developing the students' composition skills. However, during this service-learning project, BE112 NSE students were required to read and comprehend extensive literature before they tutored the low-level ELL who used this information to compose letters to support an on-campus historical site. In addition, the NSE did not receive any special reading lessons or guidance to assist them as they grappled with comprehending the literature. Thus, the NSE students were forced to read, comprehend, and explain this material as they assisted their tutees in writing their letters. Moreover, both classes received frequent direct hands-on support from the director of the community-based organization who worked one-on-one with pairs of students as they read the literature and drafted their letters. Consequently, the BE112 NSE not only improved their writing skills, which was the goal of this class, but they also advanced their reading skills. However, their mean GPAs were a mere 1.65. These outcomes suggest that when advanced NSE writing students read, comprehend, synthesize, discuss, and write about thematic reading topics, the integration of these activities advance both their reading and writing skills significantly.

In contrast to the BE112SL4 learners, their ELL tutees from BE201SL5 exhibited the lowest mean reading scores of 58.09 and the second lowest mean writing score of 4.95. It is hypothesized that the ELL did not reap the same benefits as their BE112 counterparts because they were new immigrants and were placed in a more passive role by acting as the recipients of the service. Thus, it is suggested that the ELL be offered the opportunity to tutor elementary school children or adult literacy students in reading and writing inasmuch as this project level would provide the ELL the opportunity to cultivate their English language competency and their reading and writing skills in a less complex English-language environment. Moreover, this experience would permit the ELL to deliver the service so that they could take control of the project and their learning.

Although this service-learning project was replicated with a different community-based organization to support hate-crime legislation, the results among BE112SL12 and BE201SL14 were not significant. That is, although these students participated in a series of letter writing activities during this semester to support hate-crime legislation, in contrast to students who participated in briefer service-learning projects, these learners did not evidence statistically enhanced GPAs, ACT reading scores, or ACT writing scores. The contrast in findings implies that perhaps the hate-crime reading and writing topics may not have intrigued the students as much as the on-campus historical site, or perhaps the project and the readings were too abstract for the students to bond with the project. Thus, it is suggested that the service-learning projects be more tangible and concrete so that students can develop a direct visual or physical connection with their projects.

During another service-learning project, the advanced ELL reading students in BE226SL1 were required to tutor low-level reading students in an NSE class to help them locate the main idea in a short article. For this project, the ELL (1) selected a passage, (2) read it and located the main idea, (3) created a lesson on main ideas, (4) reviewed and revised their lessons with their instructor and a tutor, and (5) taught their lessons to their tutees. The mean reading score in BE226SL1 was 67.58, which fell below the passing score of 70. These results imply that a one-time tutoring experience did not present the BE226SL1 students enough opportunities to enhance their reading skills. Therefore, it is suggested that this project be expanded to include several tutoring sessions and the development of a few different reading skills so that the participants benefit from the opportunity to engage in more trial and error as they struggle with imparting new reading skills to their tutees.

During the spring of 2009, one instructor taught a special class that offered ELL the opportunity to complete both BE203SL7 and BE205SL8 in one semester. This service-learning project linked these ELL writing students with a special on-campus program called Project Prize, which strives to prevent at-risk youth from dropping out of high school. The Queensborough Community College service-learning students met with the Project Prize youngsters on Saturday mornings during the semester to read, write, and discuss healthy food choices. During the last Saturday meeting, the class traveled to Whole Foods to shop for healthy foods. At the end of the term, this service-learning project demonstrated statistical significance among GPAs (2.83), and ACT Writing Sample Assessment scores (7.29). Their ACT reading scores were also significant (69.78), although they were slightly below the passing score of 70. This service-learning experience demonstrates that frequent thematic reading and writing activities yield improved achievement among developmental ELL because these students assumed the role of the teacher or expert and were relied upon to impart accurate knowledge and information to young people who looked up to them for guidance.

During the fall 2009, two classes, BE121SL13 and BE121SL14, participated in a service-learning project to research healthy eating and to present their findings to an advanced NSE reading class. After each presentation, the advanced reading students evaluated each presentation. A t test of independent means between the two service-learning classes and all of the other BE121 courses offered that semester displayed no statistical significance. It is theorized that when students participate in a service-learning project only once, they do not engage in repeated practice that hones their skills. Thus, once again, it is suggested that the BE121 students complete several investigations and presentations in order to perfect the new skills they develop during this project.

In the summer 2008, an advanced ELL reading class, BE226SL3, worked with the Alley Pond Environmental Center (APEC) to learn about and endorse environmental change in their local community. After APEC provided reading literature and presentations, the students crafted letters to the local community board and produced flyers to promote tree plantings in Queens, New York. The analyses of these participants' transcripts indicated that they demonstrated the highest mean GPAs and ACT Writing Assessment scores of all the developmental students who had participated in service-learning since its inception. In addition, their mean *ACT Reading Compass* scores were also the third highest. Once again, it should be noted that BE226 is a reading course; however, by engaging in semester-long reading and writing activities, these students enhanced both their reading and writing skills. These findings suggest that when students engage in semester-long authentic, thematic, reflective activities that require them to read, analyze, organize, and write about real issues that touch their communities, they acquire significantly improved reading and writing skills while they also advance their academic achievement.

Conclusion

This investigation reveals that service-learning is an effective pedagogy for developmental students. In contrast to developmental students who did not participate in service-learning, students who did were more likely to remain enrolled in college, complete more college credits, and earn higher GPAs. Additional findings include the importance of connecting the service the developmental students perform directly to their course curriculum so that they gain real-life experiences that link their classroom learning to their service-learning activities. This finding is especially important because developmental learners frequently miss the connection between what they are learning in their reading and writing classes and what they will be required to do in credit courses and real life. Thus, they fail to acquire enhanced life-long learning and study skills. However, when these students produced materials that were to be used by authentic audiences, they appreciated why these documents had to contain accurate information and be carefully edited and proofread. Consequently, they worked diligently to perfect their products because they would be viewed by real audiences.

In addition, it was observed that when the representative from the community-based organization actively engaged with the students and faculty, the students' academic performance was heightened as was demonstrated when the director of the Queens Historical Society assisted the students as they drafted their letters. The director's guidance and input assisted the students in recognizing the value of their efforts so that they maximized their performance by paying careful attention to detail.

Next, if instructors desire to develop reading or writing skills, it is unlikely that a one-session activity will bridge the students' knowledge gap. Instead, professors should design programs that permit more trial and error because these data insinuate multiple experiences lead to improved intellectual growth. Moreover, since most developmental students benefit from learning to develop and follow clear, self-directed plans, it is necessary to integrate this level of scaffolding into their service-learning projects. However, these activities will require one-on-one direction from the professor and/or a trained, experienced tutor inasmuch as most developmental students are not yet autonomous, self-sufficient learners.

Instructors should also strive to design projects that are concrete and tangible for the students as was demonstrated when two instructors executed the letter-writing campaign with the Queens Historical Society. However, when these same teachers attempted to replicate this project by having students write letters to support hate-crime legislation, they did not produce similar results. These experiences suggest when the students can visually, intellectually, and physically comprehend the need to support a project, they are better able to read and write about it with ease. In the case of the Queens Historical Society, the students toured the building, for which they composed letters of support. So, they understood the importance of this letter-writing campaign. In contrast, since many students did not have any direct experience with hate crimes, writing these letters was too disconnected from their life experiences and hence this project did not fascinate them enough. Therefore, when teachers craft developmental service-learning programs, they should seek more concrete projects that students can physically and visually appreciate so that these activities will ignite students' interest.

Some developmental educators have shied away from service-learning because when they are teaching a writing course, they fear they will not have enough time to assist their students with reading the literature, or if it is a reading class, they worry that focusing on the students' written work may distract from the enhancement of reading skills. However, the service-learning projects with the Queens Historical Society and APEC have demonstrated that a service-learning program that integrates concrete reading and writing activities can enhance both skills if they are carefully planned and scaffolded. However, it should be noted that both classes enjoyed the support of in-class and out-of-class tutors who assisted the students as they performed their service.

Finally, the service the students provide should be manageable for the participants and require them to be active learners because if the participants are only the recipients of the service, they do not become as engaged. Thus, although new immigrants with limited language skills should not tutor college students, they might profit from participation in projects in an early childhood education program or an elementary school. In contrast, advanced developmental learners can hone their skills by assisting low-level ELL.

In just a few short years, developmental service-learning practitioners at Queensborough Community College have begun to design, develop, and execute a wide range of varied programs. However, if these projects are to be effective, enjoyable, and sustainable, it is critical to reflect and learn from each experience so that these activities continue to thrive and produce positive outcomes.

Study Limitations

These results reflect the outcomes at Queensborough Community College, an urban community college with a culturally diverse population; however, they may differ in other community colleges. Thus, it is recommended that this study be replicated in another community college with a large diverse developmental population to verify if these findings can be generalized to larger populations or if they are unique to Queensborough Community College.

Note

*Portions of this chapter were originally published in 2013 in *Community College Journal of Research and Practice* 37 (5): 345–355.

References

ACT Inc. 2000. *CUNY/ACT Test Administration Manual for the Asset Writing Skills and Reading Skills Assessments and ACT Writing Sample Assessment*. Iowa City: ACT Inc.

Bailey, T., D. W. Jeong, and S.W. Cho. 2012. "Referral, Enrollment, and Completion in Developmental Education Sequences in Community Colleges." *Economics of Education Review* (March) 29: 255–270.

Eyler, J., and D. E. Giles Jr. 1999. *Where's the Learning in Service-Learning?* San Francisco, CA: Jossey Bass.

New York State Comptroller. 2006. *Queens: Economic Development and the State of the Borough Economy*. publ. nr. 3–2007. http://www.osc.state.ny.us/osdc/rpt3-2007queens.pdf.

Prentice, M. 2009. "Service-Learning's Impact on Developmental Reading/Writing and Student Life Skills Courses." *Community College Journal of Research and Practice* 33, no3: 270–282.

Prentice, M., and G. Robinson. 2010. "Improving Student Learning Outcomes with Service Learning." American Association of Community Colleges. http://www.eric.ed.gov/PDFS/ED535904.pdf.

Queensborough Community College, City University of New York. 2010. *Queensborough Community College/ CUNY Fact Book.* Accessed July 1, 2010. http://www.qcc.cuny.edu /OIRA/OIRADocs/Factbook10/B.pdf.

———. 2013. *Queensborough Community College/ CUNY Fact Book.* http://www.qcc.cuny. edu/pv_obj_cache/pv_obj_id_507807F1E804CF72AB7F096E8DD63C323F5B1A00 /filename/Factbook_2012-13.pdf.

Robinson, G. 2007. "Community Colleges Broadening Horizons through Service Learning, 2006–2009." American Association of Community Colleges. http://www.eric.ed.gov /PDFS/ED499827.pdf.

Rochford, R. A. 2013. "Service Learning for Remedial Reading and Writing Students." *Community College Journal of Research and Practice* 37 (5): 345–355.

Rochford, R. A. and Hock, S. 2010. "A Letter-Writing Campaign: Linking Academic Success and Civic Engagement." *Journal of Community Engagement and Scholarship* 3 (2): 76–83.

Roueche, J. E., and S. D. Roueche. 1999. *High Stakes, High Performance: Making Remedial Education Work.* Washington, DC: American Association of Community Colleges.

Stavrianopoulos, K. 2008. "Service Learning in the Freshman Year Experience." *College Student Journal* (June) 42 (2): 703–712.

Tinto, V. 1993. *Leaving College: Rethinking the Causes and Cures of Student Attrition.* 2nd ed. Chicago: The University of Chicago Press.

———. 1995. Taking Student Retention Seriously. *Maricopa Center for Learning and Instruction.* Tempe, AZ. http://www.mcli.dist.maricopa.edu/fsd/c2006/ docs/takingretentionseriously.pdf.

Tinto, V., and P. Russo, 1994. "Coordinated Studies Programs: Their Effect on Student Involvement at a Community College." *Community College Review* 22 (2): 16–25.

CHAPTER 8

Connect2Complete: Combining Service-Learning and Peer Advocates to Increase Student Success in Developmental Education

Shana Berger and Donna Duffy

Compared to other institutions of higher education, community colleges serve a disproportionate percentage of socioeconomically vulnerable and underprepared students (American Association of Community Colleges 2013). Unfortunately, disadvantaged students persist and graduate at lower rates than their more affluent counterparts (Bailey, Jeong, and Cho 2009). Likewise, while 60 percent of community college students test into at least one developmental education course (courses designed to prepare students for college-level coursework), only 25 percent of these students graduate within eight years (Bailey 2009).

In response to these graduation rates, President Obama set a goal that by the year 2020 America would have the highest percentage of college graduates in the world. To reach this target, Obama has called for five million more community college graduates by the year 2020 and a variety of powerful private foundations have committed funds to this effort known as the "completion agenda." While increasing graduation rates is certainly an important goal, many higher education professionals have pointed out that the completion agenda's singular focus on time to degree may emphasize efficiency to the detriment of high-quality learning (Humphreys 2012). Aware of this critique as one of many of the completion agenda, community colleges are seeking innovative strategies to increase graduation rates while also improving the quality of student learning.

One such strategy is the Connect2Complete (C2C) program, which was developed by Campus Compact, a national coalition of 1,200 college presidents—representing some six million students—committed to fulfilling the civic purposes of higher education. Nine community colleges in Florida, Ohio, and Washington are piloting C2C programs that combine peer-assisted service-learning and peer advocacy to reduce the barriers that cause economically disadvantaged developmental education students to struggle in college while also empowering these students to fully participate as members of their various communities.

For the C2C program, student success in developmental education is defined by measures of semester-to-semester retention, indicators of retention such as credit hours earned versus attempted, and student self-reporting on academic success, future aspirations, and campus connections. We define peer advocates as enrolled college students who, in addition to serving as leaders of service-learning, are mentors, advocates, and advisors to their peers in developmental education courses. The term "C2C students" refers to low-income students enrolled in at least one developmental education course.

In this chapter, we review the theories that ground the C2C program and describe the program's component parts and implementation. We then discuss the research questions that guided our evaluation of the C2C program's impact on student success, as well as the methods used in that evaluation. We conclude with a review of our findings and lessons learned.

Grounding Theories

In the most widely used framework for understanding student success, Tinto (1993) argues that of the factors that are amenable to intervention and change on campus, a student's ability to integrate with their institution both academically and socially has the most direct influence on that student's decision to remain at or leave an institution. A review of the literature reveals that the strategies of peer advocacy and service-learning encourage both academic development and social integration—Tinto's key factors for retention (Cress et al. 2010; Crisp 2010; Bringle, Hatcher, and Muthiah 2010).

In terms of academic development, service-learning has an impact on complexity of understanding, problem analysis, critical thinking, and cognitive development (Eyler and Giles 1999) and its greatest influence is on intention to persist through engaging and challenging course content (Gallini and Moely 2003). Likewise, mentoring, an important part of the peer advocate role, has been found to have a positive impact on student performance, intellectual and critical thinking skills, grade point average, and persistence rates (Pagan and Edward-Wilson 2003; Campbell and Campbell 1997).

In terms of social integration, students involved with service-learning report stronger faculty relationships and greater interaction with faculty and staff than those not involved with service-learning (Keup 2005–2006; Astin and Sax 1998). Service-learning students indicate they are more socially active and engaged with their peers (Wolff and Tinney 2006; Eyler and Giles 1999). Similarly, mentoring directly impacts students' ability to integrate socially through key relationships and support networks (Crisp 2010) and by helping students feel more connected and engaged on campus (Community College Survey of Student Engagement 2009; Pascarella 1980).

Despite the lessons of Tinto's retention theory, critics argue that his theory is based on the experiences of white, middle-class students attending private residential institutions (Karp 2011; Yeh 2010). Yeh (2010) establishes that a more complete picture of the range of ways in which service-learning impacts the most vulnerable college students, like those enrolled in community colleges, emerges through a critical examination of traditional retention theory. Critical retention theory calls attention to the ways that acculturation of students to the dominant college environment leads to maintaining the status quo and may devalue students' cultural identity. An alternative perspective draws simultaneously on Tinto and critical theory in calling on students to develop knowledge, skills, and social networks, build community ties, and adopt the forms of cultural and social capital needed to be successful *while* also maintaining cultural identity and challenging social and institutional norms (Maldonado, Rhoads, and Buenavista 2005).

Service-learning provides many of the benefits described in this alternative retention theory. In addition to developing new skills and building social networks as described previously, service-learning can strengthen one's cultural identity when students participate in service projects with communities similar to their own or that are culturally validating (Yeh 2010). One study (Lockeman and Pelco 2013) revealed that students of color and low-income students who took service-learning classes graduated at significantly higher rates than the same population of students who did not take service-learning courses (71 percent vs. 29 percent for students of color, and 72 percent vs. 28 percent for low-income students). The authors hypothesize that service-learning courses provide students of color and low-income students with experiences that increase person-culture "match" in the college context. Person-culture match theory holds that when the context is relevant to an individual, the person will experience greater well-being, be more engaged in the setting, and perform better (Fulmer et al. 2010).

While service-learning promotes students' academic integration through the acquisition of relevant cultural and social capital, it also provides tools to critique the structural inequalities within that very same culture. Through service-learning, students develop critical consciousness and use their education as a tool for social change, key elements of the alternative retention perspective (Yeh 2010). Yeh quotes Myers-Lipton (2002, 204) who states:

> Critical theory and service-learning are both interested in the development of a curriculum and pedagogy that transform school into an agent of social change. [They assume] that students should actively question power relationships in society, and that through this questioning transformational change of the student and society is possible.

Peer advocacy can also play a role in addressing issues raised by critical retention theory. Tinto (1993) argues that students must internalize the unwritten rules of college to persist and, if they do not, they will experience incongruence and find it challenging to continue. Critics of Tinto's model contend that students should not have to choose between their home cultures and the dominant college culture and argue that many ethnically diverse students benefit from valuing their home culture (Guiffrida 2006; Rendon, Jalomo, and Nora 2000; Tierney 1999). At the same time, these critics also recognize that the culture of higher education privileges certain knowledge and behaviors and that students need support in learning how to navigate college if they are to be successful. Savitz-Romer and Bouffard (2012) write about the importance of helping students explore their multiple identities, life experiences, and self-concepts to develop a college-staying identity. Peer advocates can facilitate this exploration. Studies by Walton and Cohen show that increasing a student's feeling of belonging "can have dramatic effects, particularly on students most likely to face stereotypes and a sense that they do not 'fit in' to academic settings" (Silva and White, 2011, 12).

Similarly, service-learning and peer mentoring have also been found to facilitate students' personal development and their ability to find personal meaning. Service-learning impacts students' sense of personal efficacy, personal identity, interpersonal development, ability to work well with others, spiritual and moral development, and leadership and community skills (Eyler et al. 2000). Mentoring has been found to have a positive impact on students' self-confidence, latent abilities, self-actualization, expectations, and future aspirations (Mangold et al. 2003). Yeh (2010) points out that in the field of higher education the process of making meaning of one's experiences is often associated with spiritual development. She notes that, in her study, spirituality emerged as a key theme for low-income first-generation college students reflecting on their service-learning experiences. Furthermore, she suggests that spirituality is a significant factor in the psychological health and resilience of low-income and culturally diverse populations, and she advocates for further examination of its role in retention.

The Connect2Complete (C2C) Program

In 2011, with funding from the Bill and Melinda Gates Foundation, Campus Compact launched the C2C program. Through subgrants distributed by the national Campus Compact office, nine community colleges and their related state Campus Compact affiliates participated in the C2C pilot: Broward College, Miami Dade College, and Tallahassee Community College (Florida Campus Compact); Cuyahoga Community College, Lorain County Community College, and Owens Community College (Ohio Campus Compact); and Big Bend Community College, Edmonds Community College, and Green River Community College (Washington Campus Compact). During the two-and-a-half year C2C pilot (January 2012 to May 2014), campuses engaged more than 4,500 underprepared, low-income students in service-learning experiences and peer advocacy.

C2C combines peer-assisted service-learning and peer advocates in order to improve student success in developmental education courses. The pilot phase of the C2C program gave the campuses the opportunity to test unique peer-to-peer models that reflect the culture of their campus. For example, early on, a few campuses experimented with co-curricular models of service-learning, while the majority designed course-based models. Now, all campuses have adopted a course-based model that more effectively reaches students who are not privileged with free time due to job, family, and study responsibilities.

For the service-learning component of the model, developmental education faculty work with campus service-learning staff and peer advocates to integrate service-learning pedagogy into their college-preparation courses. To select courses and faculty for C2C, campuses examine institutional data and identify developmental education courses with historically low pass rates or focus on college success courses that developmental education students are required to take. College success courses address the nonacademic skills that many students come to college lacking. These courses teach students how to take notes, take tests, and manage their time, and help students explore their learning styles and develop plans for college and careers. Campuses then reach out to developmental education and college success faculty who teach those courses and who are interested in working with peer advocates and utilizing service-learning. For the C2C model, faculty participants are expected to follow guidelines for service-learning:

- Faculty *require* student participation in service-learning activities.
- Critical reflection occurs before, during, and after service activities.
- Service activities are connected to coursework and course objectives.
- Coursework incorporates civic learning outcomes.
- Learning is documented through writing, video, photography, or other artifacts.

For the peer advocacy component, peer advocates serve as mentors and leaders of service-learning for the developmental education students, or C2C students, by attending the developmental education/college success courses with which they are matched. The peer advocate's regular presence in the classroom creates familiarity and accessibility for the C2C students. Peer advocates also support C2C students during service-learning activities and through social media and online platforms, office hours, and campus events. All campuses offer incentives to peer advocates in the form of federal work-study funds, credited or noncredited leadership development training, AmeriCorps Educational Awards, scholarship funds, stipends, or some combination of the aforementioned incentives.

Across the nine campuses peer advocates are identified in different ways: by faculty and peer advocates who recognize leadership potential in C2C students and through campus-wide outreach efforts, including contact with student leadership groups. Peer advocate application procedures vary by campus; most require interviews and reference letters. Selection criteria also vary by campus; most, but not all, peer advocates are former developmental education students, some are former C2C students, and some meet minimum GPA requirements. Demographic data gathered by the C2C program evaluators at Brandeis University reveal that peer advocates are similar to C2C students in terms of race and income level. Moreover, these data also reveal that the challenges (personal, financial, work, academic, and social) faced by C2C students are reflected in the experiences of peer advocates, as well.

As mentors, peer advocates assist C2C students with building relationships with peers, faculty, and advisors, connecting with campus and community resources, and becoming comfortable with the unwritten rules of college (Crisp 2010). As leaders of service-learning, peer advocates receive training and work closely with developmental education faculty and community engagement staff to support C2C student participation in service-learning activities. They introduce C2C students to service-learning pedagogy, develop and maintain relationships with community or campus partners, and facilitate reflection. At some campuses the program coordinator works with peer advocates and faculty to design a standard set of peer advocate–led workshops and resources around service-learning and student persistence; at other campuses the faculty and peer advocate pairs, supported by a "tool belt" of resources/activities/handouts, customize the peer advocate classroom role. The amount of time the peer advocates spend in the course varies across campuses.

Evaluation Questions

Empirical studies demonstrate the positive impact that service-learning has on intervening variables (self-efficacy, sense of civic responsibility, course grades, racial and cultural understanding) that impact student success (Celio, Durlak, and Deymnicki 2011; Astin and Sax 1998; Batchelder and Root 1994; Markus, Howard, and King 1993). There are also a limited number of studies that corroborate the impact of service-learning on semester-to-semester retention (Cress et al. 2010; Bringle, Hatcher, and Muthiah 2010) and degree completion (Lockeman and Pelco 2013). There is a need for additional research that examines the impact of service-learning on retention and degree completion, particularly among at-risk, low-income students (Yeh 2010).

Kuh (2008) cites service-learning as one of the ten high-impact educational practices effective in increasing student retention, and more educators now acknowledge the "need to move from 'boutique' programs that provide these kinds of high-impact practices for selected students to new curricular pathways that provide multiple, scaffolded encounters with high-impact practices for all students" (Schneider and Humphreys 2013, n.p.). Koring and Campbell (2005) suggest that contact with peer advisors can lead to increased involvement with the institution, academic success, and retention.

In this chapter we focus on the results of our evaluation of the C2C pilot project. The evaluation, which aimed to ascertain the impact of peer-assisted service-learning and peer advocacy on the success of low-income, developmental education community college students, was guided by two questions. The first question is grounded in the aforementioned research on service-learning and peer advocates: Is a strategy of combining service-learning and peer advocates effective in increasing the success of low-income, developmental education community college students? The term "success" is operationalized by the measures used to evaluate the C2C program: semester-to-semester retention and indicators of retention such as credit hours earned versus attempted, and student self-reporting on academic success, future aspirations, and campus connections.

The second question reflects research indicating that a one-size-fits-all approach will not work when campus climates vary, and that for something to be a best practice it needs to be adapted to a local setting (e.g., Reason 2013). As the nine colleges in the C2C project represent a diverse group of community colleges in terms of size, setting (urban versus rural), student demographics, and geography, we also ask: Will adapting the C2C model in unique ways at diverse community colleges lead to increased success of low-income, developmental education community college students across these colleges?

Campus Compact values service-learning not only for its instrumental value of increasing retention, but also for its intrinsic value in encouraging students' sense of civic responsibility and action for the public good. As a result, the C2C evaluation does measure the impact that service-learning has on civic-learning outcomes for both students and their mentors; however, those findings along with findings related to the positive impacts of the C2C experience on peer advocates are beyond the scope of this chapter.

Evaluation Methods

Together with the pilot sites and partner evaluators at Brandeis University, Campus Compact collected data to evaluate the success of C2C and to identify promising practices and essential elements of a C2C model. Evaluation methods included collection of student record data, administration of retrospective C2C student surveys, administration of retrospective peer advocate surveys, and facilitation of phone interviews. At the time of writing, the evaluation is ongoing and data is available only from Fall 2012 and Spring 2013 cohorts.

Student Record Data

Partner evaluators at Brandeis University gathered student record data from C2C students and comparison groups of similar students not receiving the C2C "treatment." Our partner evaluators examined the success of C2C students in contrast to this comparison group on various measures, including semester-to-semester retention rates, GPA, and success rates (credits earned/credits attempted).

C2C Student and Peer Advocate Surveys

At the end of each term, the nine campuses administered C2C student and peer advocate surveys to students associated with the program. Surveys track student attitudes and experiences with C2C. Together, the campuses administered 961 C2C student surveys and 196 peer advocate surveys during Fall 2012 and Spring 2013 terms.

Phone Interviews

In order to gain greater insight into the experiences of participants in this pilot study, Campus Compact conducted phone interviews with a select sample of C2C students (12), peer advocates (15), and faculty (8). Campus Compact staff reviewed the interviews to find themes and unique observations from the participants.

Findings

Retention and Success Rates

The Fall 2012 to Spring 2013 retention rates for six of the eight campuses were higher for the C2C students than the comparison groups. Retention rates were higher for the C2C students than the comparison groups at all three community colleges in Ohio (72.4 percent for C2C students versus 66 percent for comparison group), and all three community colleges in Florida (84.6 percent for C2C students versus 78.5 percent for comparison group) but not for the two community colleges in Washington. One of the Washington community colleges had a delayed start-up due to challenges with model implementation and began providing data in Winter 2013. Success rates (credits earned/credits attempted) were also higher for all three colleges in Ohio and all three colleges in Florida, but not for the two colleges in Washington for which we have data.

Faculty shared positive outcomes of peer-assisted service-learning around retention. It is important to note that students in service-learning courses did not know in advance that service-learning was a required component of their developmental education/college success courses. A C2C math faculty fellow at Lorain County Community College, commented, "I had two sections of the same course, one with service-learning and one without. Service-learning students performed better and were more successful overall." A C2C English Faculty Fellow at Edmonds Community College, noted, "I see positive outcomes in my class with students more engaged with writing assignments. They are more eager now that they've been involved in campus and community life. More enthusiastic for coursework that involves these pedagogies."

Academic Success and Goal Attainment

Academic success and goal attainment are key indicators for student retention and C2C student survey data reveal that the C2C model holds real promise in this area. C2C student survey responses reveal that the C2C model is associated with students believing that they will be academically successful and achieve their goals. When examining the data, it is important to note that due to challenges with institutional readiness and a steep learning curve, variations existed across the nine-campus implementation so that not all students were receiving the full C2C "treatment." It is not uncommon in a pilot project, and especially in its first year, to find uneven application of model components. Using C2C student responses to the retrospective survey, our partner evaluator Brandeis University disaggregated the students' experiences and the impact of the primary model components—peer-assisted service-learning and peer advocacy—into six "buckets" based on the C2C students' experience with the two primary C2C model components. The six buckets and the number of students in each are shown in table 8.1. The final group of students not receiving the "treatment," labeled "No Peer Advocate and No Service-Learning," serve as a control group.

Table 8.1 All Possible Combinations of Student Experience with C2C

Student Experience	N	%
Peer Advocate and Class-Based Service-Learning	202	22.1%
Peer Advocate and Co-Curricular Service-Learning	44	4.8%
Peer Advocate and No Service-Learning	275	30.0%
No Peer Advocate and Class-Based Service-Learning	104	11.4%
No Peer Advocate and Co-Curricular Service-Learning	27	2.9%
No Peer Advocate and No Service-Learning	264	28.8%

Our partner evaluator, Brandeis University, analyzed the impact of the buckets (all the combinations of elements in the program model) across two question domains—academic and career aspirations and feelings of connectedness to the campus community—by comparing the first five buckets to the control, "No Peer Advocate and No Service-Learning." This analysis allows us to ascertain the likelihood that a C2C student with a particular combination of program experience will respond in a positive way to particular questions. Questions within the student aspirations domain asked students how likely they were to achieve certain goals, using a five-point scale from 1, "not at all likely," to 5, "very likely." Our partner evaluator, Brandeis University, looked at the odds that students in the various buckets would say they were "very likely" to achieve a particular academic or personal goal. In this analysis, with one exception,[1] the only statistically significant "bucket" was C2C students who had both a peer advocate and class-based service-learning. This is a significant finding that indicates it is the combination of service-learning and peer advocacy and not one or the other that is associated with students believing they will be academically successful and achieve their goals. When compared with the control group, students with both a peer advocate and course-based service-learning were two times more likely to report they would achieve their academic and career goals and nearly two times more likely to report they would pass their reading and writing developmental education courses.

These results can be explained in part by the sense of confidence students gained from program participation. In Campus Compact interviews C2C students explained this: "With C2C, I intellectually felt confident. Before, I didn't feel confident to have a voice. At C2C we were learning and teaching others, and it developed a sense of confidence for everyone involved. Without C2C, I wouldn't be aware of my potential voice in the community." A C2C student particularly focused on the service-learning portion of the program commented: "I don't think I could've gotten through college without C2C. If C2C was here earlier, I would've finished school the first time. C2C turned what I fantasized about doing into a reality. A Ph.D. program is not a far off dream."

Campus Connections

Questions in the Campus Connections domain of the C2C student survey asked students about their personal interactions and experience with various groups on campus by using a scale that ranged from 1, "unfriendly, unsupportive, alienating," to 5, "friendly, supportive, and inclusive." Here again, when we refer back to the six buckets in table 8.1, having both a peer advocate *and* class-based service-learning is associated with the greatest likelihood that students will experience their campus as a friendly, supportive, and inclusive place. For example, students with both a peer advocate and course-based service-learning are nearly two-and-a-half times more likely than the control group (the bucket labeled "No Peer Advocate and No Service-Learning") to experience faculty as friendly, supportive, and inclusive. This makes sense given that course-based service-learning often allows students to interact more with faculty, and the support of a peer advocate likely enhances this interaction (Keup 2005–2006; Astin and Sax 1998). Additionally, C2C students with both a peer advocate and course-based service-learning, more than the control group, find staff in financial aid offices, advising, math labs, counseling, and writing labs to be friendly, supportive, and inclusive.

These results can be explained in part by the critical role of peer-assisted service-learning in fostering important connections. On bus rides to community sites, through peer advocate–led group reflection projects that encourage collaboration, and in the midst of service projects where students are pushed beyond their comfort zones, peer-assisted service-learning projects help to facilitate opportunities for students to connect with their peers and with faculty in a way that is unlikely to happen in a classroom setting. A C2C student notes:

> When you get a classroom together and you all go on a trip, you really interact with your classmates. Sitting in a classroom all quarter, you don't get to know people behind you or across the class. [With service-learning] you learn to communicate. It creates a bond. You develop skills within yourself. There are more learning experiences when you take the class somewhere else.

Analysis

Findings from the C2C model suggest that the combination of peer-assisted service-learning and peer advocacy provides a promising model for increasing retention in developmental education classes. C2C students in six of the eight colleges demonstrated higher rates of semester-to-semester retention when compared with the control group. Success rates were also higher for all three community colleges in Ohio and all three community colleges in Florida. The evaluation data show that having peer advocates in the class and participating in service-learning helped students to feel socially tied to peers, faculty, and the course. From the more authentic learning environments of community settings, C2C students could begin to recognize that their courses have value and that they have the skills, habits, and know-how to succeed in a college setting. The role of peer advocate as a cultural broker between students and faculty and between the college and community suggests that the C2C model may provide a strong and unified institutional support for student success.

Results for the two Washington campuses were less straightforward. There are at least three possible reasons for these findings. First, of all of the nine C2C colleges, those in Washington have the smallest student bodies, at approximately 2,100 (Big Bend Community College), 11,000 (Green River Community College), and 12,000 (Edmonds Community College) students. The other colleges range in size from 13,000 to 164,378 students. With a smaller student body, the Washington colleges have fewer faculty available for implementing innovative practices and fewer student services staff to help with the administration of new programs.

Second, across all campuses, there existed a range in institutional readiness to implement service-learning and/or peer advocacy. According to administrators and faculty at the Washington campuses, fewer systems existed to support both C2C components. For example, two campuses did not have an active service-learning program at the time they began implementing C2C; others had not completed enhancements to their data systems that were necessary to support C2C. Third, two of the

Washington campuses faced challenges in targeting Pell-eligible students in developmental education courses: eligible students were both difficult to identify (due to the data issues mentioned above) and scattered throughout various classes. Despite these challenges, the Washington campuses, like all the C2C pilot campuses, have made strides in developing program capacity, including program champions, and it is quite possible that the trend will shift in future semesters. For example, one campus has integrated C2C into a campus-wide change initiative to support the success of underserved students. At another, C2C is part of a larger effort to incorporate high-impact practices into the curriculum and co-curriculum. At a third, developmental education courses taught by C2C faculty have been integrated with credit-bearing courses with peer advocates representing the essential link between the two.

Although the six colleges in Florida and Ohio used a variety of models for incorporating service-learning and peer advocates into their developmental education courses, the combination of service-learning and peer advocates was effective in increasing success of developmental education students across many different formats. This is an important finding since innovations at any college are more likely to be sustained if they are woven into an institution's existing structures and goals. Community colleges interested in adapting the C2C model will need to follow effective practices for incorporating service-learning and the use of peer advocates into courses, but they can create their own approaches for aligning the C2C model with the unique needs of their particular community college setting.

Conclusion

Colleges seek to increase student retention while also improving the quality of student learning. Low-income, developmental-education community college students face many hurdles in successfully completing college. They may struggle figuring out how to acclimatize to the institutional culture of the college while maintaining their own identity. The combined use of peer-assisted service-learning and peer advocacy provides an avenue for helping these vulnerable students integrate with their institution academically and socially (Tinto 1993). This integration helps students operate within the culture of higher education at the same time while critical service-learning provides opportunities to confront systemic inequality on their campuses or in communities.

Connect2Complete brings new value to traditional approaches for improving student success by utilizing an incredibly underutilized resource—students themselves—to partner with faculty while developing student leaders in the community college setting. Connect2Complete is a flexible model crafted with essential elements that can be adapted for different types of classes (math, English, college success) and unique campus cultures.

Note

1. The response from students with class-based service-learning and no peer advocate was also statistically significant. These students were 1.7 times more likely to indicate that they would achieve their career goals.

References

American Association of Community Colleges. 2013. "Community College Fact Sheet 2013." Accessed September 26, 2013. http://www.aacc.nche.edu/AboutCC/Pages/fastfactsfactsheet.aspx.

Astin, Alexander W., and Linda J. Sax. 1998. "How Undergraduates Are Affected by Service Participation." *Journal of College Student Development* 39 (3): 251–263.

Astin, Alexander W., Lori J. Vogelgesang, Elaine K. Ikeda, and Jennifer A. Yee. 2000. "Executive Summary: How Service-Learning Affects Students." Los Angeles: Higher Education Research Institute, 2000. Accessed October 17, 2012. http://heri.ucla.edu/service_learning.html.

Bailey, Thomas. 2009. "Challenge and Opportunity: Rethinking the Role and Function of Developmental Education in Community College." *New Directions for Community Colleges* 145: 11–30.

Bailey, Thomas, Dong Wook Jeong, and Sung-Woo Cho. 2009. *Referral, Enrollment, and Completion in Developmental Education Sequences in Community Colleges.* Community College Research Center Working Paper No. 15.

Batchelder, Thomas H., and Susan Root. 1994. "Effects of an Undergraduate Program to Integrate Academic Learning and Service: Cognitive, Pro-social Cognitive and Identity Outcomes." *Journal of Adolescence* 17: 341–355.

Bringle, Robert G., Julie A. Hatcher, and Richard Muthiah. 2010. "The Role of Service-Learning on the Retention of First-Year Students to Second Year." *Michigan Journal of Community Service Learning* 16 (2): 38–49.

Campbell, Toni A., and David E. Campbell. 1997. "Faculty Mentor Programs: Effects on Academic Performance and Retention." *Research in Higher Education* 35 (6): 727–742.

Celio, Christine, Joseph Durlak, and Allison Dymnicki. 2011. "A Meta-Analysis of the Impact of Service-Learning on Students." *Journal of Experiential Education* 34 (2): 164–181.

Community College Survey of Student Engagement. 2009. *Making Connections: Student Engagement. 2009 Findings.* Austin, TX: Center for Community College Student Engagement.

Cress, Christine, Cathy Burack, Dwight E. Giles, Julie Elkins, and Margaret Carnes Stevens. 2010. *A Promising Connection: Increasing College Access and Success through Civic Engagement.* Boston, MA: Campus Compact.

Crisp, Gloria. 2010. "The Impact of Mentoring on the Success of Community College Students." *Review of Higher Education* 34 (1): 39–60.

Eyler, Janet, and Dwight E. Giles Jr. 1999. *Where's the Learning in Service-Learning?* San Francisco, CA: Jossey-Bass, 1999.

Eyler, Janet, Dwight E. Giles Jr., Christine M. Stenson, and Charlene J. Gray. 2001. *At a Glance: What We Know about the Effects of Service-Learning on College Students, Faculty, Institutions, and Communities, 1993–2000.* Accessed October 17, 2012. http://www.compact.org/wp-content/uploads/resources/downloads/aag.pdf.

Fulmer, C. Ashley, Michele J. Gelfand, Arie W. Kruglanski, Chu Kim-Prieto, Ed Diender, Antonio Pierro, and E. Tory Higgins. 2010. "On 'Feeling Right' in Cultural Contexts: How Person-Culture Match Affects Self-Esteem and Subjective Well-Being." *Psychological Science* 21 (11): 1563–1569.

Gallini, Sarah M., and Barbara E. Moely. 2003. "Service-Learning and Engagement, Academic Challenge, and Retention." *Michigan Journal of Community Service Learning* 10 (1): 5–14.

Guiffrida, Douglas A. 2006. "Toward a Cultural Advancement of Tinto's Theory." *Review of Higher Education* 29 (4): 451–472.

Humphreys, Debra. 2012. "What's Wrong with the Completion Agenda—And What We Can Do About It," *Liberal Education* 98 (1): 8–17.

Karp, Melinda M. 2011. *Toward a New Understanding of Non-Academic Student Support: Four Mechanisms Encouraging Positive Student Outcomes in the Community College* (CCRC Working Paper No. 28). New York: Columbia University, Teachers College, Community College Research Center.

Keup, Jennifer R. 2005–06. "The Impact of Curricular Interventions on Intended Second Year Enrollment," *Journal of College Student Retention* 7 (1–2): 61–89.

Koring, Heidi, and Susan Campbell, eds. 2005. *Peer Advising: Intentional Connections to Support Student Learning (Monograph No. 13).* Manhattan, NY: National Academic Advising Association.

Kuh, George D. 2008. *High-Impact Educational Practices: What They Are, Who Has Access to Them, and Why They Matter.* Washington, D C: Association of American Colleges and Universities.

Lockeman, Kelly S., and Lynn E. Pelco. 2013. "The Relationship between Service-Learning and Degree Completion." *Michigan Journal of Community Service Learning* 20 (1): 18–30.

Maldonado, David, Robert Rhoads, and Tracy L. Buenavista. 2005. "The Student-Initiated Retention Project: Theoretical Contributions and the Role of Self-Empowerment." *American Educational Research Journal* 42 (4): 605–638.

Mangold, William D., Luann G. Bean, Douglas J. Adams, William A. Schwab, and Scott M. Lynch. 2003. "Who Goes? Who Stays? An Assessment of the Effect of a Freshman Mentoring and Unity Registration Program on College Persistence." *Journal of College Student Retention* 4 (2): 95–122.

Markus, Gregory B., Jeffrey P. F. Howard, and David C. King. 1993. "Integrating Community Service and Classroom Instruction Enhances Learning: Results from an Experiment." *Educational Evaluation and Policy Analysis* 15 (4): 410–419.

Myers-Lipton, Scott J. 2002. "Service Learning and Success in Sociology." In *Sociology: Learning Climates That Cultivate Racial and Ethnic Diversity*, edited by C.W. Berheide, J. Chin, and D. Rome, 202–218. Washington, DC: American Association for Higher Education.

National Academic Advising Association, eds. 2005. *Peer Advising: Intentional Connections to Support Student Learning*, edited by H. Koring, and S. Campbell (Monograph No. 13). Manhattan, NY: National Academic Advising Association.

Pagan, Ralph, and Runae Edwards-Wilson. 2003. "A Mentoring Program for Remedial Students." *Journal of College Student Retention* 4 (2): 207–225.

Pascarella, Ernest T. 1980. "Student-Faculty Informal Contact and College Outcomes." *Review of Educational Research* 50: 545–595.

Reason, Robert D. 2013. "Creating and Assessing Campus Climates That Support Personal and Social Responsibility." *Liberal Education* 99 (1) (Winter). Accessed June 14. http://www.aacu.org/liberaleducation/le-wi13/reason.cfm.

Rendon, Laura, Romero E. Jalomo, and Amaury Nora. 2000. "Theoretical Considerations in the Study of Minority Student Retention in Higher Education." In *Reworking the Student Departure Puzzle*, edited by J. M. Braxton, 127–156. Nashville, TN: Vanderbilt University Press.

Schneider, Carol Geary, and Debra Humphries. 2013. Foreword to *Ensuring Quality & Taking High-Impact Practices to Scale*, edited by George D. Kuh and Ken O'Donnell. Washington, DC: Association of American Colleges and Universities. https://secure2.aacu.org/AACU/pubExcerpts/HIPQUAL.html.

Silva, Elena and Taylor White. "Pathways to Improvement: Using Psychological Strategies to Help College Students Master Developmental Math." Washington, DC: Carnegie

Foundation for the Advancement of Teaching, 2013. Accessed June 14, 2013. http://www.carnegiefoundation.org/spotlight/productive-persistence-pathways-improvement

Tierney, William G. 1999. "Models of Minority College-Going and Retention: Cultural Integrity Versus Cultural Suicide." *Journal of Negro Education* 68 (1): 80–91.

Tinto, Vincent. 1993. *Leaving College: Rethinking the Causes and Cures of Student Attrition* Chicago: University of Chicago Press, 2nd ed.

Wolff, Michele K., and Shannon M. Tinney. 2006. "Service Learning and College Student Success." *The Academic Exchange Quarterly* 10 (1): 57–61.

Yeh, Theresa Ling. 2010. "Service-Learning and Persistence of Low-Income, First-Generation College Students: An Exploratory Study." *Michigan Journal of Community Service Learning* 16 (2): 50–65.

CHAPTER 9

Promoting Community College Student Transfer: The Role of Service-Learning

Jaime Lester and Carrie Klein

Community colleges are often referred to as the "people's college" due to their status as open access institutions that provide a gateway for an increasingly diverse student population (Cohen and Brawer 2003). Each year, community colleges educate almost half of all undergraduates in the United States, totaling more than 8.3 million students with a variety of educational goals (Knapp, et al. 2012; Mullin 2012). Among these goals is the desire of students to transfer from the two-year community college to a four-year college or university in order to obtain a bachelor's degree. Over 70 percent of students entering two-year institutions intend to complete a bachelor's degree (Bailey et al. 2006) with over one-third planning on transferring to a four-year university (Horn, Nevill, and Griffith 2006). While students engage in a number of transfer behaviors that allow them to move from institution to institution, vertical transfer allows students to follow a linear process toward graduation via "the capacity of community...colleges to assist students in the transition to a four-year college or university" (Townsend 2001, 29). Thus, successful transfer is transfer that leads to baccalaureate degree-completion (Bahr et al. 2013).

Students have engaged in transfer activities since the dawn of the credit hour (Shedd 2003). Yet, the number of students seeking transfer has increased as higher education becomes costlier and students become savvier about attaining their degrees with less cost and greater efficiency. Cost of college and time to obtain a degree are the two most frequently cited reasons for students to engage in transfer activities (Mullin 2012; Cejda and Kaylor 2001; Townsend 2001). Indeed, cost-savings is a significant driver for students transferring from two-year to four-year institutions. Mullin (2012) estimates that for the 2011–12 cohort "...$1.9 billion was saved for students transferring to public institutions with an additional $1.7 billion saved for those transferring to private institutions" (8). In addition to saving money, students also use the transfer process to complete their degree programs more quickly and to take courses or engage in opportunities that are not available at their home institutions (Mullin 2012).

Despite the benefits of transfer, only one-third of community college students who transfer go on to graduate from four-year institutions (Hossler et al. 2012). Research on transfer students identifies several barriers to transfer success, including a lack of collegiate-level academic preparation that results in large number of students in no-credit developmental courses, a need to work full-time, and significant family responsibilities that hinder engagement in collegiate life—engagement that is known to have a positive impact on student success. Barriers like these pull students away from their educational studies and hinder successful transfer (Bahr et al. 2013). Moreover, structures and policies of two-year and four-year institutions often make transfer cumbersome. Complicated articulation agreements, a lack of support services on evenings and weekends, limited- or nontransfer-focused advising services, and a growing number of adjunct faculty impact a student's success in the transfer process (Jaeger 2008; Townsend and Wilson 2006).

To continue to explore student success and to find new methods to promote student transfer, perhaps it is time to consider how other aspects of the community college mission can be leveraged to prepare students to successfully transfer to a four-year university. Community colleges are mission-driven to connect with their local communities by educating and serving those very communities in which they reside (Weglarz and Seybert 2004). As Levinson (2004) states, "community colleges are the sites of numerous cultural and civic activities" (99). These characteristics make community colleges ideal for service-learning initiatives that incorporate meaningful community work with teaching, learning, and reflecting in order to enhance students' academic experiences, knowledge of civic responsibility, and commitment to their communities. Research indicates that over 60 percent of community colleges offer service-learning in their curricular programs, up from 50 percent in 2001 (Prentice, Robinson, and Patton 2012). Weglarz and Seybert (2004) found that more than 75 percent of students indicated that service-learning experiences increased their awareness of community needs, helped them to appreciate differences, created awareness of community impacts, increased empathy for others, and helped increase their ability to relate to others. The majority of student respondents reported that service-learning was important to their interpersonal, personal, career, academic, and intellectual development. Overwhelmingly, service-learning has a positive impact on students, as experienced by the community, by the faculty, and by the students themselves.

Despite the depth of research on service-learning that finds positive outcomes experienced by students and faculty, little is known about how these activities can be intentionally leveraged to promote successful student transfer. In fact, the literature on student transfer has largely ignored co-curricular efforts and collaborative partnerships, instead focusing rather strictly on the community college environment and the individual student attributes and behaviors that lead to successful transfer. This chapter presents a theoretical model of service-learning and student transfer that incorporates empirical literature on student transfer and service-learning with an emphasis on ways to support student integration on their pathway toward degree completion. Agreeing with Laanan (2004), community college transfer students must engage in "significant social and psychological relearning in the face of a new encounters, new teachers, new opportunities, and new academic, personal, and social demands" (332). We propose that service-learning can help transfer students make the transition and be successful in the face of these new demands.

Literature on Student Transfer

Attendance at community colleges is an integral part of the pathway to college completion for many American students. Almost half of students in higher education in the United States are enrolled in community colleges and 47 percent of those who earn bachelor's degrees completed a course, or more, at a community college (Mullin 2012). Student transfer and degree attainment have garnered increased attention because of both the increasing attendance and shifting demographics of students at community colleges and the recent completion agenda championed by federal and state governments (College Completion Toolkit 2011; Boswell 2004). This attention underscores the perceived importance of successful transfer, that is, transfer that ultimately yields a degree. Yet, despite the importance of successful transfer, there are numerous barriers to the process, both on institutional and individual levels.

On an individual level, students can face significant difficulty successfully transferring from their two-year institutions and completing a degree at the receiving institution. Degree completion post-transfer is not just affected by student "characteristics, goals and commitments, but also by their experiences academically and socially" (Townsend and Wilson 2006, 440). An individual student's level of integration, his or her "sense of identification with an institution and an adoption of the norms and values of the campus" (Bahr et al. 2013, 466–467), in combination with the level of involvement, the physical and psychological energy invested, directly impacts the student's success. Thus, for successful transfer to occur, students must be prepared and be supported both academically and socially through the entirety of the transfer process, to include their time at the community college and the transition to the four-year university (Bahr et al. 2013; Flaga 2006; Townsend and Wilson 2006).

Student integration is often focused around students' perception of their institution(s) and the faculty, staff, and peers with whom they interact. This perception of the level of support and quality of investment is vital to student success, as studies indicate that most transfer students experience difficulty integrating socially, particularly early in their transfer transition (Bahr et al. 2013, 478; Townsend and Wilson 2008; 2006; Laanan 1996). Transfer students who do not integrate well are less likely to retain at the community college and transfer to receiving universities. The environmental pull factors facing transfer students, many of whom are balancing multiple responsibilities outside of the classroom, serve as barriers to successful academic and social integration, including significant family responsibilities (Reyes 2011; Townsend and Wilson, 2008; 2006; Glass and Bunn 1998); living off-campus (Bahr et al. 2013; Flaga 2006; Townsend and Wilson 2008; 2006); part-time enrollment (Ishitani and McKitrick, 2010); and working more than 20 hours per week (often off-campus) while in college (Reyes 2011; Owens 2010; Townsend and Wilson 2006; Berger and Malaney 2003; Bers et al. 2001).

These factors pull transfer students away from the campus activities and events that are important in establishing academic and social integration at their receiving institutions (Bahr et al. 2013; Reyes 2011; Owens 2010; Townsend 2001; Townsend and Wilson 2008; 2006). For example, transfer students are often focused solely on their academics because they have less time and energy (due to employment, family responsibilities, commuting, etc.) than their nontransfer counterparts to devote to campus life (Bahr et al. 2013, 483–485; Reyes 2011; Owens 2010; Townsend and Wilson 2008; 2006). Further, because transfer students from community colleges often have more out-of-class demands and because many of these students are first-generation college students, they often lack the social capital of "family connections, institutional resource, and peer networks" that nontransfer students have (Bahr et al. 2013, 495).

Another pull for transfer students is their participation, at higher rates than their nontransfer peers, in developmental courses like mathematics and English, which are found to have a dramatically negative impact on eventual student academic success (Bailey, Jeong, and Cho 2010). Several studies, primarily by Bahr and colleagues (2013), conclude that enrollment in developmental courses often leads to lower rates of retention as students are unable to achieve a passing grade, thus moving them to a higher-level developmental course rather than to credit-bearing college-level work. Participation in developmental courses also creates social barriers for transfer students, as these courses often take additional academic focus and are not part of the mainstream curriculum. Developmental courses thus have the unintentional consequences of separating transfer students from their nontransfer peers.

Other pulls are related to demographic characteristics but yield the same results of complicating academic and social integration, particularly once students transfer to the four-year university. Students who are nontraditionally aged (older than 18–22 years old), from lower socioeconomic class, members of racially or ethnically underrepresented groups, and female tend to have greater difficulty in transitioning to the receiving institution (Owens 2010; Harbin 1997). Reyes (2011) found that the interaction of these characteristics creates an even greater barrier to social integration as many majors and programs are overwhelmingly populated by men of Caucasian and upper-class backgrounds. Transfer students can experience social discrimination or exclusion (Reyes 2011), alienation (Bahr et al. 2013; Reyes 2011), and resentment (Bahr et al. 2013; Harrison 1999) all due to their minority status in a mostly white and economically privileged student environment. As Bahr and colleagues (2013) note: "Although there were many exceptions, even within individual studies, students of nontraditional age and/or from historically underrepresented groups appear to face more challenges integrating socially than do middle-class, traditional-aged, white students" (478).

Racial and ethnic diversity of the faculty in relation to student demographics also has an impact on student success. Hagedorn, Chi, Cepeda, and McLain (2007) found in a study of the relationship between faculty and students racial composition that students are more successful when the faculty are more racially representative of the student population. Given the diversity of the transfer student population, Reyes (2011) noted that they may feel less alienated and socially isolated with more visible diversity in the faculty and staff ranks at the receiving institution.

Faculty demographics, beyond demographic representation, can play a role in student integration. Another faculty-related structural barrier comes from the large numbers of contingent faculty teaching in community colleges and, increasingly, in four-year universities. While the research is not entirely conclusive, studies that use community college populations and nationally representative data sets find that student outcomes are negatively impacted as the number of courses taken with part-time instructors increases (Eagan and Jaeger 2009). Conversely, faculty-student interaction is found to have a positive impact on student success; the more the students interact with faculty related to academic or social activities, the greater their likelihood of academic success (McKay and Estrella 2008). As Bahr and colleagues (2013) note: "Of all the ways in which community college transfer students become academically involved, interactions with faculty may be the most daunting but also the most rewarding" (486). Full-time faculty often have greater structural capacity to engage with students outside of the classroom, as they have the benefit of having office-space and organizational incentives that support such interaction. Unfortunately, adjunct faculty members are often without these spaces and incentives, which makes student interaction more difficult and, in turn, less likely (Jaeger 2008).

While faculty demographics and role status impact integration, other institutional barriers, often in the form of structural and organizational cultural differences, are also significant to transfer student success. Research has identified funding and articulation agreements as barriers to the "seamless transition" between the various educational components of higher education (Flaga 2006; Boswell 2004; Ignash and Townsend 2000, 16). While funding continues to be a source of constraint and articulation agreements are generally focused solely on traditional forms of transfer, there have been improvements in articulation coverage and alignment in the past two decades, particularly in statewide agreements. Yet, statewide agreements are generally not mandatory for private sector colleges, and students often find different curricular requirements depending on their academic program (e.g., English vs. engineering). Ignash and Townsend (2000) argue that these inconsistencies may be "one of the most difficult articulation tasks to tackle at a state level" (17). For students, these inconsistencies can create added confusion, cost, and time in the transfer process, all of which affect successful degree completion.

Without clear policies, processes, and programs at both two-year and four-year institutions, transfer students are unable to achieve the integration and acquire the social capital necessary for academic success. Simply put, academic and social support for students before, during, and after transfer that allows for their integration into and involvement in the new system is critical for their success (Bahr et al. 2013; Tinto 1993). Successful student support requires a host of interventions that rely on clear and sensible articulation agreements, engagements at both ends of the transfer process, and attention to the key factors of successful student transfer—integration, involvement, and engagement of students. Among practices that assist with post-transfer support are collaborative academic advising and orientation between two-year and four-year institutions; articulation agreements that move beyond the transfer of credits toward the transfer of the individual; better alignment and improved communication between institutions; and priority admission of community college students (Handel 2007; Flaga 2006; Townsend and Wilson 2006; Boswell 2004; Townsend 2001; Ignash and Townsend 2000).

Model of Effective Service-Learning Strategies to Promote Student Transfer in Community Colleges

To achieve the goal of fostering successful student transfer, we argue that students need to be supported throughout their path toward degree completion. This can be done through opportunities presented in service-learning partnerships and collaborations that bridge community colleges, universities, and communities. Transfer students' perceptions of the receiving institution have a significant impact on social and academic integration (Bahr et al. 2013) and can be aided by interaction across community colleges and receiving institutions. Service-learning is also found to have a positive impact on student academic success and engagement, which promotes the self-efficacy and interest needed to retain community college students and promote transfer to universities (Bahr et al. 2013). Although connection between the transfer function and service-learning has not been fully researched, there is a strong synergy between the two. This synergy suggests that student transfer success can be enhanced by the intentional integration of service-learning into the transfer process.

Our model weaves together service-learning and student transfer at both the initiative (community college) institution and the receiving (four-year college) institution by focusing on student social and academic integration and structural integration and partnerships. The unifying factor in this model is the role of service-learning faculty and staff as active agents in creating opportunities for integration and partnership, throughout. The model is grounded in the work of Jeandron and Robinson (2010), Prentice (2002), and Robinson and Barnett (1998), who outline a series of recommendations, based on the American Association of Community Colleges (AACC) Horizons Project, that contribute to successful integration of service-learning within community colleges. While the list of recommendations is vast and does not explicitly make reference to the transfer function, we suggest a focus on a few areas that directly address the barriers to transfer student success outlined in the literature, specifically: learning that supports student self-efficacy and academic integration; increased quantity and quality of faculty-student interaction to better support student success; and integrating campus structures and partnerships between community colleges, universities, and community stakeholders. Each area of the model is supported by the literature on student transfer and identifies the potential of service-learning activities and strengths to address student-transfer barriers. Of note is the role of faculty throughout each area of the model. Faculty serves as strong connectors across each part of the model, supporting learning within the classroom and creating the internal and external partnerships and collaborations necessary for individual and institutional transfer success. In this regard, the model is more integrated than distinct separate pieces.

Individual Integration: Learning and Self-Efficacy

Our model's first area of focus is on service-learning to support student social and academic integration, via promotion of self-efficacy and collaborative learning experiences. As illuminated in the literature, community college students are often first-generation, from lower-income families, and are returning to college after a long absence from formalized education (Cohen and Brawer 2003). These characteristics can lead to low levels of academic capital and self-efficacy, or belief in one's academic abilities, all of which negatively impact student transfer. Service-learning, by virtue of connecting out-of-class learning to traditional learning and formal course-based evaluations, creates positive, integrated, and relevant learning experiences that support student retention and reinforce self-efficacy.

Astin et al. (2000) note that service-learning creates opportunities for positive academic experiences and success by promoting students' gains in credits earned, higher grade point averages, and higher scores on ACT writing assessments. For example, Elwell and Bean (2001) found that English Language Learners (ELL) experienced significant gains in presentation and research skills, as well as exhibited better language skills, by participating in service-learning activities as part of their ELL courses. Research on adult learners also found that service-learning assists students in learning material more quickly by connecting academic concepts to active experience (Trotter 2006). Rochford's (2013) study on service-learning and students in developmental courses shows similar gains for participation in service-learning. In an experimental study, students who participated in service-learning while taking developmental courses received positive gains in credits earned, higher grade points averages, and higher scores on ACT writing assessments. These gains were largely attributed to the connection between service-learning and course curriculum and active engagement of representatives from the community-based organization.

Related to student self-efficacy is social and academic integration. In their extensive research on transfer students, Townsend and Wilson (2008) noted that community college transfer students tend to have a "desire for socially-oriented academic integration" at the four-year institution (419). The students found social support through academic activities, such as study groups and activities within the context of course curriculum. Other studies found that transfer students will prioritize academic involvement over social activities, particularly given their limited time to participate in college-related activities outside of the classroom (Bahr et al. 2013). Service-learning provides students with an academically based social opportunity that helps them build communities of learning and support with their peers, faculty, and staff.

Research suggests that community college transfer students tend to prefer smaller academic communities, including smaller departments and classes (Reyes 2011; Owens 2010; Townsend and Wilson 2008; Gray Davies and Dickmann 1998). Further, Townsend and Wilson (2008) concluded that these academic communities, like in-class collaborative learning and co-curricular experiences, can create combined opportunities for academic and social integration. Jeandron and Robinson (2010), in their research on service-learning in community colleges, identified that students in the freshman experience–based learning communities retained at higher rates than the general population and indicated that the service-learning component of the courses kept them enrolled. In a related study, community college students who engaged in service-learning activities scored higher on multiple learning outcomes, including critical thinking, communication, career and teamwork, civic responsibility, and academic development (Jeandron and Robinson 2010).

Learning communities and service-learning promote smaller collaborative academic experiences that impact how transfer students perceive of and experience their social and academic integration at both their initiative and receiving institutions. These experiences create connections between students' course experiences, interests, and learning motives and can help students connect with others who share similar academic and career interests (Reyes 2011; Flaga 2006). Thus, service-learning integrates student learning on a number of levels, leading to greater self-efficacy and probability of degree completion. Further, students can make ongoing connections between their interests, experiences, and the appropriate academic majors to help achieve those career goals. Key in this process of connection via service-learning is the role of the faculty, who act both as mentors and facilitators in the service-learning and transfer process.

Integration Agents: Faculty-Student Interaction and Engagement

Faculty act as agents of connection and integration in service-learning and in the transfer process by creating and facilitating opportunities for greater student and institutional integration. While the first area of integration refers to a need to support students academically in order to create opportunities for academic and social integration, the second addresses the active role of faculty in creating points of connection and engagement with students and with the structures of their organizations. In this model, their role is expanded and extended to facilitate greater academic engagement by students and stronger collaborations across the boundaries within and between higher education institutions.

Assisting in the process of student integration is engaged faculty, who design courses and academic programs. Not only are faculty key to the success of service-learning programs (Jeandron and Robinson 2010), but also their meaningful interactions with students both inside and outside of the classroom have a known positive impact on student success (Umbach and Wawrzynski 2005). Research on transfer students consistently notes the positive impact of faculty engagement in academic success; however, it is often difficult for part-time and commuter students to make these connections, as they are less likely, due to their schedules and outside demands, to attend faculty office hours or events that include opportunities for faculty interaction (Bahr et al. 2013; Ishitani and McKitrick 2010; Laanan et al. 2010; Matlock and Wade-Golden 2009; Townsend and Wilson 2006).

The more often that transfer students interact with faculty, the more likely they are to experience positive academic gains, such as degree completion (Townsend and Wilson 2006). McKay and Estrella (2008) in a study of first-generation students found that service-learning provided a link to improving the quality of faculty-student interactions. Having active pedagogy in and outside the classroom facilitated more opportunities for students to engage with faculty in meaningful discussions, which had a positive impact on student integration and retention. When faculty intentionally use out-of-class learning opportunities to engage with students they are building a stronger sense of academic integration and a foundation for educational success before and after the transfer process for all students.

However, most faculty are focused on work in their own institution or they are hindered by barriers that reduce opportunities for integration and collaboration between the initiative and receiving institutions (Kezar and Lester 2009). Thus, faculty involved in service-learning programs must be cognizant not just of the opportunities for student integration and the active role faculty involvement plays in that integration, but also of collaboration between their institutions and those institutions into which their students will eventually transfer.

Structural Integration and Partnership: Working across Boundaries

The third part of the model focuses on structural integration and partnership, within initiative and receiving institutions, between initiative and receiving institutions, and in the community. We have focused on structural integration and partnership because integrating structures within two-year and four-year institutions (i.e., offices, units, policies, and faculty involvement incentives) and creating partnerships with the surrounding community can create seamless co-curricular experiences, like service-learning activities, that have the potential to mitigate institutional transfer barriers to student success (Flaga 2006; Boswell 2004; Ignash and Townsend 2000). As an example of integrating structures and creating partnerships, Jeandron and Robinson (2010) found that successful service-learning programs in community colleges developed advisory boards with individuals from across the college, linked service-learning to institutional goals, and built internal collaborations. Such collaboration helped to frame service-learning as a campus priority. Advisory boards of this nature, suggested by Jeandron and Robinson (2010), can be extended and leveraged to create stronger partnerships between initiative and receiving institutions and their communities, as boards can comprise members from the community college, the local university, and community agencies. This inclusive approach to program advising builds partnerships and fosters communication across the involved institutions and the community stakeholders with whom their programs work—ultimately leading to stronger service-learning programs and transfer student success.

Partnerships, like advisory boards, are significant to supporting service-learning programs, their associated local communities, and student learning and integration. Successful service-learning projects and programs require collaboration between community organizations and higher education institutions (Jeandron and Robinson 2010). The collaboration must be based on reciprocal partnerships within and outside the individual institutions. Jeandron and Robinson (2010) note that "colleges should emphasize the quality of partnerships rather than the quantity to achieve a deeper, long-term impact in the community" (27). The emphasis is not just on doing something for the community that addresses a short-term need but also on helping students reach learning goals and objectives while assisting with a long-term need in the community. By doing so, the boundaries of higher education institutions become more permeable and students gain greater knowledge of community needs and opportunities, which can expose them to potential career paths and opportunities for academic and social engagement.

Related to partnerships is the opportunity to address one of the specific structural challenges noted in the literature on student transfer and cross-institutional partnerships—articulation agreements. Often, students begin their courses at community colleges without a clear academic major, taking courses based on interest or following a generalized curriculum that helps to fulfill the general education credits at a university. However, if a student is interested in engineering or any other specific major, courses taken at the community college or initiative institution may not count toward degree requirements at the receiving institution. This lack of integration can add time, expense, and frustration to the student experience, and it can hinder a student's transition from one institution to another (Flaga 2006; Ignash and Townsend 2000). In contrast, appropriate and accurate academic advising and clear and student-focused (not credit-focused) articulation agreements help to support student transfer (Ignash and Townsend 2000).

As stated previously, service-learning can help shape student interests and thereby can assist them in identifying academic majors by providing the real work experience to understand potential job opportunities in an academic discipline or subject area. Elwell and Bean (2001) found that ELL students found service-learning valuable because it "possessed real-world relevance" (59). Astin and colleagues (2000) found that "students thus feel challenged both affectively and cognitively in their service-learning courses because they are given an opportunity to apply what they are reading to a real-life experience, which, in turn, stimulates them to examine and reflect not only on the reading itself but also on their personal values and beliefs" (89).

Another opportunity related to partnerships concerns the transition from the initiative to receiving institution. If multiple higher education institutions engage with the same community-based organizations simultaneously, students have the opportunity to meet other students, faculty, and staff at the receiving or transfer institution. A barrier noted in the transfer student literature concerns the difficulty that students experience in integrating academically and socially when moving from a community college to the receiving institution (Bahr et al. 2013, 478; Townsend and Wilson 2008; 2006; Laanan, 2004, 1996). Service-learning aids in reducing these difficulties, as students may develop friendships or find mentors at the receiving institution, by virtue of exposure to common interests rooted in community needs.

Recommendations

Inherent in the definition of service-learning and framed by an understanding of the most effective service-learning practices is the importance of linking service-learning activities to course curriculum. We extend this knowledge and apply to transfer success by adding an additional element of *curricular intentionality that enhances student integration and self-efficacy.* Placing service-learning in the context of curriculum, often course based, creates a structure to support student reflection and critical thinking. Students are able to achieve academically, gain a better understanding of their career goals, and increase their interaction with faculty, which are all related with transfer student success. Moreover, in order to mitigate the barriers related to student integration and self-efficacy, curriculum needs to address proper behavior, including a discussion of implicit or explicit bias and to contain advising, psychological, and emotional support mechanisms that prepare and contextualize service-learning experiences for students. Given that transfer students may also experience alienation and social stigma while in the receiving university (Bahr et al. 2013; Reyes 2011; Harrison 1999), service-learning's reflection opportunities may help students establish the self-efficacy skills that are important once they transfer. These reflective opportunities can also be designed to encourage students to focus on career goals, explore interests, consider potential majors, and investigate academic policies and offerings at the initiative and receiving institutions. Peer learning and support also help to achieve the goals of academic and social integration. Students experience the classroom as a site of social and academic integration; classes are where they interact with peers. Creating service-learning teams or groups and providing peer review of reflective exercises are two methods of intentionally creating peer-to-peer contact through service learning.

Related to the first recommendation, integrating service-learning into course curriculum can occur across institutions and support partnerships. To foster a partnership with a four-year (or receiving transfer) institution, *bridging of curriculum is needed between the initiative and receiving institutions*. To do this, institutions and faculty would need to collaborate on a shared service-learning experience that places students at both institutions in the same physical space at the same time. Sharing of readings, course discussion prompts, and assignments would facilitate more opportunities for students to begin with a common understanding and potentially develop relationships that would transcend the service-learning program and support successful transition across institutions. Importantly, efforts to create these types of opportunities must be intentional and integrated; thus, they are most likely to occur in contexts where faculty and staff are encouraged and incentivized to promote and model cross-institutional partnerships. To engage and support faculty beyond their traditional roles, the American Association of Community Colleges (AACC) found through their project, Community Colleges Broadening Horizons through Service-Learning, that recognition in the form of course credit, awards, and professional development assists in supporting faculty engagement in service-learning (Prentice, Robinson, and Patton 2012). In addition, creating institutional support through centers for teaching provides the incentive and opportunity for faculty engagement and staff partnership, which has significant influence on transfer student success.

In order to achieve curricular integration, faculty involvement, and student success, *multiple structures (i.e., offices, units, and policies) must engage in internal and external collaborations* to better support student success via service-learning. Internal and external collaborations within and between two-year and four-year institutions are vital to supporting successful service-learning programs that bridge institutions and create successful pathways for students. As mentioned previously, service-learning advisory boards are an effective means for sharing information and mitigating structural barriers within higher education institutions. We argue that these boards could function similarly *across* higher education institutions, increasing efficacy by including colleagues from both the community college and receiving institutions.

By creating partnerships that bridge institutions, information on best practices, student integration, structural barriers, and future directions can be more easily shared. Further, by bringing in multiple perspectives from the two- and four-year campuses, the cognitive complexity of advisory boards is enhanced. This complexity brings with it the ability to better address the needs of students engaged in service-learning and in the transfer process. Better understanding the student perspective can further the operational complexity of the group and is critical to program and transfer success. Thus, students involved in service-learning and the transfer process should be included in advisory boards as active participants. Finally, community partners should also be actively engaged in the advisory board process, as they provide an additional perspective of the needs outside of the campus community and can assist in providing points of meaning, engagement, and future opportunity for students.

Partnership between institutions and with community stakeholders is key to student success. Therefore, schools should *intentionally partner with their communities to support student success.* In order to integrate community involvement in the service-learning and transfer process, faculty and staff should work with community partners to structure projects that incorporate student learning and service over the course of their two- and four-year college experiences. For example, a service-learning project could be designed over the course of a two-to-three-year period, during which students begin their work while taking courses at the community college and in conjunction with a course at a local university. The relationship with the community agency would continue in subsequent courses allowing for a continued relationship before, during, and after the transfer process. To achieve this level of integration and partnership, faculty and administrators from both two-year and four-year institutions would need to actively work with these organizations beyond the initial planning and final assessment stages of a service-learning project. Although faculty and staff often attend service-learning events with their students via their home institutions and programs, in a partnership model, planning, assessment, and attendance would take place at both the initiative and receiving institutions and would bridge the two- and four-year experiences. As a result, in this model, transfer students would have an opportunity to work with faculty, staff, and peers at the receiving institution early on in their community college careers. These interactions stand to promote greater academic engagement and integration and increased social capital and self-efficacy in students, which are crucial to their successful transfer.

Conclusion

Transfer from a community college to a baccalaureate program is a complex process with many considerations ranging from support to student self-efficacy to advising on career goals to mediating transfer shock. Addressing these areas requires intentional action and engaged partnerships across internal units and programs and between multiple higher education institutions. Our model of student transfer via service-learning creates an environment in which social and academic integration for the individual student and structural integration for the institutions and community stakeholders is intentionally crafted to support students transitioning from two- to four-year institutions. Service-learning encourages academic integration, career preparation, and self-efficacy in students, and institutional integration and partnerships via service-learning create the opportunity for structurally integrated, supported, and successful student transfer. With the continued focus on community colleges as sites to create more college-going and workforce-prepared students, identifying beneficial current practices and creating new partnerships is imperative in supporting student success. Service-learning can provide the bridged and integrated experiences to gird student success during the transfer process and, ultimately, toward degree completion.

References

Astin, Alexander W., Lori J. Vogelgesang, Elaine K. Ikeda, and Jennifer A. Yee. 2000. *How Service-Learning Affects Students*. Los Angeles: Higher Education Research Institute, University of California.

Bahr, Peter Riley, Christie Toth, Kathryn Thirolf, and Johanna C. Massé. 2013. "A Review and Critique of the Literature on Community College Students' Transition Processes and Outcomes in Four-Year Institutions." In *Higher Education: Handbook of Theory and Research*, 459–511. Netherlands: Springer.

Bailey, Thomas, Dong Wook Jeong, and Sung-Woo Cho. 2010. "Referral, Enrollment, and Completion in Developmental Education Sequences in Community Colleges." *Economics of Education Review* 29 (2): 255–270.

Bailey, Thomas R., D. Timothy Leinbach, and Paul Davis Jenkins. 2006. "Is Student Success Labeled Institutional Failure? Student Goals and Graduation Rates in the Accountability Debate at Community Colleges." http://academiccommons.columbia.edu/catalog/ac:145053.

Berger, Joseph B., and Gary D. Malaney. 2003. "Assessing the Transition of Transfer Students from Community Colleges to a University." *NASPA Journal* 40: 1–23.

Bers, Trudy, Joseph W. Filkins, and Gerald W. McLaughlin. 2001. "Understanding Transfers: A Collaborative Community College and University Research Project." *Journal of Applied Research in the Community College* 8: 93–105.

Borden, Victor. 2004. "Accommodating Student Swirl: When Traditional Students Are No Longer the Tradition." *Change: The Magazine of Higher Learning* 36 (2): 10–17.

Boswell, Katherine. 2004. "Bridges or Barriers? Public Policy and the Community College Transfer Function." *Change: The Magazine of Higher Learning* 36 (6): 22–29.

Cejda, Brent D., and Alice J. Kaylor. 2001. "Early Transfer: A Case Study of Traditional-Aged Community College Students." *Community College Journal of Research and Practice* 25: 621–638.

Chitgopekar, Anu, and Joseph Swaba. 1999. "Where Is the Common Ground? Insights into Service-Learning Collaborations between Community Colleges and Universities." *Campus Compact National Center for Community Colleges*. http://www.mesacc.edu/other/engagement/CommonGround/CommonGround.pdf.

Cohen, Arthur M., and Florence B. Brawer. 2003. *The American Community College*. San Francisco, CA: Jossey-Bass.

College Completion Toolkit. 2011. *College Completion Toolkit*. United States Department of Education. http://www.whitehouse.gov/sites/default/files/college_completion_tool_kit.pdf.

Eagan Jr., M. Kevin, and Audrey J. Jaeger. 2009. "Effects of Exposure to Part-Time Faculty on Community College Transfer." *Research in Higher Education* 50 (2): 168–188.

Elwell, Marelene D., and Martha S. Bean. 2001. "Editors' Choice: The Efficacy of Service-Learning for Community College ESL Students." *Community College Review* 28 (4): 47–61.

Flaga, Catherine T. 2006. "The Process of Transition for Community College Transfer Students." *Community College Journal of Research and Practice* 30 (1): 3–19.

Glass Jr., J. Conrad, and Catherine E. Bunn. 1998. "Length of Time Required to Graduate for Community College Students Transferring to Senior Institutions." *Community College Journal of Research and Practice* 22 (3): 239–263.

Gray Davies, Timothy, and Ellyn M. Dickmann. 1998. "Student Voices in the Transfer Process: Do We Hear Them? Do We Listen?" *Community College Journal of Research and Practice* 22 (5): 541–557.

Hagedorn, Linda Serra, Winny YanFang Chi, Rita M. Cepeda, and Melissa McLain. 2007. "An Investigation of Critical Mass: The Role of Latino Representation in the Success of Urban Community College Students." *Research in Higher Education* 48 (1): 73–91.

Handel, Stephen J. 2007. "Second Chance, Not Second Class: A Blueprint for Community-College Transfer." *Change: The Magazine of Higher Learning* 39 (5): 38–45.

Harbin, Carey E. 1997. "A Survey of Transfer Students at Four-Year Institutions Serving a California Community College." *Community College Review* 25 (2): 21–40.

Harrison, Patricia Lynne. 1999. "Transition Experiences of Community College Transfer Students: A Qualitative Study." *Unpublished Doctoral Dissertation.* Charlottesville: University of Virginia.

Horn, Laura, Stephanie Nevill, and James Griffith. 2006. "Profile of Undergraduates in US Postsecondary Education Institutions, 2003–04: With a Special Analysis of Community College Students. Statistical Analysis Report. NCES 2006–184." *National Center for Education Statistics.*

Hossler, Don, Doug Shapiro, Afet Dudar, Mary Ziskin, Jin Chen, Desiree Zerquera, and Vasti Torres. 2012. Signature Report. Transfer and Mobility: The National Review of Pre-Degree Student Movement in Post-Secondary Education. *National Student Clearinghouse Signature Report.* http://nscresearchcenter.org/wp-content/uploads/NSC_Signature_Report_2.pdf.

Ignash, Jan M., and Barbara K. Townsend. 2000. "Evaluating State-Level Articulation Agreements According to Good Practice." *Community College Review* 28 (3): 1–21.

Ishitani, Terry T., and Sean A. McKitrick. 2010. "After Transfer: The Engagement of Community College Students at a Four-Year Collegiate Institution." *Community College Journal of Research and Practice* 34 (7): 576–594.

Jacoby, Barbara. 1996. Service-Learning in Higher Education: Concepts and Practices. *The Jossey-Bass Higher and Adult Education Series.* San Francisco, CA: Jossey-Bass.

Jaeger, Audrey J. 2008. "Contingent Faculty and Student Outcomes." *Academe* 94 (6): 42–43.

Jeandron, Carol, and Gail Robinson. 2010. "Creating a Climate for Service Learning Success." *American Association of Community Colleges.* http://files.eric.ed.gov/fulltext/ED513943.pdf.

Kezar, Adrianna, and Lester, Jaime. *Organizing Higher Education for Collaboration: A Guide for Campus Educators.* San Francisco, CA: John Wiley & Sons, 2009.

Knapp, Laura G., Janice E. Kelly-Reid, and Scott A. Ginder. 2012. "Enrollment in Postsecondary Institutions, Fall 2011; Financial Statistics, Fiscal Year 2011; and Graduation Rates, Selected Cohorts, 2003–2008: First Look (provisional data)." U.S. Department of Education. Washington, DC: National Center for Education Statistics. Accessed April 14, 2013. http://nces.ed.gov/pubsearch/pubsinfo.asp?pubid=2012174rev.

Laanan, Frankie Santos. 1996. "Making the Transition: Understanding the Adjustment Process of Community College Transfer Students." *Community College Review* 23 (4): 69–84.

———. 2004. "Studying Transfer Students: Part I: Instrument Design and Implications." *Community College Journal of Research and Practice* 28 (4): 331–351.

Laanan, Frankie Santos, Soko S. Starobin, and Latrice E. Eggleston. 2010. "Adjustment of Community College Students at a Four-Year University: Role and Relevance of Transfer Student Capital for Student Retention." *Journal of College Student Retention: Research, Theory and Practice* 12 (2): 175–209.

Levinson, David L. 2004. "Introduction to the Special Issue on Community Colleges as Civic Institutions." *Community College Journal of Research & Practice* 28 (2): 99–103.

Matlock, John, and Katrina Wade-Golden. 2009. "University of Michigan Transfer Student Experience: Perceptions, Opinions, and Experiences of Community College Transfer Students." *Jack Kent Cooke Community College Transfer Initiative Final Report.* Ann Arbor: The University of Michigan, Office of Academic Multicultural Initiatives.

McKay, Valerie C., and Jeremy Estrella. 2008. "First-Generation Student Success: The Role of Faculty Interaction in Service Learning Courses." *Communication Education* 57 (3): 356–372.

Mullin, Christopher M. 2012. "Transfer: An Indispensable Part of the Community College Mission." *American Association of Community Colleges Policy Brief 2012–03PBL.* http://www.aacc.nche.edu/Publications/Briefs/Documents/AACC_Transfer_to_LUMINA.pdf.

Owens, Karen R. 2010. "Community College Transfer Students' Adjustment to a Four-Year Institution: A Qualitative Analysis." *Journal of The First-Year Experience and Students in Transition* 22 (1): 87–128.

Prentice, Mary. 2002. "Institutionalizing Service-Learning in Community Colleges." American Association of Community Colleges. *American Association of Community Colleges Research Brief AACC-RB-01–3.* http://aacc.nche.edu/Resources/aaccprograms/horizons/Documents/prentice_rb.pdf.

Prentice, Mary, Gail Robinson, and Madeline Patton. 2012. "Cultivating Community beyond the Classroom." *American Association of Community Colleges.* Retrieved from http://www.aacc.nche.edu/Resources/aaccprograms/horizons/Documents/CultivatingCommunities_Aug2012.pdf.

Reyes, Marie-Elena. 2011. "Unique Challenges for Women of Color in STEM Transferring from Community Colleges to Universities." *Harvard Educational Review* 81 (2): 241–263.

Robinson, Gail, and Lynn Barnett. 1998. "Best Practices in Service-Learning." *American Association of Community Colleges Project Brief,* AACC-PB-98–3. http://www.aacc.nche.edu/Resources/aaccprograms/horizons/Documents/bestprac.pdf.

Rochford, Regina A. 2013. "Service-Learning for Remedial Reading and Writing Students." *Community College Journal of Research and Practice* 37 (5): 345–355.

Shedd, Jessica M. 2003. "The History of the Student Credit Hour." *New Directions for Higher Education* 2003 (122): 5–12.

Tinto, Vincent. 1993. *Leaving College: Rethinking the Causes and Cures of Student Attrition* Chicago: The University of Chicago Press. 2nd ed.

Townsend, Barbara K. 2001. "Redefining the Community College Transfer Mission." *Community College Review* 29 (2): 29–42.

Townsend, Barbara K., and Kristin B. Wilson. 2006. "A Hand Hold for a Little Bit: Factors Facilitating the Success of Community College Transfer Students to a Large Research University." *Journal of College Student Development* 47 (4): 439–456.

———. 2008. "The Academic and Social Integration of Persisting Community College Transfer Students." *Journal of College Student Retention: Research, Theory and Practice* 10 (4): 405–423.

Trotter, Yvonne D. 2006. "Adult Learning Theories: Impacting Professional Development Programs." *Delta Kappa Gamma Bulletin* 72 (2): 8.

Umbach, Paul D., and Matthew R. Wawrzynski. 2005. "Faculty Do Matter: The Role of College Faculty in Student Learning and Engagement." *Research in Higher Education* 46 (2): 153–184.

Weglarz, Shirley G., and Jeffrey A. Seybert. 2004. "Participant Perceptions of a Community College Service-Learning Program." *Community College Journal of Research & Practice* 28 (2): 123–132.

CHAPTER 10

The Prism Effect of Service-Learning

Mary Prentice and Gail Robinson

Community colleges have offered service-learning since the 1960s (Robinson and Barnett 1996), but the vast majority of curriculum-based programs got underway in the 1990s and 2000s due to federal funding from the Learn and Serve America program of the Corporation for National and Community Service. Funding from Learn and Serve America created the two largest community college service-learning consortium programs in the country, at the American Association of Community Colleges (AACC) and the Community College National Center for Community Engagement (CCNCCE). These two organizations provided grants for program development and training for faculty, staff, and administrators from more than 130 community colleges from 1994 through 2012.

Most of these colleges developed service-learning programs from the ground up and focused on a multitude of disciplines. Additionally, in the case of AACC's consortium, they shared their knowledge and experience with other institutions through an innovative institutional mentor-mentee design. The focus of the AACC college grants ranged from improving science, technology, engineering, and mathematics (STEM) opportunities to looking at local effects of immigration and multilingual services; from community policing to strip-mined land reclamation; from using social media to preventing childhood obesity. The common element among all the programs was the integration of community-based learning into academic coursework. Each three-year cohort of grantee colleges had to achieve particular performance measures and address pertinent issues in their home communities.

We began our collaborative research in 2001 by comparing AACC and CCNCCE grantee colleges to non-grantees to determine what factors influenced service-learning institutionalization on community college campuses (Prentice 2002). That work led us to look more intentionally at AACC grantee colleges for three successive Learn and Serve America–funded cohorts, from 2003 through 2012.

We studied each three-year cohort of AACC grantee colleges under different lenses. The first cohort (2003–2006) used survey instruments that focused on the effects of service-learning on student civic engagement; the second (2006–2009) focused on the effects of service-learning on academic learning outcomes; and the third (2009–2012) focused on the effects of service-learning on retention and persistence. Each cohort's surveys not only contained different questions that addressed the particular outcome, but also asked a few questions about service-learning that were consistent over the nine-year period. The comparison of the combined results over nine years demonstrated the prism effect of service-learning.

Our cumulative years of research led us to an eye-opening yet unsurprising conclusion: in the same way that a beam of light is refracted into a greater spectrum of colors through a prism, students who participate in service-learning may enter their academic and community-based experiences with limited goals, but achieve a broad array of personal and professional benefits. Some of these benefits are planned by faculty; others are unintentional and sometimes life changing. This is both unsurprising and a revelation when we consider the uniqueness of the community college experience juxtaposed with the dimensions of service-learning. Should we assume that service-learning findings from four-year colleges and universities automatically apply to community colleges? Should we assume that community college students—with perhaps different goals, demographics, and backgrounds—respond to service-learning the same way university students do? Does the effect of service-learning differ when students are at a college for only two years, when compared to university students who have the potential to experience service-learning for four or more years? In our series of studies, we came to understand that community colleges do provide unique service-learning experiences to students because both the mission of the community college and the profile of the community college student are unique.

Service-learning is often described as a triad of factors—community engagement, reflection, and academic learning. Service-learning thus provides the structure for the prism; in past research, including our own initial studies, the outcome of service-learning was portrayed as two-dimensional, that is, service-learning leads to an outcome. Because we were able to conduct a series of studies on service-learning outcomes, what we saw emerge is the three-dimensionality of service-learning. And because we were able to conduct these studies in community colleges, we were able to see a diverse student body report multiple outcomes when asked about a single service-learning experience.

In this chapter, we first present some of the past research that guided our work—both what has been done and what scholars say still needs to be done. We then contextualize the focus of our research by presenting an overview of community colleges as distinct from other postsecondary institutions. Next we present an overview of the grant projects that spurred our research and follow it up with a specific presentation of each of the three research studies. We then gather our findings and present our conclusions about the overall impact of service-learning on community college students.

Background

The trajectory of research on service-learning has been both widespread and specific. Benefits for elementary, secondary, and postsecondary students have been and continue to be explored (Billig 2007; Eyler, Giles, Stenson, and Gray 2001). Students in universities, four-year colleges, and community colleges have been included in these studies. The institutions range in size from small to large; they comprise private, faith-based, and publicly funded colleges and universities. Changes in students' social awareness, interpersonal awareness, academic learning, and civic involvement have all been represented in these studies. The path of this plethora of research has led to meta-analyses of service-learning outcomes and identification of service-learning as one of ten high-impact strategies that foster retention and higher levels of academic achievement in postsecondary students (Kuh 2008).

The vast majority of published service-learning research has been conducted in four-year institutions. Some studies refer to their subjects in higher education with no mention of whether community college students were included. This research is rich and compelling and has led faculty and administrators to, for the most part, accept service-learning as an effective teaching tool that augments classroom instruction. As Eyler (2009) concluded, the culmination of research has substantiated service-learning's impact on students' "personal, academic, and social outcomes" (25).

Three areas that seem to be the focus of much of this research are civic engagement, academic learning outcomes, and college retention, persistence, and completion. From the beginning, a central focus of the integration of service-learning into college courses was the development of greater civic commitment in students while still in school and after graduation. Eyler's review of studies that compared students who participated in service-learning with those who did not found convincing evidence for the increase in civic engagement among service-learners. These studies demonstrated that students had acquired both an increased political interest as well as a sense of connectedness and responsibility to community (there have been debates about whether service-learning can lead to political efficacy in addition to community involvement; see Walker 2000).

No less important are the findings about service-learning's connection with academic outcomes. Beginning with a longitudinal study conducted by Astin, Vogelgesang, Ikeda, and Yee (2000), the impact of service-learning on student learning became clearer. Using data from more than 22,000 undergraduates, the researchers found that service-learning students had higher academic performance when compared to students who participated in community service, and both groups had higher performance than students who had not participated in service-learning. Similarly, in a study conducted at about the same time, Eyler and Giles (1999) interviewed students before and after participation in service-learning. They found that students who had experienced well-designed service-learning activities demonstrated "increased complexity in analysis of both causes and solutions to social problems" (75). Following this, research conducted in specific disciplines has also identified academic gains in those participating in service-learning. More specifically, it appears that while service-learning does not increase fact-based knowledge as measured by standardized tests, it does increase higher-order analytical skills (Felten and Clayton 2012).

Confirming and expanding on academic learning outcomes, three meta-analyses of research on service-learning in higher education have been conducted. A 2007 analysis by Novak, Markey, and Allen focused on the effect of service-learning on cognitive learning outcomes. They reviewed findings from nine studies that quantitatively compared courses with and without service-learning to ascertain the impact on cognitive learning outcomes in various forms such as understanding and application. The conclusions drawn from this meta-analysis were outstandingly in favor of service-learning. As the researchers stated, "The evidence indicates that service-learning offers improvement; in fact, the failure to provide students an opportunity to participate in the exercise reduces the level of student improvement" (153).

Warren (2012) conducted another meta-analysis of the research on service-learning and student learning. Warren selected 11 studies for analysis, 6 of which were also included in the Novak et al. analysis. Results confirmed the Novak et al. findings. Warren concluded that "not only does service-learning have positive benefits such as increased multicultural awareness and enhanced social responsibility, but it also increases student learning outcomes, the gold standard when measuring pedagogical practices" (59).

Research on student retention and persistence has proliferated over the past ten years, yet the number of studies that have included service-learning as a possible impact variable has been small and almost exclusively focused on universities. Research also has found links between service-learning and students' greater engagement and integration into college, which has been found to be directly linked to student retention (Tinto 1997). Only one study (Bringle, Hatcher, and Muthiah 2010) directly demonstrated the connection between service-learning participation and subsequent persistence and retention; however, the connection was weak. At this point in the service-learning research trajectory, it is unclear whether service-learning has its own unique impact on retention beyond that of engagement and integration in college. With this disclaimer, three recent studies establish this indirect link between service-learning and increased retention and persistence.

First, in a study on three curricular interventions on first-to-second-year retention, Keup (2005–2006) used Cooperative Institutional Research Program (CIRP) data as well as a follow-up survey of first-year undergraduate students to investigate first-to-second-year retention factors. Keup found a marginally significant relationship between service-learning participation and intention to re-enroll the next year at the same institution. The effect, however, depended on the "quantity and quality of faculty interactions" and the "use of good academic practices" (82).

Two other studies more directly assessed the link between service-learning and retention and persistence. Bringle, Hatcher, and Muthiah (2010) studied 805 students across 11 Indiana Campus Compact member institutions. They found that students in service-learning courses were more likely to have a greater intention to return to college for a second year, but found only a weak relationship between service-learning and actual second-year retention. They postulated that this outcome was due to the increased integration and engagement of students socially and academically. Also appearing in 2010, a qualitative study by Yeh found—through interviews with six low-income, first-generation students—that students perceived service-learning as increasing their engagement and participation in college and thus increasing their persistence.

Uniqueness of Community Colleges

While community colleges are different from four-year colleges and universities, until recently, the difference had not been noted as significant in the service-learning research. In the fall of 2011, Taggart and Crisp published a synthesis of empirical work done on service-learning in community colleges. In their introduction, they stated that "research focusing specifically on four-year institutions is problematic as there is a wealth of empirical support for the assertion that a community college setting uniquely impacts student outcomes" (26). They concluded that, "as such, it is not appropriate to assume that a service-learning experience will impact students attending two-year colleges and four-year institutions in the same ways" (26).

As they suggest, the profile of a typical community college student is different from the traditional university student. The average community college student is 28 years old. Fifty-nine percent of community college students attend college part-time; 40 percent are the first in their families to attend college; 46 percent receive some type of financial aid; 16 percent are single parents; 61 percent are employed full-time while going to college; and 55 percent have had previous college experience. The community college student population is also racially and ethnically diverse. Of all Latino or Hispanic undergraduate students attending postsecondary institutions, 56 percent attend community colleges, as do 49 percent of all Black undergraduates, 44 percent of all Asian/Pacific Islander undergraduates, and 42 percent of all Native American undergraduates (AACC 2013).

Previous studies on community college service-learning outcomes, while limited in number, confirm the findings of research conducted on higher education institutions in general. Similar to the studies cited previously, research on civic engagement in community college students has illustrated the gains made through service-learning. In Taggart and Crisp's (2011) synthesis paper, key areas in which community college students benefit are civic engagement, learning outcomes, application of classroom-acquired knowledge, and increased course satisfaction. However, Taggart and Crisp noted in their critique that the majority of studies were limited to a single community college or just a few classes within a single community college, thus restricting the generalizability of these findings to a broader segment of community college students. They found that studies also varied in describing service-learning; some mentioned students participating in 20 hours of service-learning per course, while others looked at projects that involved the whole class in a single effort that might have been more time-limited. Finally, often more than one intervention was measured at the same time, which called into question which intervention (or what combination of interventions) correlated with the measured changes in students. In their recommendations for future community college service-learning research, Taggart and Crisp called for the use of a control group to reduce the number of extraneous variables that might have an impact on student outcomes beyond that of service-learning itself. They also suggested that future studies substantiate the link between community college service-learning and student outcomes such as civic engagement, academic learning, critical thinking, and college completion.

Research with AACC Grantee Colleges

Over the course of ten years, we set out to investigate the impact of service-learning on community college students. Following the initial study on program institutionalization (Prentice 2002), each successive three-year AACC Learn and Serve

America grant focused on a particular research question, each different from the previous grant. AACC selected participating institutions through a nationally competitive process for its "Community Colleges Broadening Horizons through Service Learning" projects; hence the grantees were known as the Horizons colleges.

A total of 26 colleges from 18 states participated in the studies, with different colleges in each three-year Horizons cohort. (Four colleges participated in more than one cohort due to their selection in more than one Horizons grant.) The number of students and courses differed from college to college, and from cohort to cohort, due to varying institutional sizes and course offerings.

Each project cohort was guided by a research question. In the 2003–2006 study on civic engagement, the question we tested was what impact, if any, do service-learning experiences have on community college students' civic knowledge and commitment. The research question guiding the 2006–2009 study was what impact, if any, do service-learning experiences have on community college students' acquisition of academic learning outcomes. The question framing the 2009–2012 study was what impact, if any, do service-learning experiences have on community college students' retention in individual courses and persistence in enrolling from semester to semester.

For each research question, we created specific research tools. We developed pre- and post-course surveys for the 2003–2006 Horizons colleges that gathered data on students' levels of civic engagement. For the 2006–2009 group, we surveyed faculty and students regarding intended and actual learning outcomes. For the 2009–2012 Horizons cohort, we surveyed students on factors that lead to retention and persistence. Each study compared service-learners to non-service-learners. We also gathered qualitative data using focus groups from each cohort. The results of each three-year study were summarized and published by AACC (Prentice, Robinson, and Patton 2012; Prentice and Robinson 2010; 2007).

Summary of Findings

While the research projects happened linearly and separately, by the end of the last study, the takeaway about service-learning was that—no matter what reason a faculty member had for engaging students in service-learning—multiple simultaneous benefits accrued to students. In the first cohort, we focused on civic engagement and found evidence that service-learning affected this outcome. In the second cohort, we found that service-learning had positive effects on academic learning outcomes as well as civic engagement. This led us to the third cohort, which focused on student retention and persistence and found that service-learning had impacts beyond the civic engagement and academic learning outcomes of the first two cohorts.

It was the accumulation of these research findings that revealed to us the multidimensionality of service-learning. In other words, the service-learning focus might be about civic engagement, but students will develop civic engagement *and* academic learning *and* commitment to completing college, and so forth. Just like the hyphen between service and learning links the two concepts into something more than each is on its own, there is an "and" that follows each service-learning outcome. Thus, as explained earlier, service-learning is like a prism that takes in one beam of white light and separates it into a spectrum of colors. To see all the colors of the light spectrum, it is not necessary to have multiple prisms that produce one color of light each; a single prism can produce all the colors. Students come into the prism of service-learning as the beam of light, and when they emerge, they reflect the multiple benefits that were simultaneously brought out through the "service-learning as prism" experience.

Trajectory of Studies: Civic Engagement

With our focus on civic engagement as the intended service-learning outcome, the 2003–2006 study's design included the use of both pre-course and post-course surveys (see Gottlieb and Robinson [2006] for the survey instruments) and inclusion of a comparison group of non-service-learners. Survey questions were created to reflect direct political knowledge and involvement (such as voting and knowing when city council meetings are held) as well as more general community involvement (e.g., likelihood of volunteering in the following year and awareness of local community service agencies).

The 12 participating community colleges in the 2003–2006 cohort ranged from small and rural to large and urban. (This was also the case in the following two cohorts, although each subsequent cohort responded to a different research question.) The service-learning director at each college chose both the service-learning and comparative non-service-learning courses in which to survey students. Multiple disciplines were represented through the college project directors' choices of courses.

By the end of the three-year grant period, ten of the colleges returned 424 matched pre- and post-course survey pairs. Of these, 279 pairs were completed by service-learning students. The non-service-learning students returned 145 pre- and post-course survey pairs; of these, 56 students had previously participated in one or more service-learning courses. For analysis purposes, we removed these students from the non-service-learning group so that only students with no service-learning experience were compared to students that had participated in service-learning in the surveyed academic term.

Interestingly, 111 of the service-learning students also reported that they had previously participated in one or more service-learning courses. This additional breakdown allowed us to investigate two questions. The initial question that formed the study was tested through analyses of the impact of service-learning (the intervention) on civic engagement, compared to no service-learning (a regular course). The second question regarding the impact of multiple service-learning courses was tested through analysis of impact on civic engagement experienced in just one service-learning course, compared to the culmination of experiences from two or more service-learning courses.

What emerged from these analyses were differences among students based on previous service-learning involvement. First-time service-learning students experienced the greatest gains in civic engagement as measured by the difference in pre-course survey scores compared to post- course survey scores over the course of the academic term, followed by the experienced (more than one course) service-learners.

Non-service-learning students had the lowest gains. When the post-course surveys for all three groups (non-service-learning, first-time service-learning, and experienced service-learning) were compared, the highest average post-course survey scores came from the experienced service-learners, followed by first-time service-learners, and then—once again scoring lowest—the non-service-learning students (see Prentice and Robinson [2007] for specific details).

What this pattern suggested to us is that the first-time service-learning students had the greatest gains over time (from the beginning to the end of the course), perhaps because, since they had no previous service-learning experience, they initially scored similarly to the non-service-learners and thus they had the most room to gain in civic engagement. However, when looking at the highest post-course civic engagement scores, it was the experienced service-learners that stood out (this mirrors the findings of Chesbrough [2011] on students in a four-year institution). If initial service-learning experiences in their past had already produced a gain in civic engagement, then these students would already have higher average survey scores at the beginning of this subsequent service-learning experience. These students did not show the greatest gains over the course of the semester, but since they were already higher in civic engagement at the beginning of the semester due to their previous initial experience, the gains that they did make, while smaller, still resulted in the highest average post-course survey scores. From these findings, we surmised that there is a relationship between multiple service-learning experiences and increased civic engagement.

We followed up these surveys with seven focus groups at four of the colleges. Overall, students perceived that service-learning participation had increased their knowledge of and commitment to community involvement. Students also told us how initial community involvement morphed into political interest and social justice concerns. As one student said, "I have aspirations to find out what's going on in the county. What's happening with my taxes?... We're talking about homeless people... We're talking about senior citizens. So what's going on in the county... that funds can't get to where they need to go? I still have to have that answer."

Through the combination of surveys and focus groups, our analyses revealed the existence of one "color" of the service-learning prism: civic engagement. At the end of the 2003–2006 grant, we were able to report that service-learning was related to increases in students' civic and community knowledge, commitment to community involvement, and understanding of their role as community members. At this point in our conceptualization, we had found support for the use of service-learning when the desired outcome for students was civic engagement.

Academic Learning Outcomes

In 2006, Learn and Serve America funded another AACC Horizons consortium grant. Our research focus for this three-year project was on student learning outcomes. We surveyed students and faculty members from ten community colleges (see Prentice and Robinson [2010] for the survey questions and specific details). As in the 2003–2006 civic engagement cohort, project directors from each college chose service-learning and comparative non-service-learning courses for survey distribution. We asked directors to choose non-service-learning courses that were as similar as possible to the service-learning courses in topic, discipline, level (freshman or sophomore), and instructor. Larger colleges were able to match courses more closely; smaller colleges matched courses to the degree they were able. For example, if only one section of a particular sophomore-level biology course was offered in a given semester, the director chose as the comparison course a similar sophomore-level biology course. At times this meant that different instructors were teaching the two comparison courses, but we believed that the level and disciplinary topic of the courses were the more important criteria for selecting comparison courses.

The academic learning outcomes were chosen from a review of institutional learning outcomes that were listed on a sample of community college websites across the nation. Six learning outcomes were listed most often and are represented in the survey: critical thinking, communication, career and teamwork, civic responsibility, global understanding and citizenship, and academic development and educational success. In this study, civic responsibility or civic engagement was a learning outcome that was measured along with other learning outcomes. The survey asked both service-learners and non-service-learners to report how much of a particular ability or skill (each of which related to one of the six learning outcomes) they believed they had gained as a result of taking that course. For example, students responded on a six-point Likert-type scale to questions such as, "As a result of taking this course, I can communicate more effectively using writing skills." To contextualize students' responses, we also asked faculty members to report, via survey, the degree to which their courses focused on each skill or ability. By the end of the three-year grant period, 2,317 student surveys were returned. Of those, 1,687 surveys were completed by service-learners and 630 by non-service-learners. Faculty completed 67 surveys; 46 of these were completed by service-learning faculty and 21 were completed by faculty who did not use service-learning in the surveyed courses.

The results again supported the impact of service-learning. Using an alpha level of .05 for all statistical tests, once we took into account the instructors' reported degree of learning outcomes in their courses, we found that students who participated in service-learning scored statistically higher (i.e., their perceptions of learning these outcomes were greater) than non-service-learners on all learning outcomes except global understanding and citizenship. Most likely this was because few faculty included the global understanding outcome as an intentional part of their teaching. The greatest difference occurred between the service-learning and non-service-learning groups on the career and teamwork outcome. The service-learners' average score was 4.737 compared to the non-service-learners' average of 4.566 on a six-point scale. The outcome with the highest scores was academic development and educational success (average service-learning score was 5.033, average non-service-learning score was 4.909). These results do not seem surprising because, in addition to being two frequently listed learning outcomes, two of service-learning's hallmarks are the exposure of students to potential careers and the need for students to work with others in their service-learning activities (Astin et al. 2000; Eyler and Giles 1999).

In the last year of the 2006–2009 grant, we conducted five student focus groups and three faculty focus groups with participants from seven of the colleges. Service-learning students' comments fell into five categories. First, students reported that service-learning helped them understand their course material better. Students' sentiments were illustrated in statements such as, "You can apply what you read in the textbook, and that's how you learn it so much better," and "it ups the excitement of the whole class. It made you want to learn it more."

Second, students told us that service-learning helped them learn specific skills or knowledge that they might not learn in a course that did not offer service-learning. As one student explained, service-learning "teaches every student how to get into a real-life situation and think about it critically and logically." Third, students felt that without service-learning, they would have missed the excitement and passion that service-learning added to the classroom learning. Fourth, they also believed that there was information that they could have learned only through service-learning, such as character building, compassion, and understanding. For example, a dental hygiene student explained that she could "read the book about tooth decay and how income can affect that. But then to actually go out and put a face to that really did affect us."

Finally, students reported that service-learning had motivated them toward higher degree attainment, shown them a much greater range of employment options than presented in class or in textbooks, and confirmed their career choices before they graduated with the related degree.

If students were enthusiastic about service-learning, faculty were even more so. They reported that service-learning students learned the course content better than non-service-learners; they agreed with students that there were skills and knowledge that students learned that they would not otherwise have learned without service-learning; and they saw the benefits for both their students and themselves. As a business management instructor explained,

> I integrated service-learning for the first time as a self-preservation tool.... I got so tired of reading semester after semester about [the same well-known company]. I am pleased to have results in the classroom, but I'll be selfish too. My relationship is better with my students...you become a mentor for them as they learn these new life skills.

Additionally, faculty described how service-learning provided the unique benefit of allowing students to practice applying their academic knowledge. One instructor explained, "Learning takes place when the student is engaged with the subject and the concepts, and [sees] the direct application in the community and the civic engagement." Another instructor stated, "The great advantage of service-learning is that it's realistic. It's life itself happening." Faculty participants also believed that these benefits of service-learning motivated students to stay enrolled and go to class and, as students had told us, develop aspirations for higher degrees.

By the end of the 2006–2009 grant, students and faculty had described benefits of service-learning that went beyond the single academic learning outcomes focus we had planned to assess. The service-learning prism had begun to appear. In addition to civic engagement (one of the six learning outcomes and a benefit mentioned by students and faculty in focus groups), we heard about service-learning's benefits in career exploration and development, workforce preparation, personal development, social development, and college and course persistence when staying in school got tough.

Retention and Persistence

The final project we undertook focused on student retention and persistence. We defined retention as staying in a course from the beginning to the end of the semester, and persistence as semester-to-semester enrollment. To complete college, students must persist in their courses until degree or certificate attainment. Our research question for the 2009–2012 Horizons grant project was whether service-learning had an impact on students' retention or course completion, and students' persistence in college from one semester to the next. To assess this, we developed a survey crafted from the literature regarding the factors that put students most at risk for dropping out of college, as well as factors that have been found to motivate students to stay in college even when doing so becomes difficult.

We asked the new set of eight Horizons college project directors to administer the survey in courses with service-learning and in comparative courses that did not include service-learning. A total of 659 surveys were completed after two years: 527 by service-learners and 132 by non-service-learners. Analyses demonstrated that by the end of the course service-learners scored statistically higher on each of five retention-positive factors (see Prentice, Robinson, and Patton [2012] for specific details): commitment to obtaining educational goals, confidence of success in academics, connection with students, connection with faculty, and involvement in campus activities.

Unfortunately, Congress eliminated funding for Learn and Serve America in 2011, thus ending the Horizons program and preventing us from completing the third year of the study. Without this funding, we were unable to collect and analyze the actual retention and persistence rates of the students surveyed. Nonetheless, students' scores and focus group comments led us to conclude that there is a positive relationship between service-learning participation and retention and persistence.

In six focus groups, we asked students whether service-learning played a role in motivating them to stay in college. They told us three things. First, students responded that service-learning increased their confidence and motivation to learn. One student reported, "I've seen that I can do it, and I knew that I could finish this program." Another student explained, "Service-learning was such a rewarding experience... It made dropping out not an option."

Second, students told us that service-learning provided them with application and experience in ways that were impossible with just textbooks and lectures. For example, one student said, "When I'm taking a class now, I can see how it applies to the bigger picture. I'm just not being thrown information. I can actually take that and go... 'I understand that now.' It's neat to see the connectedness between your work and your studies."

Third, students told us that service-learning prepares them for employment and success in their careers. As one student illustrated, "Especially now that I'm approaching graduation and we're doing résumés, the service work is great. Nobody wants to give you a job unless you have experience, and service-learning is free experience." Another student said that, with service-learning, "we walk into a job competent and confident." One student felt so strongly about service-learning's benefits that she declared, "Everyone should have to do service-learning whether they want to or not. If you're not aware of what's out there, you're kind of going into college blind."

Yet again, in addition to the civic engagement and learning outcomes that were already appearing, more "colors" of the prism revealed themselves, this time with shades of workforce readiness, career development, self-confidence, and personal effectiveness.

Conclusion

It was at the end of the retention study, when we were reflecting back over the years of research, that we began to conceptualize service-learning as a prism. As we concluded in our final Horizons publication (Prentice, Robinson, and Patton 2012), "Service learning is an intervention that accomplishes many things in just one semester's experience" (24). The three studies that came out of the nine years of grant projects resulted in a total of 4,015 surveys and 21 focus groups. The trajectory began with a focus on community college service-learning and civic engagement, moved to learning outcomes, and finally to retention and persistence.

Over the course of our studies, we identified several different aspects of the service-learning prism: academic outcomes, civic engagement, community impact, community relationships, critical thinking, leadership development, personal effectiveness, retention and completion, social capital, and workforce development and job preparation. The breadth of the prism was confirmed in our conversations with students, faculty, staff, administrators, and community partners. Horizons faculty and staff overwhelmingly reported that the most valuable outcome of service-learning was increased student retention, followed by increased leadership and confidence among students. They also identified strategies that helped deepen their students' outcomes across the spectrum, such as communicating and working with diverse audiences; developing interdisciplinary service-learning opportunities; connecting with general education outcomes; focusing on social justice; and maintaining a limited number of deeper, more reciprocal service-learning community partnerships.

The experiences of Horizons participants at every level confirmed that service-learning encompasses more than just the traditional benefits to students and community. The key to broadening students' horizons is to align service-learning with larger initiatives and ideas, such as college-wide student success and completion efforts; program and institutional accreditation; workforce and economic development; and—perhaps most importantly—living in and contributing to a diverse democratic society.

Of course, circumstances differ from college to college and each institution has its own pathways and challenges. But given the variety of outcomes that the service-learning prism offers, there is no reason not to incorporate this pedagogy across the curriculum in every community college. It is not a matter of faculty not knowing how to teach with service-learning, as plenty of examples and training opportunities exist locally and online, and plenty of faculty are happy to show their colleagues how to get started. It is not a matter of funding, as most instructors decide on their own how they will teach their course objectives. It is certainly not a lack of willing partners, with so many community-based organizations and K-12 schools requesting help to meet their everyday needs. It is a matter of departmental and institutional focus: ensuring that students receive the best and most useful education possible and ensuring that local communities contribute to and benefit from the students' future.

One of the many things we learned is that in each of our studies, while we were focused on one specific outcome, students were reporting the development of multiple outcomes from a single experience. Service-learning is far more powerful than we first thought. The work of a prism is not to create colors but merely separate colors that are already there. This is what makes the analogy so much richer. Service-learning is not the creator of something from nothing; it is the catalyst for bringing out what already exists within us.

References

American Association of Community Colleges. 2013. *Community College Fast Facts*. http://www.aacc.nche.edu/AboutCC/Documents/2013facts_fold_revised.pdf.

Astin, Alexander W., Lori J. Vogelgesang, Elaine K. Ikeda, and Jennifer A. Yee. 2000. *How Service Learning Affects Students*. Los Angeles, CA: UCLA Higher Education Research Institute.

Billig, Shelley H. 2007. "Unpacking What Works in Service-Learning: Promising Research-Based Practices to Improve Student Outcomes." In *Growing to Greatness 2007: The State of Service-Learning*, edited by James C. Kielsmeier, Marybeth Neal, and Nathan Schultz. St. Paul, MN: National Youth Leadership Council.

Bringle, Robert G., Julie A. Hatcher, and Richard N. Muthiah. 2010. "The Role of Service-Learning on the Retention of First-Year Students to Second Year." *Michigan Journal of Community Service Learning* 16 (2): 38–49.

Chesbrough, Ronald D. 2011. "College Students and Service: A Mixed Methods Exploration of Motivations, Choices, and Learning Outcomes." *Journal of College Student Development* 52 (6): 687–705.

Eyler, Janet. 2009. "The Power of Experiential Education." *Liberal Education* 95 (4): 24–31.

Eyler, Janet, and Dwight E. Giles Jr. 1999. *Where's the Learning in Service-Learning?* San Francisco, CA: Jossey-Bass.

Eyler, Janet, Dwight E. Giles Jr., Christine M. Stenson, and Charlene J. Gray. 2001. *At a Glance: What We Know about the Effects of Service-Learning on College Students, Faculty, Institutions and Communities, 1993–2000*. Nashville, TN: Vanderbilt University. 3rd ed. http://www.compact.org/resources/downloads/aag.pdf.

Felten, Peter, and Patti H. Clayton. 2012. "Service-Learning." In *Evidence-Based Teaching: New Directions for Teaching and Learning* (no. 128), edited by William Buskist and James E. Groccia. San Francisco, CA: Jossey-Bass.

Gottlieb, Karla, and Gail Robinson, eds. 2006. *A Practical Guide for Integrating Civic Responsibility into the Curriculum*. Washington, DC: American Association of Community Colleges. 2nd ed.

Keup, Jennifer R. 2005/2006. "The Impact of Curricular Interventions on Intended Second Year Re-enrollment." *Journal of College Student Retention: Research, Theory & Practice* 7 (1–2): 61–89.

Kuh, George D. 2008. *High-Impact Educational Practices: What They Are, Who Has Access to Them, and Why They Matter*. Washington, DC: Association of American Colleges and Universities.

Novak, Julie M., Vern Markey, and Mike Allen. 2007. "Evaluating Cognitive Outcomes of Service Learning in Higher Education: A Meta-Analysis." *Communication Research Reports* 24 (2): 149–157.

Prentice, Mary. 2002. *Institutionalizing Service Learning in Community Colleges*. Washington, DC: American Association of Community Colleges.

Prentice, Mary, and Gail Robinson. 2007. *Linking Service Learning and Civic Engagement in Community College Students*. Washington, DC: American Association of Community Colleges.

Prentice, Mary, and Gail Robinson. 2010. *Improving Student Learning Outcomes with Service Learning*. Washington, DC: American Association of Community Colleges.

Prentice, Mary, Gail Robinson, and Madeline Patton. 2012. *Cultivating Community beyond the Classroom*. Washington, DC: American Association of Community Colleges.

Robinson, Gail, and Lynn Barnett. 1996. *Service Learning and Community Colleges: Where We Are*. Washington, DC: American Association of Community Colleges.

Taggart, Amanda, and Gloria Crisp. 2011. "Service Learning at Community Colleges: Synthesis, Critique, and Recommendations for Future Research." *Journal of College Reading and Learning* 42 (1): 24–44.

Tinto, Vincent. 1997. "Classrooms as Communities: Exploring the Educational Character of Student Persistence." *Journal of Higher Education* 68: 599–623.

Walker, Toby. 2000. "The Service/Politics Split: Rethinking Service to Teach Political Engagement." *PS: Political Science and Politics* 33 (3): 647–649.

Warren, Jami L. 2012. "Does Service-Learning Increase Student Learning? A Meta-Analysis." *Michigan Journal of Community Service Learning* 18 (2): 56–61.

Yeh, Theresa Ling. 2010. "Service-Learning and Persistence of Low-Income, First-Generation College Students: An Exploratory Study." *Michigan Journal of Community Service Learning* 16 (2): 50–56.

CHAPTER 11

Service-Learning's Role in Achieving Institutional Outcomes: Engagement, Learning, and Achievement

Yao Zhang Hill, Tanya Renner, Francisco Acoba, Krista Hiser, and Robert W. Franco

Kapi'olani Community College (KCC) is a medium-sized urban public community college that has been developing a cycle of pedagogical innovation, implementation, and evaluation in service-learning since 1995 (Franco forthcoming; 2010; 2007; 2002; Axlund and Renner 2010; Renner 2008, 2007, 2003; Baratian, Duffy, Franco, Hendricks, and Renner 2007; Renner and Bush 1997).+ In this chapter, we show how this community college organizes and utilizes internal service-learning research to form a coherent understanding of the relationship between service-learning and student success. We refer to our multifaceted evaluation framework as the KELA—Kapi'olani Engagement, Learning, and Achievement—model.

We begin this chapter with an introduction to KCC, a description of our service-learning program, and an explanation of the KELA model. Then we discuss service-learning evaluation research in higher education. Finally, we report on research we conducted to evaluate the relationship between service-learning and student success within the KELA model of engagement, learning, and achievement. We organize our *engagement* investigation around two questions: (1) Are service-learners more engaged in their academic career than non-service-learners? (2) Are service-learners more sensitive to social justice and diversity than non-service-learners? We address *learning* with the question: (3) How well do participating students achieve service-learning outcomes? We address *achievement* with the question: (4) Do service-learning students have higher academic achievement than non-service-learners? We conclude with suggestions for future programmatic evaluation on service-learning, especially in community colleges.

Institutional Background

The College

Located on the slopes of Diamond Head, on the island of O'ahu, in urban Honolulu, KCC is the second largest of ten public higher education institutions in the University of Hawai'i (UH) system, with an enrollment of 8,376 in fall 2013. The college serves diverse ethnic groups. Native Hawaiian students are the largest ethnic group on the campus (18 percent). Students of diverse Asian ethnic backgrounds (Japanese, Chinese, Korean, Vietnamese, other) comprise 41 percent of the student population; mixed race, Pacific Islanders, and "other" students comprise 28 percent of the student population; and racially Caucasian students make up 13 percent of the student population. International students account for 8 percent of the student population. The college provides nationally competitive liberal arts and career programs including Nursing, Health Science, Hospitality, Culinary, Pre-Education, and Science, Technology, Engineering, and Math (STEM). Our strategic plan is designed around an "ecology of learning" framework in which the community is situated close to the center of the student-learning environment. The ecology of learning framework (Franco 2010, 16) promotes ongoing awareness of our role in communities both on and off-campus.

The Kapi'olani Service-Learning Program (KSLP) is designed to ameliorate pressing problems in the community through issue-based, interdisciplinary pathways in education, environment, health, long-term care, intercultural perspectives, art, history, and culture. These pathways ensure that students will (1) have the opportunity to deepen their understanding of specific issues; (2) be encouraged to continue their service-learning across multiple semesters and thus have time to become more deeply engaged with a given community; (3) provide increasingly skilled service to a given community; and (4) develop career-relevant skills.

The KSLP is grounded in choice: first faculty members *choose* to offer service-learning, then students *choose* service-learning as an option within the course, and together, students and faculty work with the KSLP to *choose* an appropriate pathway and community partner for their service. Nearly 100 service-learning course sections are offered each semester, and 250–300 students complete 25 hours of service-learning in those classes. The program is managed by a full-time outreach coordinator, who supervises six to ten paid student pathway leaders, facilitates student service-learning experience, and assists with data tracking. In addition, there are two faculty coordinators who receive release time to oversee faculty development, ongoing pedagogical improvement, and the learning-outcomes assessment process. In addition, a service-learning leadership team, comprising staff, faculty, and student leaders, assesses student reflection essays each semester.

The KSLP's pedagogical approach is grounded in Vygotsky's (1978) constructivist theory and principles, which focuses on the role of social interaction in the development of cognition and emphasizes that learning is enhanced through scaffolding and social interaction during a problem-solving process. Structured service-learning experiences, social interaction, and reflection are all needed in order to discover connections between new information and prior personal experiences. To maximize the learning potential for our service-learning students, the KSLP is guided by principles for effective pedagogy derived from a large study of pedagogical practices

Table 11.1 Seven Principles for Effective Pedagogy and KSLP Aligned Practices

Seven Principles for Effective Pedagogy	KSLP Aligned Practices In KSLP Students Are Encouraged or Asked to:
1. Learning with understanding is facilitated when knowledge is related to and structured around major concepts and principles of a discipline.	apply knowledge and skills learned in the classroom to their service-learning experiences and then asked to reflect on the connection;
2. A learner's prior knowledge is the starting point for effective learning.	draw upon prior knowledge to make meaning of their service-learning experience;
3. Metacognitive learning (self-monitoring) is important for acquiring proficiency.	self-monitor and use other metacognitive forms of learning through reflective writing;
4. Recognizing differences among learners is important.	choose site and service based on their own academic and career interests and make own interpretations of the experience;
5. Learners' beliefs about their ability to learn affect learning success.	analyze and solve programs in a real-world environment and see their own impact of their actions; and
6. Practices and activities in which people engage shape what is learned.	work together with community partners, service recipients, other students, and faculty, in which social interactions enhance and shape learning.

(National Research Council [2002]). Table 11.1 lists these principles and shows how KSLP practices are aligned with them.

We also recognize the importance of critically assessing the learning that occurs and providing additional scaffolding for students as needed (Schweitzer and Stephenson 2008). We guide the KSLP based on evidence obtained from regular qualitative and quantitative assessment of our intended learning outcomes. This "data-driven" strategy has evolved over the life of the program.

Initial assessment or evaluation efforts were limited to data tracking (e.g., number of students, hours served, the number of faculty, course sections, community partners). Faculty later used surveys, student reflections, and institutional data to investigate student personal development, social understanding, and academic success in the form of GPA and retention rates (Renner and Hasager 2004; Renner 2003). In the current phase, the assessment work is guided by the KELA model, which focuses our efforts on engagement, learning, and achievement. We assess academic engagement using the Community College Survey of Student Engagement (CCSSE); learning through rubric evaluation of end-of-semester capstone essays; and academic achievement through the tracking of students' successful course completion, re-enrollment rate, and graduation/transfer rates.

Literature Review

Community colleges are in a unique position to be on the cutting edge of the service-learning paradigm (Elwell and Bean 2001), since their very mission emphasizes the role of the institution in serving the community (Taggart and Crisp 2011). A large body of service-learning research attests to its effectiveness in promoting students' academic, cognitive, personal, and social development, evidenced in research reviews and meta-analyses (Yorio and Ye 2012; Celio, Durlak, and Dymnicki 2011; Conway, Amel, and Gerwien 2009; Eyler, Giles, Stenson, and Gray 2001). For example, Eyler, Giles, Stenson, and Gray (2001) reviewed 76 research studies published between 1993 and 2000 that investigated the effect of service-learning on student-related outcomes. This body of research provided evidence that service-learning is positively associated with students' personal, social, and learning outcome achievement, career development, and relationship with the institution.

A recent meta-analysis by Yorio and Ye (2012) showed a medium-sized effect on students' cognitive development and a small effect on students' understanding of social issues and personal insights. The result confirmed previous findings in a meta-analysis conducted by Celio, Durlak, and Dymnicki (2011) that examined the effect of service-learning in both the K-12 and higher education settings. Their findings showed that service-learning had more of an effect on academic achievement than on other outcomes (attitudes toward self, school, and learning; civic engagement; and social skills), though all the effects were small. Conway, Amel, and Gerwien (2009) found that service-learning has a small but significant effect on personal, social, and citizenship outcomes in K-12, higher education, and adult/mixed education settings.

However, most of these meta-analyses focus on a four-year college setting; service-learning research in community college settings is still lacking. In Eyler et al. (2001), only 7 percent of the studies in the review focused on community colleges, and no studies included in the three other meta-analyses indicate a community college setting. Therefore their findings may not be generalizable to community colleges. As McClenney (2007) correctly stated:

> Community colleges, we all know, are diverse institutions that serve remarkably diverse student populations. These students typically contend with competing priorities – juggling jobs, family responsibilities, financial struggles, and community commitments along with their academic endeavors. (vii)

These unique conditions call for a specific body of service-learning assessment and evaluation research situated in a community college context at community colleges.

Taggart and Crisp (2011) brought to light 17 empirical studies of service-learning at community colleges. Through their review, they concluded a positive association between service-learning and civic involvement, perceived personal benefits, and application of knowledge. They found mixed effects of service-learning on student success as indicated by course completion, grades, or students' decisions to persist.

Many of the studies in their review were limited to samples from one or just a few classes. A majority relied heavily on locally developed survey instruments with unknown reliability and validity information. No studies reported results of rater consistency or procedures to reduce bias in reflection journal or essay evaluation. Only a few studies investigated student academic engagement (Gallini and Moely 2003) and academic achievement in terms of retention, transfer, and graduation

(Prentice 2009; Hodge et al. 2001). None of the studies reviewed by Taggart and Crisp investigated all three of the KELA success domains: engagement, learning, and academic achievement.

Engaging the KELA Model at KCC: Implementation and Analysis

At KCC, four studies were conducted following the evaluation framework of KELA. Study 1 compared service-learning and non-service-learning students' academic engagement using the Community College Survey of Student Engagement (CCSSE) benchmark scores. Study 2 examined service-learning and non-service-learning students' personal grown in such areas as self-esteem and sensitivity to social justice and diversity using a pre- and post-course evaluation with a locally developed survey. Study 3 investigated service-learning students' learning outcomes using rubric-based assessment of capstone essays. Study 4 used institutional data to compare service-learning and non-service-learning students' course success rates, next-semester re-enrollment rates, and graduation/transfer rates. These studies are described in turn.

Study 1: Measuring Engagement Outcomes Using CCSSE Benchmark Areas

Research Question
Are service-learners more engaged in their academic career than non-service-learners?

Instrument
CCSSE is a national survey that aims to measure areas of student engagement associated with student success in community colleges (www.ccsse.org). CCSSE survey items have five benchmark areas: active and collaborative learning (ACL); student effort (SE); academic challenge (AC); student-faculty interaction (SFI); and student support (SS). Each area consists of about ten items.

Participants
Every other even-numbered year, a set of randomly selected classes at KCC participate in CCSSE. This study included data from 1,739 nonduplicated survey respondents in the two most recent cohorts: 2010 and 2012. Among these respondents, 40 percent were service-learners and 60 percent were non-service-learners.

Analysis
The service-learners in this study were defined as respondents who self-reported as participating in community projects as part of a regular class sometimes, often, or very often on CCSSE Item 4.i. Self-identified nonparticipants were considered non-service-learners. These two groups were compared on their raw benchmark scores (RBS) in the five benchmark areas, while controlling for self-reported demographic background (i.e., gender, age, ELL status) and academic background (i.e., GPA range, and total earned credits). For the purpose of analysis, each CCSSE benchmark item score is rescaled from 0 to 1, called rescaled score. RBS are the average of the item rescaled scores under each benchmark. The RBS for ACL was recalculated with Item 4.i removed. Five general linear model (GLM) regression analyses were conducted

in SAS 9.3 with one RBS as an outcome variable at a time. For example, the GLM equation for the ACL outcome can be written out as:

ACL = Intercept + Gender + Age Group + ESL + GPA + Total Credits + Service-Learning.

Due to the exploratory nature of the study, the significance level was kept at alpha = .05.

Results

All five GLM regression models were statistically significant. The models account for 12.9 percent, 5.4 percent, 5.9 percent, 11.0 percent, and 4.1 percent of the variance in the five outcomes, respectively. In all five models, participating in service-learning showed a statistically significant positive relationship with the engagement outcomes. After controlling for participants' demographics and academic background, service-learning respondents scored 10.7 percent higher on the recalculated ACL benchmark (with the item related to service-learning participation removed), 5.4 percent higher on SE, 6.1 percent higher on AC, 10.8 percent higher on SFI, and 4.5 percent higher on SS. The service-learners seemed to be more engaged than non-service-learners, most evidently in ACL and SFI.

Discussion

Regarding the results on ACL, we believe that service-learners are more actively engaged in learning because they are presented with real-world problems that create a demand for deeper levels of thinking, knowledge seeking, and application. At KCC, the finding that service-learners reported more interaction with faculty also came as no surprise. Students interact with service-learning faculty and staff in and outside of classroom, in the field and community, and through one-on-one in-person communication and feedback on reflection journals. These activities all translate into a higher student-faculty interaction compared with non-service-learners.

Study 2: Measuring Sense of Social Responsibility through Survey

Research Question

Are service-learners more sensitive to social justice and diversity than non-service-learners?

Instrument

We used a locally developed survey instrument that measures understanding of social justice (eight items, adopted from Moely et al. 2002) and attitude toward diversity (five items, Renner 2003). A pre-course survey and a post-course survey were administered in 23 service-learning classes in spring 2012.

Participants

In spring 2012, 512 students took the pre-course survey and 383 students took the post-course survey. The analysis used 102 students with matching IDs on the pre- and post-course surveys. Among them, 28 were self-identified service-learners in that semester and 74 were non-service-learners.

Analysis
After removing one item found detrimental to the reliability of the pre-course survey, the Cronbach Alpha reliability was 0.57 on the social justice scale and 0.64 on the understanding of diversity scale. While relatively low, these values prove acceptable for further analysis.

Twelve two-way repeated measures of ANOVAs were conducted on each of the survey item scores using the Proc Mixed procedure in SAS 9.3. The between-group main effect is the group (service-learners vs. non-service-learners). The within-group main effect is the survey (pre-course survey versus post-course survey). The interaction effect is the group by survey. The interaction effect tells us whether the pre- to post survey rating change is significantly different between the two groups. The significance levels were set at alpha = .05 due to the exploratory nature of the study.

Results
Significant interaction results were found in two items; both were on the social justice scale. On these two items, the service-learners showed improved sensitivity, more than the non-service-learners. On the item "in order for problems to be solved, we need to change public policy," the average service-learning respondent scored 3.46 on the post-course survey ($SD = 0.96$), higher than on the pre-course survey ($M = 3.04, SD = 0.74$). The non-service-learners scored 3.50 ($SD = 0.80$) on the post-course survey, almost no change compared to their pre-course survey scores ($M = 3.58, SD = 0.88$). The change difference between the two groups was statistically significant, $F(1, 100) = 5.26, p = .02$.

On the second social justice item "we need to institute reforms within the current system to change our communities," the service-learners improved in their average score on this item by the end of the semester, from 3.52 ($SD = 0.80$) to 3.71 ($SD = 0.71$), but the non-service-learners showed a slight decline by the end of the semester, from 3.81 ($SD = 0.70$) to 3.65 ($SD = 0.75$), resulting in a significant interaction effect, $F(1, 99) = 4.59, p = .03$.

Discussion
It is interesting to observe that the service-learners had a lower-level understanding of social justice measured by these two items at the beginning of the course compared to non-service-learners. Still, the increase in understanding reflected in higher ratings at the end of the semester may be due to participation in the KSLP. For example, every semester, over 100 students are exposed to Native Hawaiian land issues and issues of capitalism and development. Dozens of students work with children in poverty in nearby public housing. Through working with the people they served and community partners, it is quite likely that they gained a deeper understanding that inequality is more of a structural issue at the societal level than an issue of culture differences or individual fault.

There was no difference between service-learners and non-service-learners on understanding of diversity, which relates to the global understanding and citizenship outcome defined by American Association of Community Colleges. This finding is consistent with Prentice and Robinson (2010) who found no statistical difference between service-learners and non-service-learners on this outcome. Different service activities undoubtedly lead to different learning. It is possible that when service-learners have a more interactive role with the people or communities they serve, they develop a deeper understanding of cultural differences and others' perspectives. For example, Gutheil et al. (2006) found that after service-learners conducted one-on-one personal interviews with elderly individuals, learning about their life and perspectives, the learners experienced important positive shifts in attitudes and perceptions about older adults, combating prevailing stereotypes. Providing opportunities for meaningful personal interaction between service-learners and the people they serve may help improve this outcome.

Study 3: Measuring Learning Outcomes through Rubric-Based Assessment of Capstone Essays

Research Question

How well do service-learners achieve KSLP student learning outcomes (SLOs) by the end of the service-learning course?

Instrument

The assessment instrument is a four-page end-of-semester essay that fulfills both service-learning program and course requirements. Each essay has the following outcome components: (1) Problem: statement of the social problem that the student has helped to ameliorate; (2) Learning: course concepts that were applied in service-learning; (3) Change: change in point of view about the community served; (4) Goal: the students' future academic/career goals; and (5) Affect: the development or change of values as a result of the service-learning participation.[1]

Outcome 1 is related to critical thinking skills that evaluate whether students are able to identify and describe the social problem and articulate how they contributed to the solution. Outcome 2 is an academic development outcome that asks students to articulate how they applied course knowledge to solve real-world problems. Outcome 3 is related to global understanding and citizenship. Outcome 4 is about career and academic goal setting. Outcome 5 is a noncognitive outcome that focuses on personal insights and transformation. Students' essays are evaluated each semester using a five-dimension rubric with five levels of performance from Level 0 to Level 4. Level 1 demonstrates emerging evidence of critical thinking. Level 2 indicates that students can substantiate their arguments with examples and illustrations. Although a score of 1 demonstrates meeting minimum competencies on the outcomes, Level 2 is our target based on various early attempts to assess general education outcomes.[2]

Participants

Every semester, about 10 percent of the over 300 student reflection essays collected as part of the KSLP are randomly selected for the SLO assessment. We include the results of 60 essays from the most recent two semesters, fall 2012 and spring 2013, in this study.

Fifteen raters score the essays each semester; three raters for each of the five dimensions. Raters go through a training and score-norming procedure led by the assessment coordinator. Raters discuss their scores for each essay, agreeing on a final score. (If the raters cannot agree, the lower score is taken.) The norming at the start and the discussion during the assessment promote consistency.

Results

Table 11.2 SLO Results for Fall 2012 and Spring 2013 Cohorts (*n* = 60)

		Problem	*Learning*	*Change*	*Goals*	*Affect*
Mean Score (standard deviation)	Fall 2012	0.9 (0.9)	1.9 (0.9)	1.1 (1.3)	1.5 (1.1)	1.9 (1.2)
	Spring 2013	2.0 (1.2)	1.3 (0.8)	1.9 (1.4)	1.3 (1.1)	1.6 (1.0)
	Overall	1.5 (1.2)	1.6 (0.9)	1.5 (1.4)	1.4 (1.1)	1.8 (1.1)
% with minimum competency	Fall 2012	63	97	53	83	87
	Spring 2013	83	87	90	73	87
	Overall	73	92	72	78	87
% Meeting Target	Fall 2012	23	63	40	33	63
	Spring 2013	73	40	43	37	47
	Overall	48	52	42	35	55

Analysis

Table 11.2 presents the results of service-learning SLO assessment for the fall 2012 and spring 2013 cohorts. The performance was not consistent across the two investigated semesters. The overall (*n* = 60) mean scores are above 1, the minimum competency level, but the variation among students is very large, with standard deviations ranging from 0.9 to 1.4. While none of the mean scores reached the target level of 2 in this year's assessment, scores on Learning and Affect are very close to 2 in fall 2012 and scores on Problem and Change are close to 2 in spring 2013. When looking at percentages meeting minimum competency, overall, about three quarters of service-learners reached this level on critical thinking (SLO One: Problem), global understanding and citizenship (SLO Three: Change), and academic/career goal setting/adjustment (SLO Four: Goals). A high percentage of service-learners reported knowledge application (SLO Two: Learning) in their service (92 percent) and experienced personal sights/transformation (SLO Five: Affect) (87 percent). Lower percentages of learners met the target level, with the lowest achievement areas being global understanding and citizenship (SLO Three: Change) and academic/career goal setting/adjustment (SLO Four).

Discussion

Perhaps the small sampling percentage (10 percent) and diverse student background (e.g., courses taken, sites served, academic preparation) may account for the variation in performance across semesters. The relatively low achievement on global understanding and citizenship was consistent with our finding in the survey project (Study 2) and the finding in Prentice and Robinson (2010). The lower achievement on academic/career goal setting/adjustment is affirmed by Hodge et al. (2001), who found that only between 30 to 40 percent of the service-learning survey respondents at Collin County Community College reported that service-learning affected their career plans and major selection (i.e., they questioned, confirmed, or changed the plan). One possibility is to arrange more personal interaction with the people/community served. For example, a 20-minute interview of an immigrant's life in the United States can help students recognize immigrant contribution to the society to a greater extent; a short meeting with the staff talking about essential job skills and main duties can help students form more concrete ideas of personal/academic improvement needs and career interest.

Study 4: Measuring Academic Achievement through Course Success, Re-Enrollment, and Graduation Rates

Research Question
Do the service-learners have higher academic achievement than non-service-learners, as measured by successful course completion, next-semester re-enrollment, and transfer/certificate/graduation rates?

Instrument
The data used for analysis are from the service-learning tracking system that provides service-learning enrollment data and from the student data warehouse where institutional data (e.g., enrollment, GPA) are recorded.

Participants
The service-learners in the study were from fall 2010, spring 2011, and fall 2011 semesters. The number of service-learners is 343, 292, and 284 in the three semesters, respectively, with an average of 304. The comparison group comprised non-service-learners who enrolled in the same classes but did not choose the service-learning option. The average number of non-service-learners is 1215 per semester, and 1355, 1131, and 1159 in each of the three semesters, respectively.

Analysis
The study examined the following rates between service-learners and non-service-learners: (1) the successful course completion (C or better) rate in all the courses; (2) the next-semester re-enrollment rate; and (3) graduation/transfer rates between the service-learners and non-service-learners. The graduation status was obtained in spring 2012 and the transfer status in fall 2012. The three indicators were calculated for each semester, and then averaged.

Results
The three-semester average showed that compared with the non-service-learners in the service-learning offering classes, the service-learners had a higher course success rate (88.9 percent out of a total of 1,031 grades granted) in the service-learning semester than non-service learners (64.9 percent out of 2,729 grades given). Even though the service-learners in general were more successful students, with a pre-service-learning-semester overall success rate at 86.9 percent, compared with the non-service learners (72.6 percent), service-learners maintained their success in the service-learning semester, while non-service-learners had a decrease in their success rate.

Regarding performance in developmental courses, by examining the average success rates across three semesters, we found that among 47 grades that service-learners received, 79.7 percent were successful grades. In comparison, of 171 grades received by non-service-learners, only 58.4 percent were successful. Again, service-learners maintained and continued their success from the previous semester (80.5 percent), whereas non-service-learners' success rate had decreased from the previous semester (65.2 percent).

The three-semester average next-semester reenrollment rate was higher for the service-learners (76.1 percent) than it was for the non-service-learners (61.0 percent). The service-learners also had higher graduation/transfer rates (13.1 percent) than the non-service-learners (10.5 percent). This pattern holds true for students in each semester.

Discussion
When examining the success of service-learning students, we need to consider the self-selection issue—more successful students seemed to choose service-learning components in the course than non-service-learners. However, given that the service-learners maintained their success in the service-learning semester, while non-service-learners had decreased success in all the courses as well as in the developmental courses, it is our interpretation that through service-learning experience students are exposed to enhanced learning conditions that lead to increased success.

Conclusion

To evaluate service-learning and its relationship with student success, KCC used the KELA institutional effectiveness model to investigate the *engagement* of service-learners and non-service learners on CCSSE benchmarks (Study 1), the *learning* (i.e., cognitive and noncognitive outcomes) for service-learners after their service experience, using previously validated survey questions and student reflection essays scored using a rubric (Study 2 and Study 3); and academic *achievement* of service-learners and non-service-learners through course success, reenrollment, and graduation rates (Study 4).

Results indicate that service-learners were more engaged than non-service-learners, especially in areas of active and collaborative learning and student-faculty interaction, even with demographic and academic background variables held constant. The service-learners in the study had higher course success rates and maintained their success better from the previous semester in all courses, including developmental courses, in comparison with non-service-learners. The service-learners also had a higher next-semester reenrollment rate and graduation/transfer rate than non-service-learners.

For learning outcomes, service-learning respondents showed greater improvement in understanding of social justice on two out of seven survey items than non-service respondents. The results of the service-learners' reflection essays showed that a majority of the service-learners met the minimum competencies for critical thinking, knowledge application, global understanding and citizenship, academic/career goal setting/adjustment, and personal insight/transformation (fall 2012 and spring 2013). Yet, less than 80 percent of the study students achieved the target level in any of the outcomes in either semester. Since global understanding and citizenship and academic/career goal setting/adjustment were the two outcomes that had the lowest percentage of service-learners meeting the target, these will receive the most attention in program improvement.

The studies were designed and implemented within institutional and data constraints. Despite our effort to control for student background variables (Study 1) and prior academic performance (Study 4), identifying control groups (Study 1, 2, and 4), using pre- and post-course survey strategies (Study 2), and using rubric and training to ensure rater objectivity and consistency (Study 3), we recognize limitations in our studies. First, the student participants in these studies were not from the same cohort and not all studies used random sampling. This makes the results hard to generalize across cohorts. Second, it is possible that the service-learning students in the study were already engaged and successful learners.

Despite these and other limitations, this research provides positive evidence in favor of service-learning as an effective educational practice at the community colleges. We attribute the success of KSLP to the practices developed based on effective pedagogical principles, as well as social support provided by the service-learning coordinator, student leaders, and interdisciplinary faculty working collaboratively to ameliorate real community problems. Further, the urgency of these problems provides a compelling context for students' coursework. Students want to construct a learning experience that engages real-world issues and sharpens their focus on academic and career goals. Multisemester service pathways scaffold courses across the general education program and connect students to a strong structure of community partnerships. Relevance and urgency drive greater student engagement for their own success.

We suspect that service-learning works for students who are already engaged and successful. Moving forward, our action involves extending service-learning to less engaged students who do not choose service-learning, focusing on the potential of service-learning as a pedagogical strategy for developmental and first-year courses, while building leadership skills in students who join service-learning in multiple semesters or across multiple courses.

We believe the KELA model will serve as a useful evaluation framework for community colleges. First, much of the data employed in the framework—like the CCSSE data on engagement and institutional achievement data—are readily available. Second, the framework allows examination of service-learning effectiveness using indicators that matter most to student success. The KELA model makes the conclusions more actionable. Meanwhile, the results from multiple sources and perspectives suggest solutions for improvement that may elude a single study. To advance the KELA model for service-learning evaluation at KCC, we plan to evaluate the same cohort of students for all three domains: engagement, learning, and achievement. Since we started collecting student IDs on CCSSE, we can now use students' actual service-learning status, rather than their self-reported status, to evaluate engagement outcomes. We also plan to compare the results from multiple cohorts to ensure the generalizability of the conclusions.

By focusing on engagement, learning, and academic achievement outcomes through the KELA model, KCC is able to evaluate service-learning on the outcomes that matter most to student success. The KELA model brings together disparate internal research and assessment of service-learning to form a more coherent picture of the positive association between service-learning and student success. The overall results have driven continuous improvement on campus, promoting service-learning as an effective pedagogy and positioning the college to leverage both external funding and internal resources to support KSLP. The college strives to utilize both internal and external resources to continue to improve service-learning evaluation methods within the KELA model.

Notes

1. For details see the KCC Office for Institutional Effectiveness web page at: http://ofie.kapiolani.Hawaii.edu
2. See a sample rubric http://ofie.kapiolani.hawaii.edu/wp-content/uploads/2013/01/Gen_Ed_Slos_WITH_AACU_ELOS_AND_S-L_ALIGNMENT.revised.docx.

References

Axlund, R., and T. Renner. 2010. "Faculty Engagement in Service Learning and Community-Based Research: A Seven State Snapshot." Poster presented at the American Association of Colleges & Universities' Faculty Roles in High-Impact Practices Conference in Philadelphia, Pennsylvania.

Baratian, M., D. Duffy, R. Franco, A. Hendricks, and T. Renner. 2007. *Service-Learning Course Design for Community Colleges*. Providence, RI: Campus Compact.

Celio, C. I., J. Durlak, and A. Dymnicki. 2011. "A Meta-Analysis of the Impact of Service-Learning on Students." *Journal of Experiential Education* 34 (2): 164–181.

Center for Community College Student Engagement. 2013. *A Matter of Degrees: Engaging Practices, Engaging Students: High-Impact Practices for Community College Student Engagement*. Austin: The University of Texas at Austin, Community College Leadership Program.

Conway, J. M., E. L. Amel, and D. P. Gerwien. 2009. "Teaching and Learning in the Social Context: A Meta-Analysis of Service Learning's Effects on Academic, Personal, Social, and Citizenship Outcomes." *Teaching of Psychology* 36 (4): 233–245.

Elwell, M. D., and M. S. Bean. 2001. "Editors' Choice: The Efficacy of Service-Learning for Community College ESL Students." *Community College Review* 28 (4): 7–61.

Eyler, J., D. E. Giles Jr., C. M. Stenson, and C. J. Gray. 2001. *At a Glance: What We Know about the Effects of Service-Learning on College Students, Faculty, Institutions and Communities, 1993–2000*. Nashville, TN: Vanderbilt University. http://ewucommunityengagement.pbworks.com/w/file/fetch/62951195/aag.pdf.

Franco, R. W. 2002. "The Civic Role of Community Colleges: Preparing Students for the Work of Democracy." *Journal of Public Affairs*, Supplement 1, 6. Reprinted by Campus Compact.

———. 2007. "The Next Nexus: Classroom and Community, Community and World; Democracy Collaborative." *The Anchor Dashboard: Aligning Institutional Practice to Meet Low-Income Community Needs*. Takoma Park, MD: Campus Compact.

———. 2010. "Faculty Engagement in the Community Colleges: Constructing a New Ecology of Learning." In *Handbook of Engaged Scholarship: Contemporary Landscapes, Future Directions*, edited by H. Fitzgerald, C. Burack, and S. Seifer, 149–163. East Lansing: Michigan State University Press.

———. (forthcoming). *Discourses of Civic and Community Engagement*. Honolulu, HI: Asia-Pacific Higher Education Research Program.

Gallini, S. M., and B. E. Moely. 2003. "Service-Learning and Engagement, Academic Challenge, and Retention." *Michigan Journal of Community Service Learning* 10: 5–14.

Gutheil, I. A., R. H. Chernesky, and M. L. Sherratt. 2006. "Influencing Student Attitudes toward Older Adults: Results of a Service-Learning Collaboration." *Educational Gerontology* 32 (9): 771–784.

Hodge, T. L., K. Kramer, and R. Hughes. 2001. "Collaboration for Excellence: Engaged Scholarship at Collin County Community College." *Community College Journal of Research and Practice* 25 (9): 675–690.

Kuh, G. D. 2008. *High-Impact Educational Practices: What They Are, Who Has Access to Them, and Why They Matter.* Washington, DC: Association of American Colleges and Universities.

McClenney, K. M. 2007. "Forward: On the Purposeful Engagement of Community College Students." In *Service-Learning Course Design for Community Colleges*, edited by M.Baratian, D. K. Duffy, R. Franco, A. Hendricks, and T. Renner. Providence, RI: Campus Compact.

Moely, B. E., S. H. Mercer, V. Ilustre, D. Miron, and M. McFarland. 2002. "Psychometric Properties and Correlates of the Civic Attitudes and Skills Questionnaire (CASQ): A Measure of Students' Attitudes Related to Service-Learning." *Michigan Journal of Community Service Learning* 8 (2): 15–26.

National Research Council. 2002. *Learning and Understanding: Improving Advanced Study of Mathematics and Science in U.S. High Schools.* Washington, DC: National Academy Press.

Prentice, M. 2009. "Service-Learning's Impact on Developmental Reading/Writing and Student Life Skills Courses." *Community College Journal of Research and Practice* 33 (3–4): 270–282.

Prentice, M., and G. Robinson. 2010. *Improving Student Learning Outcomes with Service Learning.* American Association of Community Colleges. http://ceas.calstatela.edu/wp-content/uploads/2010/07/Student-Learning-and-Service-Learning.pdf.

Renner, T. 2003. "Converging Data: Demonstrating Service Learning Effectiveness on Our Campus." Paper presented at the Third International Conference on Service-Learning Research, Salt Lake City, Utah.

———. 2007. "Assessment: Service Learning and Indigenous Communities Forum." Paper presented at the 10th Annual Continuums of Service Conference, San Jose, CA.

———. 2008. "Authentic Assessment of Those Essential Thinking Skills That You Know Your Service Learners Are Developing." Paper presented at the 11th Annual Continuums of Service Conference, Portland, OR.

Renner, T., and M. Bush, eds. 1997. *Evaluation and Assessment in Service-Learning.* Mesa, AZ: Campus Compact National Center for Community Colleges.

Renner, T., and U. Hasager. 2004. "Service Learning and Depth of Understanding." Paper presented at the Seventh Annual Continuums of Service Conference, San Diego, CA.

Schweitzer, L., and M. Stephenson. 2008. "Charting the Challenges and Paradoxes of Constructivism: A View from Professional Education." *Teaching in Higher Education* 13: 583–593.

Taggart, A., and G. Crisp. 2011. "Service Learning at Community Colleges: Synthesis, Critique, and Recommendations for Future Research." *Journal of College Reading and Learning* 42 (1): 24–44.

Vygotsky, L. 1978. *Mind in Society.* Translated by M. Cole. Cambridge: Harvard University Press.

Yorio, P., and F. Ye. 2012. "A Meta-Analysis on the Effects of Service-Learning on the Social, Personal, and Cognitive Outcomes of Learning." *Academy of Management Learning & Education* 11 (1): 9–27.

Weglarz, S. G., and J. A. Seybert. 2004. "Participant Perceptions of a Community College Service-Learning Program." *Community College Journal of Research & Practice* 28 (2): 123–132.

PART IV

Service-Learning as Community and Community College Nexus

CHAPTER 12

Community College Service-Learning Programs: The Well-Traveled Path to Civic Engagement

Mary Prentice

How does service-learning impact civic engagement in community college students? To what extent is it mediated by multiple service-learning experiences? In what, if any, areas of civic engagement are these impacts most profound? In order to investigate these three research questions, surveys measuring civic engagement levels were developed and administered to community college students who participated in service-learning and those who did not. These surveys were administered in courses at eight community colleges each semester for two years.

To best contextualize and address the questions posed above, this chapter will begin with a review of the literature on civic engagement, community colleges, and service-learning. Following a description of the methods used in the study and an analysis of survey data, the chapter will conclude with conclusions, limitations, and suggestions for future research.

Literature Review

The scholarship on civic engagement in higher education reveals a debate about what "civic engagement" even means. In one camp are scholars who commit to the definition of civic engagement as direct political involvement. In the other camp are scholars who commit to the definition of civic engagement as direct political involvement as well as involvement in activities that support the general welfare of a community. In practical terms, scholars are divided as to whether volunteering in a homeless shelter or picking up trash in community parks should count as a measure of civic engagement in the same way as voting for elected officials or attending city commissioner meetings. While this debate among researchers continues, this chapter engages the more inclusive definition of civic engagement as participation in political or community affairs and includes the development of "civic and moral knowledge, skills and values" (Boyd and Brackmann 2012, 40). Similarly guiding this study is the American Association of Community Colleges' definition of civic engagement: "active participation in the public life of a community in an informed, committed, and constructive manner, with a focus on the common good" (Gottlieb and Robinson 2006, 1).

Why Community Colleges?

Higher education has traditionally played a role in preparing students to become active citizens (Knefelkamp 2008). Community colleges are one type of higher education institution (HEI), but research rarely reports on community colleges as separate entities. Almost exclusively, when studies are reported, researchers do not clarify whether community college students were included in their HEI participants. While the dearth of research on community college students requires this clarification, the validity of researchers' efforts to understand HEI participants demand it: it might not be valid to assume that community college students respond as four-year college and university students do to course and campus activities. So, when, in discussing higher education's role in furthering the civic nature of its students, Hartley, Saltmarsh, and Clayton (2010) note that a growing number of people claim that HEIs have failed in this role, does this also indict community colleges? The reports that posit this failure do not mention the role that community colleges play in the development of students' civic engagement.

Community colleges, with their strong emphasis on workforce preparation, may at first appear not to be a place where civic engagement is actively developed. Yet, community colleges are also known as "democracy's colleges" because of their open-access admissions policies, which have "broadened access to higher education and training opportunities to students who would not otherwise have had the opportunity to attend college due to economic, mobility, and social barriers" (Boggs 2010, 2). Instead of only educating the "intellectual elite," community colleges have become "the means by which every citizen youth and adult in enabled and encouraged to pursue higher learning" (2). As a result, the students who attend community colleges often come from the marginalized communities that are the beneficiaries of others' community engagement efforts. Who else is better positioned to translate the theoretical academic content of college into practical civic knowledge and commitment that can be used to transform a community?

As an early definition of community college illustrated "The [community college] may, and is likely to, develop a different type of curriculum suited to the larger and ever-changing civic, social, religious, and vocational needs of the entire community in which the college is located" (Bogue 1950, xvii). Students who attend community colleges typically work full time, attend college part-time, have children, and may even be the single parent raising these children (Mullin 2012; IWPR 2010). Because of these characteristics, community college students are more likely to live in the community, work full time in the community, and have children attending day care, school, and after-school activities in the community (Mullin 2012). They are also less likely to live on campus or have time to participate in many extracurricular campus activities. In other words, community colleges students are not connected to campus or community in the same ways that four-year and university students tend to be connected. Who else is better situated to understand the needs of a community or to recognize the potential impact of community involvement on the daily lives of those who live in the community?

Service-Learning and Civic Engagement

Research studies have consistently found that college graduates are more civically engaged that non-college graduates. While there are factors outside of the educational experience that can impact a person's civic engagement level (Brown and Ferris 2007; Rotolo and Wilson 2004), researchers such as Warchal and Ruiz (2004) point to the college courses and campus experiences that help students develop the self-confidence, critical thinking skills, and social knowledge that lead to greater civic involvement. One of the most often-mentioned academic practices in relation to civic engagement development is service-learning (Cress, Burack, Giles, Elkins, and Stevens 2010). Warchal and Ruiz (2004) found that service-learning experiences are a significant factor in postgraduate community engagement. Hatcher (2011) claims, "Although there are many forms of community involvement and civic engagement, service-learning represents one of the best approaches for reaching the most central goals of teaching students civic knowledge, skills, and habits" (85–86). Likewise, Gallini and Moely's (2003) research indicates that students who have greater civic engagement development have greater college outcomes, and that service-learning is most typically the vehicle that gets students civically involved. The connection between service-learning and civic engagement development thus appears solid. What is less clear is how multiple service-learning experiences might impact students' civic engagement. Intuitively, more would seem better, but this remains to be ascertained. Given that a review of the literature uncovered no research on the impact of multiple service-learning experiences, this study aims to address that gap.

While the connection between service-learning and civic engagement is strong, the studies establishing this connection did not specify what type of HEIs were used in these studies. Thus, what also remains uninvestigated is whether this connection also occurs within the community college sector. In fact, community college service-learning programs are perhaps the least studied of all service-learning programs in the United States. The practice of service-learning in community colleges is based primarily on studies conducted in four-year colleges and universities. Benefits found in these institutions are assumed to also occur in community colleges, but little research has been done to verify the validity of this assumption. As a result, this study also attempts to fill this gap in the literature.

Methods

In 2003, Gail Robinson, who was then the director of service-learning at the American Association of Community Colleges (AACC), and I began what was to be a ten-year research collaboration. When AACC's service-learning office was awarded three years of grant funding by Learn and Serve America to help competitively selected community colleges develop service-learning programs, we chose to investigate service-learning's role in civic engagement development as the grant's primary outcome measure.

Instrument

As previously stated, scholars continue to debate what counts as/for civic engagement. To create a survey instrument to assess the civic engagement levels of community college students, researchers must choose one side or the other of the debate. Options for conceptualizing what is being debated can be found in the literature on civic engagement in HEIs. As an example, Westheimer and Kahne (2004) posited a framework of three types of citizenship: personally responsible citizenship, participatory citizenship, and justice-oriented citizenship. Battistoni (2006) introduces the United Kingdom's model of active citizenship, which they define as "citizens taking opportunities to become actively involved in defining and tackling" community problems to improve quality of life (6). The model both defines the dimensions of active citizenship and defines what it is not (i.e., community service without any underlying understanding and desire to initiate change or to purposely reflect on what was learned through the community experience). Fiume (2009) emphasized the need to foster an ethic of actions in addition to knowledge when developing civically engaged students. As he explains, "Talking about acting for the common good is not enough; people must actually act for the common good" (91). More indicative of the common conceptualizing of civic engagement, Keeter, Zukin, Andolina, and Jenkins (2002) differentiated between civic engagement and political engagement, surmising that the first is represented in direct involvement in the community toward its betterment while the second is represented by direct involvement in political activities such as campaigning for politicians, running for local office, or engaging in specific issues being considered by legislators or other elected officials.

Adopting the more common conceptualization of civic engagement as civic or community involvement and political involvement, we began reviewing the civic engagement surveys available online. We found a variety of civic engagement surveys, but none that were applicable to the study's participant demographics. For example, some focused on "youth," a construct that tends to include young people from 15 to 24 years old, but did not include questions relevant for older survey-takers. Others focused on adults, but not on adults who were going to college. Still others focused on college students, but presumed these students were seeking a bachelor's degree. All surveys were reviewed and analyzed for common themes and questions, and these were used to create a civic engagement survey that would be relevant to adults attending community colleges.

The survey developed for this study included three demographic questions about enrollment status (full-time or part-time), employment status (full-time, part-time, no work), and caretaker responsibilities. Following these questions were 19 core questions that represented civic/community knowledge and behavior (7 questions), and political knowledge and behavior (12 questions). To assess the development of civic engagement over the span of a college term, both a pre-course survey and a post-course survey were developed. All questions on the survey were framed as multiple-choice items.

Instructional Settings

To select the colleges that would participate in the three-year grant project, AACC released a national call for proposals at the beginning of the first year of the grant. All community colleges in the country had the opportunity to submit a proposal outlining the service-learning projects that would be developed and linked to civic engagement activities. The eight competitively selected community colleges represented the range of community colleges across the nation; some were rural, some were suburban, some were urban, some were small, and some were large. All eight colleges engaged in this study were new to service-learning.

Participants

By the end of the study, 424 community college students had completed matched pre-course and post-course surveys. Students in courses that included service-learning completed 279 matched surveys and students taking non-service-learning courses completed 145 matched surveys. Participants were enrolled in courses representing the academic disciplines of biology, communication, English, environmental science, history, management, math, nursing, and sociology. In total, across all of the colleges, there were 23 courses in which surveys were distributed. The courses included topics such as speech, public health, anthropology, psychology, technical writing, math, environmental science, human development, nursing, management, family and consumer sciences, and video production.

Procedures

For this research, a quasi-experimental design was used. This was necessary because study participants were not randomly selected from the population of all service-learning participants or the population of all non-service-learning participants. Additionally, participants were not randomly assigned to the treatment and comparison groups. To create the treatment and comparison groups, each academic term, project directors were asked to choose for survey dissemination at least three courses that included service-learning, and a comparison set of three courses that did not include service-learning. While this design was necessary for the research study, it came with the cost of a loss of control over extraneous variables. These variables remain unknown in the study but may have an effect on the outcome variable of civic engagement. It is important to note here that without the control of extraneous variables through random selection and random assignment, this study's conclusions about service-learning's impact on civic engagement will be more exploratory and less conclusive.

The first step in beginning the study was the selection of service-learning and similar non-service-learning courses. The degree to which a chosen service-learning course and the comparison non-service-learning course were similar depended on the size of the college. Two colleges were in rural communities, four were in suburban communities or in small cities, and two were in urban communities. The small rural colleges often only had one section of one course offered in a particular semester on a particular topic. When a project director selected such a class for survey administration, he or she was instructed to select as similar a class as possible to survey for the comparison group. Thus, for example, if only one section of sophomore level biology 210 was offered, the project director was instructed to select another sophomore level biology course that was being offered. If a course with two sections were offered (one with service-learning and one without) but were taught by different instructors, then students in the service-learning section would be surveyed and included in the treatment group, while students in the non-service-learning section would be surveyed and included in the comparison group. Because of the constraints of surveying similar but not identical courses, the comparison group and the treatment group may have differed in characteristics that remain unknown but that may have had an impact on the results of the study. Given that one of the common problems in service-learning research is the lack of comparison groups, we decided that including such a group, even if it was not identical, was important to the research (Steinberg, Bringle, and Williams 2010).

Each academic term, once the project director at a college had identified the courses that would be surveyed, he or she would give directions to the instructor of the class for the distribution of the pre-course survey. This distribution would typically occur within the first month of the term. Toward the end of the term, the project director again gave directions to the instructors for distribution of the post-course survey. This was most often accomplished during the last month of the term. Completed surveys were returned to the project directors, who then sent them by mail to the researcher responsible for analyses. Project directors repeated this process each academic term in the last two years of the three-year grant period.

Results

The surveys were analyzed cumulatively at the end of the grant period; service-learners were compared to non-service-learners in their civic engagement development from the beginning of the course to the end as measured by average survey scores on the pre-course and post-course surveys. Both descriptive and inferential statistics were used to analyze the data. An alpha level for significance was set at 0.05 for all tests. *ANCOVA*s were conducted to compare the mean survey scores of the service-learners with the mean survey scores of the non-service-learners from the beginning of the course to the end, and *t*-tests were conducted to analyze differences between average scores on the civic/community knowledge and behavior questions and the political knowledge and behavior questions.

Before beginning the analyses, data were separated for the various statistical comparisons. Descriptive statistics were conducted on responses to the survey question regarding the number of previous service-learning courses taken by students. Surveys of students who responded that they were not participating in service-learning during that semester were selected for inclusion in the comparison group of non-service-learners. Of the total number of students who were not participating in service-learning in the surveyed course, 39 percent indicated that they had actually experienced service-learning in one or more previous courses. For the comparison to be cleanest, these students were removed from the non-service-learning group when conducting analyses. The remaining surveys of the comparison group thus represented only students who had never experienced service-learning in any courses.

Similarly, through the analyses of responses to the question regarding previous service-learning experiences, the treatment group was broken into subgroups. Of the 40 percent who indicated that they had previously participated in service-learning, 23 percent had previously taken one service-learning course, 9 percent had previously taken two courses, 3 percent had previously taken three courses, 2 percent had previously taken four courses, and 3 percent had previously taken five or more courses. From this breakdown, surveys were separated into two groups: experienced service-learners (operationally defined in this study as two or more service-learning courses, including the course that the student was taking in the surveyed semester), and first-time service-learners (the course in which they were surveyed was their first service-learning experience).

After the narrowing down of surveys to be included in the control group, and the creation of two subgroups of the treatment group, analyses of the data were conducted in order to address the three research questions: How does service-learning impact civic engagement in community college students? To what extent is it mediated by multiple service-learning experiences? In what, if any, areas of civic engagement are these impacts most profound? To assess the first research question focusing on service-learning's impact on civic engagement, service-learners were compared to non-service-learners. An *ANCOVA* was conducted using the pre- and post-course surveys of both groups. Results revealed a significant difference between the service-learners ($n = 279$, $M = 6.67$) and the non-service learners ($n = 89$, $M = 4.99$), $F = 19.61$, $p = 0.00$, one-tailed.

With the knowledge that there was a statistical difference in average survey scores between service-learners and non-service learners, to answer the second research question, which focused on what, if any, impact multiple service-learning experiences would have on civic engagement, an *ANCOVA* was conducted using only service-learning data. First-time service-learners were compared to the experienced service-learners. Results demonstrated a significant difference between the experienced service-learners ($M = 7.21$) and the first-time service-learners ($M = 6.30$), $F = 5.66$, $p = 0.02$.

To address the final research question regarding the impact of service-learning on the two types of involvement measured by survey questions: civic/community knowledge and behavior and political knowledge and behavior. Topics of the civic/community-focused questions included previous community volunteering, probability of volunteering in the future, whether the student would organize a group to address a community problem, whether the student would know where in the community to refer someone who was homeless, and so forth. Political questions focused on areas such as whether students were registered to vote, whether they had voted in nation elections, whether they had voted in local elections, whether they had attended a meeting of their town, city, or tribal council, and whether they would volunteer their time for a candidate that they believed in. Two t-tests were conducted using data from first-time service-learners and non-service-learners. One t-test was conducted using only post-course data from the service-learners to compare the average scores on the political questions and the civic/community questions. This was done to ascertain if service-learning was most closely aligned with one of the two types of civic engagement measured by the survey.

First, using data from the 12 questions measuring political knowledge and involvement, the post-course scores of the first-time service-learners were compared to the post-course scores of the non-service-learners. Results demonstrated a statistical difference between the first-time service-learners (M = 6.21) and the non-service-learners (M = 5.01), $t(255)$ = 3.79, p = 0.00 on the political questions. Next, using data from the seven questions measuring civic/community knowledge and behavior, the post-course scores of the first-time service learners were again compared to the post-course scores of the non-service learners. Again, results demonstrated a statistical difference between the first-time service-learners (M = 6.43) and the non-service-learners (M = 4.93), $t(255)$ = 4.72, p = 0.00 on the civic/community questions. Finally, when the two types of civic engagement were compared using the first-time service-learning data, average scores were statistically higher for civic/community knowledge and behavior (M = 6.43) than for political knowledge and behavior (M = 5.71), $t(334)$ = 3.65, p = 0.00.

Conclusion

This chapter focused on answering three research questions: How does service-learning impact civic engagement in community college students? To what extent is it mediated by multiple service-learning experiences? In what, if any, areas of civic engagement are these impacts most profound? When the findings from this study are looked at as holistically, they tell the story of how one service-learning experience can be linked to a statistical increase in civic engagement, and that more than one service-learning experience increases the gain. Additionally, in looking at whether particular areas of civic engagement are impacted to a greater extent by service-learning, average scores on the civic/community questions were statistically higher than average scores on the political questions.

Previous research had identified a link between service-learning participation and civic engagement development in higher education students. However, civic engagement advocates report that civic and political engagement overall remains low. These advocates have recently claimed that HEIs have failed in their role in preparing future citizens, but whether this claim also indicted community colleges was unknown. Additionally, studies done on civic engagement have used various definitions of civic engagement. A number of models of civic engagement have been proposed (see, e.g., Westheimer and Kahne 2004; Keeter, Zukin, Andolina, and Jenkins 2002), but no consensus has emerged regarding whether "civic engagement" should refer only to political involvement or whether it should also refer to involvement in the community. Because of this lack of consensus, it is also unclear whether HEIs have failed to develop a particular type of engagement or failed in developing all types described in the civic engagement research. This study set out to explore both of these uncertainties by studying student civic engagement outcomes in community college courses that included service-learning. What was found was evidence that civic engagement can be developed in community college students through service-learning experiences, that more experience with service-learning is associated with greater civic development in community college students, and that experience with service-learning is associated with both types of civic engagement explored in this study.

Finding a correlation between community college students' participation in service-learning and civic engagement is informative in and of itself, but it might also speak to larger/other connections/ideas. First, perhaps the ambiguity of findings about what service-learning promotes—civic, political, community involvement—reveals confusion about what practitioners intend service-learning to promote. The death knells of civic engagement have been sounding for decades, but perhaps that is because the definition of the concept has not been updated, or contemporized, or even clarified. Hartman (2013) explains that the connection of education to the development of a democracy began with the ideas of Thomas Jefferson, Benjamin Rush, and Noah Webster. Each believed that educational institutions should be the vehicle to create "citizens fully prepared for participation in the democratic governance of a republic" (61). John Dewey (1916), in considering the connection between education and civic democracy, confirmed the ideas of Jefferson and others, but he posited that there was meaning beyond that of "democratic governance" in the connection. Dewey provided a glimpse into that meaning in the following argument:

> A democracy is more than a form of government. It is primarily a mode of associated living, of conjoint communicated experience. The extension in space of a number of individuals who participate in an interest so that each has to refer his own action to that of others, and to consider the action of others to give point and direction to his own is the equivalent of breaking down those barriers of class, race, and national territory which kept men from perceiving the full import of their activity. (100)

If service-learning inspires students to feel connected to a community and committed to its well-being, then perhaps their definition of civic engagement is more in line with Dewey than it is with that of the founders of the country. Certainly, students in this study grew in civic/community knowledge and behavior more than in political knowledge and behavior.

This is not to say that our efforts to encourage students to vote, work on a candidate's election, attend meetings with elected officials, petition for legislative changes to be made, and so forth are not important or should be set aside. If civic engagement could be viewed as developmental, then service-learning experiences can continue to develop students' definition of civic engagement. Knowing where students are in terms of community awareness allows those in community colleges to be purposeful in what civic engagement outcomes they wish to foster through the use of service-learning. Likewise, and as the findings regarding the benefit of multiple service-learning experiences suggest, each introduction to civic engagement through service-learning can be one step toward the educational goal of ensuring the continuance of civic engagement in all of its definitions.

Limitations

With these results come cautions. In the *Service-Learning Research Primer*, Steinberg, Bringle, and Williams (2010) list ten common problems in research on service-learning and civic engagement. This study includes three of these: nonrandom assignment, use of measures that are self-report based, and "creaming the crop" (17). First, and as described previously, this study was not a controlled experimental study; rather, it employed a quasi-experimental design. Quasi-experimental research has value in that it offers researchers a method to investigate questions when it would be unethical or impossible to assign participants to groups randomly. The drawbacks, however, include concerns regarding the validity of findings associated with the treatment variable. Results from research that is not conducted using a controlled experimental design should be accepted cautiously.

As second limitation is that, like most service-learning research on students, this study used a self-report measure of assessment. Limitations of such usage include the fact that students' self-reports may not correspond with their actual behavior, that students may be affected by inaccurate or biased memories, and that students are subject to social desirability responses sets (i.e., they are inclined to make themselves look good). Solutions to these limitations include the use of longitudinal follow-up studies, participant observation methods, and the collection of multiple data sources. Significantly, the use of a comparison group might also help to reduce these limitations because the limitations then occur in both the treatment and the comparison groups.

A third limitation in this study is not identifying whether service-learning students chose to participate in service-learning or were required to participate in service-learning. Thus, whether this study assessed only the "cream of the crop" (i.e., those students who were already interested, motivated, and involved in volunteering in the community) is unknown. If, in fact, the "cream" were the participants in this study, then caution must be used when interpreting the results to draw conclusions about the impact of service-learning on the civic engagement of all students.

Future Research

Research on community college student civic engagement is new. More of it is needed to understand whether or how the research conducted with four-year college and university students applies to community college students. For example, how community college students compare to their four-year college and university counterparts on the trajectory of civic engagement is unknown. Perhaps at the end of their first two years, four-year and university students' civic engagement outcomes are identical to those of community college students. Or perhaps, as discussed earlier, these outcomes differ according to the variables—of age, race/ethnicity, work and enrollment status, etc.—that distinguish community college students from their peers in their first two years of study in baccalaureate-granting institutions. Community colleges themselves are also different from other HEIs in their open-access admissions policy. While this study confirmed that in addition to four-year and university students, community college students also grow in civic engagement through participation in service-learning, it did not compare and contrast the college experiences of community college service-learners with those of four-year college and university students.

Also lacking is research on the relationship between service-learning and the development of civic engagement among community college students. While comparisons are worthwhile, research specific to community colleges is also needed. For example, this study did not investigate the characteristics of community college students' service-learning experiences: length of service, frequency of service, and variety of service-learning placement sites. Additionally, community college faculty characteristics and faculty's purpose in integrating service-learning within the content of a course were also not investigated. Faculty design the service-learning component of their courses, guide students in reflection, and are responsible for helping students link the service-learning experience with the course content, and more understanding is needed regarding community college faculty variables.

Research should also be conducted to ascertain whether there are outcome differences in students who choose to participate in service-learning and students who are required to participate in service-learning. Removing the "cream of the crop" service-learning research validity problem would go far in assessing the impact of service-learning on civic engagement. While a 2010 study on service-learning and learning outcomes in community college students revealed higher learning outcomes scores for those students who are required to participate in service-learning (Prentice and Robinson, 2010), these findings remain tentative and underexplored.

Finally, further research is also needed to investigate what aspects of the service-learning experience change community college students into civically engaged community members. Perhaps most importantly, longitudinal research is needed to investigate the civic engagement of community college graduates who participated in service-learning while in college. Since approximately a quarter of students who start their education at a public community college continue on to a four-year college or university and complete their bachelor's degree (AACC 2014), longitudinal research should also investigate the service-learning experiences of students after community college graduation. Do these students have additional service-learning experiences? If so, do these solidify and build upon the gains that students accrued through community college service-learning experiences? Is two years of exposure to service-learning enough to ingrain long-term civic engagement habits, or do these habits fade as the number of postgraduation years increase?

As is typical, the results of this study have provoked more questions than answers. While this study provides tentative evidence for a connection between service-learning participation and civic engagement in community college students, whether these results represent students' entry onto the path of civic engagement or represent a road more traveled is not clear. What is clear, however, is that the bulk of our knowledge on HEIs comes from studies of baccalaureate-granting institutions. While community colleges educate half of all American undergraduates, research on community colleges is scarce. When higher education is called on to foster civic engagement or decried for failing at the task, it is important to be clear about which students need to grow in civic engagement and what institutions these students attend. If targeted interventions to develop civic engagement in students are to be made in higher education, these interventions should be based on research that represents all post-secondary students, both in two-year as well as four-year institutions. Community colleges are distinctive among HEIs and research on these colleges may produce results that are both unique and beneficial to the growth of all students.

References

American Association of Community Colleges. 2010. *Democracy's College: The Evolution of the Community College in America*. Washington, DC: Accessed on July 11, 2013. http://www.aacc.nche.edu/AboutCC/whsummit/Documents/boggs_whsummitbrief.pdf.

———. 2013. *Community College Fact Sheet*. Washington, DC: Accessed on December 11, 2013. http://www.aacc.nche.edu/AboutCC/Documents/fastfacts13_full.jpg.

———. 2014. Data Points: Outcomes for Students Starting at Public Two-Year Institutions. Washington, DC: Accessed on January 15, 2014. http://www.aacc.nche.edu/Publications/datapoints/Pages/default.aspx.

Battistoni, Rick. 2006. "Approaching Democratic Engagement: Research Findings on Civic Learning and Civic Practice." In *Advancing Knowledge in Service-Learning: Research to Transform the Field*, edited by Karen McKnight Casey, Georgia Davidson, Shelley H. Billig, and Nicole C. Springer. Greenwich: Information Age Publishing.

Boggs, George R. 2010. "Democracy's Colleges: The Evolution of the Community College in America." Paper prepared for the White House Summit on Community Colleges, American Association of Community Colleges.

Bogue, Jesse Parker. 1950. *The Community College*. New York: McGraw-Hill.

Boyd, Karen D., and Sarah Brackmann. 2012. "Promoting Civic Engagement to Educate Institutionally for Personal and Social Responsibility." In *Special Issue: Facilitating the Moral Growth of College Students* (no.139), edited by Debora L. Liddell and Diane L. Cooper. San Francisco, CA: Jossey-Bass.

Brown, Eleanor, and James M. Ferris. 2007. "Social Capital and Philanthropy: An Analysis of the Impact of Social Capital on Individual Giving and Volunteering." *Nonprofit and Voluntary Sector Quarterly* 36 (1): 85–99.

Cress, Christine M., Cathy Burack, Dwight E. Giles Jr., Julie Elkins, and Margaret Carnes Stevens. 2010. *A Promising Connection: Increasing College Access and Success through Civic Engagement*. Boston, MA: Campus Compact.

Dewey, John. 1916. *Democracy and Education*. New York: The Free Press. Accessed on July 29, 2013. http://www.studenthandouts.com/01-Web-Pages/New%20Folder/John-Dewey-Democracy-Education.html.

Fiume, Peter Francis. 2009. "Community College Service Learning Pedagogy." *Community College Enterprise* 15 (2):75–93.

Gallini, Sara M., and Barbara E. Moely. 2003. "Service-Learning and Engagement, Academic Challenge, and Retention." *Michigan Journal of Community Service Learning* 10 (1):5–14.

Gottlieb, Karla, and Gail Robinson, eds. 2006. *A Practical Guide for Integrating Civic Responsibility into the Curriculum*. Washington, DC: American Association of Community Colleges Community College Press.

Hartley, Matthew, John Saltmarsh, and Patti Clayton. 2010. "Is the Civic Engagement Movement Changing Higher Education?" *British Journal of Educational Studies* 58 (4): 391–406.

Hartman, Eric. 2013. "No Values, No Democracy: The Essential Partisanship of a Civic Engagement Movement." *Michigan Journal of Community Service Learning* 19 (2):58–71.

Hatcher, Julie A. 2011. "Assessing Civic Knowledge and Engagement." *Special Issue: Assessing Complex General Education Student Learning Outcomes* 2011 (149): 81–92.

Keeter, Scott, Cliff Zukin, Molly Andolina, and Krista Jenkins. 2012. *The Civic and Political Health of the Nation: A Generational Portrait*. College Park, MD: The Center for Information and Research on Civic Learning and Engagement.

Knefelkamp, Lee L. 2008. "Civic Identity: Locating Self in Community." *Diversity and Democracy: Civic Learning for Shared Futures* 11 (2): 1–3.

Miller, Kevin. 2010. *"Fact Sheet: Child Care Support for Student Parents in Community College Is Crucial for Success, but Supply and Funding Are Inadequate."* Institute for Women's Policy Research Accessed on July 31, 2013. http://www.iwpr.org/publications/pubs/child-care-support-for-student-parents-in-community-college-is-crucial-for-success-but-supply-and-funding-are-inadequate.

Mullin, Christopher. 2012. *Why Access Matters: The Community College Student Body*. Washington, DC: American Association of Community Colleges.

Prentice, Mary, and Gail Robinson. 2010. *Improving Student Learning Outcomes with Service Learning*. AACC-RB-10-1. Washington, DC: American Association of Community Colleges.

Rotolo, Thomas, and John Wilson. 2004. "What Happened to the Long Civic Generation? Explaining Cohort Differences in Volunteerism." *Social Forces* 82 (3):1091–1121.

Steinberg, Kathryn S., Robert G. Bringle, and Matthew J. Williams. 2010. *Service-Learning Research Primer*. Scotts Valley: National Service-Learning Clearinghouse.

Warchal, Judith, and Ana Ruiz. 2004. "The Long-Term Effects of Undergraduate Service-Learning Programs on Postgraduate Employment Choices, Community Engagement, and Civic Leadership." In *New Perspectives in Service-Learning: Research to Advance the Field*, edited by Marshall Welch and Shelley H. Billig. Greenwich: Information Age Publishing.

Westheimer, Joel, and Joseph Kahne. 2004. "What Kind of Citizen? The Politics of Teaching for Democracy." *American Educational Research Journal* 41 (2): 237–269.

CHAPTER 13

Service-Learning and the Acquisition of Social Capital in the Community College Setting

Amy Pucino and Thomas Penniston

This chapter engages a conversation on community college service-learning participation and the impact of such experiences on students' social capital development. We analyze ten interviews with community college service-learners to provide the context for an improved understanding of this development. Driving this research, are two main research questions: (1) What kinds of relationships (formal and informal) do students develop through their service-learning experiences? (2) How do these relationships help students access institutional resources that are academically or professionally beneficial?

In this chapter, social capital is defined as relationships from which an individual may gain institutional knowledge and resources (Stanton-Salazar 2011; Stanton-Salazar and Spina 2003; Stanton-Salazar and Dornbusch 1995). Institutional knowledge and resources include information and opportunities about college programs, jobs, etcetera that can benefit the individual academically and professionally (Stanton-Salazar and Dornbusch 1995). Research has shown that service-learning supports students' development of peer, institutional, and community relationships (Eyler and Giles 1999).

Literature has also specifically explored social capital as an outcome of service-learning (D'Agostino 2010; Howard 2006; Kahne, Chi, and Middaugh 2006; Campbell 2000). Such research has been promising, suggesting that service-learning can contribute to the development of social capital. For example, Kahne, Chi, and Middaugh (2006), using a quasi-experimental design, tested a high school civic engagement curriculum program, which involved a service-learning component, to reveal that the program built students' civic engagement, social trust, and awareness of networks. D'Agostino (2010), through her quantitative study of college graduates' social capital development, also found that service-learning programming can predict the development of students' social trust and awareness of social networks. However, research has not specifically focused on community college students' development of social capital through service-learning, nor has it deeply explored some of the tangible resources students might gain from their newly developed networks established through their service-learning experiences.

Community colleges, more so than four-year colleges, educate greater numbers of students with economic challenges (Century Foundation 2013; 2004). In fact, at some four-year colleges and universities, high-income students outnumber low 14:1, but at two-year colleges, the population of low-income students doubles that of their high-income counterparts (Century Foundation 2013). Low-income status can affect a myriad of student success outcomes, and it is correlated with students' higher dropout rates and limited mobility to four-year colleges and universities. Since community college students' economic capital may be limited, supporting their development of other forms of capital might aid their success.

Service-learning may support important new social relationships by connecting diverse individuals. For example, students may build connections with faculty and community partners through their service-learning projects, which may lead to the students' acquisition of support, knowledge, and resources that they may not have received otherwise. Because of the lower socioeconomic status of the traditional student body served, such opportunities to incorporate social capital goals into programming (i.e., to take the professional development and networking[1] frames of "internships" and implement them through service-learning participation) may be especially beneficial. In turn, these involvements are at the core of Dewey's (1926) contention that education is the process of living, rather than preparation for future living. Students gain access to social capital through real-world experiences that allow them to learn and connect with people and resources through life in practice rather than as an abstraction. Didactic educational models do not typically involve intentional scaffolding of the same types of connections. Rather, it is through authentic experiences, such as those supported by service-learning participation, that students encounter opportunities for growth of social capital.

Literature Review

Social capital refers to connections among individuals (Putnam 2000; Coleman 1988; Bourdieu 1986) and the resources available through these relationships (Stanton-Salazar 2011; Lin 2001; Bourdieu 1986), which can contribute to individual or societal growth. While some social capital scholars point to advantages, such as the importance of social capital for building the connectedness of societies and communities at large (Putnam 2000; Coleman 1988), this chapter focuses on the importance of social capital for the advancement of the individual, the kinds of resources that individuals can access through relationships, the ways in which individuals may access important resources through social capital ties, and individuals' unequal access to networks that build social capital.

According to Bourdieu (1986; 1977), some individuals may have access to resource-yielding relationships, which secure them higher economic position in society, while others may not. Also, Bourdieu acknowledged that social capital could protect the higher social class status of the elites (Philip 2008), since they may be likely to network with other advantaged individuals. These aspects of networking, hegemony, and social reproduction may be especially relevant in a community college context where students are most likely to experience poverty (Century Foundation 2013). Since community college students may not have these well-formed, socially beneficial networks, intentionally scaffolding communities of practice (Wenger 1998) might support their social capital development and improve their opportunities for success.

When considering the context of an academic setting, particular resources might be most useful for students. Individuals who are integrated into and familiar with the institution, called institutional agents, can potentially transmit resources to others (Stanton-Salazar 2011). Institutional resources and knowledge acquired through connections with institutional agents may help students become successful in the academic and, later, professional worlds (Stanton-Salazar 2011; Stanton-Salazar and Spina 2003; Stanton-Salazar 2001; Stanton-Salazar and Dornbusch 1995). Institutional knowledge and resources may include information about institutions and opportunities within those institutions, such as school programs or job opportunities, as well as items, tools, or skills, such as letters of recommendation and skill training that might benefit individuals within institutions. For example, a student who sustains a relationship with a previous instructor might gain knowledge about an academic program about which the instructor is familiar and, in turn, request a recommendation letter from that instructor. In this example, the instructor is the institutional agent, the information about the academic program and the recommendation letter are the institutional resources, and potentially, the student is able to generate social capital through this relationship. Additionally, this social capital may contribute to the development of human capital (Coleman 1988). Human capital is the collection of knowledge and skills that may lead one to access economic capital. In other words, through relationships with institutional agents, students may build their skill set and be better equipped to compete successfully in the job market.

In what ways can we facilitate community college students' access to relationships and resources that will help support their upward social mobility? Coleman (1990) believed that individuals across various economic backgrounds could benefit from social capital ties. In fact, such relationships could be especially important for individuals who, outside of school, have limited access to information about school and employment. Relationships can connect individuals with less access to social capital to those who have greater access to it. These connections can, for example, lead to acquisition of resources, which lead to societal advantages that may not otherwise be accessible to an individual or group without these relationships (Stanton-Salazar 2011; Putnam 2000; Coleman 1988; Bourdieu 1986). To support the establishment of these connections that yield social capital, students need to actively engage within the community.

The literature supporting service-learning is grounded in John Dewey's philosophy of American Pragmatism (e.g., Eyler and Giles 1999; Stanton, Giles, and Cruz 1999). Dewey (1944; 1938) contended that Western epistemologies and ontologies based upon notions of a priori Truth are flawed because knowledge is bound to experience.[2] According to Dewey (1963; 1957), experiences occur everywhere, and therefore education should actively link different contexts to learning, including the school and the community. Since all of life's elements are interwoven (Dewey 1958; 1944; 1938), educators need to find ever-improving ways to promote practices that benefit students' long-term chances of success, such as intentionally structuring their connections to institutional agents and social capital. Service-learning, in turn, is a particular pedagogy that provides participants with authentic learning opportunities by tying service to learning and the school to the community.

Student experiences through service-learning participation might help them build networks, connections to institutional knowledge and resources, and pathways toward upward mobility. As Pierre Bourdieu (1986) contends, social capital may provide invaluable access to resources. To Bourdieu, social capital is

> the aggregate of actual or potential resources which are linked to possession of a durable network of more or less institutionalized relationships of mutual acquaintance and recognition—or in other words, to membership in a group—which provides each of its members with backing of the collectively-owned capital, "credential" which entitles them to credit. (248–249)

In accordance with Bourdieu's (1986) definition, the benefits that one can accrue through these relationships are contingent upon the knowledge, prestige, and social assets of the individuals to whom s/he is connected. This dynamic is why Bourdieu purported that social capital most often benefited elites because it is privileged and becomes increasingly consolidated with those who already have access to it. However, relationships forged between individuals who possess desirable assets (e.g., institutional agents) and those who lack them can link the latter to beneficial yet otherwise restricted resources. For example, if a student completes service-learning with an organization for which she wishes to later work, then her service might connect her with individuals who possess skills and knowledge beneficial to her future employment.

Finally, these resources can be accrued through various types of relationships. Putnam (2000) distinguished between two types of relationships: *bridging* relationships, which occur between individuals who are not part of close and homogenous circles, and *bonding* relationships, which occur between like individuals. Bridging relationships may allow individuals to access skills, knowledge, and resources that are beyond the purview of their close-knit circles (Onyx and Bullen 2000). For example, a student may connect with a service-learning site coordinator who does not share her same race, social class, social position, and/or societal experiences. In so doing, the student may learn new and different information and garner more diverse resources than what she would receive through relationships with her family and friends. This relationship bridges the world of the student and the world of the community partner.

Methodologies

This research engaged several important sampling, recruiting, data collection, and analysis procedures in order to address the research questions: (1) What kinds of relationships (formal and informal) do students develop through their service-learning experiences? (2) How do these relationships help students access institutional resources that are academically or professionally beneficial? Because one of the researchers conducting this study is a community college instructor and had taught at the community college in which the research took place, a convenience sampling method was implemented to recruit ten interview participants.

The group of ten interviewees was diverse, with six female students and an equal representation of white and black students. Four of the interviewees were of nontraditional age: Arlo, Dwayne, Natalie, and Stephani. The study demographics are similar to those of the overall institution, where just over half of students are white, almost 40 percent of students are black, and 40 percent of students are male. At this community college, about half of the students receive financial aid and close to 60 percent work 20 or more hours per week. The students of the sample were recruited from one of three 100 level sociology courses. Regardless of the course, students completed about ten hours of service; however, their projects ranged depending on the course. From our sample, one student participated in a course in which the whole class completed service-learning at a community garden and soup kitchen. The other nine students participated in classes where they were able to choose their own service-learning site. Three of these nine, however, were also required to serve several hours, together as a class, in a community garden. Confidentiality statement and consent forms were discussed and signed prior to the interviews. Additionally, to protect the confidentiality of interview participants, researchers had respondents select pseudonyms; thus, no names or identifiers such as the school, course, or semester are included in this chapter. Interviewees also received a monetary incentive as thanks for participation in this research, and to offset the participants' potential expense in terms of time and travel.[3]

Data were collected using a semistructured interview format. This type of interview was suitable for the research agenda for two reasons. First, it ensured some consistency between interviews, which was necessary given the specific focus on social capital and resources. Also, it allowed for some flexibility if students wished to elaborate on matters important to them. Each interview lasted less than 45 minutes and was audio-recorded. The researcher who had previously been the interviewees' sociology course instructor administered the interviews. The researchers chose this dynamic hoping that respondents would feel most comfortable having known the instructor. However, the researchers recognize that through this approach interviewee responses may have been susceptible to social response bias because students might have wished to craft the image they portrayed to their instructor. This is one reason why the researchers chose to interview students after the course was over so that no grades would be affected by the research.

The data analysis was conducted through a multilevel process that began by preliminary assessment of the audio recordings through transcription and note taking. After the preliminary analysis, the two primary investigators collaboratively established codes. Given the exploratory nature of this research, preliminary codes were informed by the social capital and service-learning literatures. To illustrate the coding process, if the respondent mentioned having received a letter of recommendation, the researchers coded this "institutional resources"; if the respondent mentioned building a professional or academic relationship with someone, the researchers coded this "formal network"; and so on.

Each of the researchers separately coded the interviews as either having themes from the literature or lacking the given themes. The researchers each included supplementary notes describing how the given themes were actualized through the interviewees' contributions. After independently coding, the researchers compared and reconciled codes in order. This process helped ensure consistency and reliability through a process similar to the constant comparative method. The constant comparative method means that the researchers take multiple reads through their interview transcriptions, code each time, and constantly compare the codes and analysis with each consecutive read (Roulston 2010; Glaser and Strauss 1967).

Findings

This chapter reveals an underlying narrative that service-learning helps students develop social capital through improved relationships with their professors, enhanced connections between classroom content and the real world, and deeper engagements on campus and within the greater community. For example, all but one student were able to establish informal networks (e.g., student or peer connections) through their service engagement, while seven of the ten were able to establish formal networks (e.g., professional connections). These connections helped over three quarters of the students connect to resources (e.g., a letter of recommendation).

However, factors beyond the service-learning itself may also contribute to whether and how social capital develops. Interviews revealed that just over half of interviewees had personal characteristics developed prior to their service engagement that led them to seek out resources. The remaining students were empowered through their service-learning experience and development of personal characteristics to seek out resources.

Networks and Resources

Students established both formal and informal networks through their service-learning experiences. Half of the students mentioned developing informal networks with students from their service-learning class. In fact, some were connected through Facebook or other social networking sites at the time of the interviews. The majority of the networks built tended to be more formal. For example, upon the course instructor's recommendation, Vanessa was asked by the service-learning committee at the community college to participate in a service-learning conference presentation as a student representative. She cited this as an example of networking. Coincidentally, Vanessa's English professor, who happened to be attending the conference, learned of Vanessa's interest in service-learning through her presentation. Being part of service-learning allowed her to strengthen her relationship with this professor. Arlo was able to network with someone connected with the Board of Education. Erin was also part of a formal online network put together by the local office of the political party with which she is affiliated.

These formal networks often led to access to institutional resources as well. Most of the respondents indicated that they had either received or felt empowered to ask for a recommendation from either the course instructor or someone from their service-learning site. Prior to the interviews, Vanessa had already asked for and received a recommendation letter from her sociology professor,[4] and Sam and Dwayne had inquired about receiving recommendations in the future.[5] Likewise, just under half of the respondents expressed confidence that someone from their service-learning site would recommend them.[6]

Mae is an example of a student who was able to access a letter of recommendation from site personnel. She completed her service-learning project at a museum with which she had been volunteering for over ten years. After having shared her service-learning paper with someone in leadership at the museum, she was informed that he would write her a recommendation letter. She revealed that her experience with service-learning, above and beyond her previous volunteer work with the organization, was what got her access to that letter. In this case, Mae had already known the people with whom she was volunteering for several years; however, by connecting her work and course requirements through her service-learning experience, Mae was able to expand the nature of her professional network.

Arlo shared a similar story related to receiving a recommendation letter. He explained that, when he was looking for a service-learning site, his instructor had recommended that he look in to an afterschool educational program. While he was unable to complete his service-learning hours there, he later volunteered with the program and found that the program coordinator was well-networked with the local educational administration. Recognizing these networks, Arlo mentioned that he would feel comfortable asking this coordinator for a recommendation or reference should he need one when applying for jobs as a teacher in the school system. In addition, Arlo also gained professional resources in the process of volunteering with this afterschool program:

> I think for institutional resources, especially for someone who wanted to, like future educators, because you have to go downtown and get fingerprinted and get your picture taken and all of that is now out of the way. So now, as soon as I graduate I am going to send my application in for substitute teacher...so now my fingerprints are done. I have my ID badge. The same thing I would have to go through if I were going to be a substitute teacher just coming in off the street.

Arlo and Mae made these connections specifically because their service-learning experience provided connections between classroom content and the real world. Notably, although all recommendation letters are resources, not all resources are recommendation letters. Such tangible and quantifiable outcomes, however, help exemplify the potential benefits for students forming connections and improving access to social capital through service-learning.

Another resource accrued by respondents was information about programs in the community. In particular, every respondent mentioned knowledge they had acquired, that they had not previously known, about their service-learning site and the issues the site addressed. Erin explained that her work with the national presidential election made her feel more informed as a first time voter in the 2012 elections:

> I learned about the issues. When I went to vote I felt extremely proud of myself because I knew what was going on...I knew what most of the questions were...they were trying to vote in different bills for schools and education but people seemed to only care about the one main one that was being televised. So it was just like, I felt rewarded knowing that I knew what was going on.

At the time of the interview, which was several months after her completion of the service-learning project, Erin was still receiving informative updates via email from the service-learning site coordinator regarding personal and professional experiences and opportunities. Similarly, at the time of the interview, which was also conducted several months after project completion, Stephani was still receiving updates from her service-learning site coordinator. As a result, she had remained actively involved in events at the site, even after the service was no longer required for a class. This additional engagement deepened her relationships with the coordinators of the site and potentially contributed to her confidence in their willingness to recommend her.

Not only did students learn about their service-learning site, but they also learned about other organizations through the process of finding a site or listening to class reflections about other students' sites. For example, when Vanessa began searching for a service-learning site, her sociology instructor recommended that she connect with a tutoring program for refugees. Although she was unable to complete service-learning hours at the program that semester, Vanessa still followed the program, kept up with their fundraisers, and posted about them on her Facebook page. Similarly, additional respondents reported learning about relevant community college campus information during or as a result of their service-learning courses. For instance, Natalie, who had completed part of her service-learning hours in the community garden, which was then part of the horticulture program on campus, mentioned learning about a campus food resource because she had kept up with horticulture news since taking the service-learning course. After participating in service-learning in his sociology course, Dwayne also completed a service-learning project with his health class. This experience taught him about free health programs on campus. Sam explained that service-learning had allowed him to connect with another student who was applying to the same academic program, and that they could talk about that program with each other. In each of these cases, students were either able to access tangible resources or learn about programs in their own community or on campus that could potentially benefit them in their academic or professional lives.

Participant Characteristics and Transformative Practice

While this research seems to show that service-learning does in fact help students develop social capital, interviewees also reported a number of personal characteristics that may have mediated this development. These characteristics were either held by the interviewee prior to his/her service, or developed through the service engagement. In this section, we describe these student characteristics and reveal how they served to aid or hinder the development of social capital. In cases where students held characteristics that hindered their ability to make connections, service-learning seemed to offer a vehicle for developing skills to compensate for their initial challenges. In turn, through these developed capacities students were able to access key relationships and resources.

Personal characteristics held prior to service varied widely among interviewees. For example, a student who is curious, open to new experiences, or liked to help people may be more likely to prosper in courses with a service requirement than one who is not similarly disposed. As a salient example of student predispositions to service, Natalie was glad to engage in service at a soup kitchen as a component of her course, most specifically because she had previously benefitted from similar assistance. She distinctly remembered and recounted how she felt in receiving donations of clothes, food, and presents at Christmas time when she was a child. For her, service was not just a giving experience; it also carried with it an element of repayment.

Arlo, like Natalie, was a nontraditional-age student, and he partly attributed his excitement to participate in service to his age (43). Service-learning exposed him to different organizations, which subsequently provided him with the opportunity to fulfill institutional requirements for working in the public school system, such as fingerprinting and a background check (e.g., for substitute teaching post graduation). He now has positive relationships with institutional agents in these organizations, and would, for example, feel comfortable asking at least one of them for a letter of recommendation.

Yet, students also exhibited characteristics that seemed to impede their integration within the community and, in turn, their successful service-learning participation. However, in these cases, students reported that service-learning actually helped them begin to overcome such challenges. Jamie, for example, experienced anxiety about her service, running "What if?" and contingency scenarios through her head. Outside of befriending her teachers, she found it generally difficult to approach people. Service-learning presented Jamie with an opportunity for slow, controlled acclimation and socialization through a proximal safety net. As Jamie explained, her experience was "like testing the waters." She felt she was able to gradually ease into relationships at her service site.

Sam was similarly shy and felt awkward when it came to communication. His introduction to his service site, which was a food preparation and distribution program for persons with terminal illnesses, felt very formal to him, "like a job interview." Additionally, when Sam initially arrived at the site, he felt left out of some casual conversations among other more experienced volunteers. Sam believed service-learning experiences such as his require students to form relationships with diverse people through authentic social situations. When asked if students should be forced to engage in service, Sam said,

> I still say yea...you never know how their perception is affected or how their judgment is affected...You're forced to work with people of different backgrounds and you get to know them better more than just their behaviors.

Of all of the skills and knowledge interviewees developed through service-learning, the most constant theme was that these experiences helped them to gain confidence by getting *into* the real world and *out* of their comfort zone. In this way, service-learning might also help students to forge beneficial relationships and pursue academic success. As Jamie described this dynamic:

> It's like testing the waters. You know it's like when you go into the pool and some go full force cannonball and others go down the steps...Volunteering was baby steps. It tested me out for other things I would do further in schooling or outside of schooling.

Dwayne believed he benefitted from his service-learning experience on a personal level because, as he explained, he tended to find it difficult to connect with others. He talked about his level of social comfort prior to his service-learning experience and how he, at times, acted the way he perceived others thought he should act. His service experience, on the other hand, felt "therapeutic" to him, and it was rewarding in this regard because he felt he could be authentic. To him, the informal nature of the service-learning setting was preferable to a more restricted formal or clinical setting of an externship, which, from his perspective, lacked the intentional feedback and reflective component that defines service-learning.

Stephani provides perhaps the most compelling example of service-learning's impact on student growth, including social capital access and development. Stephani's service site, an organization for families headed by previously incarcerated parents, was located in her old neighborhood. Initially concerned about this connection, she was later empowered by her service experience to work for change in her old neighborhood:

> Honestly, it went from volunteering to second nature. And even if I'm not there, I'm back in my own neighborhood which was something that once I received...once I gained a point in my career I was just like "Why do I want to go back around there?" Like I couldn't...I couldn't understand why I would want to stay there because it was just like...You know I'm...I...I believe I've grown above that. But then it made me realize, it is like if you just abandon where you come from then no one will ever receive the chances that you had. Because,...even though it may be ten students that don't want to hear your story, it's that one kid in there who's life you can change. Change it.

Since her service-learning project concluded, Stephani has kept in contact with a number of institutional agents from whom she would feel comfortable requesting a recommendation letter. She also continues to engage in service at the organization and to receive information about organizational programming. Stephani's situation is unique to the students interviewed because, not only did she build her own social capital, she can now also serve as a resource for young people from her old neighborhood, building their social capital.

Conclusion

This exploratory research introduces the idea that service-learning has multiple functions. While oriented toward student learning of course material and meeting a community need, service-learning might also help students build skills and access resources. For example, interviewees reported that service-learning facilitated their access to several different types of institutional resources, including recommendation letters, information about their service-learning site and other community programs, and information about campus programs. When students stepped out of their comfort zones, they were able to build and connect with social capital, which may be of special importance to community-college students. In a setting where half the students are receiving financial aid and most must work 20 hours or more per week, students in this community college may benefit from added access to institutional resources that may help them ultimately garner financial resources. Students' characteristics also played a role in their service-learning experiences. For instance, the characteristics they held prior to service, such as shyness or confidence, mediated their integration within the service site. How students related with others through their service in turn affected what they valued about these experiences.

If we are aware that social capital is central to the development of human capital, we must help students develop these ties wherever, whenever, and however possible. While our research contributes to an understanding of social capital growth through service-learning, more research on this topic is required. Future investigation might help disentangle the impact of various elements influencing social capital development, including how the structure of the service-learning courses, type of service-learning projects, characteristics of the instructors, and additional student characteristics impact the extent to which students acquire institutional resources. Additionally, future inquiry might investigate the purposeful establishment of social capital through service-learning programming.

Notes

1. A network is a web of people and their relations (Wasserman and Faust 1994).
2. Plato's cave allegory in *The Republic*, for example, implies that there is an inherent Truth underlying knowledge that is obscured by human senses.
3. The researchers paid the respondents out of pocket.
4. This professor was one of the current study's coauthors.
5. Future research would need to uncover the extent to which instructor qualities, student qualities, or the service-learning itself have an influence on whether or not students seek recommendation letters from their service-learning faculty.
6. Stephani, Arlo, Erin, and Mae indicated they would feel comfortable seeking a recommendation from service-learning site representatives.

References

Astin, Alexander W., and Linda J. Sax. 1998. "How Undergraduates Are Affected by Service Participation." *Journal of College Student Development* 39 (3): 251–263.
Bourdieu, Pierre. 1977. "Cultural Reproduction and Social Reproduction." In *Reproduction in Education, Society, and Culture*, edited by Pierre Bourdieu and Jean Claude Passerson, 257. Beverly Hills, CA: Sage, 1977.
———. 1986. "The Forms of Capital." In *Handbook of Theory and Research for the Sociology of Education*, edited by John G. Richardson, 241. New York: Greenwood.
Campbell, David E. 2000. "Social Capital and Service Learning." *PS: Political Science and Politics* 33 (3): 641–645.
Century Foundation. 2004. *Left Behind: Unequal Opportunity in Higher Education*. Accessed July 9, 2013. http://tcf.org/assets/downloads/tcf-leftbehindrc.pdf.
———. 2013. *Bridging the Higher Education Divide: Strengthening Community Colleges and Restoring the American Dream*. Accessed July 9, 2013. http://tcf.org/assets/downloads/20130523-Bridging_the_Higher_Education_Divide-REPORT-ONLY.pdf.
Coleman, James S. 1988. "Social Capital in the Creation of Human Capital." *American Journal of Sociology* 94: S95–120.
———. 1990. *Foundations of Social Theory*. Cambridge: Belknap Press of Harvard University Press.
D'Agostino, Maria. 2010. "Measuring Social Capital as an Outcome of Service Learning." *Innovative Higher Education* 35 (5): 313–328.
Dewey, John. 1926. "My Pedagogic Creed." *Journal Of Education* 104 (21): 542.

Dewey, John. 1938. *Experience and Education*. New York: Macmillan Publishing.
——. 1944. *Democracy and Education*. New York: Macmillan Publishing.
——. 1957. *Reconstruction in Philosophy*. Boston, MA: Beacon Press.
——. 1958. *Experience and Nature*. New York: Dover Publications.
——. 1963. *The Child and the Curriculum, and the School and Society*. Chicago, IL: University of Chicago Press.
Eyler, Janet, and Dwight Giles. 1999. *Where's the Learning in Service-Learning?* San Francisco, CA: Jossey-Bass.
Giles, Dwight E., and Janet Eyler. 1994. "The Impact of a College Community Service Laboratory on Students' Personal, Social, and Cognitive Outcomes." *Journal Of Adolescence* 17 (4) (August): 327–339.
Glaser, Barney G., and Anselm L. Strauss. 1967. *The Discovery of Grounded Theory: Strategies for Qualitative Research*. Chicago, IL: Aldine Pub. Co.
Howard, Robert W. 2006. "Bending towards Justice: Service Learning and Social Capital as a Means to the Tipping Point." *Mentoring & Tutoring* 14 (1): 5–15.
Kahne, Joseph, Bernadette Chi, and Ellen Middaugh, 2006. "Building Social Capital for Civic and Political Engagement: The Potential of High School Civics Courses." *Canadian Journal of Education* 29 (2): 387–409.
Lin, Nan. 2001. *Social Capital: A Theory of Social Structure and Action*. Cambridge: Cambridge University Press.
Onyx, Jenny and Paul Bullen. 2000. "Measuring Social Capital in Five Communities." *The Journal of Applied Behavioral Science* 36 (1): 23–42.
Philip, Kate. 2008. "She's My Second Mum: Young People Building Relationships in Uncertain Circumstances." *Child Care in Practice* 14 (1): 19–33.
Prentice, Mary, Gail Robinson, and Colleges American Association of Community. 2010. "Improving Student Learning Outcomes with Service Learning." Washington, DC: American Association of Community Colleges.
Putnam, Robert D. 2000. *Bowling Alone: The Collapse and Revival of American Community*. New York: Simon & Schuster.
Roulston, Kathryn. 2010. *Reflective Interviewing: A Guide to Theory and Practice*. Los Angeles, CA: Sage Publications.
Stanton, Timothy, Dwight Giles, and Nadinne I. Cruz. 1999. *Service-Learning: A Movement's Pioneers Reflect on Its Origins, Practice, and Future*. San Francisco, CA: Jossey-Bass Publishers.
Stanton-Salazar, Ricardo D. 2001. *Manufacturing Hope and Despair: The School and Kin Support Networks of U.S.-Mexican Youth*. New York: Teachers College Press.
——. 2011. "A Social Capital Framework for the Study of Institutional Agents and Their Role in the Empowerment of Low-Status Students and Youth." *Youth & Society* 43 (3) (September 1): 1066–1109.
Stanton-Salazar, Ricardo D., and Sanford M. Dornbusch. 1995. "Social Capital and the Reproduction of Inequality: Information Networks among Mexican-Origin High School Students." *Sociology Of Education* (2): 116.
Stanton-Salazar, Ricardo D., and Stephanie Urso Spina. 2003. "Informal Mentors and Role Models in the Lives of Urban Mexican-Origin Adolescents." *Anthropology & Education Quarterly* (3): 231.
Vogelgesang, Lori J., and Alexander W. Astin. 2000. "Comparing the Effects of Community Service and Service-Learning." *Michigan Journal Of Community Service Learning* 7: 25–34.
Wasserman, Stanley, and Katherine Faust. 1994. *Social Network Analysis: Methods and Applications*. Cambridge: Cambridge University Press.
Wenger, Etienne. 1998. *Communities of Practice: Learning, Meaning, and Identity*. Cambridge: Cambridge University Press.

CHAPTER 14

Service-Learning as a Pedagogical Tool for Career Development and Vocational Training

Sharon Ellerton, Cristina Di Meo, Arlene Kemmerer, Josephine Pantaleo, Mary Bandziukas, Michael Bradley, and Victor Fichera

Workforce development has been one of the key missions of community colleges nearly from their inception in the beginning of the twentieth century (Vaughan 2006). Community college curricula are replete with vocational programming to serve high school graduates, adults changing careers, students with poor academic standing, as well as the traditionally underserved groups, including low-income, first-generation college attendees and minority students. For these markedly different populations, community colleges offer a chance for economic security since individuals with more education tend to have lower rates of unemployment (USNCES 2012a) and greater earning potential (USNCES 2012b). Unfortunately, it is the underserved that are most likely to drop out and never complete a college degree (Burns 2010) thereby perpetuating a negative cycle that keeps these populations in lesser-skilled jobs with lower earnings. Mechanisms that will help retain these students in the community colleges are of vital importance.

The twenty-first century has brought new challenges to employability, even for students who attain a college degree. The globalization of the economy, the outsourcing of jobs, and the recession have contributed to increased rates of unemployment. In spite of these systemic changes, many middle-skilled jobs requiring some college credit or an associate's degree remain unfilled (Carnevale and Smith 2013). President Obama (2009) issued a mandate to community colleges to address twenty-first century workforce development, stating that "...in the coming years, jobs requiring at least an associate degree are projected to grow twice as fast as jobs requiring no college experience. We will not fill those jobs—or keep those jobs on our shores—without the training offered by community colleges" (paragraph 5). Further, Arne Duncan (2010), US Secretary of Education, stated that community colleges "have a new mission...to prepare students to compete successfully in the twenty-first century knowledge economy and participate in civic society" (paragraph 5).

Although the government's charge to community colleges is clear, the means to best prepare community college students for twenty-first century jobs are less so. While community colleges may teach the industry-specific technical skills needed to enter the workforce, additional skills are necessary to remain competitive and function effectively within the workplace. The US Department of Labor (2013) recognizes general areas of "soft skills" necessary for workforce development, which include: oral and written communication skills, teamwork skills (i.e., respect for differing opinions and customs), problem-solving and critical-thinking skills, and professionalism (i.e., responsibility, accountability, and integrity). It is logical that students with the "hard skills" or technical knowledge would be most successful if they also have "soft skills" or the nontechnical knowledge needed in the workplace (Bancino and Zevalkink 2007).

As agencies involved in workforce development were recognizing the importance of "soft skills," a parallel line of thinking was developing in higher education. Through the LEAP initiative (2007), the Association of American Colleges and Universities (AACU) developed a set of "Essential Learning Outcomes" that all colleges should provide their students as part of a liberal education. Many of these learning outcomes are the same "soft skills" deemed important for workforce development, although some skills are framed in slightly different language. The AACU's essential learning outcomes include: written and oral communication skills, teamwork skills, problem solving skills, civic knowledge and engagement skills, intercultural knowledge and competence, and ethical reasoning skills. Employers reviewed this list of "essentials" and the majority considered these outcomes important for student success in the workplace (AACU and Hart Research Associates 2010). In a similar survey (AACU 2013) nearly all employers agreed that the ability to think critically and communicate clearly is more important than the student's major. They prefer to hire employees who demonstrate ethical judgment, integrity, and intercultural skills. Employers also stated that colleges should emphasize "...written and oral communication, and applied knowledge in real-world settings" (AACU 2013, 2). It is this confluence of thinking about the importance of "soft skills" in the workplace and essential learning objectives in higher education that places colleges at the center of student workforce development.

Kuh (2008) provides a pathway for college students to achieve these essential learning outcomes/"soft skills" by aligning each learning outcome with one or more of ten identified high-impact pedagogies. Within this framework, curriculum development at four-year institutions could include these pedagogies in designated elective courses. In contrast, curricula in two-year associate or certificate technical programs are tightly proscribed, with very few elective credits available. This would suggest that in the community college setting, the pedagogies that provide "soft skill" learning be incorporated into existing "hard skill" coursework. For multiple reasons, service-learning stands out among the high-impact practices as a pedagogy that can be readily incorporated into community college curricula and best serve career and technical students in this way.

Research has demonstrated that service-learning positively impacts many student learning outcomes (Astin et al. 2000), including those we identify as "soft skills," and is a pedagogy that positively impacts the traditionally underserved (Finley and McNair 2013). It is also a pedagogy that can be incorporated into virtually any technical classroom. Furthermore, service-learning provides students the opportunity to engage in experiential learning: a methodology that creates knowledge through real-life work experience (Kolb 1984).

Many technical industries have recognized that the combination of "soft skill" acquisition and experiential education are essential elements for students preparing to become part of their workforce. The Accreditation Board of Engineering and Technology (ABET) (2005) has gone so far as to incorporate "soft skill" and experiential education as required program criteria for accreditation. It is therefore not surprising that service-learning is recognized as a promising mechanism to instill both "soft skills" and work experience into engineering technology programs (Shuman et al. 2005). In a similar fashion, other career programs identify service-learning as a means to meet programmatic goals. For example, service-learning has been recognized as a means to expand the narrow scope of business programs (Zlotkowski 1996), and the American Association of Colleges of Nursing (AACN 2008) views service-learning as a mechanism for instilling in their students "professionalism and professional values" (9).

Despite the fact that service-learning is situated within so many varied career-oriented programs, the literature linking this pedagogy to positive gains in students' development of "soft skills" (e.g., writing, critical thinking, interpersonal skills, increased awareness of the world, civic responsibility) has focused primarily on baccalaureate programs (Astin et al. 2000). Although approximately two-thirds of the nation's 1,200 community colleges offer service-learning in their various curricular programs (American Association of Community Colleges), far less data are available from community colleges.

Much of what we do know about the impact of service-learning on acquisition of "soft skills" within the two-year colleges comes from Prentice and Robinson's (2010) AACC national survey research, which indicates that students' service-learning experiences are correlated with gains in career and teamwork, civic responsibility, academic development and educational success, critical thinking, and communication and learning of career skills. This research also indicates a positive relationship between service-learning and students' intent to continue their education (i.e., their retention/persistence).

This AACC study suggests that community college and baccalaureate students benefit from service-learning in similar ways, but much more remains to be studied, particularly with regard to differing community college student populations. Considering the key role community colleges play in workforce development, research on the impact of service-learning on students in the career and technical fields is vital.

In this chapter, we contend that service-learning can influence community college student success in career and technical education (CTE). To do so, we draw on mixed-methods data collected during the 2012–2013 academic year from career and technical courses that incorporated service-learning into curricula at Queensborough

Community College (QCC), the City University of New York (CUNY). The impact of service-learning will be presented through the results of student surveys, retention rates, and student, faculty, and community partner reflections. Presented evidence will demonstrate that the acquisition of "soft skills" needed to enter the job market can be learned through service-learning in technical courses. The results will also illustrate the efficacy of this teaching strategy and the numerous observed benefits of an education based in real-life community settings where academic learning is transformed into practical, vocational knowledge. We hope, in this way, to contribute to the community colleges' response to President Obama's challenge, preparing students to succeed in the twenty-first century workforce.

Methods

Institutional and Instructional Context

QCC is one of seven community colleges within the City University system of New York and is located in Queens County, one of the most diverse areas in the United States (CUNY 2014). The approximately 16,000 students enrolled represent 139 countries and nearly 40 percent speak a language other than English at home. Since the campus is open-admissions, more than 70 percent of the students require at least one developmental course. Approximately half of all students receive financial aid. The ethnic composition of the student body is very diverse, with 28 percent Hispanic, 25 percent Asian, 25 percent black, and 22 percent white (QCC Office of Institutional Research and Assessment 2012–2013).

Service-learning at QCC operates through the Office of Academic Service-Learning (OASL) under the Office of Academic Affairs and comprises a program director, part-time staff, and a faculty liaison. The OASL develops and maintains collaborative partnerships between the faculty and community partners (nonprofit organizations off-campus or college programs on-campus); collects data on the students, faculty, community partners, and courses participating in service-learning; monitors and implements projects; provides professional development for faculty; assesses the impact of service-learning on students; and gathers feedback from community partners and faculty. Vaknin and Bresciani (2013) contend that such characteristics lead to sustainable, high-quality service-learning programs.

Before faculty incorporate service-learning into their courses, their projects are vetted through the college's OASL to ensure alignment with both course and general education objectives and that the project meets a need of the community partner. Course objectives refer to the academic learning that is occurring within the course while general education objectives refer to basic competencies the college expects of all students, including, but not limited to, the ability to communicate in oral and written form, work effectively with others, follow directions, and think critically.

Service-learning at QCC takes on many forms. Faculty may choose to incorporate it as a course requirement for all students, create an option for those students who choose to participate, use it to replace an existing assignment, or offer it as an extra credit "add-on." All students in a class may work on a particular project or multiple projects may occur concurrently. Projects address issues of adult literacy, senior services, advocacy, the environment, health and nutrition, mental health, homelessness, hunger, K-12 education, and the formerly incarcerated. The college's courses are not identified as service-learning courses at the time of registration, thereby reducing the likelihood that students self-select into these courses.

Despite the broad variation in how and where the service-learning is implemented, Stachowski and Frey's (2005) "3 Rs" (i.e., *R*eal, *R*eciprocal and *R*eflective) are steadfast consistencies in the application of this pedagogy. The service performed by the students must fulfill a *real* community need, generate *reciprocal* benefits for both students and the community partner, and directly connect to learning through student *reflection*.

Data Sources and Procedures

Information assessing the service-learning experience was obtained from all of the key stakeholders—the students, faculty, and community partners. A quantitative survey was administered to students in three semesters—fall 2012, spring 2012, and fall 2013. Data were self-reported, that is, students were asked for their views on their attainment of skills and knowledge based on a five-point Likert scale. Qualitative data, including student, faculty, and community partner reflections, and open-ended responses from the student surveys over the three semesters, were used to gain descriptive information from each group. Students completed post-project reflections comprising short-answer questions on workplace skills they learned and their application of course content during the project. The survey included an open-ended question in which students were asked to describe a specific project experience. Faculty members were asked to evaluate students' attainment of workplace skills as a result of their project. Community partners completed short-answer questions to assess the project's effectiveness in meeting the organization's needs. The student retention data further validate both the quantitative and qualitative data and provide an additional measure of program effectiveness.

Study Respondents

During the fall of 2013, 141 CTE students from the following ten courses participated in the student survey: Architecture Design Fundamentals, Database Management Systems, Health of the Nation, Introduction to Microcomputer Applications, Introduction to Physical Fitness, Introduction to Robotics, Massage Practicum, Nursing Care of Clients III, Surveying and Layout, and Yoga. The survey respondents comprised students in business, engineering technology, health, massage therapy, and nursing program. The sample consisted of 51 percent males and 49 percent females. Ethnically, the student sample was diverse, reflecting the overall makeup of the college, with 31 percent Hispanic, 29 percent Asian, 19 percent black, 12 percent white, 7 percent biracial, and 2 percent Native American/Alaska Native/Native Hawaiian/Pacific Islander.

A prior student survey was administered in fall 2012 and spring 2013 for a total of 14 CTE classes. The data from these two semesters were combined into one sample, resulting in 145 survey respondents. Although the student demographics and types of classes assessed from these 14 classes were similar to those in the fall 2013 cohort, the fall 2013 data are presented separately due to changes in the question format.

Surveys: CTE Service-Learners Self-Report on the Acquisition of Skills
After completion of their projects, CTE students were asked to rank the impact of the service-learning experience on their acquisition of "soft skills" and academic knowledge. During the fall 2013 semester, the post-only survey consisted of 22 questions with graded responses on a five-point Likert scale, as well as an open-ended question asking students to provide an example of their experience during the service-learning project. Thirteen questions pertained to "soft skill" acquisition and students were asked to self-report if the service-learning project helped them feel more confident in areas such as being a member of a team, problem solving, or expressing themselves orally and in writing. Possible student responses included "Not at all," "A little bit," "Somewhat," "Quite a bit," and "A lot," with a sixth option to indicate that the question was not applicable to their service-learning experience. The percentage of students indicating that service-learning helped them with a particular skill was calculated by adding the number of "Quite a bit" and "A lot" responses.

During the fall 2012 and spring 2013 semesters, the post-only survey consisted of 26 and 28 questions respectively, with graded responses on a five-point Likert scale, as well as open-ended questions. Students were asked whether they attributed growth in workplace competencies to their participation in service-learning. The percentage of students responding negatively were compared to the percentage of positive student responses.

The student survey was approved by CUNY's Community College Institutional Review Board, which oversees human subjects research including research on students within an educational setting. Surveys were administered to students after the service experience. Survey administration, collection, and storage were all performed by members of the OASL. The survey data are anonymous and only identified by course. Analysis was done by office staff and reviewed by the QCC Academic Learning Outcomes Assessment Manager.

Reflections: Student, Faculty, and Community Partners Report on CTE Student Skill Acquisition
CTE student reflections on their service-learning experience were collected from multiple sources, but were primarily gathered from an open-ended question on the student survey. Over the course of the three semesters, students responded to the instruction: "Please provide a specific example of your experience during your service-learning project." Content analysis was performed searching responses for themes such as acquisition of course knowledge or improvement in a "soft skill." The percentage of students addressing each theme was calculated. Additional reflections were obtained from writing assignments collected by faculty and submitted to the QCC OASL. Quotations were derived from these reflections but content analysis was not performed since the writing assignments greatly varied.

Although the OASL did not formally gather CTE faculty reflections on "soft skill" acquisition, some of the CTE faculty provided their thoughts on this topic for the purposes of this chapter. Faculty were asked to evaluate student gains due to their service-learning project in "soft skill" areas such as teamwork, problem solving, expressing ideas verbally or in writing, following directions, meeting deadlines, respecting diversity and the opinions of others, accepting criticism, and preparedness for entering a career. A reflection was also drawn from a faculty publication.

The quality and effectiveness of selected projects were also discussed in exit interviews with community partners at the end of each semester. Community partners included a homeless shelter for families, a community center, local K-12 schools, senior centers, public parks, and an environmental center. Comments were reviewed for specific references to student acquisition of "soft skills."

Retention Data: CTE Service-Learners' Retention Patterns

Retention data for fall 2012 students were derived from the CUNY Institutional Research Database.[1] A student is considered retained when he or she returns to the institution the following semester. Data were collected for CTE students who participated in service-learning and CTE students who did not participate in service-learning. A chi-square test was performed to analyze the relationship between service-learning and retention.

Results

Surveys: CTE Service-Learners Self-Report Gains in Acquisition of Skills

In the fall 2013, CTE students reported that service-learning helped them feel more confident in their ability to engage in critical workplace skills. Survey results are listed in table 14.1.

Table 14.1 Fall 2013 Impact of Service-Learning on CTE Students' Increased Confidence in Workplace Skills

Workplace Skill	N	*Students Responding "A Lot" or "Quite a Bit"*
Follow directions completely	141	85%
Communicate with people of different backgrounds or cultures	139	84%
Complete projects or assignments on time	138	83%
Respect the opinions of others who may disagree with you	136	82%
Understand values of people different than you	134	81%
Work with others as a member of a team	140	78%
Compare different approaches to solving a problem	138	78%
Analyze and critically evaluate ideas, arguments, and points of view	133	75%
Solve challenging problems	138	71%
Express ideas, opinions, and facts verbally	139	70%
Ask questions in class	136	70%
Express ideas, opinions, and facts in writing	136	65%
Make a presentation in front of a class or speak in public	136	58%

Note: Student responses were based on a five-point Likert scale and results, listed here, were determined by collapsing the highest responses into a single percentage.

After their participation in a service-learning project, the majority of CTE students reported increased confidence in their abilities, including following directions completely (85 percent), completing projects on time (83 percent), and comparing problem solving approaches (78 percent).

CTE students who participated in service-learning also reported an increased confidence in their ability to engage in interpersonal behaviors that would be beneficial in the twenty-first century workplace. For example, 84 percent of CTE students who participated in service-learning reported greater confidence when communicating with people from different backgrounds or cultures. Additionally, 82 percent of CTE students felt more confident in their ability to respect the opinions of others who disagreed with them and 81 percent of CTE students felt more confident in their ability to understand the values of people different from themselves.

In addition to increased self-assurance, 80 percent of students surveyed indicated that their service-learning project helped them learn their course material more effectively, and 82 percent indicated that they applied what they learned in class during the service-learning experience. These results suggest that the knowledge and skills students acquired in the classroom are reinforced by practical application.

While the fall 2013 survey measured the impact of service-learning on student confidence in their ability to perform workplace skills, the fall 2012 and spring 2013 surveys measured student belief that service-learning directly increased their workplace skills. These results complement the student confidence survey, though responses were less pronounced. For example, in fall 2013, 85 percent of students indicated that as a result of service-learning they were more confident in their ability to follow directions, while only 61 percent of students surveyed in fall 2012 and spring 2013 stated that service-learning helped them follow directions "a moderate amount" or "a lot." Similarly, in fall 2013, 83 percent of students reported increased confidence in their ability to complete projects or assignments on time; in fall 2012 and spring 2013, 62 percent of students responded that service-learning helped them meet deadlines "a moderate amount" or "a lot." These differences may be due to students' perceptions of their workplace skills based on the survey question. *Expressing confidence* in an ability to perform a skill may be less intimidating than noting an *increased ability* to perform a skill.

Reflections: Student, Faculty, and Community Partners Report Positive Impacts on CTE Student Skill Acquisition

During the three semesters that the survey was administered, 118 of the 286 CTE students responded to the reflection question about their service-learning experience. The open-ended nature of the question generated some very vague and some very specific responses. The frequency of response content was analyzed and most comments revolved around students' learning and application of course content (32 percent), as well as students' increased civic awareness and an interest in community (30 percent). Fewer students commented on specific "soft skills," though 12 percent mentioned improved interpersonal communication skills and an understanding of other viewpoints, and 6 percent indicated that their perception of others changed. In this latter group, this change refers to the respective populations served by students' different service-learning projects: depending on the project, students indicated a change in their perception of the elderly or the very young, of people from diverse cultures, or of those with differing socioeconomic status. Other aspects of "soft skill" acquisition were expressed by individuals, indicating increased gains in public speaking skills, ability to accept criticism, ability to focus, organizational skills, and ability to follow directions. One student remarked on the experience of working collaboratively toward a goal: "The process of forming a database took a coordinated effort. Our class was able to argue perspectives and arrive at an agreed upon agenda." Another student described how creating a presentation on health careers for high school students strengthened the group's skills: "Presenting...helped me and other students get more comfortable with public speaking and talk about our interests relating to the health field."

Reflective statements collected from writing assignments also demonstrate that service-learning improves skill acquisition. When asked which skills the students applied to the service-learning project that would prepare them for future jobs, health students responded they learned public speaking, interacting with others, and "...working collaboratively with people from diverse backgrounds." Engineering Technology students responded that they learned "...to take criticism, opinions of other people," and "...to design a project given certain parameters." When asked about challenges they faced working with others and how they addressed these challenges, an Engineering Technology student wrote, "I learned how to work with time limitations." CTE students also expressed that course academic content was incorporated into their projects. One student wrote, "Learning through experience taught me more."

CTE faculty reflections further support the notion that service-learning provides students with skill acquisition. A professor of Biotechnology[2], who pairs her students as mentors to high school students on a service-learning DNA fingerprinting project, related:

> I saw tremendous gains in the level of maturity, responsibility and problem solving skills in students. They followed directions to prepare the lab material...Then a few of them took a leadership role...[used] critical thinking skills to explain why the results don't match the predicted hypothesis. These gains are hard to make in a traditional learning environment.

A professor in Massage Therapy reflected on how students in real-world settings learn to adapt to situations as they arise:

> Students had to use problem solving skills to accommodate individuals who could not negotiate getting in and out of a massage chair. This experience encouraged them to think about proper body positioning and safety issues...Massage students had to work effectively and efficiently, they learned to time themselves to get the chair massage done within the allotted time.

In his abstract for the First Year Engineering Experience conference, a Computer Programming professor reflected on how the experience of working for a community partner changed students' approach to the project:

[Students] have now had a memorable experience in which they were asked by a client—not just their professor—to create a program, have met with the client for comments and criticism, and have re-written their programs to meet with their clients' needs, some of which may have been changed or clarified. The difference in the attitude of the students toward their work from when I taught this class without service learning is gratifying. (Schwartz 2013)

Most community partner reflections centered around the positive impact the service-learning students had on the community they serve. Fewer statements centered on the CTE students themselves, though a few comments noted students' professionalism, levels of preparation for their project, and good interpersonal skills. One community partner observed, "The QCC nursing students came dressed in their nursing uniforms which impressed the high school students. Their presentation was clear, and it was evident that they had worked hard to prepare. They interacted well with the high school students." Another community partner commented that "the students have met with our staff and provided a professional presentation of the challenges and solutions."

Retention Data: CTE Service-Learners More Likely to Be Retained Than Non-Service-Learners

CTE students enrolled in fall 2012 who participated in service-learning were retained at QCC at a higher rate than CTE non-service-learners enrolled in fall 2012, as illustrated in table 14.2.

These data indicate a positive relationship between service-learning and students' retention at QCC. Of the 316 students who were enrolled in fall 2012 and participated in service-learning, 255 (80.7 percent) were retained in spring 2013. A chi-square test of independence was performed and the relationship between having a service-learning experience in fall 2012 and QCC retention in spring 2013 was found to be very significant, χ^2 (1, N = 6,656) = 7.73, p < .005. This test ruled out the possibility that the difference in enrollment outcomes between the service-learning and comparison group was due to chance.

Table 14.2 Retention Rates of CTE Students, Service-Learning, and Non-Service-Learning

Participation in Service-Learning	*Fall 2012 Student Cohort*	*Students Retained in Spring 2013*	
	N	N	Percent
Service-Learning	316	255	80.7%
Non-Service-Learning	6,340	4,659	73.5%

Note: CTE students enrolled in fall 2012 who participated in service-learning were retained at QCC at a higher rate than CTE non-service-learners enrolled in fall 2012.

Source: QCC Office of Institutional Research and Assessment.

Discussion

Community colleges have long been the appropriate venue for those seeking career and technical training. In fact, it is at the community college level that specific skills necessary for highly specialized jobs are most frequently taught and learned. Students who enroll in career and technical programs at community colleges do so to learn the hard skills needed for job market entry, but that is not enough. Community colleges must provide "soft skills" education and retain students so that they can enter the workforce with both the skills and certification required to perform and maintain their jobs.

If community colleges wish to answer the government's call to prepare the modern workforce, we contend that career and technical training work best when supported within the framework of service-learning. Further, we contend that service-learning is better than other high-impact practices at promoting the success of career and technical student success. Although all the high-impact practices provide "soft skill" education (Kuh 2008) and particular benefits to underserved community college populations (Finley and McNair 2013) only two of these practices, service-learning and internships, also provide experiential education. There are two important advantages of service-learning for the community college CTE student that sets it apart from internships. One advantage is that, unlike internships, service-learning can be readily incorporated into "hard skills" coursework without impacting the program's course or credit load. A second advantage is that, unlike internships, service-learning can be incorporated into multiple courses within a program. Participation in multiple service-learning courses provides increased benefits to students (Eyler and Giles 1999).

At QCC, the faculty is committed to using service-learning pedagogies as a means to benefit CTE students. Service-learning integrates academic learning with community service; in the process students learn the "soft skills" that are so crucial to the twenty-first century workplace. Interactions with community organizations give students the opportunity to apply classroom knowledge in real-life settings. During service-learning projects, students work collaboratively to: accomplish goals and meet real community needs; communicate with their peers and community partners; improve their reading, writing and speaking skills; and critically analyze their projects as they reflect on their activities within the classroom. These skills will help students successfully persist in the workforce, increasing their chance for future advancement and success.

In this chapter, we have used data from student surveys, from student, faculty, and community partner reflections, and from CUNY's Institutional Research Database to support these contentions. Many of the gains identified are consistent with findings on the impact of service-learning in baccalaureate students (Astin et al. 2000) and in the general population of community college students (Prentice and Robinson 2010). These findings also contribute to a developing body of research that demonstrates how service-learning supports CTE students in workforce development. In addition, given that the student body at QCC consists of the traditionally underserved, our data contribute to discussions regarding the experiences of students of color, first-generation students, and low-income students in service-learning.

Future efforts at QCC will focus on providing students with guidance to help them think critically about their service-learning experiences. Reflection affords students a venue to explore what they have learned through their project; it facilitates their ability to identify achievement of "soft skills" and make connections between their project and course material. This opportunity for critical analysis helps students develop knowledge in their specific CTE content area, as well as in "soft skill" acquisition. The OASL is piloting a set of structured pre- and post-project reflection questions as a further attempt to capture students' experiences and to identify the benefits community college students gain through service-learning.

Limitations

This research involved a small sample of community college students enrolled in a variety of classes across different CTE disciplines. These classes were taught by different faculty members whose students worked on different class projects. These variations may confound the results of the study. Further studies should be conducted with larger sample sizes to determine if the results are consistent. Also, the addition of a control group would help rule out the possibility that the student growth presented was a result of some other process. The student survey data were self-reported. Future studies should add a more objective measure of workplace-readiness skills, including a faculty assessment of students' competencies. The collection of faculty and community partner reflections was limited and a more focused approach should be utilized to gather these reflection data in the future.

Notes

*The authors would like to acknowledge that the study's research on CTE students and service-learning was funded through the OASL by a three-year Carl D. Perkins grant from the New York State Education Department, *Building and Bridging Service-Learning into the Career and Technical Academies and Disciplines,* which was designed to support a service-learning program with the goal of increasing retention and graduation rates of students enrolled in CTE programs. The OASL utilized these funds to enrich career and technical courses with service-learning and assess the outcomes of inserting this pedagogy into CTE curricula. The authors would also like to thank Dr. Ian Beckford, academic assessment manager, Learning Outcomes, QCC Office of Academic Affairs, for his support for the OASL and his analysis of the study's student data.

1. The data included in this chapter come from the following report: QCC Office of Institutional Research and Assessment (2014), "Half-Year Enrollment Outcomes for Students Participating in Service-Learning Activities in Fall 2012.
2. Biotechnology was included as a CTE program during this study, but has subsequently been reclassified as non-CTE.

References

American Association of Community Colleges (AACC). 2013. Accessed January 7, 2014, http://www.aacc.nche.edu/resources/aaccprograms/horizons/Pages/default.aspx.

American Association of Colleges of Nursing (AACN) Faculty Tool Kit. 2008. "The Essentials of Baccalaureate Education for Professional Nursing Practice." Accessed January 1, 2014, http://www.aacn.nche.edu/education-resources/BacEssToolkit.pdf.

Association of American Colleges and Universities (AACU). 2013. "It Takes More Than a Major: Employer Priorities for College Learning and Student Success." Accessed January 7, 2014, http://www.aacu.org/leap/documents/2013_EmployerSurvey.pdf.

AACU and Hart Research Associates. 2010. "Raising the Bar: Employers' Views on College Learning in the Wake of the Economic Downturn." Accessed January 7, 2014, https://www.aacu.org/leap/documents/2009_EmployerSurvey.pdf.

Accreditation Board for Engineering and Technology (ABET). 2005. Accessed January 4, 2014, http://www.foundationcoalition.org/home/keycomponents/assessment_eval/ec_outcomes_summaries.html.

Astin, Alexander W., Lori J. Vogelgesang, Elaine K. Ikeda, and Jennifer A. Yee. 2000. *How Service Learning Affects Students*. Los Angeles: Higher Education Research Institute, University of California.

Bancino, Randy, and Claire Zevalkink. 2007. "Soft Skills: The New Curriculum for Hard-Core Technical Professionals." *Techniques: Connecting Education and Careers* 82 (5): 20–22. Accessed January 7, 2014. http://files.eric.ed.gov/fulltext/EJ764824.pdf.

Burns, Kimberly. 2010. "Community College Student Success Variables: A Review of the Literature." *Community College Enterprise* 16 (2): 33–61. Accessed January 22, 2014. http://eds.a.ebscohost.com/ehost/detail?sid=92a3bcd0-f86f-4b94-a3bb-4262c427590f%40sessionmgr4003&vid=1&hid=4108&bdata=JnNpdGU9ZWhvc3QtbGl2ZSZzY29wZT1zaXRl#db=eue&AN=508190682.

Carnevale, Anthony, and Nicole Smith. 2013. "Skills Match." *Community College Journal* 83 (3): 20–25. Accessed January 7, 2014. http://www.ccjournaldigital.com/ccjournal/20121201?pg=22#pg22.

CUNY. 2014. Colleges and Schools. Accessed January 7, 2014. http://www.cuny.edu/about/colleges.html.

Duncan, Arne. 2010. "The Linchpin: The New Mission of Community Colleges." Accessed January 1, 2014. http://www.ed.gov/news/speeches/linchpin-new-mission-community-colleges.

Eyler, Janet, and Dwight E. Giles Jr. 1999. *Where Is the Learning in Service-Learning?* San Francisco, CA: Jossey-Bass, 1999.

Finley, Ashley and Tia McNair. 2013. *Assessing Underserved Students' Engagement in High-Impact Practices*. Washington, DC: Association of American Colleges and Universities. Accessed January 5, 2014. https://www.aacu.org/assessinghips/documents/TGGrantReport_FINAL_11_13_13.pdf.

Kolb, David A. 1984. *Experiential Learning: Experience as the Source of Learning and Development*. Englewood Cliffs, NJ: Prentice-Hall.

Kuh, George D. 2008. *High-Impact Educational Practices: What They Are, Who Has Access to Them, and Why They Matter*. Washington, DC: Association of American Colleges and Universities.

LEAP. 2007. *College Learning for the New Global Century: A Report from the National Leadership Council for Liberal Education and America's Promise*. Washington, DC: Association of American Colleges and Universities. Accessed January 7, 2014. http://www.aacu.org/leap/documents/GlobalCentury_final.pdf.

Obama, Barack. 2009. "Excerpts of the President's Remarks in Warren, Michigan Today and a Fact Sheet on the American Graduate Initiative." Accessed January 5, 2014. http://www.whitehouse.gov/the_press_office/Excerpts-of-the-Presidents-remarks-in-Warren-Michigan-and-fact-sheet-on-the-American-Graduation-Initiative.

Prentice, Mary and Gail Robinson. 2010. *Improving Student Learning Outcomes with Service Learning.* Washington, DC: American Association of Community Colleges. Accessed January 7, 2014. http://www.aacc.nche.edu/Resources/aaccprograms/horizons/Documents/slorb_jan2010.pdf.

QCC Office of Institutional Research and Assessment. *Fact Book 2012–2013.* Accessed January 7, 2014. http://www.qcc.cuny.edu/pv_obj_cache/pv_obj_id_507807F1E804CF72AB7F096E8DD63C323F5B1A00/filename/Factbook_2012-13.pdf.

Schwartz, Jeffrey L. 2013. "Extended Abstract: Teaching Computer Programming to a Diverse Student Body through Service-Learning." Paper presented at the 5th First Year Engineering Experience (FYEE) Conference, Pittsburgh, Pennsylvania, August 8–9, 2013. Accessed January 8, 2014. http://fyee.org/fyee2013/papers/1012.pdf.

Shuman, Larry J., Mary Besterfield-Sacre, and Jack McGourty. 2005. "The ABET 'Professional Skills': Can They Be Taught? Can They Be Assessed?" *Journal of Engineering Education* 94 (1): 41–55.

Stachowski, Laura L., and Christopher J. Frey. 2005. "Student Teachers' Reflections on Service and Learning in Navajo Reservation Communities: Contextualizing the Classroom Experience." *School Community Journal* 15 (2): 101.

Taggart, Amanda, and Gloria Crisp. 2011. "Service Learning at Community Colleges: Synthesis, Critique, and Recommendations for Future Research." *Journal of College Reading and Learning* 42 (1): 24–44.

US Department of Labor (DOL). 2013, Accessed January 8, 2014. http://www.dol.gov/odep/topics/youth/softskills.

USNCES. 2012a. U.S. National Center for Education Statistics. Table 427. *Digest of Education Statistics*: 2012. Accessed January 1, 2014. http://nces.ed.gov/programs/digest/d12/tables_5.asp#Ch5Sub2.

USNCES. 2012b. U.S. National Center for Education Statistics. Table 438. *Digest of Education Statistics*: 2012. Accessed January 1, 2014. http://nces.ed.gov/programs/digest/d12/tables_5.asp#Ch5Sub2.

Vaknin, Lauren Weiner, and Marilee J. Bresciani. 2013. "Implementing Quality Service-Learning Programs in Community Colleges." *Community College Journal of Research and Practice* 37: 979–989.

Vaughan, George B. 2006. *The Community College Story.* Washington, DC: American Association of Community Colleges.

Zlotkowski, Edward. 1996. "Opportunity for All: Linking Service-Learning and Business Education." *Journal of Business Ethics* 15 (1): 5–19.

CHAPTER 15

Mapping Routes to Our Roots: Student Civic Engagement in Transportation Planning

Rebecca M. Townsend

The best assets of any community college are their students. Students learn, grow, thrive, and, often, remain in their community to help others do the same. They are vital to the development of their communities. Their voices, unfortunately too often silent to policy makers, can contribute to sustainable futures for the cities and towns in which they dwell. Their experiences and stories can enlighten others about how people live in a place and how those places can be made better for those who live there. How can these voices be heard? Can students at a community college help to generate public participation in government planning? Can they use their roots in the community to help their community find a voice? In this chapter, I discuss the theoretical and conceptual grounding for the "Partnership for Inclusive, Cost-Effective Public Participation" (PICEP2), a model of curriculum for Communication courses at Manchester Community College (MCC) in Manchester, Connecticut, that was designed to amplify citizen voices in government public engagement efforts. This project, which I created through funds from the Federal Transit Administration, is an example of using service-learning with community college students (and their networks) to bring previously silenced voices into efforts to solve/satisfy community/public (transportation) needs. It also indicates: (1) the direct connection between service-learning and participatory action research; (2) the direct role theory can play in project design; and (3) the real and unique contributions community college students, as community members, can make to mandated community-participation processes (as network bridges to additional participants).

The Project: Partnership for Inclusive, Cost-Effective Public Participation (PICEP2)

The PICEP2 developed out of studying public voice in community governance. While in graduate school for my PhD in communication, I studied public involvement in government. I became fascinated by the work of Danish planning scholar Bent Flyvbjerg, particularly his ability to draw on theory to help describe and explain massive infrastructure projects and produce critical work of tremendous value. Having always been fascinated by civic and community life, I volunteered to serve as my hometown's alternate representative to my regional planning agency, the Pioneer Valley Planning Commission. In addition to learning about the broad spectrum of activities in which planning agencies engage, I gained a great deal of knowledge about the dearth of transportation options in Western Massachusetts. Though there was a rail line running parallel with the Connecticut River, the train did not run with enough frequency to spur the economic development that would come with linking (via Connecticut) to rail connected to New York City. Citizens would have to demand it, I learned, so I initiated a region-wide citizens' activist group, the Pioneer Valley Advocates for Commuter Rail. In doing so, I became aware of how little citizens believed their opinions mattered. Soon I became known in my community for my understanding of both transportation and communication. While serving on another town board, a fellow board member who worked for an international transportation planning firm informed me of a grant that the Federal Transit Administration (FTA) was offering to scholars who could help address a key problem in transportation planning: getting people with low incomes, racial and ethnic minorities, and youth engaged in legally required public involvement efforts. He shared a study with me that demonstrated the kinds of efforts planners used to engage these "hard-to-reach" groups. He offered his pro bono assistance on the grant application for the FTA's Public Transportation Participation Pilot Program (PTP-4), and another colleague who had done a great deal of community engagement work joined the team.

With my background as a transportation activist, community member, and college professor at MCC in Manchester, Connecticut, I wanted to create a model of curriculum that would address planners' needs for public engagement, community members' needs to have a say in the kinds of transportation modes, services, schedules, and funding systems that are designed to meet their needs, and college students' needs to participate in meaningful coursework. Thus, at its core, I developed PICEP2 to engage community college students' existing connections with their own community groups (whether through work, social life, religious affiliation, or other) as bridges for public participation in planning or government engagement.

In 2009, the PTP-4 funded the PICEP2 at $77,368.65. With these funds, I was able to hire project staff members, purchase a sturdy high-quality audio recorder, supply food for meetings, and obtain a course release each semester of the project. The project involved students in two of my communication courses at MCC, Public Speaking and Group Communication. In each course, students traditionally learn the discipline's central ideas of understanding audiences, crafting effective and appropriate messages, and sensitivity to context. Through PICEP2, these ideas were applied to understanding community groups, crafting questions and responses that helped elicit discussion about transportation within these groups, and comprehending how cultural background and life situations help to shape people's responses in the discussion.

My spring 2010 Public Speaking classes assisted staff in conducting a kick-off meeting for the project with 47 government, community, and business leaders, students, faculty, and administration. Students promoted this event, helped with implementing it, and were active members of the discussions. MCC's president, Dr. Gena Glickman, opened the meeting, which included a multicourse meal prepared and served by MCC's Culinary Arts students (and funded by the President's Innovation Fund). Participants at each table talked about the scope of students' fall 2010 and spring 2011 PICEP2 work. Working across the tables, participants then decided that students would focus on understanding transportation needs across all modes (walking, biking, bus, car, rail, etc.) in the Greater Hartford region. To do so, students would connect with community groups to conduct discussions about transportation at the times and places where the groups already meet, recording their discussions digitally and via field notes.

In the fall of 2010, the project got underway. On the first day of class, students enrolled into two sections of Public Speaking and a single Group Communication course learned that their sections would be doing service-learning to assist their communities and regional planners in public engagement on transportation planning. The Public Speaking students would be researching, writing, and conducting speeches on transportation and helping to facilitate the group discussions noted above. The Group Communication course's students had additional work. In addition to conducting two discussions, they would draw on insights from ethnography of communication and consultations with planners to develop a discussion guide, and they would also analyze their own class-based group communication dynamics. Guest speakers on transportation planning were invited to speak to both the Public Speaking and Group Communication courses.

The major work for students' preparation and leadership of the discussions involved the following steps. Students learned about transportation planning and public involvement. They learned about the International Association for Public Participation (IAP2) Spectrum of Participation (International Association of Public Participation 2007b), and they agreed to adhere to IAP2 Core Values and Code of Ethics for Public Participation Practitioners (International Association for Public Participation 2007a; International Association of Public Participation, n.d.). Students worked in research teams based on the geographical proximity of their residences. Each research team generated a list of groups to which they belonged, from family to religious organizations, sports to work. Students selected a community group and contacted a non-class member representative of that group to ask for permission to conduct a 30–60 minute discussion on transportation needs at a time and place where the group normally meets. Students conducted the discussions, recording observations in ethnographic field notes. They administered written questionnaires to community group participants, assisting if needed. For example, if some people had trouble reading, students would read the questions aloud. They also audio-recorded the discussions, which were transcribed by a paid professional service. Students presented findings related to transportation needs at an end-of-semester symposium. The symposium included group posters, dinner, and select student speeches. Audience members included community group members, planners, academics, transit providers, and government and business leaders. This process was refined and repeated with three Public Speaking classes in the spring 2011 semester. Since Group Communication had a low enrollment that semester, the course was canceled.

Theoretical Bases for PICEP2

Various literatures helped to shape the PICEP2. Since the FTA was looking for whether certain kinds of innovative methods of public participation would be effective, I drew upon theories of service-learning and participatory action research within communication studies, ethnographies of communication and group deliberation, and public participation and transportation sources. Through this review of the theoretical bases for the project, I will demonstrate how service-learning can be a form of action research, and how theoretically informed design can craft a project that meets (and exceeds) legal mandates for public involvement.

Participatory Action Research and Service-Learning

PICEP2 emerged out of a need for improved public participation in policy planning and a need for engaged student learning. Students, involved as co-researchers and as members of the community groups with which they met, amplified community group voices and connected those who had been labeled as "hard-to-reach" with those who need to reach them. This type of pedagogy, which is "translational" (Frey 2009, 205) or "makes a difference" (Kahl Jr. 2010, 298), affects how professors present material, how knowledge of communication practices become present to students, and how improved communication becomes manifest within a community:

> Communication is not only the outcome of learning an individual skill (through which one's competence in society can be measured) but is also central to the process of learning, and key to constructing engaged participation in a civil society. If individuals make meaning of themselves and society through communicative processes, then participation is itself defined in and through communication; without communication, participation in society would be impossible. (Cooks, Scharrer, and Castaneda Paredes 2004, 44)

Service-learning is one such example of such this type of pedagogy: students learn about communication while engaging in communication in service to their communities. They apply what they learned to real-world situations and needs.

Service-learning is often coupled with participatory action research. Schensul and Berg (2004) link service-learning and participatory action research in the following way:

> Action research as service-learning is an activist oriented participatory approach to addressing social problems that utilizes ethnographic research methods

together with the critical theories of anthropology, sociology, and education to involve community members in identifying, conducting research on, and working to resolve social problems that affect them, their peers and their communities. (76)

Paired together, service-learning and participatory action research contribute to students' understanding of local political communication dynamics (in contrast with national political communication) (Townsend 2006) and engaged students' intellects, bodies, and senses of selves as civic agents.

Ethnography of Communication

The PICEP2 is based in ethnography of communication (Hymes 1962) and cultural discourse analysis (Carbaugh 2007). Ethnography of communication is both a theory and a method of conducting research that "embraces cultural diversity and uses this diversity to understand what is particular and what is general in discourse and communication across cultures" (Scollo 2011, 5). It seeks first to understand how it is that people communicate. Often using native informants, ethnographers of communication engage in intense participant observation while recording observations and making initial interpretations in field notes. In order for this research to approach validity, participant observations must involve close and careful knowledge of the scene, setting, participants, acts, act sequence, emotional tone, means, norms, and genres in speaking events. This holistic view of the broad and specific contexts that shape communication requires the researcher to demarcate the boundaries of her or his observations.

Cultural discourse analysis (Carbaugh 2007) is a further development of the ethnography of communication where the major focus is on the ways of being, acting, relating, feeling, and dwelling in a speech community. This theoretical framework, elaborated elsewhere (Townsend 2013), presumes that because native members of a speech community already know, understand, and have the trust of their community members, they will choose those ways of communicating when in that community. In other words, because an outsider may not understand the rules for speech and social interaction in a community, they may have less success in communicating with that community. In the PICEP2, students, who were members of many of the groups with which they met, led group discussions using a discussion guide that they helped to create using ethnography of communication concepts like setting, scene, participants, ends/outcomes, among others.

Group Communication

While ethnography of communication can address any communicative actions, group discussions are a particular kind of interaction that has its own literature in the discipline of communication. Group communication and deliberation scholarship and (Gastil 2009) the practice of public involvement or engagement (International Association of Public Participation 2009) also informs this work. Groups across the world communicate in ways that seem natural to them and enact different forms of making decisions. The PICEP2 asked group members to make decisions, to be *deliberative*, on a subject that government needs them to discuss. To be deliberative, a discussion "establishes a solid information base, prioritizes the key values at stake, identifies a broad range of solutions, looks carefully at the advantages, disadvantages, and tradeoffs among choices, and ultimately makes the best judgment" (Gastil 2009, 2). Students' crafting of the discussion guide included deliberative activities where group members needed to weigh what was most important to them, whether government dollars should go toward one mode of transportation over another, or whether a particular mode of transportation was deemed to be better for the environment.

Because deliberation has been so strongly aligned with democracy, and because some organizations realize the importance of having *everyone* participate in democratic discussions, community colleges are an ideal place for students to serve as facilitators of group decision making and deliberation. Yet even Carcasson, Black and Sink's (2010) exhaustive review of work in communication on deliberation in higher education ignores how community college students in communication classes can create or use deliberative spaces in their communities of origin. Thankfully, one network of organizations affiliated with the National Issues Forum Institute does include community colleges. The National Issues Forum Institute (and other organizations like it, e.g., the National Coalition for Dialogue and Deliberation) draws upon communication research and supports other institutions, like colleges, in the conducting of public deliberation. Most notable is Arizona's Maricopa Community College Center for Civic Participation. In an interview, its director, Alberto Olivas, a national leader among deliberation researchers and practitioners, noted that community colleges are less prominent among colleges that engage in deliberative forums. Yet, he also cited distinct benefits of deliberation at community colleges:

> On any effort where you need to try and attract members of the community to a public event on an issue, community colleges make more sense. A lot of times in the past, people would host these things in official government offices, like the County Board of Supervisors auditorium, or the Secretary of State's offices. Most members of the public don't know where those places are. But everybody knows where the community college is, even if you've never taken a class there. Most people know what their local community college is and how to get there. And it seems available to people in a way that state university campuses oftentimes do not. [...] community colleges tend to enjoy a high degree of confidence, a trust, by the community members. We're trusted. We're seen as a resource. And people know how to get to us. (Olivas 2010, n.p.)

The significant role that community colleges play in communities helped shape the PICEP2. In the PICEP2, I sought to connect the orientation provided by ethnography of communication and cultural discourse analysis with knowledge about group deliberation at community colleges as a way to meet a need for participatory engagement in planning process. Yet I did not limit discussion location to the community college; instead students were asked to hold discussions in those places where community groups regularly gather.

Transportation Planning and Community College Engagement

Developed with funding from the US Department of Transportation Federal Transit Administration's (FTA) Public Transportation Participation Pilot Program (PTP-4), the PICEP2 aims to fulfill and surpass legal mandates for minimum public involvement, mandates that developed in 1946 (McComas 2001). Public involvement became part of transportation planning starting with the Intermodal Surface Transportation Efficiency Act (ISTEA) of 1991 through the Transportation Equity Act for the 21st Century (TEA-21) in 1998, and expanded in the 2005 Safe, Accountable, Flexible, Efficient Transportation Equity Act: A Legacy for Users (SAFETEA-LU) (Smith 2006). The current legislation, the Moving Ahead for Progress in the 21st Century Act (MAP-21) (P.L. 112–141), continues where SAFETEA-LU left off. Metropolitan Planning Organizations are required to have a plan detailing how they will involve the public. Before a project is developed, environmental review processes mandated by the National Environmental Policy Act (NEPA) require public involvement. And transit agencies in relation to FTA programs must also conduct public involvement that is environmentally "just" or fair and equitable to all.

This notion of environmental justice, which is part of Environmental Justice Executive Order 12898 signed in 1994, refers to "the fair treatment and meaningful involvement of all people regardless of race, color, national origin, or income with respect to the development, implementation, and enforcement of environmental laws, regulations, and policies" (US Environmental Protection Agency 2012). The Environmental Protection Agency explains that meaningful involvement entails that "people have an opportunity to participate in decisions about activities that may affect their environment and/or health" (US Environmental Protection Agency 2012). It also calls for the provision of public participation for minority and low-income communities. The efforts of transportation planners and those focused on transit seem to be thoughtful and reflective about their need to engage these various publics. For example, the PTP-4 was designed to fund innovative research projects that would deepen and broaden public participation in transit planning. In particular, it emphasizes the development of specific ways to connect with "hard-to-reach" populations and remain sensitive to cost. The PICEP2 addressed these concerns by engaging community college students, who are members of the communities sought by planners, as leaders of and partners in public engagement. In so doing, it evidenced how community colleges can serve as cost-effective resources for future and different public engagement efforts.

Conclusion

At the onset of PICEP2, I applied for and received Institutional Research Board approval from MCC to study this project. As a result, I would like to conclude this chapter with a brief summary of the project's findings. In total, PICEP2 engaged 95 students as trained facilitators and ethnographic recorders of group deliberation. In turn, these students engaged 29 different community groups, including Spanish-speaking church parishioners; a fantasy soccer league; nursing home staff; a senior center belly-dancing class; high-school students in a social studies class; members of a male minority group mentoring association; a ballroom dancing club; volunteer firefighters; a college women's basketball team; student study groups; social service agency staff; a junior police group for middle-school aged youth; clients at a homeless shelter; a dentist's office staff; and more. Nearly every group queried granted students' requests to conduct a discussion.

As indicated in the project's Final Report (Townsend 2012), participants' post-discussion questionnaires ($n = 108$) yielded interesting descriptive data about the breadth of public involvement in students' transportation discussions: 42 percent of participants were in either high school or college; 47 percent were male; 53 percent were female; 56 percent lived in Manchester or Hartford; 59 percent self-identified as nonwhite; 16 percent spoke a language other than English at home; 25 percent took their own vehicle to school or work; 53 percent took a bus to school or work; 8 percent had previously contacted a government agency; and 8 percent had previously attended a public meeting. The mean age of participants was 28; the mode age was 17; and the median age was 18. The questionnaires also asked participants to describe their prior interest in participating in local transportation planning issues in their community at a level of 1.5 out of 5 (where 1 = not interested; 5 = very interested). Subsequent to the discussion, participants reported that their current interest level in participating in local transportation planning issues in their community increased to 2.6 out of 5.

Participants had much to say about transportation needs, reporting major concerns with bus availability, promptness, driver-rider interaction, and safety and comfort. Those with the lowest, or no, income were particularly concerned about bus ticket prices, arguing that free bus passes ought to be provided to seniors and the homeless. Students' ethnographic data revealed that participants' concerns spanned the following issues: respect for users of public transportation; the convenience, time, affordability, route and mode of availability of public transportation; the comfort, cleanliness, and safety of public transportation; passenger interactions on public transportation; their ability to have a voice and feel valued in discussions of transportation planning; bicycles, children and strollers; walking and sidewalks; and public involvement and efficacy in shaping transportation policy and practice.

As evidenced, participants wanted to be involved and to have a say in how their communities are structured. A primary concern holding many participants back from full expression of their democratic rights in this regard was their perception that they were insignificant to transit providers or to government more broadly. Thus, the first major finding of this project is that group discussion sessions can help to both involve and value the input of community members on matters of transportation. Student reflections also provided data for project analysis. In these writings, students expressed surprise at how participants responded to them and with their success in the assignment. In some of the writing, students noted their own transformation: "It was a great experience for me. I have never had to speak to a large group of people outside of class. It was good to feel that we were able to engage them even if it was only for a short period of time. I felt that they respected us and we even got some handshakes on our way out." Transformations focused on their developing communicative abilities. However, they were not convinced that it would work, as this student's reflection shows: "At first I thought this was a pointless exercise in public speaking, but I quickly realized you know what you are doing and that it was very valuable for me. It is something that will help me in life not just in your class." Participatory action research can bring powerful changes to people's ways of interacting with the world.

Beyond how the experience could benefit them personally, students also noted the importance that public participation has for people who are traditionally marginalized in such processes. Some students were aware that their role in connecting two spheres—the public, and the planners and service providers—was a position of importance, as this student's writing demonstrates: "I am also grateful for the privilege of being their voice on improving the fairness, convenience and safety of public transportation because many of them are non-participants of meetings like this." A different student explained, "It was nice for kids who can't get their voices heard to actually have that happen, they seemed surprised that people actually do care about how they feel. They also seemed shocked that what they think really does matter." The potential for transformation moved from "self" to "other people" sometimes also resulted in a third shift, a move to "society." This student was able to see the bigger picture of the role of public participation in a democratic society: "Connecticut cannot fix its transportation until it fixes communication. It has to reach out to those most affected by our state's numerous transportation issues, as there is no point in living in a democracy if your voice cannot be heard." And lastly, this student's reflection summarizes the entire experience:

> I think the most important part was we the students were almost like teachers in a way. We had to gather the information by ourselves to have a meeting based around the information we gathered and we needed to attend meetings out of class to get the information. This is a lot of responsibility that you don't receive in other classes. I think this was the key to the amazing learning environment that we had. We felt that what we did mattered and that what we were doing in and out of class not only mattered to our grades but it mattered to the community. What we did in class was going to make a positive effect on something more than us and that was honestly a really great feeling. I felt like this was more than school for once. I was doing something for a greater cause and going into it I was a little nervous thinking how the hell am I going to do this, I don't know anything about transportation but that wasn't the case at all and I was delighted with the end results that we made.

As indicated, students learned core topics and methods in communication through direct action in their communities. They also engaged "hard-to-reach" (or "under-heard") publics in ways that have proven difficult—but essential—to public planning efforts in the past. Having the trust of "hard-to-reach" (or "under-heard") groups eased students' participation; they were seen as liaisons that could be trusted to both receive the opinions and then share them with the transit providers and transportation planners. This trust was generated in several ways: (1) students were themselves part of the "under-heard" population already connected to the community groups with which they partnered and (2) students were prepared theoretically and practically for an intervention in their communities that had the potential for development of both themselves and their communities. Thus, the second major finding of this study is that, when armed with the appropriate theoretical knowledge and practical training, community college students can serve as effective network bridges between community members and planners.

Area planners have since informed students that they plan to use the project's findings in future work to improve transportation services. They also indicated that they would use the strategy of partnering with community college students as a part of their public involvement efforts in the future. As a result of this feedback and their more general experience with PICEP2, many of the students involved in the project have gone on to positions of leadership, internships, and further involvement in community organizations. For example, after calling out the local bus service provider in a semester's end symposium, one student received an internship with that organization. Another student, who had been uninterested in school, sought greater involvement in school and the community after his participation in PICEP2: he became student government president and had internships with a US Senator and the Governor's Office. He is pursuing further education and a public service career (in transportation or logistics, and the armed forces). Significantly, all PICEP students can indicate on their resumes that they were assistant researchers in a federally funded study. Numerous other outcomes resulted from this work. College-community partnerships were strengthened. Any college is concerned about outreach. Community colleges in particular have partnerships with multiple organizations as part of their foundations. The premise that people will talk with whom they trust was upheld. Where consultants and planners, no matter how well meaning, have difficulty in gaining people's trust to speak with them, this "trust gap" was bridged through the use of students' social networks. Public participation became more deliberative and inclusive. Students saw they were able to bring more people into policy conversations now than previous to their efforts. Interest and involvement amplified while costs were reduced. Typically, consultants who do public engagement work cost tens of thousands of dollars. The PICEP2 dollar costs were under $1000; several hours of student research and faculty time in setting this project up were the personnel costs. Student leadership abilities and civic involvement increased.

Students reflected on their own learning and civic engagement in final speeches for the courses. They were amazed at their own growth, often puzzled that they found such a "random" topic like transportation policy interesting. They felt responsible and engaged in the civic infrastructure of their communities. I was curious about the effects this had on their success in school, if any. In addition to seeking student evaluations in the middle of the course I sought information about how my projects have improved student retention. According to research that the Institutional Research Office at MCC conducted at my request, new and full-time students who took Public Speaking with me in specific semesters where I used community service learning in 2010 were more likely to earn a degree or certificate in the time since their Public Speaking class, 12 percent versus 5 percent.

To conclude, community college student participation in leading deliberative, democratic discussions allows them to exercise civic muscles that they may not have known they had. It can also have a significant impact on the communities from which they come and to which they return. Students' pride in their growth, strength, and accomplishments was heartening for me to witness. Civic participation, once experienced, can become habit-forming. Community college student engagement with their communities through service-learning is one habit that will increase the power of their communities.

Note

*The work for the project described herein has benefitted from the advice and consultation of many people. Specifically, I would like to thank all the students plus Stephen Gazillo; David Elvin; Shelby Brown; Martin Hart; Tim Woods; Matthew Robinson; Joanne Waszczak; Elizabeth Murphy; Angel Williams; Martín Carcasson; and Tom, Tommy, and Charlie Townsend. A special note in honor of her memory, Valerie Scott created the title for this work; her words help me to communicate the meaningfulness of the students' efforts.

References

Black, Laura W. 2009. "Stories of North Omaha: Conveying Identities, Values, and Actions through Storytelling in a Public Meeting." *International Journal of Public Participation*: 36–55.
Black, Laura W., H. T. Wesler, D. Cosley, and J. M. DeGroot. 2011. "Self-Governance through Group Discussion in Wikipedia: Measuring Deliberation in Online Groups." *Small Group Research* 42: 595–634.
Bureau of Labor Statistics. 2013. *Urban and Regional Planners.* Accessed September 8. http://www.bls.gov/ooh/Life-Physical-and-Social-Science/Urban-and-regional-planners.htm.
Capitol Region Council of Governments. 2010. "CRCOG Transportation Planning Program Annual Assessment of Public Involvement Efforts." *Capitol Region Council of Governments.* December 22. http://www.crcog.org/publications/TransportationDocs/FY2010-PI-Assessment.pdf.
Carbaugh, Donal. 2007. "Cultural Discourse Analysis: Communication Practices and Intercultural Encounters." *Journal of Intercultural Communication Research* 36 (3): 167–182.
Carbaugh, Donal, Ute Winter, Brion van Over, Elizabeth Molina-Markham, and Sunny Lie. 2013. "Cultural Analyses of In-car Communication." *Journal of Applied Communication Research* 41 (2): 195–201.
Carcasson, Martín. 2010. *Facilitating Democracy: Centers and Institutes of Public Deliberation and Collaborative Problem-Solving* 152, in *New Directions for Higher Education: Educating for Deliberative Democracy*, edited by Nancy L. Thomas, 51–57. San Francisco, CA: Jossey-Bass.
———. 2011. "Facilitating Democracy through Passionate Impartiality: Communication Studies Programs and Students Should Serve as Local Resources." *Spectra*: 3–7.
Carcasson, Martín, Laura W. Black, and Elizabeth S. Sink. 2010. "Communication Studies and Deliberative Democracy: Current Contributions and Future Possibilities." *Journal of Public Deliberation* 6 (1).
Center for Civic Participation. 2013. *Curriculum Infusion Project.* Accessed January 13, 2014. http://www.maricopa.edu/employees/divisions/publicaffairs/ccp/civic-responsibility-curriculum-infusion-project/.
Conrad, Elizabeth, Louis F. Cassar, Michael Jones, Sebastian Eiter, Zita Izaovičová, Zuzana Barankova, Mike Christies, and Ioan Fazy. "Rhetoric and Reporting of Public Participation in Landscape Policy." *Journal of Environmental Policy & Planning* 13: 1, 23–47.
Cooks, Leda, Erica Scharrer, and Mari Castaneda Paredes. 2004. "Toward a Social Approach to Learning in Community Service Learning." *Michigan Journal of Community Service Learning* 10: 44–56.

Creighton, Sean. 2013. "Today's Civic Mission for Community Colleges." *Higher Education Exchange*: 69–77.
Federal Transit Administration. 2012. "Environmental Justice Policy Guidance for Federal Transit Administration Recipients." Vol. FTA C 4703.1. Washington, DC: US Department of Transportation, July 14.
Frey, Lawrence R. 2009. "What a Difference More Difference-Making Communication Scholarship Might Make: Making a Difference from and through Communication Research." *Journal of Applied Communication Research* 37: 205–214.
Gastil, John. 1993. *Democracy in Small Groups: Participation, Decision Making and Communication.* Philadelphia: New Society Publishers.
———. 2000. *By Popular Demand: Revitalizing Representative Democracy through Deliberative Elections.* Berkeley: University of California Press.
———. 2009. "The Spirit and Practice of Deliberative Democracy." March/April. Accessed January 2014. http://www.la1.psu.edu/cas/jgastil/pdfs/SpiritAndPractice.pdf.
Gastil, John, E. Pierre Deess, Philip J. Weiser, and Cindy Simmons. 2010. *How Jury Deliberation Promotes Civic Engagement and Political Participation.* New York: Oxford University Press.
Hymes, Dell. 1962. "The Ethnography of Speaking." In *Anthropology and Human Behavior*, by Thomas Gladwin and William C. Sturtevant, 13–53. Washington, DC: Anthropological Society of Washington.
———. 1972. "Models of the Interaction of Language and Social Life." In *Directions in Sociolinguistics: The Ethnography of Communication*, edited by John Gumperz and Dell Hymes, 35–71. New York: Holt, Rinehart & Winston, 1972.
———. 1978. *What Is Ethnography?* Working papers in sociolinguistics. Vol. 45. Austin: Southwest Educational Development Laboratory.
International Association for Public Participation. 2007a. "IAP2 Core Values of Public Participation." *IAP2*. Accessed April 16, 2013. http://www.iap2.org/associations/4748/files/CoreValues.pdf.
———. 2007b. "Spectrum of Participation." *IAP2*. Accessed April 16, 2013. http://www.iap2.org/associations/4748/files/IAP2%20Spectrum_vertical.pdf.
———. 2009. "Painting the Landscape: A Cross-Cultural Exploration of Public-Government Decision-Making." Thornton.
———. n.d. "IAP2 Code of Ethics for Public Participation Practitioners." *IAP2*. Accessed April 16, 2013. http://iap2.affiniscape.com/associations/4748/files/CodeofEthics.pdf.
Kahl Jr., David H. 2010. "Making a Difference: (Re)Connecting Communication Scholarship with Pedagogy." *Journal of Applied Communication Research* 38 (3): 298–302.
Keyton, Joann, Stephenson J. Beck, Amber S. Messersmith, and Ryan S. Bisel. 2010. "Ensuring Communication Research Makes a Difference." *Journal of Applied Communication Research* 38 (3): 306–309.
Leighter, James L., Lisa Rudnick, and Theresa J. Edmonds. 2013. "How the Ethnographer of Communication Provides Resources for Design." *Journal of Applied Communication Research*: 209–215.
McComas, Katherine A. 2001. "Theory and Practice of Public Meetings." *Communication Theory* 11: 36–55.
Molina-Markham, Elizabeth. 2013. "Finding the 'Sense of the Meeting': Decision Making through Silence among Quakers." *Western Journal of Communication* 78 (2): 155–174.
Mosher, Heather. 2013. "A Question of Quality: The Art/Science of Doing Collaborative Public Ethnography." *Qualitative Research* May 30: 428–441.
Olivas, Alberto, interview by Scott London. 2010. *Civic Engagement at Maricopa Community Colleges: An Interview with Alberto Olivas.* Parts of it were featured in a public radio program titled Education for Democracy. October 5.

Schensul, Jean J., and Marlene Berg. 2004. "Youth Participatory Action Research: A Transformative Approach to Service-Learning." *Michigan Journal of Community Service Learning*: 76–88.

Scollo, Michelle. 2011. "Cultural Approaches to Discourse Analysis: A Theoretical and Methodological Conversation with Special Focus on Donal Carbaugh's Cultural Discourse Theory." *Journal of Multicultural Discourses* 6: 1–32.

Smith, Darren W. 2006. "Evolving Involvement: New Public Participation Requirements of SAFETEA-LU." Presentation to the TPB Citizens Advisory Committee.

Sprain, Leah, Danielle Endres, and Tarla Rai Petersen. 2010. "Research as a Transdisciplinary Networked Process: A Metaphor for Difference-Making Research." *Communication Monographs* 77 (4): 441–444.

Sprain, Leah and David Boromisza-Habashi. 2013. "The Ethnographer of Communication at the Table: Building Cultural Competence, Designing Strategic Action." *Journal of Applied Communication Research* 41 (2): 181–187.

The National Task Force on Civic Learning and Democratic Engagement. 2012. *A Crucible Moment: College Learning and Democracy's Future*. Washington, DC: Association of American Colleges and Universities.

Townsend, Rebecca M. 2006. "Review Essay: Local Communication Studies." *Quarterly Journal of Speech* 92 (2): 202–222.

———. 2009. "Town Meeting as a Communicative Event: Democracy's Act Sequence." *Research on Language and Social Interaction* 42 (1): 68–89.

———. 2012. *Partnership for Inclusive, Cost-Effective Public Participation Final Report*. Washington, DC: US Department of Transportation, Federal Transit Administration.

———. 2013. "Engaging 'Others' in Civic Engagement through Ethnography of Communication." *Journal of Applied Communication Research* 41 (2): 202–208.

Tracy, Karen. 2010. *Challenges of Ordinary Democracy: A Case Study in Deliberation and Dissent*. State College: Penn State Press.

Tracy, Sarah J. 2007. "Taking the Plunge: A Contextual Approach to Problem-Based Research." *Communication Monographs*: 106–111.

US Department of Transportation Federal Highway Administration. 2006. "How to Engage Low-Literacy and Limited-English-Proficiency Populations in Transportation Decisionmaking." February. Accessed July 5, 2012. http://www.fhwa.dot.gov/planning/publications/low_limited/index.cfm.

———. 2013. "Public Involvement Techniques for Transportation Decision-Making." May 16. Accessed September 8. http://www.fhwa.dot.gov/planning/public_involvement/publications/techniques/chapter02.cfm.

US Department of Transportation Federal Transit Administration. 2011. *Transit Cooperative Research Program Synthesis 89 Public Participation Strategies for Transit: A Synthesis of Transit Practice*. Washington, DC: US Department of Transportation.

US Environmental Protection Agency. 2012. *Environmental Justice: Basic Information*. May 24. Accessed June 1, 2013. http://www.epa.gov/environmentaljustice/basics/index.html.

———. 2012. *Environmental Justice: Basic Information Background*. May 24. Accessed June 1, 2013. http://www.epa.gov/environmentaljustice/basics/ejbackground.html.

Witteborn, Saskia, Trudy Milburn, and Evelyn Y. Ho. 2013. "The Ethnography of Communication as Applied Methodology: Insights from Three Case Studies." *Journal of Applied Communication Research* 41 (2): 188–194.

PART V

Future Directions and Considerations in Service-Learning and Service-Learning Research at Community Colleges

CHAPTER 16

Overcoming Obstacles for Involving Part-Time Faculty in Service-Learning

Daniel Maxey and Adrianna Kezar

One of the main challenges facing community colleges in creating and sustaining service-learning curricula and programs is their growing reliance on part-time non-tenure-track faculty. Although research suggests there is strong interest among non-tenure-track faculty in civic engagement and utilizing service-learning in their courses, these faculty members often face obstacles that limit their involvement (Garcia and Robinson 2005; Antonio, Astin, and Cress 2000). Studies have demonstrated how the working conditions of part-time faculty constrain their ability to provide a high-quality learning environment for their students, including their utilization of high-impact practices, teaching strategies, and pedagogies such as service-learning (Baldwin and Wawrzynski 2011; Umbach 2007). In addition to receiving inequitable compensation and benefits, they are often hired at the last minute and given little time to prepare for teaching their courses, lack opportunities for professional development, and may not have access to materials, support personnel, office space, or email addresses to help them fulfill their duties for instruction effectively. They may also be excluded from departmental faculty meetings or from making contributions to curriculum design. These are only a few factors that constrain the work of non-tenure-track faculty. While much has been written about part-time faculty over the last several years, only a few publications such as the American Association of Community Colleges' *Creating a Climate for Service Learning Success* (Jeandron and Robinson 2010) and *Transcending Disciplines, Reinforcing Curricula: Why Faculty Teach with Service Learning* (Garcia and Robinson 2005) have called attention to positive steps that can be taken to help them to utilize high-impact practices, effective teaching strategies, or pedagogies such as service-learning in a better manner.

Still, on many community college campuses across the country, faculty and staff leaders are working to change policies and practices that impose limits on part-time faculty members' work; many are at the forefront of efforts to integrate part-time faculty into activities and the broader life of the campus. In our work with organizations such as Achieving the Dream and the American Association of Community Colleges (AACC) through the Delphi Project on the Changing Faculty and Student Success, we have learned from and helped to share positive examples from colleges that are improving their policies and practices for supporting part-time faculty.[1] What we have seen is that it is not only possible to improve conditions for non-tenure-track faculty, but that by purposefully connecting these faculty members to professional development, providing feedback to enhance their teaching, giving them resources and access to support staff, and involving them in decision making and curriculum development, faculty members are often better prepared to provide a high-quality learning experience for their students.

In this chapter, we aim to foster greater awareness about some of the challenges faced by part-time faculty in order to help service-learning advocates and others consider ways to improve conditions that will lead to greater adoption and more effective use of the pedagogy. First, we provide a brief overview of the changing composition of the community college professoriate. Second, we highlight encouraging research findings about non-tenure-track faculty and service-learning. Third, we review some of the challenges that specifically relate to part-time faculty members' ability to implement service-learning in their courses. Finally, we present a case involving a campus that has sought to change these conditions as a model. By doing so, we intend to call attention to areas where community college leaders, including department chairs, directors of centers of teaching and learning, and service-learning professionals can focus on efforts to provide better support to these faculty members.

Literature Review

The Growing Numbers of Part-Time Faculty in Community Colleges

Reliance on part-time faculty has increased across all higher education institution types, but community colleges utilize part-time faculty in greater numbers than the others and have been employing large numbers of individuals in these positions since the 1980s (AFT 2009; Eagan 2007; Gappa and Leslie 1993).[2] The numbers of part-time faculty members continue to grow. In 1997, part-time faculty members were 65.6 percent of the instructional faculty among community colleges. According to the most recent provisional data available from the National Center for Education Statistics' (NCES 2012) Integrated Postsecondary Education Data Survey (IPEDS) from fall 2011, part-time faculty now comprise approximately 69.2 percent of instructors at these institutions. And, they are responsible for teaching between half and two-thirds of all course sections (CCCSE 2009). Still, in working with community college faculty members on this issue, we have often heard of community colleges where 80–90 percent or more of the faculty are employed on a part-time basis; the 2011 provisional IPEDS data show that part-time faculty represent 80 percent or more of instructional faculty at 11 percent of community colleges in the United States (NCES 2012). The growth in the number of part-time faculty has largely occurred as a result of two related changes that have shaped community colleges and the work of their faculty over the last several decades—the expansion of their missions and increases in enrollments.

Since their inception, the mission of what we now call community colleges has evolved to include a broader set of important academic and programmatic offerings for vocational training, developmental and continuing education, and community service (Cohen and Brawer 2008; Twombley and Townsend 2008, 15; Bragg 2001). As community college missions expanded to encompass a broader range of activities, service-learning and other forms of civic engagement have come to be viewed as essential components of a reformed community college function as well (Cohen and Brawer 2008, 377–379). Faculty work and composition have been shaped by these changes. For example, as the mission of the community college expanded, the employment of part-time faculty served an important role in bringing professionals from business and industry, government, and nonprofit organizations with real-world experience and connections with community organizations into the classroom (Cohen and Brawer 2008; Twombley and Townsend 2008, 15; Wallin 2004). These individuals often teach in order to give back to their fields and share skills and knowledge with the next generation; they are typically seen as a valuable part of the faculty because they offer students practical skills and knowledge that other faculty members might not possess (Levin, Kater, and Wagoner 2006). And yet, these part-time faculty members who have been hired in increasing numbers to help meet the demands of an expanded mission have not always been used to help to advance service-learning efforts.

In addition to expanding their missions, community colleges have periodically experienced surges in enrollment, which have stretched the capacity of the existing faculty. Institutions have often needed to find ways to accommodate fluctuating student enrollments. In many ways, community colleges have been more limited in their options to respond to these pressures compared with traditional four-year institutions, as they have had to maintain lower tuition and greater flexibility in hiring and scheduling (Cohen and Brawer 2008; Christensen 2008; Levin, Kater, and Wagoner 2006; Brewster 2000). Hiring part-time faculty instead of full-time faculty has been one significant way to cut costs; the practice has also given administrators greater flexibility in hiring faculty to teach courses amid fluctuations in enrollments (Levin, Kater, and Wagoner 2006; Anderson 2002; Gappa 1984).

For the most part, the introduction of instructors from business and industry, government, and nonprofits has usually been regarded as a positive addition to the faculty; they allowed community colleges to be more responsive to the demands of a changing mission and supplemented the full-time faculty by bringing practical knowledge and skills. Hiring increasing numbers of part-time faculty as a response to fluctuations in enrollments or budgets, though, has typically been engaged as a cost-saving measure (Kezar and Sam 2010; Cohen and Brawer 2008). Too often, part-time faculty are hired instead of traditional tenure-track or full-time faculty simply because they are less expensive, they give administrators greater flexibility with regard to staffing academic programs, and they are not provided the same types of benefits or support.[3] But, it is important to recognize the substantial contributions these individuals make to the academic mission of community colleges and their potential for advancing service-learning when they are properly supported and involved. For example, like most of their full-time colleagues, part-time faculty members at community colleges aren't typically hired through national searches, but come from the local community (Cohen and Brawer 2008). So, they often maintain connections with community organizations and are invested in the health and prosperity of the neighborhoods, towns, and region that their colleges serve from the time they are hired.

Since part-time faculty are often already involved with community organizations, they are in a good position to help bridge the divide between their institutions and potential service-learning partners (Garcia and Robinson 2005). Perhaps on a more fundamental level, though, research continues to show that part-time faculty members are highly committed and talented educators (Leslie and Gappa 2002); they are knowledgeable about their fields of study and care just as deeply about the success of their students as other educators do. Many go above and beyond what is expected of them and work in excess of the time for which they are paid in order to provide a high-quality educational experience for students (Street, Maisto, Merves, and Rhoades 2012). They are often interested in learning new skills and strategies for improving the effectiveness of their teaching, but may have very few, if any, opportunities to do so.

Part-Time Faculty in Service-Learning

Although utilization of service-learning has grown among community colleges since the 1990s, many colleges still struggle with how to involve part-time faculty, who comprise a majority of the faculty and sometimes teach most of the courses on campus (Cohen and Brawer 2008, 377; Garcia and Robinson 2005; Abes, Jackson, and Jones 2002). Part-time faculty involvement in service-learning has received very little attention in research, but some of the few studies and project reports that do address this topic, particularly reports from the AACC Broadening Horizons through Service Learning initiative, are encouraging. For example, a study by Antonio, Astin, and Cress (2000) suggested that non-tenure-track faculty often report a strong interest in community service and engagement activities, as well as integrating these concepts into their courses. Garcia and Robinson (2005) noted that more than just being interested, part-time faculty are also often already involved with community organizations that could become partners in service-learning efforts; so, they have an interest and existing networks and should be recruited and included in training and development opportunities. And, several reports have tried to encourage colleges to invite more of their part-time faculty members to participate in service-learning initiatives, calling attention to important forms of support that facilitate their inclusion, such as having access to professional development and receiving logistical support from campus civic engagement programs and development staff (Jeandron and Robinson 2010; Garcia and Robinson 2005). Garcia and Robinson (2005) note:

> Adjunct instructors are an ideal target group and should not be excluded from instructional training. Part-time faculty may also be involved with community agencies where students can do their service. Recruitment efforts should be

designed for both daytime and evening hours—whenever most adjunct faculty members are on campus. Service learning coordinators should meet with department deans to determine which instructors may be good candidates for service learning. (6)

Yet, something that is usually missing in the recommendations that are issued is a broader examination of how the nature of part-time work, the working conditions part-time faculty members experience, and the support they do or do not receive can affect their use of high-impact practices, teaching strategies, and innovative pedagogies like service-learning.

Policies and Practices Affecting Part-Time Faculty Instruction

The expansive literature on service-learning notes a wide range of factors that motivate or deter faculty members (mostly tenured, tenure-track, or full-time faculty) from utilizing the pedagogy; deterrents include limited time, the challenges of logistics and obtaining funding, reward structures, and level of comfort with utilizing innovative, high-impact practices (Abes, Jackson, and Jones 2002; Bringle and Hatcher 1997). The working conditions and lack of support experienced by part-time faculty members, though, add an additional layer of complexity. For example, although many full-time faculty initially lack knowledge about service-learning or the skills to implement it effectively, they are usually able to improve their knowledge and confidence by participating in workshops, grant-funded service-learning programs, or through interactions with other faculty members who have used the pedagogy (Jeandron and Robinson 2010; Christensen 2008). Part-time faculty, though, often cannot access similar programs and workshops, mentoring, or funding to travel to an off-campus conference about civic engagement and service-learning. Addressing some of these obstacles and supporting part-time faculty as professionals can go a long way toward advancing the effective implementation of service-learning at community colleges and ensuring that its benefits can be realized by the community, faculty, and students. In this section of the literature review, we outlined several ways in which part-time faculty members are limited by institutional or departmental policies and practices, and we reviewed some opportunities to mitigate or remove existing obstacles. With this information in mind, community college leaders can consider ways to access untapped potential among part-time faculty for service-learning by addressing constraints created by their working conditions.

Hiring

Many institutions and departments hire part-time faculty members within days of the start of the semester (Street, Maisto, Merves, and Rhoades 2012; Baldwin and Chronister 2001). Last minute hiring affords faculty very little time to prepare for the term ahead by doing things such as updating course readings, defining learning goals, and developing a course plan, which diminishes the quality of instruction a faculty member is able to provide to students (Kezar 2012). The short time frame between hiring and beginning work also denies part-time faculty important opportunities to receive a formal orientation to the institution, department, colleagues, and campus policies (including policies related to instruction, grading, and students). Since implementing service-learning requires time for identifying partners and projects, planning, selecting readings, and integrating classroom activities and assignments into the course curriculum, hiring faculty with more advanced notice ensures that they have time for preparation and can take the steps necessary to properly integrate service-learning into their course plans and assignments.

Professional Development and Mentoring
When community college faculty members participate in professional development to improve their teaching strategies and learn about pedagogy, they are more likely to utilize high-impact educational practices such as service-learning, first-year seminars, learning communities, and collaborative assignments that help to promote active learning, engagement, and the development of critical thinking and intercultural skills (Kuh 2008; Keim and Biletzky 1999). Marits (1996) notes, "the professional development of adjunct faculty involves all formal or informal activities that ultimately help faculty to improve instructional quality" (221). A 2005 AACC report found professional development to be one of the most important institutional factors motivating community college faculty members to offer service-learning (Garcia and Robinson 2005). Specific forms of developmental support such as attending professional conferences and receiving mentoring or advice from colleagues help faculty in their implementation of service-learning (Abes, Jackson, and Jones 2002; Bringle and Hatcher 1997). Mentoring programs that pair part-time faculty members with an experienced full-time or part-time peer are another way to ensure that faculty members have the chance to exchange knowledge, strategies to improve their teaching, syllabi, and other useful course materials to improve their utilization of high-impact practices (Kezar and Sam 2010; St. Clair 1994, 31). Yet, part-time faculty members often lack access to or the same opportunities as their full-time or tenure-track peers for professional development programs, workshops, or mentoring (Kezar and Maxey 2012; Conley and Leslie 2002; Schell and Stock 2001; Gappa and Leslie 1993).

On some of the campuses we have engaged with in our work on the Delphi Project on the Changing Faculty and Student Success, including William Rainey Harper College and Tallahassee Community College (the latter being the focus of the case presented later in this chapter), centers for teaching and learning and other programs specifically set up to provide support for part-time faculty are helping to ensure faculty members have access to development opportunities (Maxey and Kezar 2013a, b). Department chairs and deans can also help by encouraging their part-time faculty to participate and recognize their efforts to improve the quality of instruction. When planning professional development opportunities such as workshops for part-time faculty, certain factors should be considered to encourage their participation. First, programming should not only be offered during normal business hours, but also in the evening, on weekends, or online to make it easier to participate for faculty members who may teach or be on campus at different times (Jeandron and Robinson 2010). Second, it is important that workshops or other programs are attentive to the unique circumstances related to part-time work. Since their working conditions are different, and because they may require additional support due to the time and logistics involved with planning, implementing, and evaluating service-learning, part-time faculty might have different programming needs than other faculty. Experienced part-time faculty are sometimes recruited and paid to lead professional development alongside staff to help with this. A third consideration is that part-time faculty are usually only compensated for the time they spend in the classroom. Providing some form of stipend for the time they spend participating in professional development, offering meals, or recognizing their efforts in evaluation and promotion can help to increase interest.

Access to Instructional Resources and Support Personnel
In order to fulfill even their most basic responsibilities as instructors, faculty need to have access to instructional resources, space on campus, and administrative or support personnel. However, access to these resources is not always granted for part-time faculty members (Kezar and Sam 2010). A variety of studies have shown that part-time faculty members have only limited access to resources that support their roles as instructors (Street, Maisto, Merves, and Rhoades 2012; Outcalt 2002; Gappa and Leslie 1993). Having access to instructional resources and support personnel is particularly important for faculty members who want to use service-learning in their courses; and, part-time faculty members often require extra support (e.g., one-on-one consultation or mentoring; access to sample syllabi and other instructional resources; help identifying and connecting with community partners or evaluating students' work) because the time demands involved with designing and planning, implementing, and evaluating service-learning for their courses are common deterrents to implementing the pedagogy (Antonio, Astin, and Cress 2002). Centers for teaching and learning, service-learning professionals, department chairs, and other support and administrative staff should be attentive to the needs of part-time faculty.

Communicating with Part-Time Faculty
Creating a strong professional development program or providing access to support staff and resources may not be successful if part-time faculty members never learn about the offerings. Distributing information about service-learning programs is one way to encourage faculty to learn about and utilize the pedagogy in their courses (Bringle and Hatcher 1996). On some campuses, part-time faculty members do not have access to institutional email addresses or are not included in faculty meetings or email communications where important information is shared. They also may not receive an orientation or introduction to services and programs that are available on campus. As a result, they may be unaware of the various programs and support services that are available to them and their students. And, they may not receive announcements and invitations about events that would help to expose them to service-learning faculty and programs. Many of the campus centers for teaching and learning we have worked with have been able to enhance the success of their professional development offerings by working with human resources and information technology offices to ensure that all faculty have email addresses, creating email lists and websites to disseminate important information, and working with department chairs, who can help to encourage part-time faculty to participate. This

can also create opportunities to connect part-time faculty who are utilizing service-learning to share ideas and best practices, circulate information about possible projects, and involve these faculty members more directly in developing service-learning partnerships.

Involving Part-Time Faculty in Curriculum Development
Another major concern for part-time faculty is the circumscribed nature of teaching; they have little input into curriculum design and implementation (Kezar and Sam 2010). They are often excluded from contributing to the creation of course syllabi, textbook selection, projects to integrate curricular or pedagogical reforms, or other curricular decisions, sometimes even for their own courses (Baldwin and Chronister 2001). These conditions have been found not only to affect their morale, status, and efficacy as professionals, but also to make it difficult for them to bring their knowledge and experience with service-learning or other forms of community engagement into the classroom. Where they are not already included, involving part-time faculty in curriculum design not only brings to the table faculty members who are often teaching a majority of the courses, but it also incorporates faculty who may have a strong interest in and experience with service-learning, as well as valuable connections with community organizations (Garcia and Robinson 2005).

Evaluation
Improving part-time faculty evaluations is one way to help part-time faculty identify areas where they can enhance the quality of their instruction, courses, and ways they can better integrate high-impact practices, teaching strategies, and pedagogies like service-learning. Usually, the only feedback part-time faculty members receive about their teaching comes from student evaluations (Marits 1996). Some campuses have sought to improve the evaluations of part-time faculty members by creating formal or informal opportunities for department chairs or faculty colleagues to observe and provide feedback about their instruction and possible areas for improvement. These evaluations can help faculty members to enhance their performance or make improvements to the courses that they teach, regardless of their level of experience or the discipline in which they teach. They can also give institutions and service-learning programs a basis for evaluating the success and outcomes of service-learning, balancing student evaluations, identifying and recognizing exceptional part-time faculty members through awards and opportunities for promotion, and determining areas where more professional development opportunities are needed, in general.

Pulling It All Together: Comprehensive Support for Part-Time Faculty in Service-Learning at Tallahassee Community College

In order to have a better understanding of how to involve part-time faculty, we conducted a case study of a community college campus that is currently engaged in expanding service-learning by including these faculty members in greater numbers and in new ways. Our focus was to examine barriers that were encountered and ways the institution overcame them through new or amended practices and policies. We utilized a single case study approach, described by Merriam (1988) as "an intensive, holistic description and analysis of a single instance, phenomenon, or social unit" (27). Case study research is useful for capturing the complexity of a case and providing in-depth contextual information about the underlying processes and outcomes in order to inform practices and policy development (Merriam 1998; Stake 1995). Multiple sources of data are typically used in case study research to gain an in-depth understanding of the case at hand (Creswell 1998). In this study, primary data collection approaches included both structured and unstructured interviews and document analysis. Interviews were conducted with a variety of individuals involved, including members of the college administration, program directors and coordinators, and part-time faculty members. The documents reviewed included the college's strategic plans, reports, videos pertaining to its academic programs and service-learning approaches, official websites, and resources created for part-time faculty.

The institution we selected to profile in this case has both an established service-learning program and professional development and support programs for part-time faculty, which have recently been connected as part of a broad effort to increase civic engagement and service-learning activities on campus. Located in Florida's capital city, Tallahassee Community College (TCC) serves more than 21,000 students from three nearby counties. The college mostly serves transfer students, but is also home to a host of developmental, vocational, and continuing education programs. More than 80 percent of TCC's students are degree-seeking students, and many continue their education at one of the state's universities. Part-time faculty are an important part of the campus community, comprising 77.2 percent of instructors, with tenured or tenure-track and full-time non-tenure-track faculty making up 20.8 percent and 2 percent of the faculty, respectively.

Involving part-time faculty in service-learning at TCC did not happen overnight. Rather, a foundation was set up over several years, which has helped to create the right conditions for current and future success. The college has been an active member of Florida Campus Compact for several years. Although there has also been a strong program for supporting part-time faculty at the college for nearly a decade, the service-learning initiatives and efforts to better support non-tenure-track faculty coexisted without ever being formally connected to one another. So, much like on other campuses, most part-time faculty members at TCC never had much formal exposure to service-learning, were never taught how to utilize it in their courses, nor did they know about its benefits for their students. One part-time faculty member reported that although she had been an active participant in community organizations and even engaged in service-learning years ago as a student, she was not really aware of what service-learning was. When she was finally approached about utilizing the pedagogy in the courses she taught at TCC, it seemed like just another demand on her already limited time. But, as she started to gain knowledge and practice through workshops, attending service-learning retreats and conferences, and actually using the pedagogy in courses, she started to view it as "not another thing to do, but a different way of doing things." And, she started to witness how service-learning helped her students to connect knowledge from the classroom to their day-to-day lives.

Efforts to expand the utilization of service-learning at TCC began in 2010, as campus leaders sought to integrate some of the college's student affairs functions, including volunteerism and service-learning, and academic programs. Two key strategies were utilized: involving a variety of service-learning advocates, and presenting what one program coordinator described as a "salad bar of options" that were accessible for faculty and students. In 2011, the college was awarded a Campus Compact Connect2Complete (C2C) program grant (see chapter 8 in this book), which helps campuses to utilize peer mentoring and service-learning to support the most vulnerable community college students in achieving academic success and engaging with their peers, the college, and the broader community. Although a handful of staff and faculty service-learning mentors had worked to promote the pedagogy among their peers up until this point, C2C helped TCC to involve students and part-time faculty members to a greater extent. Work-study students and recipients of the college's Board of Trustees Scholarship were recruited to help their faculty members integrate service-learning into their own courses and class assignments. And, as students got more involved, so did more faculty members. C2C coordinators also sought to make service-learning more accessible to students and faculty by providing models that could be utilized as templates to help integrate the curriculum and impactful civic engagement projects. For example, students in one developmental course were engaged in coursework that asked them to consider the various types of knowledge and skills necessary to succeed in college; students then used their findings to develop poster projects and deliver presentations to underserved students in local high schools. Through these activities they examined their own understanding of the importance of success in college and helped their community by contributing to efforts to build college knowledge in local schools. In another course, students leveraged their knowledge from the classroom to help local food pantries improve their infrastructure, services, and outreach to the community.

Just within the last year, the administration and board at TCC have increased their commitment to creating new opportunities for part-time faculty members to be involved. While attending a Florida Campus Compact retreat with staff and faculty members, TCC's president witnessed how other colleges were increasing their use of service-learning and the impressive results for those institutions and their students. The president wanted to reaffirm the priority of civic engagement and service-learning; the college's strategic plan was revised to advocate for further integrating them into the curriculum and academic programs. This became the impetus for establishing new connections between service-learning programs on the campus and existing programs for TCC's part-time faculty members, housed in the Center for Teaching, Learning, and Leadership. Although service-learning has been a periodic topic for workshops, book clubs, and lunch-and-learn presentations for all faculty, the increased integration of service-learning into the center's programs for part-time faculty is beginning to increase their knowledge about the pedagogy and how to utilize it in their courses, create opportunities to practice its implementation, and realize its potential for connecting the curriculum to civic engagement and the day-to-day lives of students. Service-learning has been integrated into a number of key programs for improving the quality of part-time faculty members' instruction, such as expanded professional development opportunities, formal teaching evaluations, access to support personnel, and inclusion in communications about programs and services on campus. These key programs are described next.

Professional Development Opportunities for Part-Time Faculty

Professional development is an important tool in facilitating the effective use of service-learning on a community college campus (Kuh 2008; Garcia and Robinson 2005; Keim and Biletzky 1999; Marits 1996). The Center for Teaching, Learning, and Leadership at TCC has made substantial progress in recent years with regard to improving the quality of professional development available not only to full-time faculty members but to part-time faculty as well. There are workshops and development seminars offered throughout the year. In partnership with a newly formed Department of Campus and Civic Engagement, they are able to offer a wider variety of programs that are intended to help build skills and knowledge about service-learning and expand its utilization. There is also a more comprehensive series of programs to help part-time faculty members develop and refine their skills for using service-learning and other innovative classroom strategies, interact and share their knowledge with other faculty, advance their careers, and receive recognition for their contributions to community engagement, teaching, and learning excellence. Three main programs comprise a sequence of faculty professional development opportunities: (1) the Academy of Teaching, Learning, and Success; (2) Adjunct Faculty Advancement Program; and (3) Academy of Adjunct Professors. Service-learning has been integrated into each of these programs to help expose part-time faculty to the pedagogy and learn how to effectively utilize it in their courses.

The Academy of Teaching, Learning, and Success (ATLAS) provides up to 40 part-time faculty members each year with the opportunity to connect with their peers, improve their skills for providing instruction and facilitating student learning, and learn about the resources and support services that are available for faculty and students. The semester-long program comprises eight face-to-face seminar-style workshops wherein each participant creates a portfolio with a statement of their teaching philosophy, an annotated syllabus, a sample of learning outcomes for a course and corresponding assessment tools, and reflections on their use of new teaching strategies. As a result of the college's expanded commitment to service-learning and civic engagement, the inclusion of service-learning has become an expectation in each of these workshops and the portfolios that participants develop. Participants receive a stipend as compensation for their time attending workshops and completing corresponding online modules and reflections.

Part-time faculty who are interested in further developing their skills and knowledge, as well as pursuing opportunities for career advancement, may be invited by their dean to participate in the Adjunct Faculty Advancement Program (AFAP). Applicants to the program submit their ATLAS portfolio, develop a professional growth plan, and present a teaching demonstration to a panel of deans. Each participant receives guidance from a mentor, who meets with them throughout the program, conducts classroom observations and gives feedback, and provides assistance for creating the growth plan. Increasingly, service-learning is being favored as a core component of faculty members' plans for their courses. Part-time faculty members who complete AFAP receive a stipend for their time, are promoted to the rank of adjunct professor, receive a per-credit salary increase as determined by the institution's faculty salary schedule, and are inducted into an Academy of Adjunct

Professors. In order to continue receiving the higher rate of compensation, part-time faculty members who earn this recognition must continuously update their course plans and present their proposals to their deans. Participants also complete reflection exercises that help them to learn from their experiences participating in workshops and engaging service-learning and other strategies in their courses.

Evaluations

Participants in the professional development programs described above are not the only faculty at TCC who receive formal evaluations of their instruction. In fact, all part-time faculty members are evaluated by a full-time colleague in their department. Department chairs assess each new faculty member's instruction every semester, shifting to annual evaluations once the faculty member has taught for several terms. This creates an opportunity for part-time faculty members to receive ongoing feedback from their peers to supplement student evaluations. It also serves as a way to assess their effectiveness in applying service-learning in their courses, when they are making use of it in their courses, or to learn about new opportunities for integrating service-learning and other strategies and high-impact practices when they are not. Faculty members are also able to receive additional feedback on their efforts to incorporate service-learning from the Department of Campus and Civic Engagement and the Center for Teaching, Learning, and Leadership to continually develop their skills for engaging the pedagogy.

Providing Access to Instructional Resources and Support Personnel

The leadership at TCC understands that it is important that faculty members are able to easily access information and resources in order to enhance the quality of instruction and support they provide for their students. The Center for Teaching, Learning, and Leadership has created an impressive repository to inform and support all faculty members and has been expanding its library to include a growing number of publications and resources to promote the adoption and implementation of service-learning, in particular. Recently, the center has begun creating sample service-learning syllabi that are tailored for various types of courses and specific disciplines to make it easier for interested part-time faculty to have some strong resources to use when getting started. In addition to housing a collection of physical resources, the center has also created the Faculty Online Resource Center for Excellence, which provides detailed information about everything from policy initiatives like the college's strategic plan to resources for enhancing teaching and learning. Additionally, part-time faculty have access to computers and copiers to meet the needs of providing instruction. Efforts are also underway to improve the quality of orientation programming for new part-time faculty members.

Improving Communication

Improving communication to and with part-time faculty has been another goal of the center. Part-time faculty members are provided with a phone number, email address, and office space. The center also produces a weekly newsletter, *Around the Classroom*, which highlights full- and part-time faculty and staff achievements, summaries of new research on teaching strategies, campus news and events, and resources about technology, books, and practices for improving teaching and learning. Given the college's continued expansion of civic engagement initiatives, the newsletter often features articles on service-learning pedagogies.

Building a Foundation for Future Success

At TCC, the results of the increased focus on service-learning are beginning to show, and greater attention is being given to supporting part-time faculty members' involvement. Part-time faculty members have responded by integrating service-learning into their courses with great enthusiasm. The numbers of part-time faculty utilizing the pedagogy continue to grow as their involvement and inclusion in service-learning programs has become a greater priority for the institution. One instructor noted, "The service learning integrated extremely well into my overall objectives. I am really excited about continuing this type of approach with my classes in the fall!" When surveyed about their experience, part-time faculty members reported that they are very pleased with the professional development opportunities made available to them at TCC. Student evaluations also show greater satisfaction among students as a result of expanding service-learning into courses that are typically taught by part-time faculty.

Many of the efforts to encourage part-time faculty to participate in service-learning and support their work better have only emerged in the last couple of semesters, but the early success of these initiatives is promising. A program coordinator at TCC put it best: "It's like the cement of service learning has been poured." With a strong foundation in place, TCC is continuing to expand efforts to involve part-time faculty in service-learning by improving their access to knowledge and resources and creating opportunities for them to share their experiences with other faculty members and campus leaders. Recent additions to the programming available to part-time faculty have included the creation of new workshops and sample syllabi to help faculty members begin utilizing service-learning in their courses. Together, these efforts have increased part-time faculty members' interest in and knowledge about service-learning, as well as their skills to use the pedagogy successfully.

Conclusion

Institutions such as TCC help to demonstrate for others—not just other community colleges, but universities, too—that it is possible not just to improve the working conditions of part-time faculty, but to do so as a means to make these faculty members partners in service-learning for the benefit of the community, their institutions, and faculty and students. A community college does not necessarily need to already have the sort of robust program for supporting part-time faculty that TCC has in place in order to get started. Many of the types of support that we have described—professional development and evaluation, hiring, providing access to resources, communicating with faculty, and involving them in curriculum design—are already in place and are provided for full-time faculty. Expanding these to support part-time faculty better can often be done at a relatively low cost, while yielding results with regard to the quality of instruction and student outcomes. At TCC and other institutions we have worked with, these efforts are often started with modest funds; however, this funding tends to increase as campus leaders realize the return on their investments.[4] At community colleges, where part-time faculty comprise large majorities and often teach most of the courses, these improvements can have a real impact.

Notes

1. Additional information about the Delphi Project on the Changing Faculty and Student Success and its work to help improve working conditions and support for non-tenure-track faculty can be found online at http://www.thechangingfaculty.org.
2. In 1969, tenured and tenure-track positions made up approximately 78.3 percent of the faculty, while non-tenure-track positions comprised about 21.7 percent (Schuster and Finkelstein 2006). More than 40 years later, in 2011, these proportions had nearly flipped: tenured and tenure-track faculty had declined to 29.8 percent and 70.2 percent of faculty were ineligible for tenure (National Center for Education Statistics 2013). Part-time faculty, who have experienced the most significant rate of growth over the last 30–40 years, represent the single largest subset of the professoriate in American higher education today at 51.2 percent.
3. A recent study conducted by the Coalition on the Academic Workforce in 2012 found the median per-course compensation for part-time faculty to be $2,700, far lower than what tenure-track faculty are paid for the same work. In a report released by the University of Michigan's Center for the Education of Women, Hollenshead et al. (2007) also noted that part-time faculty are often ineligible for raises or promotions. In addition to being paid less, Hollenshead et al. (2007) found that only 51 percent of part-time faculty are provided any form of benefits. Typically their health insurance plans may be of lesser quality than plans for tenure-track faculty, and they may not receive paid sick leave or access to other benefits such as retirement plans or life insurance.
4. Example cases describing practices for supporting non-tenure-track faculty can be found on the Delphi Project website at http://examplepractices.thechangingfaculty.org.

References

Abes, Elisa S., Golden Jackson, and Susan R. Jones. 2002. "Factors That Motivate and Deter Faculty Use of Service-Learning." *Michigan Journal of Community Service Learning* 9 (1): 5–17.

American Federation of Teachers. 2009. *The American Academic: The State of Higher Education Workforce 1997–2007.* Washington, DC: American Federation of Teachers, 2009. Accessed December 8, 2011. http://www.aftface.org/storage/face/documents/ameracad_report_97-07for_web.pdf.

Anderson, Eugene L. 2002. *The New Professoriate: Characteristics, Contributions, and Compensation.* Washington, DC: American Council on Education.

Antonio, Anthony Lising, Helen S. Astin, and Christine M. Cress. 2000. "Community Service in Higher Education: A Look at the Nation's Faculty." *The Review of Higher Education* 23 (4): 373–397.

Baldwin, Roger G., and Jay L. Chronister. 2001. *Teaching without Tenure.* Baltimore, MD: Johns Hopkins University Press.

Baldwin, Roger G., and Matthew R. Wawrzynski. 2011. "Contingent Faculty as Teachers: What We Know; What We Need to Know." *American Behavioral Scientist* 55 (11): 1485–1509.

Bragg, Debra D. 2001. "Community College Access, Mission, and Outcomes: Considering Intriguing Intersections and Challenges." *Peabody Journal of Education* 76 (1): 93–116.

Brewster, David. 2000. "The Use of Part-Time Faculty in the Community Colleges." *Inquiry* 5 (1): 66–76.

Bringle, Robert G., and Julie A. Hatcher. 1996. "Implementing Service Learning in Higher Education." *The Journal of Higher Education* 67 (2): 221–239.

———. 1997. "Reflection: Bridging the Gap between Service and Learning." *College Teaching* 45 (4): 153–158.

Center for Community College Student Engagement. 2009. *Making Connections: Dimensions of Student Engagement (2009 CCSSE Findings)*. Austin: The University of Texas at Austin, Community College Leadership Program.

Christensen, Chad. 2008. "The Employment of Part-Time Faculty at Community Colleges." *New Directions for Higher Education* 143: 29–36.

Cohen, Arthur M., and Florence B. Brawer. 2008. *The American Community College*. San Francisco, CA: Jossey-Bass.

Conley, Valerie Martin, and David W. Leslie. 2002. "Part-Time Instructional Faculty and Staff: Who They Are, What They Do, and What They Think. 1993 National Study of Postsecondary Faculty (NSOPF: 93). Statistical Analysis Report."

Creswell, John W. 2007. *Qualitative Inquiry & Research Design: Choosing among Five Approaches*. Thousand Oaks, CA: Sage.

Eagan, Kevin. 2007. "A National Picture of Part-Time Community College Faculty: Changing Trends in Demographics and Employment Characteristics." *New Directions in Community Colleges* 140: 5–14.

Gappa, Judith M. 1984. "Part-Time Faculty: Higher Education at a Crossroads." *ASHE-ERIC Higher Education Report* 1984 (3).

Gappa, Judith M., and David W. Leslie. 1993. *The Invisible Faculty: Improving the Status of Part Timers in Higher Education*. San Francisco, CA: Jossey-Bass.

Garcia, Rudy M., and Gail Robinson. 2005. *Transcending Disciplines, Reinforcing Curricula: Why Faculty Teach with Service Learning*. Washington, DC: American Association of Community Colleges.

Hollenshead, Carol, Jean Waltman, Louise August, Jeanne Miller, Gilia Smith, and Allison Bell. 2007. *Making the Best of Both Worlds: Findings from a National Institution-level Survey on Non-tenure-track faculty*. Ann Arbor, MI: Center for the Education of Women.

Jeandron, Carol, and Gail Robinson. 2010. *Creating a Climate for Service Learning Success*. Washington, DC: American Association of Community Colleges.

Keim, Marybelle C., and Peter Eric Biletzky. 1999. "Teaching Methods Used by Part-Time Community College Faculty." *Community College Journal of Research and Practice* 23: 727–737.

Kezar, Adrianna. 2012. "Needed Policies, Practices, and Values: Creating a Culture to Support and Professionalize Non-Tenure Track Faculty." In *Embracing Non-Tenure Track Faculty*, edited by Adrianna Kezar, 2–27. New York: Routledge.

Kezar, Adrianna, and Cecile Sam. 2010. "Understanding the New Majority of Non-Tenure-Track Faculty in Higher Education: Demographics, Experiences, and Plans of Action." *ASHE Higher Education Report* 36 (4).

Kezar, Adrianna, and Daniel Maxey. 2012. *Review of Selected Policies and Practices and Connections to Student Learning*. Los Angeles, CA: Pullias Center for Higher Education.

Kuh, George. 2008. *High-Impact Educational Practices: What They Are, Who Has Access to Them, and Why They Matter*. Washington, DC: Association of American Colleges and Universities.

Leslie, David W., and Judith M. Gappa. 2002. "Part-Time Faculty: Competent and Committed." In *Community College Faculty: Characteristics, Practices, and Challenges*, edited by C. L. Outcault. New Directions for Community Colleges 59–68. Hoboken, NJ: Wiley.

Levin, John S., Susan Kater, and Richard L. Wagoner. 2006. *Community College Faculty*. New York: Palgrave Macmillan.

Marits, Edward J. 1996. "Professional Development of Adjunct Faculty." In *The Adjunct Faculty Handbook*, edited by Virginia Bianco-Mathis and Neal Chalofsky, 221–226. Thousand Oaks, CA: Sage.

Maxey, Daniel, and Adrianna Kezar. 2013a. *The Delphi Project Database of Non-Tenure-Track Faculty Example Practices: Tallahassee Community College Adjunct Seminars and Faculty Online Resource Center for Excellence*. Los Angeles, CA: Pullias Center for Higher Education.

———. 2013b. *The Delphi Project Database of Non-Tenure-Track Faculty Example Practices: William Rainey Harper College Center for Adjunct Faculty Engagement*. Los Angeles, CA: Pullias Center for Higher Education.

Merriam, Sharan B. 1988. *Case Study Research in Education: A Qualitative Approach*. San Francisco, CA: Jossey-Bass.

———. 1998. *Qualitative Research and Case Study Applications in Education*. San Francisco, CA: Jossey-Bass.

National Center for Education Statistics. 2012. *Integrated Postsecondary Education Data System*. Washington, DC: United States Department of Education.

———. 2013. *Integrated Postsecondary Education Data System*. Washington, DC: United States Department of Education.

Outcalt, Charles Lee. 2002. *A Profile of the Community College Professoriate, 1975–2000*. New York: Routledge.

Schell, Eileen E. and Patricia L. Stock. 2001. *Moving a Mountain: Transforming the Role of Non-Tenure Track Faculty in Composition Studies and Higher Education*. Urbana, IL: National Council of Teachers of English.

Schuster, Jack H., and Martin J. Finkelstein. 2006. *The American Faculty. The Restructuring of Academic Work and Careers*. Baltimore: Johns Hopkins University Press.

St. Clair, Karen L. 1994. "Faculty-to-Faculty Mentoring in the Community Colleges: An Instructional Component of Faculty Development." *Community College Review* 22: 23–35.

Stake, Robert E. 1995. *The Art of Case Study Research*. Thousand Oaks, CA: Sage.

Street, Steve, Maria Maisto, Esther Merves, and Gary Rhoades. 2012. *Who Is Professor "Staff?" And How Can This Person Teach So Many Classes?* Center for the Future of Higher Education. Retrieved from http://futureofhighered.org/policy-report-2/.

Twombley, Susan, and Barbara K. Townsend. 2008. "Community College Faculty: What We Know and Need to Know." *Community College Review* 36 (1): 5–24.

Umbach, Paul. 2007. "How Effective Are They? Exploring the Impact of Contingent Faculty on Undergraduate Education." *The Review of Higher Education* 30 (2): 91–123.

Wallin, Desna L. 2004. "Valuing Professional Colleagues: Adjunct Faculty in Community and Technical Colleges." *Community College Journal of Research and Practice* 28: 373–391.

CHAPTER 17

Service-Learning among "Nontraditional" College Students: Contexts, Trends, and Implications

Shannon S. Fleishman, Kristina Brezicha, and Travis York

Nontraditional students account for a notable proportion of community college students, indeed of students in all of higher education. In the last in-depth, national-level exploration of nontraditional undergraduates by the US Department of Education, Choy (2002) found that only 27 percent of American undergraduates in 2000 met the criteria most commonly associated with "traditional" college students.[1] Put another way, around the turn of the twenty-first century, roughly seven in ten undergraduates were in some way "nontraditional." Nontraditional students are no longer the exception in American higher education; they are the rule. This fact becomes even more obvious when we observe the proportion of traditional versus nontraditional students by institutional type. While nontraditional students remain the majority in most cases, they are overrepresented in the community college sector. For example, though private and public four-year institutions have surprisingly high percentages of nontraditional students (50 and 48 percent respectively)—especially given the dominant narrative of such institutions as serving more traditional students—these figures were notably higher at public two-year and private for-profit institutions (90 and 89 percent respectively).

Increasing access to higher education across gender, race/ethnicity, socioeconomic status, and other historically nontraditional descriptors of undergraduates has continued in the decade since the 2002 Department of Education report was published (Baker in print). Moreover, these already convincing numbers ignore an important and growing population of community college students: students enrolled in noncredit courses and programs. Though defined differently across states and even between institutions within the same state, noncredit education at community colleges includes areas as diverse as workforce development, contract training, adult basic education, English language learning programs, and developmental courses (Cohen and Brawer 2008). In 2011, roughly five million (38 percent)[2] of the nation's thirteen million community college students were enrolled in noncredit courses and programs (as opposed to the credit-bearing programs reflected in the opening figures) (AACC 2012). Unlike requirements for for-credit students, the Federal government does not require higher education institutions to report on students enrolled in noncredit programs and courses. As such, national-level data on these students are virtually nonexistent. This is particularly problematic given the overrepresentation of nontraditional students in noncredit education. Based on state-level data on noncredit community college students in four states, Grubb, Badway, and Bell (2003) find that lower cost, greater accessibility, flexibility and responsiveness, and easier access of noncredit education hold particular advantages for some nontraditional groups of students. This finding is especially interesting in light of growing evidence of a possible "middle class takeover" of community colleges, whereby credit-bearing programs are increasingly meeting the needs of more advantaged, middle-class students (Townsend 1999).

Given the focus of this book, we are especially interested in understanding what works—and does not work—for nontraditional students involved in service-learning in the community college context (be they in credit and/or noncredit courses). Recent national data from the American Association of Community Colleges suggests that two-thirds of the 1,200 associate degree-granting institutions in the United States offer service-learning in their curricular programs (Prentice, Robinson, and Patton 2012). While a growing body of research specific to students attending four-year institutions points to a positive relationship between participating in service-learning and various student outcomes (Kuh, Kinzie, Schuh, and Whitt 2010; Eyler and Giles 1999), relatively little empirical research exists on the impacts of service-learning for community college students, much less on nontraditional community college students specifically (Buglione 2012). Taggart and Crisp (2011, see also Crisp and Taggart 2013) begin to fill this gap with their recent narrative reviews examining empirical work regarding service learning in the community college sector. Among other recommendations, they call on researchers to address the issue of external validity by parsing findings across different institutional types and student groups. Their research begins to address the former concern by distinguishing what is known about service-learning impacts based on the experiences of community college students. We add to this by attempting to further disentangle what is known about a particular group of community college students: nontraditional students attending community colleges. Given the recent attention paid to service-learning as a high-impact pedagogy and evidence that historically underserved students in the four-year sector tend to benefit more from engaged pedagogies (such as service-learning) than majority students do (Kuh 2008), we also include a careful review of what we know about service-learning and nontraditional student populations from research on four-year students as a launching point for understanding the impact of service-learning for nontraditional students in the community-college sector.

Following Taggart and Crisp's recommendations, our aim in this chapter is twofold: First, to quantify the research on nontraditional students in both the two- and four-year sectors and second, based on the categorizations of nontraditional students emerging from this meta-analysis, to review existing findings on what works—and does not work—for different categories of nontraditional students. To accomplish our first objective, we performed an analytic literature review summarizing the research literature available for nontraditional students in service-learning, whether in the two- or four-year sector. This allowed us to have a better understanding of how researchers operationalize the term "nontraditional," quantify the extent to which certain nontraditional characteristics are a focus of the relevant research, and compare the degree to which the literature that does exist on nontraditional students and service-learning intersects with the two- and four-year sectors.

We find that research on service-learning among nontraditional undergraduates tends to focus on the implications of service-learning for four groups of nontraditional students: (1) *nonwhite students*; (2) *adult students* (originally categorized as "older" in our content analysis); (3) *working students* (originally categorized as "full-time employed"); and (4) *students with varying forms of capital*. The latter—*students with varying forms of capital*—is a new construct, which we argue offers a better framework for understanding the unique challenges and opportunities of involving nontraditional undergraduates in service-learning.

To accomplish our second objective, we summarize the topline trends emerging from a content analysis of the relevant literature on the four groups of nontraditional undergraduates unearthed in the first part of our study. We find that while the research reviewed in two of these groups (adult and working students) focuses on specific service-learning impacts, research on the remaining groups (nonwhite and students with varying forms of capital) was limited to demographic detail and/or included as context only, without due attention to the extent to which service-learning as a pedagogy works for specific groups of students. Finally, we discuss the implications of these findings for practice and for future research on nontraditional students involved in service-learning.

Similar to the phenomenon by which group service-learning pedagogies are studied together with community service or other "active pedagogies," researchers often utilize broader, more ambiguous terms to refer to nontraditional students. Levin (2007) points to three dominant frameworks for understanding nontraditional students: (1) the trait framework where the focus is primarily on ascribed student characteristics; (2) the behavioral framework where the focus is primarily the academic and nonacademic experiences of students during college; and (3) the action framework where the focus is on institutional/governmental policies and how the institution treats students. Though a full discussion of our operationalization of nontraditional students is detailed in the following section, it is worth mentioning at the onset that we follow the trait framework in this study.

Methods

We employed content analysis to conduct an analytic literature review of the existing research on nontraditional students involved in service-learning. Specifically, we followed the content analysis-based coding and schemas developed by Klaus Krippendorf (2012) and Kimberly Neuendorf (2002). Given the goal of this method to "identify and record relatively objective (or at least intersubjective) characteristics of messages," it fit well with our own stated research goals (Neuendorf 2002, 141). Using content analysis allowed our team of three researchers to establish a shared understanding of the underlying construct of nontraditional students, to develop a systematic coding scheme, and to calculate our inter-rater reliability.

Prior to conducting our actual study, we first conducted a pilot study reviewing articles published in two peer-reviewed journals over the past decade. Specifically, we selected the *Journal of Higher Education Outreach and Engagement* and the *Michigan Journal of Community Service-Learning* as both focus on higher education, service-learning, and outreach research, and rank in the Web of Science's Journal Citation Reports. We chose the past decade (2002–2012) to capture the period of expanding research on service-learning pedagogy and the impact of service-learning on students. The pilot study enabled us to clarify our research methods, as well as our coding process.

Drawing heavily from Kim's (2002) review of nontraditional students in the community college context and Choy's (2002) comprehensive study of nontraditional undergraduates across institutional type, combined with what we learned in our pilot study, we established the following key descriptors or characteristics of nontraditional postsecondary students: (1) local/commuting; (2) older; (3) nonwhite; (4) first-generation; (5) enrolled in school part-time; (6) independent (i.e., financially independent from parents); (7) full-time employed; (8) parent; (9) single-parent; (10) English Language Learner (ELL); (11) not a high school graduate; (12) low income; (13) pre-college (i.e., enrolled in developmental coursework).

During our pilot study, we realized that authors frequently used "nontraditional" as an umbrella term to refer to an unspecified group of nontraditional students; therefore we added it as a characteristic to code for in our actual study. We did not apply a strict definition to any of these terms. Rather, we utilized myriad definitions that emerged from our review of the literature to help us define and explain the terms. This decision prevented our own preconceived definitions from limiting an already narrow field. Given the fairly large stand-alone bodies of literature within sociology, higher education, and the scholarship of teaching and learning related to gender, disability status, and immigration studies, we ultimately decided not to include these as characteristics we coded. This decision was based solely on our desire to maintain a manageable body of research to review and should not overshadow the importance of studying these groups in future research. Our pilot study also confirmed our hypothesis that the majority of research on nontraditional students focuses on students in a four-year institutional setting. Therefore, we included literature on nontraditional students' service-learning experiences in *either* two- or four-year higher-education institutions.

Literature Search

To perform our full content analysis, we drew from a comprehensive literature search of several academic fields such as nursing, gerontology, business, engineering, and higher education within the past ten years (2003–2013). We also utilized key word searches within EBSCO*host* Research Databases (EBSCO) and Educational Resources Information Center (ERIC) to compile refereed and edited academic literature for review. We conducted several initial literature searches using a variety of key words to determine the combination of key words that returned the most complete body of literature available. As a body of literature emerged, we utilized the Web of Science Citation Index (relative to the year of publication) and Google Scholar's citation index to identify key words of high impact. The final key words used were: "service-learning"; "nontraditional"; and "higher education." Next, we utilized the reference lists of the most highly cited works to identify other relevant literature. In effect, we employed these citation indexes to provide a measure of quality or depth to the keyword search process by exploring relevant literature and the citation loops at play in these works. Our literature search returned over 160 articles. The team jointly combed through the articles eliminating those that did not focus in some way on undergraduate, nontraditional students engaged in service-learning. We determined this by reading through the abstracts, author-supplied key words, and a cursory review. This culling of articles resulted in a final sample size of 57 articles.[3]

Coding and Analytic Process

After establishing our definition for nontraditional college students, we randomly selected 14 articles from our full sample to calculate our inter-rater reliability. Though small compared to the generally cited 30 article rule of thumb for establishing inter-rater reliability (Lombard, Snyder-Duch, and Bracken 2010), this sample allowed us to meet the random probability sample of 10 to 25 percent of the full sample considered sufficient for establishing inter-rater reliability (Lacy and Riffe 1996). Additionally, we coded the articles in two sets, with each researcher independently coding the entire article to further ensure reliability.[4] We also used Krippendorf's (2012) alpha, one of the more conservative measures of inter-rater reliability, to correct for our small sample size. As shown in table 17.1, we achieved the ideal minimum reliability score of at least 80 percent for the majority of traits studied. Even the four traits falling below 80 percent meet Lombard, Snyder-Duch, and Bracken's (2010) recommended reliability score of over 70 percent to be considered acceptable for content analysis.

Given the high rate of internal consistency between coders, the remaining manuscripts were divided between the three researchers. We coded each article

Table 17.1 Inter-Rater Reliability Scores for Coded Nontraditional Student Characteristics (*n* = 14)

Student Characteristic	*Krippendorf's α*
Married	1.00
No High School Diploma	1.00
Independent	1.00
Single Parent	1.00
Older	0.91
Parent	0.88
Local	0.88
First-Generation	0.83
Nonwhite	0.83
Part-Time Enrollment	0.78
English Language Learner	0.78
Full-Time Employed	0.75
Low-Income	0.73

independently, consulting with each other when questions arose over the coding process. Each author reviewed the article's abstract and then used an in-text key word search of the following terms to identify content worthy of further examination: "student"; "participant"; and "population." These terms were selected because they allowed us to determine the article's focus population. When the terms were identified, the reviewer then evaluated the surrounding passage to determine whether or not any discussion of nontraditional students was involved. If one of the nontraditional postsecondary student characteristics identified above was mentioned, we coded that variable as a '1' on our spreadsheet. Additionally, we coded the page number(s) where the terms were identified in a corresponding variable. If an article did not discuss that group of students, we coded that as a '0.'

While any mention fitting our categories of nontraditional postsecondary students were coded as "1," frequently students fitting those characteristics were not the *focus* of the article. We found many cases where an article would mention nontraditional students as an aside, while their focus was on myriad other aspects of service-learning. While we decided to code any and all mention of our operationalized understanding of nontraditional students, we noted when these terms appeared only descriptively in our page numbers variable. Further, we created several variables that allowed us to code for articles in which nontraditional students or service-learning were the focus of the article. We also created codes to indicate whether the article focused on the two- or four-year setting allowing us to parse out the differences between various studies in those settings. Finally, we included a variable, coded as "1," for any manuscript deemed relevant enough to trends related to service-learning and nontraditional students to warrant full and careful review by all members of our research team.

Results

Our content analysis revealed that though researchers increasingly recognize the changing demographics of students attending higher education institutions, the research on nontraditional students and service-learning has yet to reflect these new realities. While researchers acknowledge these changes by frequently mentioning characteristics of nontraditional students in the literature (table 17.2), the term nontraditional has become an umbrella term lacking a clear, universally agreed-upon definition. Recall that we added "nontraditional" as a general characteristic to code for after discovering during our pilot study that authors frequently used it to refer to an unspecified group of students. Our results clearly demonstrate this tendency as we see that the broader the characteristic, the more frequently it was used. For example, nonwhite students were mentioned in approximately 42 percent of the articles. Similarly, older students and nontraditional students were mentioned in 36 and 35 percent of articles, respectively. It's important to note that, because we were searching based on these specific terms according to the methodology laid out above, these figures represent lower bounds of inclusion. We could imagine a variety of other terms used to attain the same constructs. Our pilot research, as well as the definitions used by Choy (2002) and Kim (2002), suggested these were a good starting point, though future research should consider the utility of broader coding schemes. Table 17.2 also indicates that the more specific a characteristic is the fewer

Table 17.2 Nontraditional Student Characteristics Present in Literature: 2003–2013 ($n = 57$)

Nontraditional Student Characteristic	Number of Manuscripts	Percent of Total
Nonwhite	24	42.11
Older ("Adult")	21	36.84
Nontraditional	20	35.09
Full-Time Employed ("Working")	12	21.05
First-Generation	10	17.54
Local	9	15.79
Parent	9	15.79
Married	7	12.28
Low-Income	6	10.53
Remedial	6	10.53
Part-Time Enrolled	5	8.77
English Language Learners	4	7.01
No High School Diploma	1	1.75
Single Parent	1	1.75
Independent	0	0.00
Institutional Characteristics		
Focused on Two-Year Setting	13	22.81
Focused on Four-Year Setting	35	61.40

articles discussing those traits were present. For example, nontraditional characteristics such as being enrolled part-time, participating in an ELL program, not having a high school diploma, or being a single parent showed up in fewer than 10 percent of the articles reviewed.

Our review also demonstrated that despite numerous mentions of nontraditional students—either within the umbrella term or via more specific characteristics—many articles failed to address the differing experiences in service-learning that these students had as a result of their unique backgrounds. Many articles merely described demographic student information at an institutional level, even when writing about a specific subgroup. Though some authors acknowledged the potential for differing experiences, few engaged in a discussion of these implications. When articles did discuss the experiences of nontraditional students engaged in service-learning, it was generally noted that these students benefitted from a well-planned, carefully implemented service-learning program that included flexibility for students and real-world utility, points we elaborate on in the following sections.

As table 17.2 highlights, roughly a fifth of the articles reviewed (23 percent) focused on some aspect of nontraditional students and service-learning in the two-year sector, while nearly two-thirds (61 percent) focused on the four-year sector. These overall figures become even more noteworthy when looking at the relative focus on nontraditional students and/or service-learning within the articles exclusively on the two-year ($n = 13$) and four-year ($n = 35$) sectors (see table 17.3). Does research on community college students tend to focus more on the experiences of nontraditional students in service-learning, while research on four-year college students focuses more on service-learning effects specifically? In short, the answer is

Table 17.3 Articles That Focus on Nontraditional Students and/or Service-Learning by Sector

Article Focus	Two-Year			Four-Year		
	Number	Within-group % (n = 13)	Total Percent (n = 57)	Number	Within-group % (n = 35)	Total % (n = 57)
Nontraditional students	6	46.15	10.53	12	34.29	21.05
Service-learning	6	46.15	10.53	22	62.86	38.60
Both	5	38.46	8.77	6	17.14	10.53

yes. Table 17.3 shows that the two-year sector articles were more likely to focus on nontraditional students (+12 percentage-points) and on nontraditional students and service-learning (+21 percentage-points). Alternately, articles focused on the four-year sector were more likely to focus on service-learning specifically (+17 percentage-points). That said, of the full sample, only 9 percent of articles focused on nontraditional students engaged in service-learning in the two-year setting. Fewer than 20 percent of articles focused on the four-year context meaningfully discussed both service-learning and nontraditional students. Within the full sample, that number dropped to only 11 percent of the articles. These results highlight the scarcity of research being conducted at either the two- or four-year levels on nontraditional students engaged in service-learning.

Overall, we find a great deal of heterogeneity within the umbrella term "nontraditional" students, which needs to be teased out to more fully understand the effectiveness of service-learning for different types of students. We also find that despite overrepresentation of nontraditional students in community colleges relative to four-year colleges and universities, existing research on the experiences and outcomes of nontraditional students involved in service-learning stems primarily from studies of these students within the four-year sector. Finally, we learned that the research that does exist on service-learning among nontraditional undergraduates tends to focus on the implications of service-learning for nonwhite students (42 percent), older students (37 percent), nontraditional students (35 percent), and full-time employed students (21 percent).

In the next section we summarize the research reviewed on three of the four aforementioned groups: (1) *nonwhite students*; (2) older students (renamed *adult students* to better mirror the research reviewed); and (3) full-time employed students (renamed *working students*, again in light of research conventions). Although the umbrella term "nontraditional" was commonly invoked, most of the literature referencing nontraditional characteristics (broadly defined) did not provide meaningful analysis or findings related to these characteristics. Given the lack of utility of such research to inform what is working—and what is not working—for nontraditional students involved in service-learning, we instead draw from the remaining characteristics not included in the four aforementioned groups to highlight a new construct of interest: *students with varying forms of capital*. As discussed in greater detail next, this construct better captures the types of challenges and opportunities of which researchers and practitioners involved in service-learning in the two- and/or four-year contexts should be aware.

Trends: Nontraditional College Students Service-Learning Outcomes and Experiences

So what does the literature on nontraditional students in service-learning tell us? In this section, we describe what we know about nontraditional students and their experiences and outcomes related to participation in service-learning based upon our analytic literature review. In the first part of our study, we found that research on service-learning among nontraditional undergraduates tends to focus on the implications of service-learning for the following groups of nontraditional students: (1) *nonwhite students*; (2) *adult students*; (3) *working students*; and (4) *students with varying forms of capital*. In this section, we accomplish our second objective of reviewing what works—and does not work—for these different categories of nontraditional students. Unfortunately, we face two constraints in accomplishing this second objective. First, the limited research on nontraditional students and service-learning precludes the parsing of this research between two-year and four-year sectors in the summaries that follow. Second, in some cases the studies reviewed made reference to particular nontraditional characteristics as a demographic note and/or in contextualizing content rather than speaking specifically to the intersectionality of these particular characteristics and the impact of service-learning pedagogies upon particular student experiences. As further detailed below, this was most problematic within the articles mentioning nonwhite students and students with varying forms of capital. In these cases, we pulled relevant research external to our review to fill the gap. These constraints point to several directions for future research.

Nonwhite Students

As mentioned in the findings of our content analysis, over 40 percent of the articles mentioned nonwhite students; however, none of these articles contained findings or discussions about the ways in which nonwhite students may have varied service-learning experiences or related outcomes. Even studies including significantly diverse samples did not consider the ways race may—or may not—influence student's pedagogical experiences. This is not to say that there is no scholarship on the topic; rather, we believe that our literature search terms may not have accurately captured this section of the literature.

Here we draw on research external to our review to address this gap in the literature. In 2011, Novick, Seider, and Huguley found that within service-learning experiences, students of color often qualitatively described their experience of community differently than their white counterparts. Participants related these feelings to frustrations over troubling interactions around racial issues and ineffective communication about racial topics within the academic component of their experience. More recently, Seider, Huguley, and Novick (2013) found that, on average, students of color experienced a statistically weaker sense of community resulting from the academic component of their service-learning experience compared to their white peers. These findings illustrate the importance of faculty development in fostering learning environments where students are comfortable expressing their perspectives and perceptions, especially around race.

The findings of our content analysis more accurately serve to question the placement and use of the term "nonwhite students"—especially in total—as nontraditional for two reasons: First, there is little theoretical agreement within the literature about whether nonwhite students are considered nontraditional; although, when race is mentioned, and thereby operationalized, we find that it is often nonwhite students that are considered nontraditional. Second, the changing demographics of American college students, and especially community college students, where nonwhite students are often the majority demographic, cause us to advocate for students' race to be carefully reconsidered in related educational research. In other words, we contend it is a misnomer to consider nonwhite students nontraditional at many institutions where they are and have historically been the majority. In fact, most studies contained within our analytic review that mentioned their samples were drawn from disproportionately high nonwhite student populations were usually single-institution studies, where such a demographic characteristic is likely to have notable relationship to institutional culture and student experiences. While the recent work that Seider, Huguley, and Novick (2013) have conducted begins to address this gap in the service-learning literature, we believe this finding of our analytic literature review serves to highlight how significant that gap is within this area of research. We hope that these findings will lead researchers to consider the intersection between multiple student characteristics in future research.

Adult Students

By a far measure, the most commonly researched characteristic of nontraditional students was their age—most often operationalized as students 24 years of age and older. This preponderance in the literature may be a result of access to this data or due to the mere fact that adult students are a broad demographic of interest for many institutions, especially those with outreach missions to serve local communities. The bulk of empirical studies on adult students and service-learning were qualitative, which resulted in findings that are primarily affective in nature—this is not a value judgment but rather a factual statement about the type of data streams that have currently been examined and the resulting findings. In other words, the lack of quantitative or mixed methods findings pertaining to academic skills, such as grades or cognitive growth, should not be assumed to be nonexistent, but rather, simply absent from the literature.

Utilizing faculty open-ended surveys, adult student interviews, and document analysis of course syllabi, Largent (2013) found that faculty utilizing a service-learning pedagogy observed increases in adult students' personal and professional growth, enhanced desires for future service participation, and a stronger connection to course content for adult students. Adult students' deeper engagement with course content as a result of their service experiences is likely to be connected with a distinctive perception of service (Bauer, Moskal, Lucena, and Munoz 2007). Specifically, Bauer et al.'s (2007) research has suggested that adult students are more likely than their younger counterparts to recognize the positive impact their service participation had on others.

Research exploring adult student's moral development has found that older students, even students above the age of 20, exhibit statistically significant increases in moral reasoning related to their service-learning participation in comparison to their younger counterparts (Bernacki and Jaeger 2008; Boss 1994). These findings suggest that older students, on average, may be at developmental stages that allow for greater growth in moral reasoning related to service-learning (Bernacki and Jaeger 2008). Such findings are theoretically consistent with Smith's (2008) argument regarding the expected positive outcomes resulting from adult students' service-learning participation given the prevailing cognitive, moral-ethical, and psychosocial theoretical conceptions of adult learning.

Previous research has indicated that adult students often cite external priorities such as limited time, family, and work as barriers to their service-learning participation (Largent 2013; Hughes 2002; Fertman 1993). These commitments have caused several scholars to encourage faculty to consider nontraditional student complexities in planning their courses, provide greater flexibility in the service components of their service-learning courses, and even involve adult students in front-end decisions about their service-learning experiences (Marienau and Reed 2008; Bulot and Johnson 2006). Largent and Horniek (2004) argue that such involvement places value on student experiences and provides them with greater agency, which in turn increases adult students' satisfaction with service-learning courses. As suggested above, future research would benefit from more quantitative and mixed-methods exploration of the impact of service-learning on adult students to triangulate the rich information coming from the various qualitative studies reviewed here.

Working Students

As one might expect given the vocational obligations of working students, the literature on this subgroup suggests these students thrive in service-learning experiences where there is a high degree of applicability to students' coursework or career competencies. Working students, typically operationalized as students who are working in "more than part-time occupations," are more likely to also have other out-of-school obligations, such as spouses or children. While it is easy to assume that these busy students are less likely to partake in service-learning courses, Holland and Robinson (2008) argue that the research shows the opposite. Drawing on several studies conducted by the California State University System, they find that students who worked reported a higher level of participation in service-learning courses. The researchers argue that busy students look for greater returns on their investment of time, and that service-learning courses deliver a learning experience that resonates with working students. Holland and Robinson's research indicates that working students appreciate the practicality and relevance of service-learning courses and see them as transformative. Bulot and Johnson (2006) also note that working students' connections in the community often aid faculty with increased community resources and service-learning implementation. Taken together, the research in this area indicates that working students may be more interested in participating in service-learning than previously assumed. It would be a valuable addition to the field for future research to consider the ways in which new modes of learning popular among working students (e.g., hybrid and online courses) can integrate service-learning into the curriculum.

Students with Varying Forms of Capital

Finally, we also found references made by researchers regarding nontraditional students whose backgrounds included various forms of limited capital. Researchers did not often use the term "capital"; however, we find that this Bourdieuian construct more appropriately captures the underlying essence of interrelated characteristics like socioeconomic status and familial college knowledge. For example, students from low-income families have barriers resulting from limited financial capital, say meeting the cost of higher education. Students from low-income families are also disproportionately more likely to fall in the "first-generation" category. Being the first in their families to attend postsecondary education produces limited cultural capital, such as a lack of family knowledge regarding navigating college culture. These examples are, in fact, representative of the two types of limited capital we found specifically explored within the research. While students were limited in certain forms of capital, they also exhibited excess amounts of capital in other arenas. Similarly, especially in the community college context, many service-learning students are one and the same as the community they are serving, resulting in rich, sustainable partnerships.

Here, studies external to our search criteria that explore the service-learning experiences of low-income, first-generation (LIFG) students prove informative. These studies find that service-learning pedagogies aided LIFG students in the production of academic and affective outcomes (York 2013; Yeh 2010). A qualitative study by Yeh (2010) found that service-learning provided a learning experience where LIFG students were able to engage with and apply course content. Yeh also reports that service-learning increased LIFG student's skills to engage in academic work, their self-efficacy in that engagement, and their development of awareness to social inequities. While this study is somewhat limited in its generalizability, it is complemented by a more recent mixed methods study (York 2013) on the outcomes and experiences of LIFG college students at four-year public and private universities. The findings of York's study suggest that service-learning participation for LIFG students is positively related to increased academic outcomes such as GPA and acquisition of learning outcomes, as well as the development of affective outcomes such as civic awareness and critical consciousness. Future research should consider both the challenges and opportunities related to involving students with varying forms of capital in service-learning.

Implications for Practice and Future Research

In this chapter, we utilized Choy (2002) and Kim's (2002) definitions of nontraditional students to operationalize the term within our content analysis. This operationalization led us to parse the literature resulting from our search, via our coding, into categories such as adult students, nonwhite students, first-generation students, part-time or full-time employed students, and parents—just to name a few. Our first objective was to quantify the research on nontraditional students in both the two- and four-year sectors and, second, to use the categorizations of nontraditional students that emerged to delve further into what works—and does not work—for different groups of nontraditional students. As revealed above, research on service-learning among nontraditional undergraduates tends to focus on the implications of service-learning for the following groups: (1) *nonwhite students*; (2) older students (renamed *adult students* to better mirror the research reviewed); and (3) full-time employed students (renamed *working students*, again in light of research conventions). Although the umbrella term "nontraditional" was commonly invoked, most of the literature referencing nontraditional characteristics (broadly defined) did not provide meaningful analysis or findings related to these characteristics. Such research does not inform the extent to which service-learning is working for nontraditional students. Instead, we draw from the remaining characteristics not included in the aforementioned groups to highlight a new construct of interest: (4) *students with varying forms of capital*. In the second part of our study, we found that while the research reviewed in two of these groups (adult and working students) focuses on specific service-learning impacts, research in the remaining groups (nonwhite and students with varying forms of capital) was similarly limited to demographic detail and/or included only as context, without due attention to the extent to which service-learning as a pedagogy works for specific groups of students. What are the implications of these findings for practitioners and researchers? In this section, we highlight two programmatic messages, as well as directions for future research.

Specifically, our review of research on adult and working students suggests that community college faculty and staff developing such programming should be mindful of the need for flexibility and alternative research assignments as nontraditional students balance competing demands in their academic, professional, familial, and community lives. Additionally, given that many nontraditional students are indeed returning to school after entering the world of work and/or starting families, their educational goals are often deeply pragmatic (Hansen 2011; Robbins 2012). In addition to the academic benefits, students are able to build networks in the professional and volunteer sectors where they would not otherwise have had access. Simultaneously, the skills and connections that adult service-learning students bring to the table often result in symbiotic relationships between site providers and students. As such, focusing on the academic and practical needs of students is of utmost importance when implementing service-learning programs that link nontraditional students with the community (Hansen 2011).

Our study also suggests several directions for future research. Research speaking to the specific impacts of service-learning for adult and working students is relatively further along than similar research on nonwhite students and students with varying forms of capital. Even so, the research on adult students would benefit from more quantitative and mixed-methods studies, while the research on working students would be well-served to consider the utility of service-learning in new and emerging modes of learning such as hybrid and online courses. The lack of findings or discussions about the ways in which nonwhite and students with varying forms of capital may have varied service-learning experiences or related outcomes in many ways mirrored the issues we found with use of "nontraditional students" as an umbrella term. Future research needs to rethink how we conceptualize nontraditional college students—be they in the two-year sector, four-year sector, or simultaneously enrolled in both sectors (a trend which has been on the rise for over two decades) (Adelman 2006; 2004)—so that we can have a better understanding of the effectiveness of service-learning for different types of students.

Choy (2002) suggests that one way to go about this in research would be to consider nontraditional students on a continuum. Does the impact of, or experience with, service-learning vary based on the prevalence of nontraditional characteristics a student has, or for particular characteristics? For instance, are there particular nontraditional characteristics that, on the whole, matter more in terms of service-learning outcomes and experiences? Finally, we must resist the temptation to assume that the demographic characteristics of an institution mirror the demographic characteristics of any given classroom within that institution. It could be that the demographics of students enrolled in service-learning classes within community colleges are not reflective of the larger institution. For example, little is known about the degree to which service-learning happens in credit versus noncredit classes and/or by the time of day classes within an institution are offered. Given that we know that nontraditional students are unevenly distributed in credit versus noncredit classes, not to mention by time of day, the possibility remains of a self-selection bias in service-learning programming within the community college sector. Further, the lack of quality data on noncredit students and on students involved in service-learning programs certainly presents a challenge to disentangling these effects. By collaborating with colleagues across and within institutions, pooling service-learning data over time, and creating new ways for understanding the realities of nontraditional students, we can begin to chip away at these challenges, discover the nuances of programming in these areas, and make changes that enhance the value of service-learning in the lives of nontraditional students.

Notes

1. In *National Undergraduates*, Choy (2002) defines the traditional undergraduate as one who earns a high school diploma, enrolls full time immediately after finishing high school, depends on his/her parents for financial support, and either does not work during the school year or works part-time.
2. Given the limitations of data collection on noncredit students, we cannot know at a macrolevel the degree to which students enrolled in noncredit courses are also enrolled in credit-bearing courses.
3. Full lists of journals and articles included in our final sample are available upon request.
4. After the first set, we noted discrepancies and discussed their origins. We negotiated our understandings and recoded those articles as well as the next set of articles to establish our final inter-rater reliability.

References

AACC. 2012. *Community College Fact Sheet* Washington, DC: American Association of Community Colleges (AACC).

Adelman, Cliff. 2004. *Principal Indicators of Student Academic Histories in Postsecondary Education, 1972–2000* Washington, DC: US Department of Education.

———. 2006. *The Toolbox Revisited: Paths to Degree Completion from High School through College* Washington, DC: US Department of Education.

Baker, David P. (In press). *The Schooled Society: The Educational Transformation of Global Culture* Stanford, CA: Stanford University Press.

Bauer, E. Heidi, Barbara Moskal, Joan Gosink, Juan Lucena, and David Munoz. 2007. "Faculty and Student Attitudes toward Community Service: A Comparative Analysis." *Journal of Engineering Education* 96 (2): 129–140.

Bernacki, Matthew L., and Elizabeth Jaeger. 2008. "Exploring the Impact of Service-Learning on Moral Development and Moral Orientation." *Michigan Journal of Community Service Learning* 14 (2).

Boss, Judith A. 1994. "The Effect of Community Service on the Moral Development of College Ethics students." *Journal of Moral Education* 23: 183–198.

Brown, Bethanne, Pamela C. Heaton, and Andrea Wall. 2007. "A Service-Learning Elective to Promote Enhanced Understanding of Civic, Cultural, and Social Issues and Health Disparities in Pharmacy." *American Journal of Pharmaceutical Education* 71 (1): 1–7.

Buglione, Suzanne. 2012. "Nontraditional Approaches with Nontraditional Students: Experiences of Learning, Service and Identity Development." PhD Diss., University of Massachusetts, Boston.

Bulot, James J., and Christopher J. Johnson. 2006. "Rewards and Costs of Faculty Involvement in Intergenerational Service-Learning." *Educational Gerontology* 32 (8): 633–645.

Choy, Susan. 2002. *Nontraditional Undergraduates, NCES 2002–012.* Washington, DC: US Department of Education, National Center for Education Statistics.

Cohen, Arthur M. and Florence B. Brawer. 2008. *The American Community College.* San Francisco: Jossey-Bass Publishers, 5th ed.

Crisp, Gloria, and Amanda Taggart. 2013. "Community College Student Success Programs: A Synthesis, Critique, and Research Agenda." *Community College Journal of Research and Practice* 37 (2): 114–130.

Elwell, Maralene D., and Martha S. Bean. 2001. "Editor's Choice: The Efficacy of Service-Learning for Community College ESL Students." *Community College Review* 28 (4): 47–61.

Eyler, Janet, and Dwight Giles. 1999. *Where's the Learning in Service-Learning?* San Francisco, CA: Jossey-Bass.

Fertman, C. 1993. "The Pennsylvania Serve-America Grant: Implementation and Impact, Report no. BBB31285." Pittsburgh: Pennsylvania Service-Learning Resource and Evaluation Network.

Grubb, W. Norton, Norena Badway, and Denise Bell. 2003. "Community Colleges and the Equity Agenda: The Potential of Noncredit Education." *The Annals of the American Academy of Political and Social Science* 586 (1): 218–240.

Hansen, Matthew C. 2011. "'O Brave New World': Service-Learning and Shakespeare." *Pedagogy* 11 (1): 177–197.

Holland, Barbara, and Gail Robinson. 2008. "Community Based Learning with Adults: Bridging Efforts in Multiple Sectors." *New Directions for Adult and Continuing Education* 118: 17–30.

Hughes, Alice S. 2002. "A Study of Service-Learning at Virginia Highlands Community College and Mountain Empire Community College." PhD Diss. East Tennessee State University.

Kim, Karen A. 2002. "ERIC Review: Exploring the Meaning of 'Nontraditional' at the Community College." *Community College Review* 30 (1): 74–89.

Krippendorff, Klaus. 2012. *Content Analysis: An Introduction to Its Methodology.* Thousand Oaks, CA: SAGE Publications.

Kuh, George D. 2008. *High-Impact Educational Practices: What They Are, Who Has Access to Them, and Why They Matter.* Washington, DC: Association of American Colleges and Universities.

Kuh, George D., Jillian Kinzie, John H. Schuh, and Elizabeth J. Whitt. 2010. *Student Success in College: Creating Conditions That Matter*. San Francisco, CA: John Wiley & Sons.

Lacy, Stephen, and Daniel Riffe. 1996. "Sampling Error and Selecting Intercoder Reliability Samples for Nominal Content Categories," *Journalism & Mass Communication Quarterly* 73 (4): 963–973.

Largent, Liz. 2013. "Service-Learning among Nontraditional Age Community College Students." *Community College Journal of Research and Practice* 37 (4): 296–312.

Largent, Liz, and Jon B Horinek. 2004. "Community Colleges and Adult Service Learners: Evaluating a First-Year Program to Improve Implementation." *New Directions for Adult and Continuing Education* 118: 37–48.

Levin, John S. 2007. *Nontraditional Students and Community Colleges: The Conflict of Justice and Neoliberalism*. Hampshire, England: Palgrave Macmillan.

Lombard, Matthew, Jennifer Snyder-Duch, and Cheryl Campanella Bracken. 2010. "Practical Resources for Assessing and Reporting Intercoder Reliability in Content Analysis Research Projects." http://matthewlombard.com/reliability/.

Marienau, Catherine, and Susan C. Reed. 2008. "Educator as Designer: Balancing Multiple Teaching Perspectives in the Design of Community Based Learning for Adults." *New Directions for Adult and Continuing Education* 118: 61–75.

Neuendorf, Kimberly A. 2002. *The Content Analysis Guidebook*. Thousand Oaks, CA: SAGE.

Novick, Sarah, Scott C. Seider, and James P. Huguley. 2011. "Engaging College Students from Diverse Backgrounds in Community Service Learning." *Journal of College and Character* 12 (1): 1–8.

Prentice, Mary, Gail Robinson, and Madeline Patton. 2012. *Cultivating Community beyond the Classroom* Washington, DC: American Association of Community Colleges.

Reed, Susan C., and Catherine Marienau. 2008. "Maintaining a Steady Fire: Sustaining Adults' Commitment to Community Based Learning." *New Directions for Adult and Continuing Education* 118: 97–107.

Robbins, Christine Reiser. 2012. "Expanding Service-learning in the Humanities among First-Generation, Minority-Population, and Non-Traditional Students: A Mixed-Participation, Mixed-Assessment Model." *Interdisciplinary Humanities* 29 (3): 24–40.

Rochford, Regina A. 2013. "Service-Learning for Remedial Reading and Writing Students." *Community College Journal of Research and Practice* 37 (5): 345–355.

Seider, Scott, James P. Huguley, and Sarah Novick. 2013. "College Students, Diversity and Community Service Learning." *Teachers College Record* 115 (3): 1–44.

Smith, M. Cecil. 2008. "Does Service Learning Promote Adult Development? Theoretical Perspectives and Directions for Research." *New Directions for Adult and Continuing Education* 118: 5–15.

Taggart, Amanda, and Gloria Crisp. 2011. "Service Learning at Community Colleges: Synthesis, Critique, and Recommendations for Future Research." *Journal of College Reading and Learning* 42 (1): 24–44.

Townsend, Barbara K. 1999. *Understanding the Impact of Reverse Transfer Students on Community Colleges*. San Francisco, CA: Jossey-Bass.

Yeh, Theresa Ling. 2010. "Service-Learning and Persistence of Low-Income, First-Generation College Students: An Exploratory Study." *Michigan Journal of Community Service Learning* Spring: 50–65.

York, Travis. 2013. "Exploring Service-Learning Outcomes and Experiences for Low-Income, First-Generation College Students: A Mixed Methods Approach." PhD Diss., The Pennsylvania State University.

CHAPTER 18

Best Practices in Researching Service-Learning at Community Colleges

Amanda Taggart and Gloria Crisp

In recent years, an increasing number of community colleges have integrated some form of service-learning into their programs or courses with the idea that it will promote civic engagement, increase student satisfaction with their courses and college experience as a whole, and improve learning outcomes. There is a good amount of research published on service-learning programs and outcomes conducted at four-year institutions, though there is a dearth of studies available on service-learning at community colleges. Because community colleges serve a purpose unique from that of four-year colleges and universities, both in their mission and often in the students they serve, research on service-learning at community colleges should also be distinct from investigations at the four-year level.

This chapter details best practices in researching service-learning at community colleges. We begin with an overview of how to locate service-learning research inside and outside of academic journals. We then provide focus to key methodological issues to consider when reading and analyzing empirical work, including the role of theory. The chapter concludes with recommendations for community college faculty, staff, and administrators in applying research toward the development and/or evaluation of service-learning programming.

Locating Service-Learning Research

The following section provides suggestions for locating service-learning research at the community college level. Because the accessibility of published empirical work on this topic is now fairly limited, uncovering research on service-learning at community colleges entails conducting extensive literature searches on multiple education databases with several search term combinations. Databases such as Education

Full Text, ERIC via EBSCO, JSTOR, Project Muse, and Academic Search Premier have proven to be very useful in covering a wide range of topics in education journals. Furthermore, we recommend using combinations of key words such as "service-learning," "experiential learning," "community college," "programs," "student development," and "student success" to find articles that explicitly discuss service-learning at the two-year level. However, this requires searching through hundreds of journals and many more articles, many of which are specific to certain disciplines (e.g., *Journal of Correctional Education; Gerontology and Geriatrics Education*). Manual reviews of articles published in commonly read and top-tier higher education journals are also worthwhile. For instance, a recent search for literature on service-learning at community colleges located articles in the *Community College Journal of Research and Practice, Journal of Experiential Education, Community College Review,* and *New Directions for Community Colleges*. The reference pages of articles pertaining to service-learning should also be combed for other work pertinent to the subject.

In addition, due to the relatively small number of academic journal articles published on service-learning in community colleges, we recommend considering unpublished work to inform current service-learning research. Unpublished research is often conducted as part of program evaluations at individual institutions, reported in dissertations or theses, or presented in conference format and can be found through the same kinds of database searches as those used for peer-reviewed journal articles. For example, in our synthesis of empirical work about the impact of service-learning on community college students (Taggart and Crisp 2011), we reviewed studies that came from all of the above-named sources and found multiple articles from the *Community College Journal of Research and Practice*, as well as numerous dissertations and other papers on service-learning at the two-year level from the Dissertation Abstracts International database and the ERIC database.

Moreover, publicly accessible manuscripts may be retrieved from policy centers or other organizations and groups interested in community college students and can be found and accessed via Internet searches. In fact, the websites of these organizations are the richest source of information on service-learning in higher education. For instance, the National Service Learning Clearinghouse[1] aggregates and distributes data and research on service-learning, including specific information about service-learning at community colleges.[2]

Furthermore, the American Association of Community Colleges (AACC) offers curriculum tools for service-learning education, publications on service-learning, and many links to other service-learning information, all easily located from their service-learning home page.[3] This website also details the AACC's Community Colleges Broadening Horizons through Service Learning project (1994–2012), the intent of which was to integrate quality service-learning programming into the institutional climate of community colleges around the country. In addition, this website lists the colleges that participated in the project and also gives links to many of those schools' service-learning websites.

The Campus Compact Center for Community Colleges is another site filled with information and resources for those interested in service-learning.[4] Campus Compact is a national association dedicated exclusively to civic engagement on college campuses, including community service. Its website offers resources specific to faculty, students, association presidents, and service-learning staff. It also offers a bookstore where scholars and others can easily locate volumes on service-learning.

It is important to note that such an extensive search process as that outlined above necessitates an understanding of methodologically sound research in order to differentiate between strong empirical and nonrigorous or nonempirical work. Searches must be carefully filtered to find research that evaluates service-learning programs and experiences, as much of what has been published focuses on descriptions of various service-learning programs, suggestions for implementing service-learning in college courses or more widely on college campuses, or theoretical or opinion pieces on service-learning. As such, the subsequent portion of this chapter offers questions to contemplate when evaluating service-learning research.

Issues to Consider When Reading Empirical Work

The following section provides an overview of key methodological issues to consider when reading service-learning research. Issues are presented in the form of questions to be considered by community college administrators, faculty, and staff in analyzing empirical work. The first two questions are focused on understanding the paradigm in which the research was conducted. The third, fourth, and fifth questions are presented to discern the degree to which findings from a study may be comparable to other studies and/or are generalizable. The section concludes with two questions focused on analyzing the degree to which research findings are methodologically and theoretically sound.

What Was the Purpose of the Research?

One issue to consider when reading empirical work on service-learning is the purpose, focus, and/or goals of the research. Service-learning research is produced for a variety of reasons that may intentionally or unintentionally influence how findings are presented and the degree to which findings may be useful. It is notable that the purpose or focus of the research is not always explicitly stated and may need to be discerned by the reader. A good amount of service-learning research is conducted with the intention of contributing to knowledge and theory (termed basic research) or to provide generalizable conclusions that are able to inform the development or implementation of service-learning programming (referred to as applied or action research) (Johnson and Christensen 2012). These forms of research are most often conducted by academic researchers and have the benefit of determining the degree to which service-learning is beneficial to constituents, in what ways, for how long, and under what conditions (Howard 2003).

A subset of applied research is conducted by program evaluators with the purpose of assessing the quality, value, or worth of a program (Johnson and Christensen 2012). Program evaluation can be defined as the process of systematically gathering data about a program to obtain information and measure program outcomes (National Service-Learning Clearinghouse 2001). Program evaluations answer specific questions about a particular program (Howard 2003) and are not designed to provide findings and conclusions that are applicable to other service-learning programs.

A smaller amount of research on service-learning can be categorized as advocacy research. Advocacy work is often financially supported, published as a form of marketing and program promotion, and written to highlight the strengths of a particular program. Although valuable to service-learning practice, a critical eye should be used when reading advocacy work as it rarely uses rigorous methodological designs and may overlook or exclude negative findings.

What Type of Research Was Conducted?

A second question that readers of service-learning research should seek to understand is the methodology used by researchers and evaluators to answer research questions. A recent review identified that a combination of quantitative, qualitative, or mixed methodology paradigms are used for service-learning research conducted at the community college level (Taggart and Crisp 2011). Quantitative research is used to measure service-learning outcomes and utilizes a variety of data collection tools such as test scores, surveys, and data maintained by the college, including student grades or graduation rates (National Service-Learning Clearinghouse 2001). Quantitative research is specifically used to assess relationships between participants' experiences and outcomes, including but not limited to cause and effect relationships. In contrast, qualitative research is used to gain a more holistic understanding of students' experiences, perceptions, and opinions of service-learning. Primary data collection tools used for this purpose include personal interviews, focus groups, or observations (National Service-Learning Clearinghouse 2001). Qualitative research is typically utilized to answer questions beginning with "how" or "why," such as how service-learning promotes civic engagement among students. A growing number of studies are using a combination of quantitative and qualitative paradigms in a single research study, commonly referred to as "mixed methods research," to assess the impact of service-learning programming. Mixed methods research has the benefit of providing multiple forms of data to warrant claims and may produce findings that are more valid than research that utilizes only quantitative or qualitative methods (Johnson and Christensen 2012). *Educational Research: Quantitative, Qualitative and Mixed Approaches* provides a more detailed explanation of each of the above-mentioned paradigms and their uses.

Although there are numerous designs used in both qualitative and mixed methods research, we feel it may be worthwhile to provide more focus to methods used by quantitative researchers, as this form of research is often the most difficult to read and analyze. Quantitative research can be categorized into three primary designs including experimental, quasi-experimental, and nonexperimental research (Johnson and Christensen 2012). Experimental designs (also known as randomized control trials or comparative designs) are conducted to measure whether a service-learning program "causes" an outcome where each participant has two potential outcomes: (1) the outcome he or she would experience if offered the program, known as the "treatment outcome"; and (2) the outcome experienced if not offered the program. Because it is impossible to observe both potential outcomes for a participant, experimental designs compare outcomes of the treatment group with a control group, which is made up of a comparable group of students who did not participate in the program (Weiss, Bloom, and Brock 2013). Use of a control group allows the researcher to measure whether group differences are a product of initial differences, maturation, or participation in the service-learning experience (Hecht 2003). Experimental designs rely on a process of random assignment of participants to the treatment or control group to ensure that the groups do not systematically vary in a way that may influence the findings (Johnson and Christensen 2012).

Although considered the "gold standard" of research, for educational and financial reasons, random assignment is rarely used in studies of service-learning (Hecht 2003). In these cases, a quasi-experimental design or nonexperimental design may be used. A quasi-experimental design is a form of experimental research that does not involve random assignment and therefore makes it more difficult for researchers to establish a treatment and control group that are comparable. This is problematic, as nonequivalent groups introduce the possibility of differences between the treatment and control that unintentionally influence the findings (Johnson and Christensen 2012). For example, a service-learning study that uses an existing section of a sophomore-level sociology class as the treatment group and a group of students enrolled in a developmental English class as the control group would introduce several differences between the groups (termed "confounding variables") that may influence outcomes such as service-learning curriculum/activities, student academic preparation, and motivation, etc.

A final form of quantitative research used in service-learning research, nonexperimental designs (also referred to as pre- and post-designs), gathers data about student outcomes before and after the service-learning experience to determine whether the experience was related to the change. Although this design does not measure cause and effect relationships, it is often the preferred method of service-learning evaluation work, as it is the simplest quantitative design and does not require a comparable control group (National Service-Learning Clearinghouse 2001). A common type of nonexperimental research uses correlational designs, which are used to measure the relationship between two or more naturally occurring variables such as participation in service-learning and students' commitment to civic involvement (Clayton et al. 2013).

How Transferable/Generalizable Are the Findings?

There is growing evidence to suggest that (1) different versions of the same program may have different outcomes; (2) a program that is effective for one group of individuals may not yield positive effects for another; and (3) a program that is effective under certain conditions/settings may not work in other contexts (Weiss, Bloom, and Brock 2013).

As such, when reading and analyzing service-learning research, readers should not assume that findings will apply to other programs, students, or contexts. To begin with, although all service-learning requires some sort of community service, there is large variation in how the learning occurs (i.e., the treatment itself) (Howard 2003). For example, some service-learning research involves co-curricular service-learning, which refers to learning and service outside of a formal course curriculum, whereas other studies involve academic service-learning, defined as bounding the service experience to the academic course curriculum (Howard 2003). These two types of service-learning are likely to produce different outcomes and should not be assumed to be comparable.

Who Were the Participants?

Service-learning outcomes are also influenced by a variety of student characteristics that limit the relevance or generalizability of the findings to other student populations. Student characteristics that may impact service-learning outcomes include, but are not limited to, gender, prior academic experiences, quality of peer relationships, personality, motivation, beliefs, values, and cognitive ability (Waterman 2003). This is of particular relevance when analyzing service-learning research that was not conducted specific to community college students, as, on the whole, students attending two-year colleges have different characteristics and experiences when compared to students who begin college at a four-year university. At the same time, service-learning research focused on community college students also should not be assumed to be generalizable to all community college students, as many studies focus on subpopulations of students such as developmental students or English Language Learners (ELLs). Further, outcomes may vary among individual students within a given study, which may or may not be examined by the researchers (Furco 2003).

Along with variations in how service-learning is defined and which students are involved, service-learning research is confounded by the diverse and situational nature of service-learning settings and experiences (Furco 2003). It is impossible to standardize or control experiences students will have with service-learning because experiences occur in natural settings (Waterman 2003). Additionally, service-learning may involve a diversity of activities and tasks, even within a given activity (Hecht 2003). Further, the length and intensity of the service-learning experience vary across studies, with some experiences involving a single afternoon and others requiring a daily commitment for an extended period of time (Hecht 2003). These variations in setting and program characteristics are expected to influence outcomes (Waterman 2003). For example, findings from an exemplary service-learning program conducted at an exemplary college are likely to be largely a product of the college and/or students rather than the service-learning experience (Hecht 2003). In contrast, service-learning studies that utilize multiple sites or programs for comparative purposes are more likely to provide more generalizable findings. Therefore, attention should be given when reading service-learning research and making comparisons across studies or drawing conclusions about the relevance of findings to other contexts, such as the community college, and programs (Furco 2003). Community colleges, for example, provide unique settings for service-learning because their mission highlights serving the community (Hodge et al. 2001). However, because community college students generally have fewer opportunities to take part in academic and social events outside of their classroom experiences, it is challenging for two-year institutions to incorporate ways to engage students in civic or volunteer activities (McIntosh and Rouse 2009; Bailey and Alfonso 2005; Cohen and Brawer 2003). For this reason, community colleges often use service-learning to integrate meaningful learning experiences with their emphasis on serving the community (Berson and Younkin 1998).

How Valid/Trustworthy Are the Findings?

Beyond understanding the type of research and the relevance of findings to other studies/programs, it is also important to consider the methodological rigor of the research being conducted when reading and analyzing service-learning research. A lot of community college service-learning research is based on self-reports by staff, faculty, students, or community partners. These measures can be meaningful and useful, but should be interpreted with caution, as self-reported data are likely to be biased and the reliability or consistency in the findings, as well as the validity, may be limited (Clayton et al. 2013). Internal validity is a key measure of methodological rigor in quantitative research, and service-learning research should use techniques and measures that demonstrate validity (Clayton et al. 2013). Internal validity can be defined as the ability of a study to measure a true relationship between variables (Johnson and Christensen 2012). Although the possibility and appropriateness of the strategy will vary across studies, researchers should identify and explain the strategies used to ensure the internal validity and trustworthiness of their results (Clayton et al. 2013).

Efforts to promote internal validity are especially important in cases where the service-learning program at a community college is optional and students self-select into a service-learning enhanced course. Self-selection is a serious methodological issue plaguing service-learning research (Clayton et al. 2013), as students who choose to enroll in the service-learning course are likely to be systematically different (e.g., motivation, maturity) from students who do not choose to enroll in a service-learning course. In turn, these differences are likely to influence study outcomes. As such, caution should be used when interpreting findings from service-learning studies that involve self-selection into service-learning but do not use random assignment or utilize efforts to control for initial differences between the treatment and control groups. Further, internal validity is enhanced when researchers collect data from a variety of sources (not just students) and include both disaggregated data (specific to individual students and programs) and aggregated (combined across students and programs) (Furco 2003).

To What Extent Was the Research Design Grounded in Theory?

A final consideration when reading service-learning research is the degree to which the study design and evaluation efforts were guided by relevant theory. A theory is "a set of speculations about a phenomenon and its nature" (Clayton et al. 2013, 66). Theories are useful in service-learning research by identifying concepts and relating them in a way that assists both the reader and researcher in understanding, organizing, and predicting events. Additionally, theories pose answers to "why" questions, such as, "Why did the students change as a result of the service-learning experience?" Theories from a variety of disciplines including sociology, education, psychology, communication, and the cognitive sciences can contribute to the development and interpretation of service-learning research (Clayton et al. 2013). Unfortunately, the disconnect between program design and evaluation and existing developmental and learning theory makes it difficult to establish a cause and effect relationship between service-learning experiences and outcomes (Bradley 2003). As such, attention should be paid to assessing the degree to which experiences and outcomes are clearly linked to theory when reading and analyzing service-learning research.

Recommendations

Given the methodological issues outlined above and the growth of service-learning initiatives on community college campuses, it is vitally important to increase the research knowledge base on service-learning in order to provide evidence for service-learning program outcomes (Howard 2003). Therefore, we conclude this chapter by offering several recommendations for community college faculty, staff, and administrators in conducting service-learning research, as well as applying it toward the development and/or evaluation of service-learning programming. We also discuss directions for future research and useful resources for those interested in studying service-learning.

First, it is important for those interested in researching service-learning to familiarize themselves with the research that has already been conducted and with what outcomes that work revealed. Consumers of research should use this existing work to inform all aspects of their research design and assessment—in other words, do not attempt to reinvent the wheel. For instance, prior research can provide scales or other assessment measures that others have used. If researchers determine that an existing instrument meets their needs, using that instrument can save them and their institutions time and money that would have been used creating and testing their own measures. Unfortunately, research articles that have been published in peer-reviewed journals often do not make available more than the name of the instrument used; dissertations are much more reliable in terms of providing the entire measurement instrument. In cases where an instrument named in a study is not provided in the article, researchers should not hesitate to contact the author(s) and request the full instrument. However, there are examples of service-learning related assessment measures used in previous research. For instance, Shiarella, McCarthy, and Tucker (2000) have published an article on the development of the Community Service Attitudes Scales (CSAS), an instrument for measuring college students' attitudes about community service. Though that research instrument was not developed specifically for community college students, dissertation studies that are based at two-year campuses and provide complete copies of the measurement instruments used include modified versions of the Civic Education and Community Service evaluation questionnaire (Haines 2002), a student interview protocol to look at students' perceptions of their service-learning experiences (Hughes 2002), and an evaluation questionnaire to measure the extent to which students, faculty, and community partners met a service-learning program's objectives (Reed and Pietrovito 2000). So as to reduce time spent searching for studies on service-learning and the data collection instruments they employed, we recommend that scholars and educators in the field work to create repositories of such instruments in order to publish them and to collaborate with others on service-learning research in community college settings. This is especially important given the waning of federal support for many national service-learning initiatives.

As noted previously in this chapter, it is also key for service-learning researchers to critically consider several methodological issues when planning and conducting their research. We recommend that, first, scholars determine the purpose of their research. For instance, is the intent of the study to provide generalizable findings, to conduct a program evaluation, or to advocate for a certain type of service-learning program? Next, it is important to decide what type of research should be conducted in order to best answer the research questions (i.e., quantitative; qualitative; mixed methods) and whether the research design they choose is grounded in theory. Third, researchers should also utilize rigorous methodology that accounts for internal validity. Finally, scholars must consider how generalizable the findings of their study will be. Because service-learning outcomes are influenced by variations in student and program characteristics, it is necessary to consider whether or not the findings will be comparable across different settings. There is also large variation in how service-learning occurs across programs and campuses.

It bears repeating that community colleges differ from four-year institutions in several ways. However, when thinking about their own research, community college educators should consider work that has been conducted at four-year institutions, keeping in mind how their two-year programs may be similar to or different from those at the four-year level. Service-learning work done at four-year schools includes that conducted by Astin and colleagues, who have written much about community service and service-learning, including large-scale work on understanding how students learn in a service-learning course, how service experiences enhance college courses, and how faculty have integrated service into their curriculum (for one example, see Astin et al. 2000). In addition, we advise researchers and campus leaders to seek guidance from colleagues and others who already have been involved in researching, implementing, and/or evaluating service-learning programs in order to learn from both their mistakes and successes. This can be done through professional networks such as conferences or through the service-learning organization websites discussed earlier in this chapter. The National Service-Learning Clearinghouse website provides descriptions of and links to conferences that offer forums for presentations on service-learning.[5] Service-learning researchers and program administrators can also request information and contacts from these various organizations.

Considering the often limited resources on community college campuses, it is also important for faculty and administrators to understand where to focus their efforts. As such, it is wise to design research and assessment that seeks to understand the groups of students served by a particular institution. For instance, institutions who serve many nontraditionally aged college students should work to tailor their service-learning programs around the unique needs of this specific demographic. Doing so will be more beneficial to students and can bring significant new insight into how service-learning impacts different groups of students, an area in which we need more research to inform practice. There is also a need to understand the conditions under which service-learning is most effective, such as whether or not the service-learning is a requirement of students' degree programs or course grades.

Finally, we urge community college faculty and leaders to present and publish the research they conduct on service-learning so that others can learn from it. Again, the National Service-Learning Clearinghouse offers suggestions on where to look to publish work on service-learning,[6] including some previously mentioned in this chapter (e.g., *Journal of Experiential Education*). Moreover, conferences that often include presentations on varying types of work in community colleges include those held by the Association for the Study of Higher Education (ASHE) and the American Educational Research Association (AERA), as well as others. Information on submitting presentation proposals for these conferences is available on their respective websites. The potential for empirical research on service-learning at the community college level remains to be explored in depth and new work could provide valuable contributions to the field that would ultimately benefit students and institutions, as well as improve educational policy and practice. For those interested in furthering this work, we conclude this chapter with a description of a few resources that may prove useful in studying service-learning:

1. *The Educator's Guide to Service-learning Evaluation,* published by the National Service-Learning Clearinghouse (2001), provides additional information regarding data collection and analysis and serves as an excellent resource for community college faculty and staff engaged with service-learning programming and research.
2. *Studying Service-Learning,* edited by Billig and Waterman (2003), expands on many of the ideas presented in this chapter including issues to consider when studying service-learning, relevant developmental theories, and methodological considerations when reading and conducting research on service-learning.
3. *The Measures of Service-Learning: Research Scales to Assess Student Experiences* (Bringle et al. 2004), provides a primer on measurement theory and scales to measure a variety of service-learning outcomes including moral development and critical thinking.
4. The National Service-Learning Clearinghouse, which provides news about service-learning and information on various service-learning resources. For example, a fact sheet titled *Tools and Methods for Evaluating Service-Learning in Higher Education* (Seifer et al. 2009) enumerates issues to consider when evaluating service-learning programs and links to multiple resources for evaluating service-learning.

Notes

1. See http://www.servicelearning.org
2. See http://www.servicelearning.org/topic/demographics-settings/community-colleges
3. See http://www.aacc.nche.edu/Resources/aaccprograms/horizons/Pages/default.aspx
4. See http://www.compact.org
5. See http://www.servicelearning.org/instant_info/fact_sheets/he_facts/publishing_sl.
6. See http://www.servicelearning.org/instant_info/fact_sheets/he_facts/publishing_sl

References

American Association of Community Colleges. 2013. "Service Learning." Accessed July 25. http://www.aacc.nche.edu/Resources/aaccprograms/horizons/Pages/default.aspx.

Astin, Alexander W., Lori J. Vogelgesang, Elaine K. Ikeda, and Jennifer A. Yee. 2000. *How Service-Learning Affects Students*. Los Angeles, CA: Higher Education Research Institute, UCLA.

Bailey, Thomas R., and Mariana Alfonso. 2005. "Paths to Persistence: An Analysis of Research on Program Effectiveness at Community Colleges." *Lumina Foundation for Education New Agenda Series* 6.

Berson, Judith S., and William F. Younkin. 1998. "Doing Well by Doing Good: A Study of the Effects of a Service-Learning Experience on Student Success." Paper presented at the 23rd Annual Meeting of the Association for the Study of Higher Education, Miami, FL.

Billig, Shelley H., and Alan Waterman, eds. 2003. *Studying Service-Learning: Innovations in Education Research Methodology*. Mahwah, NJ: Lawrence Erlbaum Associates, Publishers.

Bradley, Richard. 2003. "Using Developmental and Learning Theory in the Design and Evaluation of K-16 Service-learning Programs." In *Studying Service-Learning: Innovations in Education Research Methodology*, edited by Shelley Billig and Alan Waterman, 47–72. Mahwah, NJ: Lawrence Erlbaum Associates, Publishers.

Bringle, Robert, Mindy Phillips, and Michael Hudson. 2004. *The Measures of Service-Learning: Research Scales to Assess Student Experiences*. Washington, DC: American Psychological Association.

Campus Compact Center for Community Colleges. 2013. Accessed July 25. http://www.compact.org.

Clayton, Patti, Robert Bringle, and Julie Hatcher. 2013. *Research on Service-Learning: Conceptual Frameworks and Assessment*. Sterling, VA: Stylus.

Cohen, Arthur M., and Florence B. Brawer. 2003. *The American Community College*. San Francisco, CA: Jossey-Bass.

Furco, Andrew. 2003. "Issues of Definition and Program Diversity in the Study of Service-Learning." In *Studying Service-Learning: Innovations in Education Research Methodology*, edited by Shelley Billig and Alan Waterman, 13–34. Mahwah, NJ: Lawrence Erlbaum Associates Publishers.

Haines, Dana Lee. 2002. "A Study of Community College Student Attitudes Related to Service-Learning." PhD Diss., Baylor University.

Hecht, Deborah. 2003. "Issues of Research Design and Statistical Analysis." In *Studying Service-Learning: Innovations in Education Research Methodology*, edited by Shelley Billig and Alan Waterman, 107–124. Mahwah, NJ: Lawrence Erlbaum Associates Publishers.

Hodge, Gary, Ted Lewis, Kim Kramer, and Regina Hughes. 2001. "Collaboration for Excellence: Engaged Scholarship at Collin County Community College." *Community College Journal of Research and Practice* 25: 675–690.

Howard, Jeffrey. 2003. "Service-Learning Research: Foundational Issues." In *Studying Service-Learning: Innovations in Education Research Methodology*, edited by Shelley Billig and Alan Waterman, 1–12. Mahwah, NJ: Lawrence Erlbaum Associates Publishers.

Hughes, Alice. 2002. "A Study of Service-Learning at Virginia Highlands Community College and Mountain Empire Community College." PhD Diss., East Tennessee State University.

Johnson, Burke, and Larry Christensen. 2012. *Educational Research: Quantitative, Qualitative, and Mixed Approaches*. Thousand Oaks, CA: SAGE Publishers, Inc.

McIntosh, Molly F., and Cecilia E. Rouse. 2009. "The Other College: Retention and Completion Rates among Two-Year College Students." Washington, DC: Center for American Progress.

National Service-Learning Clearinghouse. 2001. "Educators' Guide to Service-Learning Program Evaluation." Accessed July 25. http://www.servicelearning.org/filemanager/download/37/EvaluationToolkit.pdf.

———. 2013. Accessed July 25. http://www.servicelearning.org.

Reed, Carol B., and James A. Pietrovito. 2000. "Evaluation of the Service-Learning Program at Mount Wachusett Community College: History, Philosophies, and Practices of Adult Education." PhD Diss., Nova Southeastern University.

Seifer, Sarena D., Stacey Holmes, Julie L. Plaut, and Julie Elkins. 2009. "Tools and Methods for Evaluating Service-Learning in Higher Education." Accessed July 25. http://www.servicelearning.org/instant_info/fact_sheets/he-facts/tools_methods.

Shiarella, Ann Harris, Anne M. McCarthy, and Mary L. Tucker. 2000. "Development and Construct Validity of Scores on the Community Service Attitudes Scale." *Educational Psychology and Measurement* 60: 286–300.

Taggart, Amanda, and Gloria Crisp. 2011. "Service Learning at Community Colleges: Synthesis, Critique, and Recommendations for Future Research." *Journal of College Reading and Learning* 42: 24–44.

Waterman, Alan. 2003. "Issues Regarding the Selection of Variables for Study in the Context of the Diversity of Possible Student Outcomes of Service-Learning." In *Studying Service-Learning: Innovations in Education Research Methodology*, edited by Shelley Billig and Alan Waterman, 73–90. Mahwah, NJ: Lawrence Erlbaum Associates Publishers.

Weiss, Michael, Howard Bloom, and Thomas Brock. 2013. "A Conceptual Framework for Studying the Sources of Variation in Program Effects." MDRC Working Paper on Research Methodology. Accessed July 25. http://www.mdrc.org/publication/conceptual-framework-studying-sources/variation-program-effects.

PART VI

Concluding Reflections on Service-Learning and Community Colleges

CHAPTER 19

The Idea of Place

Scott Evenbeck, Paulette Dalpes, and Linda E. Merians

Students come from a place. They are studying in a place. They connect with many places. As Karen Halttunen (2006) said in her presidential address to the American Studies Association, "We live in place, make our homes and raise our families in place, vote in place, and teach, and write, and eventually die—in place" (8). In a recent interview to the *New York Times*, William Least Heat-Moon (1982), whose book *Blue Highways* is iconic in celebrating places, argues that we want to be travelers, not tourists (Caputo 2013). We need to help our students, particularly those who study at community colleges, become fully aware travelers to and from their own places—family neighborhoods, larger communities, high schools to colleges—and ultimately their futures and the various places they will come to inhabit in their personal and professional lives.

Community colleges are in and of their communities. The word "community" is definitional for the community college; it is so familiar it is often overlooked or taken for granted. Community colleges, unlike any other institution of higher education, have a unique relationship with their surrounding communities. The origins of community colleges are rooted in the placement of the school in a distinct location to serve specific communities. Indeed, many community colleges were intentionally planned to serve a specific mile radius within reach by the community where they are located or to serve districts defined by regional or county boundaries (Tull 2014). Community colleges hold a closeness and intimacy to their surrounding community because the community itself defines the mission of the college. With this mission, community colleges can engage the role of service-learning in a more personal and highly intentional approach.

This reflective chapter explores and encourages consideration of the idea of place in community colleges. Tony Hiss (1991), in *The Experience of Place*, proposes that "...the places where we spend our time affect the people we are and can become" (xi). As community college students become engaged with the curriculum and the co-curriculum, particularly with high-impact practices and specifically service-learning, how can faculty and staff engage the "place" of the college, both on and off campus, to enhance student learning? Place is more than where the college is located and the buildings where students take classes. It can also include nearby places they have never had reason or inclination to visit, places where they never felt welcome, and even electronic platforms/places. Engagement with these new places can afford students the opportunity to learn and reflect more about themselves and, crucially, to interact and integrate their academic studies with all the various places they understand can play important roles in their present and future lives.

As argued in this edited book, service-learning provides an ideal platform for engaging and connecting students with each other and their shared places, often improving their academic performance and jump-starting transformative moments of personal development. The service-learning programs that may evolve within the community college curriculum have the capacity to be based directly on the immediate needs of the community the college serves, and they can be located in community-based agencies, local businesses, city government, and faith-based organizations that serve or employ students or family members of students enrolled at the college. In this chapter, we reflect on our collective experiences at two community colleges, one in Massachusetts and one in New York, to show the fundamental importance of engaging with "place" through a variety of approaches to service-learning and how this engagement of place within the community college curriculum is central to advancing student learning during a time of critical change in higher education.

Literature Review

Service-learning in community colleges has grown significantly. The American Association of Community Colleges (AACC) conducted studies of service-learning in community colleges in 1995, 1997, and 2003. Results indicated that in 1997, 31 percent of community colleges used service-learning and this increased to 71 percent in 2003. Additionally, during this same period of time, faculty involvement and community partnerships have become more robust.

In 1994, through a grant from the Corporation for National Service, the AACC began a vigorous and committed endeavor to encourage service-learning in community colleges; this encouragement continued through 2012 thanks to ongoing support from Learn and Serve America. This initial venture, which became known as "Community Colleges Broadening Horizons through Service-Learning," developed into an extensive series of reports, publications, and evidence-based best practices expounding the impact of service-learning in community colleges. The initial goal of the grant was to develop infrastructure and faculty skills to implement service-learning within community college curriculum. In addition to this, a network of ten colleges was created, now referred to as the AACC Service-Learning Alumni Colleges. From 1994 to 2012, ten different colleges were awarded grants every three years, totaling 104 colleges, including Queensborough Community College within the City University of New York system.

In 2002, the American Association of State Colleges and Universities (AASCU) released a groundbreaking call-to-action report: *Stepping Forward as Stewards of*

Place presented a guide and strategic tool kit intended to help campuses deepen their ideas and programs related to public engagement. The report's opening section offers a four-part definition of crucial aspects of public engagement: place-related, interactive, mutually beneficial, and integrated. In so doing, it makes a crucial point about place-related public engagement, which is that the idea of place should not be thought to be limiting:

> While the demands of the economy and society have forced institutions to be nationally and globally aware, the fact remains that state colleges and universities are inextricably linked with the communities and regions in which they are located. Exercising "stewardship of place" does not mean limiting the institution's worldview; rather, it means pursuing that worldview in a way that has meaning to the institution's neighbors, who can be its most consistent and reliable advocates. (AASCU 2002, 9)

Public and community engagement efforts in higher education have gathered even more momentum since the publication of *Stewards of Place* in 2002. The Carnegie Foundation has offered a series of Community Engagement classifications and, in a forthcoming monograph, the AASCU offers a follow-up report to its 2002 document. In the introduction to this book, entitled *Becoming a Steward of Place: An Operational Guide for Institutional Leaders*, Wim Wiewel urges AASCU institutional leaders who are dedicated to stewardship of place to focus on four key areas: civic learning, work with K-12 schools, economic development, and internationalization.

The role of place is being tested to some extent by the allure of new educational technologies and issues related to access. Citing the growing cost of higher education and the increase of online educational options, Bill Gates stated, "College needs to be less place-based" (Young 2010 n.p.). No doubt, community colleges stand at the forefront of many new, "less place-based" efforts to increase affordability and accessibility in higher education. For example, massive open online courses, often referred to as "MOOCs," offer both, yet distinctly minimize the emphasis on "place." Some have embraced this minimization, extolling the virtues of open access and the absence of the bricks-and-mortar parameters of the traditional classroom. Yet, for many the idea that MOOCs will prompt radical transformations in the education sector has yet to be proven. The role MOOCS will play is a subject prompting much commentary. In a blog for *The Chronicle of Higher Education*, Clay Shirky, an associate professor of Journalism at NYU and a fellow at the Berkman Center for Internet and Society, asserts that "MOOCs are not the future of higher education—that future will be far more various and surprising than we can see now—but they do expand the horizon of the visible" (Shirky 2013, n.p.). Along the same vein, Valerie Strauss, an Education reporter and blogger for *The Washington Post* reprinted a piece from Larry Cuban's blog, which asserts that MOOCS will not be "as revolutionary as advocates hope" (Strauss 2013, n.p.).

Significantly, we shall soon be in a better position to evaluate the impact of this new delivery technology: the Bill and Melinda Gates Foundation funded 12 grants in 2012 to higher education institutions, including community colleges, to look closer at MOOCs with the explicit intention of improving the college success rates of low-income students. It makes sense for us to ask if MOOCs will serve to flatten community colleges and other institutions that serve low-income students at the expense of service-learning programs. Because they are not focused on learning or teaching, we do not perceive MOOCs as a great threat. Indeed, we are confident that service-learning is playing and will continue to play a more central and crucial role in teaching and learning at many of our community colleges.

George D. Kuh (2008) regards service-learning as one of ten high-impact activities that serve to "engage participants at levels that elevate their performance across multiple engagement and desired-outcomes measures such as persistence" (14). Like Kuh and many others, we believe that service-learning programs in community colleges help to improve the persistence rate, particularly for students in their first years of study. Since students at community colleges are most often attending schools in their communities, service-learning programs will deepen their connections to place, and thus play a role in promoting student success. We believe that community colleges must become more innovative in creating place-centered service-learning projects and pedagogies that promote deeper connections and, thus, more integrated learning experiences for students.

Service-Learning and Place at Two Community Colleges

A Campus in Western Massachusetts

Holyoke Community College (HCC) is located in Holyoke, Massachusetts, and nestled in the Connecticut River Valley. The city of Holyoke is historically notable for silk production and paper mills. Factory buildings line the canals connected to the Connecticut River, which runs along the city's border. Employment in these factories has diminished significantly and, not surprisingly, the community has suffered greatly. The website of The Care Center, a Holyoke not-for-profit, describes the city as having "alarming rates of poverty and under-education" (n.p.).

According to 2010 census data, Hispanics comprise 48.4 percent of the population in Holyoke, making up the majority of the population, surpassing the white (non-Hispanic) population of 46.8 percent for the first time since census data was collected. Additional segments of the population are 4.7 percent African American; 3.9 percent include persons of two or more races; and 3 percent are Asian or Native American (US Census 2010). Because enrollment at HCC does *not* reflect the community's constituents to the proportions detailed above, its service-learning program has great importance for town/gown relations and development. The credit student profile for fall 2013 at HCC shows enrollment at 6,740 full- and part-time students. The racial/ethnic composition of the college is predominately white (63 percent), with 22 percent Hispanic, 7 percent African American, 2 percent Asian, and 1 percent Native American. The overall minority student percentage, based on total known race/ethnicity is 34 percent (Holyoke Community College website).

Western Massachusetts can be very stratified by race in terms of geography, housing, and education. The majority of African American and Hispanic students attending HCC live in urban areas that have the largest minority populations in western Massachusetts: Springfield (over 60 percent African American and Hispanic) and Holyoke (over 54 percent African American and Hispanic). In Springfield and Holyoke, the primary and secondary school populations consist of only a small percentage of white students: 14.2 percent and 18 percent, respectively. (Massachusetts Department of Education 2011). In contrast, the majority of the white students attending HCC are more likely to live in suburban and rural areas of western Massachusetts, where the majority of the population is white: Chicopee (approximately 80 percent white); Westfield (over 88 percent white); West Springfield (over 82 percent white); Easthampton (over 91 percent white); and Agawam (over 92 percent white) (US Census Data 2010). In each of these towns, the primary and secondary school populations mirror the overall population in terms of race (Massachusetts Department of Education 2013). Thus, it is fair to conclude that the majority of white students attending HCC have lived and attended secondary school in majority white environments, while the majority of its Hispanic and African American students have lived and attended secondary school in predominantly African American and/or Hispanic environments. It is also fair to assume that HCC represents the most racially diverse environment the college's white students have encountered to date, and that HCC might encourage new feelings of underrepresentation in a school environment for the college's Hispanic and African American students.

Service-learning has existed at HCC for well over a decade, with local community partnerships providing service-learning opportunities for all HCC's students. Recent efforts include projects serving city youth, elders, and Spanish-speaking citizens, as well as projects addressing issues of food access and nutrition, teen pregnancy, literacy, health and fitness, and the environment. Service-learning projects at HCC are designed to meet the critical needs of underrepresented communities at the school and in the area. As such, they often involve partnerships with community-based organizations that are Hispanic led and/or also serve a predominately Hispanic clientele, many of whom, based on the demographics of the city, will also be low income. Given the racial composition of HCC, it is important to consider how these place and community-based projects will impact the students involved. Indeed, Lisa Mahon, an associate professor of English and the service-learning coordinator at HCC, advises that students might need help when thinking about issues related to race and class, and this prompting must happen before they engage in a service-learning experience (personal conversation with Paulette Dalpes, August 6, 2013).

Will a service-learning project on teen pregnancy, which primarily services Hispanic teens, reinforce any negative stereotypes and misconceptions that might be held by white students? How will the generally middle-class white students with limited experience across race and class effectively engage with Hispanic youth programs or with people in homeless shelters? What is the impact on low-income or Hispanic students who engage in these projects? Will they feel an increased sense of pride in supporting their community, or might their service-learning experiences create or reinforce negative perceptions of their own life or family experience and thus manifest or magnify feelings of marginalization?

At HCC, a thoughtful consideration of "place" in service-learning requires an intentional and strategic conceptualization and implementation of cultural competencies to assist students in cross-race and class interactions. The service-learning program at HCC provides opportunities and incentives for faculty. Mahon has developed a dynamic Faculty Fellows Program for faculty who either want to create new courses that incorporate service-learning activities or redesign existing courses with service-learning components. Up to three faculty members are given fellowships every semester that include either an extra stipend or a course reassignment. During the first semester of their fellowship, the faculty members work with Mahon, community partners, and among themselves to create a course and service-learning component from the ground up. During the second semester, they implement what they have planned, and in the final semester of their fellowships, they serve as mentors to a new class of faculty fellows. HCC also offers a one-credit course, called Service Learning Practicum, which can be added to any course with a service-learning component; as in the fellows program, faculty can receive credit to their course load for adding the practicum. The fellowships and practicum demonstrate that HCC's commitment to service-learning is serious and sustaining.

An example of how faculty engage place and build student skills to advance their cultural competencies can be found in an interdisciplinary HCC Learning Community titled, "Exploring Inequality: The Causes and Consequences of Hunger and Homelessness." The service-learning component of this course involves students organizing after-school activities with children at a local shelter for homeless families. Recognizing the different life experiences students bring to college, and to prepare them as they embark on service-learning projects, faculty work with students to investigate their personal biases, stereotypes, and negative internalized societal messages about self and identity while exploring issues of diversity. Prior to the service-learning component, students are provided time in class to explore their ideas about people who are or might be homeless. In the past, many students described common myths and stereotypes about homeless people: that they struggle with alcoholism and drug addiction and that they are unwilling to work. Following this initial assignment, students are asked to research statistics and factors that contribute to hunger and homelessness and then to revisit their initial thoughts and conceptions of who is homeless. These in-class assignments not only expand students' understanding of the vastness and complexity of the issues involved in someone becoming homeless, they also help students develop skills of critical thinking, self-reflection, and systemic conceptualization of a significant social issue. In turn, this learning prepares them to engage in a more informed and effective manner during the service-learning project and, no doubt, to achieve many of the Learning Community's learning objectives.

The service-learning experience at HCC has changed students' views and helped them think about their community in broader and more inclusive ways. In a text message to Linda Merians on March 12, 2014, Lisa Mahon described how students come to feel "a greater sense of agency and a stronger awareness of the needs of their community"; for example, one student whose Earth Science class studied the water quality of Tannery Brook, which runs through Holyoke, reported to Mahon that he now thinks "that's my brook."

A Campus in the Heart of New York City

Place also plays a central role at the Stella and Charles Guttman Community College, the newest community college of the City University of New York (CUNY). Initially called the New Community College, the Stella and Charles Guttman Community College welcomed its first students in the summer of 2012. Located at Bryant Park across the street from the New York Public Library in Midtown Manhattan, the college's place enlarges the definition of a community college. The students, who, for the most part, have lived and gone to school in one of New York City's five boroughs, often find the college's location unfamiliar, as it is not in a place or a "community" that they know. As a result, Guttman must somehow become their new place and community. To accomplish this, all first-year students are required to attend on a full-time basis, and all first-year students are organized into "houses" of approximately 75 students each and then placed into smaller cohorts (25 each) for their coursework.

The positive disruptions inspired by Guttman's neutral location and its internal structures have prompted the college to stress its relationship to the city and implement service-learning in several key ways. For example, all first-year students are enrolled in a two-semester foundational course called the City Seminar. This course addresses "big picture" issues important to "place" in an interdisciplinary manner: in the fall semester, students study sustainability; in the spring semester, students study immigration. In tandem, Guttman hosts two successive "Community Days," which engage students, faculty, and staff in service-learning, place-based community activities, and workshops led by community activists around the themes of sustainability and immigration. Along with a faculty member who was recruited because of her expertise in experiential education, the college's Office of Partnerships and Community Engagement works to develop these special days, as well as create, implement, and assess year-round service-learning and community service opportunities for students.

David Scobey (2013) states, "We need to help our students understand and claim the civic dimension of all the jobs they have, or may have, or aspire to, or might eventually fill over the course of their lives—teacher, electrician, coder, blogger, barrista, soldier" (13). Before students matriculate for their first fall term at Guttman, they participate in a mandatory Summer Bridge program where they begin to engage the city and to explore a range of possible careers. Building on this learning, Guttman's first-year curriculum includes a number of required courses that engage place and work. One such course, "Ethnography of Work," utilizes sociological and anthropological approaches to work to engage students in learning about future career paths and work in New York City. In addition to the Office of Partnerships and Community Engagement, the college has also hired career specialists, who work primarily with second-year students to engage them in the city and support their academic success.

The *learning* in service-learning becomes evident to Guttman students as reflected in their electronic portfolios, which often include multimedia artifacts of place (e.g., photos, prose, and video). Interestingly, this use of e-portfolio adds yet another layer to the idea of place at Guttman: students enter the platform through a home page titled "My Guttman," which symbolically claims a place for them in this shared virtual space. In this way, Guttman's adoption of e-portfolios is part of the college's larger effort to use place within service-learning and to enhance students' development of information literacy. In the age of the Internet, students often believe that "stuff is stuff," and they are particularly adept at accepting and referencing the "stuff" that fits their biases or those of authority figures. The role of Guttman's librarians is to help students confront primary sources as faculty design assignments and engage students with their places. For example, librarians help students use digitized nineteenth-century insurance maps detailing specific New York City neighborhoods to learn more about the places in which they perform their service-learning experiences and Community Days projects. Faculty then employ rubrics, which stress the learning that takes place in applied settings, especially in regard to service-learning experiences, to assess students' e-portfolios. Significantly, such an assessment is not an assessment of learning but rather an assessment for learning.

Conclusion

Every discipline can engage students by referencing place. Alfred Kazin's (1951) *Walker in the City* demonstrates the grip and effect of place on, in his case, a young boy in the Brownsville section of Brooklyn: "All my early life lies open to my eyes within five city blocks." Although Walker's work chronicles a far different time in New York City's history, his memoir's focus on how place fed his great ambition to read and to learn helps to make the content relatable to students. Similarly, in reminiscing about his years as a New York City teacher in *Teacher Man,* Frank McCourt (2005) describes the powerful lessons he learned partly by focusing his students' writing on place: "The kids are opening up in their writing and classroom discussions and I'm getting a tour of American family life from East Side townhouses to Chinatown tenements. It's a pageant of the settled and the new and everywhere there are dragons and demons" (243).

The academic landscape for place-based service-learning spans wide ground and crosses disciplines. While many might think that arts and humanities courses lend themselves more easily to service-learning components, science and social science courses can be also place-based. A real world place-based activity, like Guttman biology students' efforts to measure and graph the relationship between temperature and carbon dioxide content in Bryant Park, brings the curriculum to life. In the social sciences, students' analyses of local cases and neighborhoods can engage them in new and profound ways with their personal histories as well as acquaint them with potential careers they might develop as they pursue their programs of study. Focusing on place also has the potential to create a multiplier effect, providing students with team building and leadership skill sets and knowledge they can build on in the future.

With "community" in their name, it is imperative that community colleges own and extend the idea of place in their curricula. We believe civic engagement, as it is manifested in place-based service learning, is where we should center our attention.

Note

*The authors wish to thank Lisa Mahon for her assistance with this chapter.

References

Becoming a Steward of Place: An Operational Guide for Institutional Leaders. 2014. New York: American Association of State Colleges and Universities.

Caputo, Philip. 2013. "To See America, Be a Traveler, Not a Tourist." *New York Times*, July 11. http://travel.nytimes.com/2013/07/14/travel/a-conversation-between-philip-caputo-and-william-least-heat-moon.html?pagewanted=all&_r=0.

Fakhari, Reza, Brian Mitra and Paulette Dalpes. 2013 "Civic Learning for All students: An Institutional Priority." *Diversity and* Democracy 16 (4). Accessed August 3, 2014. http://www.aacu.org/diversitydemocracy/vol16no4/fakharI_mitra_dalpes.cfmHalttunen, Karen. 2006. "Groundwork: American Studies in Place: Presidential Address to the American Studies Association, November 4, 2005." *American Quarterly* 58 (1): 1–15. http://muse.jhu.edu/journals/aq/summary/v058/58.1halttunen.html.

Hiss, Tony. 1991. *The Experience of Place: A New Way of Looking at and Dealing with Our Radically Changing Cities and Countryside.* New York: Vintage Books.

Holyoke Community College. n.d. "Holyoke Community College Demographic Characteristics." Accessed March 7, 2014. http://www.hcc.edu/about-hcc/general-information/fast-facts.

———. n.d. "Holyoke Community College Service-Learning Program." Accessed July 17, 2013. http://www.hcc.edu/courses-and-programs/integrative-learning/service-learning-program/community-partners-and-projects.

Kazin, Alfred. 1951. *A Walker in the City.* Kindle Edition. Orlando: Harcourt, Inc.

Kuh, George. 2008. *High-Impact Educational Practices. What They Are, Who Has Access to Them, and Why They Matter.* Washington, DC: Association of American Colleges and Universities. http://www.clarion.edu/297592.pdf.

Mahon, Lisa. 2014. Personal conversation and e-mail message to Linda E. Merians. March 12.

Massachusetts Department of Elementary and Secondary Education. 2011. "2010–11 Enrollment by Race/Gender Report (School)." Last modified October 1, 2011. http://profiles.doe.mass.edu/state_report/enrollmentbyracegender.aspx?year=2011&mode=school&Continue=.

McCourt, Frank. 2005. *Teacher Man: A Memoir.* i-book edition. New York: Scribner, 2005.

Scobey, David. 2013. "Post-Traditional Undergraduates and the Copernican Moment: New Models of Engaged Learning for the New Majority Student." Speech presented at 2013 American Democracy Project and The Democracy Commitment National Meeting, Denver, CO, June 6–8.

Shirky, Clay. 2013. "MOOCs and Economic Reality." *The Chronicle of Higher Education*, July 8. http://chronicle.com/blogs/conversation/2013/07/08/moocs-and-economic-reality/.

Stepping Forward as Stewards of Place. 2002. New York: American Association of State Colleges and Universities. http://www.aascu.org/WorkArea/DownloadAsset.aspx?id=5458.

Strauss, Valerie. 2013. "Why MOOCS Won't Revolutionize Higher ED." *The Washington Post*, July 8. http://www.washingtonpost.com/blogs/answer-sheet/wp/2013/07/08/why-moocs-wont-revolutionize-higher-ed/.

The Care Center. 2014. "About—Impact." Accessed March 7, 2014. http://www.carecenterholyoke.org/about/impact.

Tull, Ashley, Linda Kuk, and Paulette Dalpes, eds. 2014. *Handbook for Student Affairs in Community Colleges.* Sterling, VA: Stylus.

United States Census Bureau. 2013. "State & County Quick Facts." June 27. Accessed August 29. http://quickfacts.census.gov/qfd/states/25/2500840.html.

———. 2013. "State & County Quick Facts." June 27. Accessed August 29. http://quickfacts.census.gov/qfd/states/25/2519370.html.

———. 2013. "State & County Quick Facts." June 27. Accessed August 29. http://quickfacts.census.gov/qfd/states/25/2530840.html.

———. 2013. "State & County Quick Facts." June 27. Accessed August 29. http://quickfacts.census.gov/qfd/states/25/2567000.html.

———. 2013. "State & County Quick Facts." June 27. Accessed August 29. http://quickfacts.census.gov/qfd/states/25/2576030.html.

———. 2013. "State & County Quick Facts." June 27. Accessed August 29. http://quickfacts.census.gov/qfd/states/25/2577890.html.

Young, Jeffrey. 2010. "Bill Gates Predicts Technology Will Make 'Place-Based' Colleges Less Important in 5 Years." *The Chronicle of Higher Education*, August 9. http://chronicle.com/blogs/wiredcampus/bill-gates-predicts-technology-will-make-place-based-colleges-less-important-in-5-years/26092.

CHAPTER 20

There Is a Reason Community Is in Our Name: Thoughts on How Service-Learning Expands Community in Community College

Robert Exley

What constitutes community? Is community a shared commitment to the common good or a physical place? Many think of community in terms of a safe space (psychologically and physically) where individuals can pursue their own goals and dreams; for others, community comes to life through the daily beliefs and actions of its members. Do values like caring, compassion, love, acceptance, sacrifice, encouragement, optimism, forgiveness, equality, and fairness contribute to the formation and sustaining of community? If so, do we have an obligation in higher education to promote comprehension of and commitment to these ideals within the educational journey of our students?

The college campus is a major component of the fabric of our overall community. In fact, by their very mission, America's community colleges intertwine with their surrounding communities in unique and compassionate ways. We in higher education simply must accept and embrace our interconnectedness with the greater community. Service-learning is a powerful means for joining our institutions and our students in this effort.

After nearly 20 years of involvement with service-learning and civic engagement, I am convinced that academically based service produces amazing and life-changing learning. Snead State Community College's recent experiences demonstrate how service and engagement enhance and improve the college experience for community college students, faculty, and staff. By responding to others in need during major crises, our college—a community in and of itself—connected to our core mission in ways that rarely happen within the traditional realm of lecture-based higher education.

The intent of this chapter is to provide thoughts and reflections regarding how my understanding of community has evolved and expanded through experience with service-learning and civic engagement. To do so, I use Palmer and Zajonc's (2010) conception of integrative education as a core framework upon which to base my observations. For, in their words, "A truly integrative education engages students in the systematic exploration of the relationship between their studies of the 'objective' world and the purpose, meaning, limits, and aspirations of their lives" (10).

Insights on Community, Higher Education, and Service-Learning Pedagogy

In *The Heart of Higher Education*, Palmer and Zajonc (2010) write separate chapters as well as coauthor the introduction and afterword. The entire work is not based on a tight definition of integrative education; instead, the focus is on understanding the concept of integrating one's education through multiple and connected experiences. Their introduction includes this quotation from Wendell Berry:

> The thing being made in a university is humanity...(W)hat universities...are mandated to make or to help to make is human beings in the fullest sense of those words—*not just trained workers or knowledgeable citizens but responsible heirs and members of human culture* (emphasis mine)...Underlying the idea of a university—the bringing together, the combining into one, of all the disciplines—is the idea that good work and good citizenship are the inevitable by products of making of a good—that is, a fully developed—human being. (1)

In Chapter 2: "When Philosophy Is Put into Practice," Palmer further identifies the pivotal issue of higher education when he says: "The real question is whether we want higher education to be about life" (36).

Service-learning is one powerful means for using integrative education to move the conversation about higher education beyond an esoteric discussion of mission and vision to one of truly making a difference through the *making of a good—that is a fully developed—human being*. It is messier than focusing solely on course content because life is unpredictable and messy too. In Chapter 2, Palmer identifies the challenge well:

> The kind of knowledge most valued in the academy is that which can be dealt with in a rational, linear, and controlled manner; words such as those define the comfort zone in academic culture. But when it comes to questions involving relational knowledge, bodily knowledge, intuitive knowledge, or emotional knowledge, more than a few academics draw a line they are loath to cross—sometimes because they feel unqualified to deal with knowledge of that sort, sometimes because they do not regard it as credible knowledge in the first place. (36)

Higher education leadership must step to the forefront and accept that it is just this type of wholeness in the educational experience—the going beyond the rational and linear with our students to facilitate knowledge in the nonlinear areas like relationships, intuition, and emotion—that is desperately needed today. Creating relationships with other members of our community through service-learning and civic engagement has shaped my vision for Snead State Community College and redefined my understanding of our local community to go beyond artificial boundaries like city limits, county and state lines, or service areas.

In Chapter 1: "Toward a Philosophy of Integrative Education," Palmer argues that community is more than a sociological phenomenon. For him, community is an ontological reality, an epistemological necessity, a pedagogical asset, and an ethical corrective. These four concepts aptly explain the power of service-learning. First, Palmer refers to ontology as "the nature of being and how we perceive it" (25). So with regard to ontology, what does make up the nature of one's experience with civic engagement and service? Is it the relationships formed during service or is it the acts of service? Reflective processes serve to answer this important question by emphasizing the connections between relationships and service acts.

Second, epistemology is our way of knowing. Civic engagement and service-learning move the predominant way of knowing from objectivism to one of accepting and honoring subjectivity in the learning experience. Third, pedagogy is the very art and science of teaching. Too often, we are guilty of teaching the way we do simply because that is the way we were taught. Integrative education requires that we craft new ways of teaching and learning that emphasize relationships on an equal footing with content knowledge, thus reinforcing active awareness of the ontological reality.

Finally, ethic is the way one lives his/her life. Successful experiences with service-learning and civic engagement definitely impact how one lives life. Service-learning shapes lifelong commitment to engagement that benefits us all. Palmer summarizes it like this, "Every epistemology, or way of knowing, as implemented in a pedagogy, or way of teaching and learning, tends to become an ethic, or way of living" (31). We simply cannot avoid the fact that when we accept the role of teacher/educator/leader we also take on some of the responsibility for shaping how our students live their lives.

Yet, to what community should students' service-learning experiences be directed? The Rev. Martin Luther King Jr. provided many poignant, truthful, and challenging words in his day, and among them are those found in his essay "On Being a Good Neighbor." When reflecting upon the question "Who is my neighbor?" Dr. King (1933) speaks eloquently to the critical importance of genuine caring and compassion for others. He also comments on the Samaritan's goodness versus universal selfishness when he states, "One of the great tragedies of man's long trek along the highway of history has been the limiting of neighborly concern to tribe, race, class, or nation" (557).

Community—tribe, race, class, or nation—is this not the same? All too often we fail to generate true community because we fail to include others. Dr. King identifies four categories where it is easy for us to have compassion because we identify only with members of our tribe, our race, our class, or our nation. Unfortunately, the more we focus on the subgroup the easier it becomes to exclude the larger whole.

Alexis De Touqueville (1993), the famous French political theorist, wrote compellingly about America based on his visit in 1831. He produced two volumes of his work *Democracy in America,* and his nearly two-centuries-old words ring true today: "If men are to remain civilized or to become so, the art of associating together must grow and improve in the same ratio in which the equality of conditions is increased"

(531). Sadly, today's community of mankind is marked by a lack of associations leading to a limiting of compassion, a lack of civility, and a preponderance of injustice. Service-learning builds associations and relationships within the academy and with the greater community and in some ways fosters the restoration of these missing associations (relationships).

Applying These Insights at Snead State Community College

Snead State Community College (SSCC) is a small, two-year college located in the northeastern corner of Alabama, in the rural town of Boaz and in a community referred to as Sand Mountain. Approximately 2,400 students attend the college—most from our surrounding community. Snead State can best be described as an example of the original junior college model. The college has residential housing, NJCAA athletics, extensive student organizations, and exceptional academic programs. The enrollment is predominately transfer students (nearly 81 percent) completing the first two years of their bachelor's degree. A majority of the students enroll directly from local high schools, with over 75 percent of the students being under the age of 25. Sixty-two percent of the students are female and only a combined seven percent are reported as African American, American Indian, or Hispanic.

The college has a long and rich history within the community; from its founding by the Methodist Church in 1898 as the first school in Boaz on through its years as a private seminary, its chartering as a junior college in 1935, and eventually its transitioning into a state institution in 1967. In fact, Snead State Community College's founders (1898) envisioned the college as always in service to its community and established a heritage recaptured in the fall of 2008 and again in the spring of 2010. Two natural disasters far from Boaz, Alabama, and the SSCC campus (Hurricane Gustav in New Orleans, Louisiana, and the earthquake in Port-au-Prince, Haiti) redefined community for the students, faculty, and staff of Snead State.

Hurricane Gustav Emergency Shelter Experience, Fall 2008

The crisis was real. Hurricane Gustav was bearing down on New Orleans and, even though the final impact was yet to be determined, the reaction to memories of Hurricane Katrina was immediate. Over two million people evacuated the greater New Orleans metro area, including thousands by bus transportation. Specific colleges of the Alabama Community College System, including Snead State Community College, were tasked with serving as emergency shelters for these evacuees. SSCC and the Sand Mountain community stepped to the forefront and provided shelter, food, and human caring for nearly 300 guests (evacuees) from New Orleans.

In just a matter of hours on Labor Day Sunday, the college gymnasium and student center were transformed into an emergency shelter. College maintenance and custodial workers set up three hundred cots. The City of Boaz mayor made available all key city services from Emergency Medical Services to Public Works to the Police Department. The Police Department moved its operational center to the campus by maintaining the mobile police command center in the parking lot next to the gym. The Fire Department and Emergency Services personnel worked with local hospitals and college nursing faculty members to equip and maintain a health clinic on-site in the gym. In addition, numerous adjoining municipalities and county services departments quickly joined the team effort.

When the approximately 300 evacuees arrived at around five o'clock Monday morning, they had spent nearly 22 hours in transit. Each evacuee was greeted by smiling volunteers and each received a freshly baked biscuit with ham, sausage, or bacon, a cold bottle of fresh orange juice or milk, and a warm welcome to Snead State. It was our desire to emphasize to them that they were our guests, that they were important to us, and that they were welcome in our community.

Over the next five days numerous challenges presented themselves to all involved. The evacuees included New Orleanians who were homeless, members of organized gangs, elderly and infirm, and/or young and energetic. They also included entire families with children, visiting business people caught up in the evacuation, and individuals with serious health issues (two evacuees required dialysis treatment and one was in the latter stages of lung cancer). We had episodes where frustration and anger boiled over into confrontations between guests requiring law enforcement intervention. In addition, we cared for guests with minor injuries from sprained ankles to skinned knees. We also experienced an overwhelming number of community organizations, churches, and individuals wanting to assist; it took a monumental effort by the Department of Human Services personnel to organize, screen, credential, and then assign these volunteers.

One of the most meaningful aspects of this experience is that we cancelled classes for the week and encouraged our faculty, staff, and students to assist in the effort. Our college students were engaged in numerous activities throughout the days, including organizing games and activities for children, accompanying our evacuees on trips to local grocery and drugstores, and playing cards or board games. Our student union building (SUB), with its pool tables, foosball tables, table tennis tables, couches, big-screen televisions, and comfortable chairs, became the hub of daytime activity. Numerous faculty and staff spent hours in the SUB visiting with our guests and providing much-needed human compassion. Our nursing faculty worked with our local EMT/Fire Department personnel to coordinate and make available community resources. At the conclusion of the week, my wife and I, as representatives of our college and community, boarded the departing buses to proclaim each evacuee an honorary alumnus of Snead State Community College and provide them with a parting college memento.

Sand Mountain, Snead State Community College, and our guests from New Orleans became one community for five days in September of 2008. Each of us experienced community in a very special way. Our desire to care for one another and to make a positive difference for others became our sole purpose. There was no "formal" service-learning during this time. In its place we lived a "real-world" learning experience through serving others and, as we did, the history and heritage of our institution came to life in a profoundly moving manner.

Port au-Prince Earthquake, Spring 2010

Since I had the honor of working at Miami Dade College for nearly ten years in the 90s, and because Miami Dade College has a significant number of Haitian immigrant students, the Haitian Earthquake of 2010 had special meaning to me. During my tenure at Miami Dade College I had the privilege of leading the establishment of the service-learning program. Thus, upon seeing the news of the earthquake, I thought of the many Haitian students, colleagues, and friends that I have in south Florida. I immediately contacted my colleagues at Miami Dade and asked what we at Snead State could do to be of assistance.

The next day our student leaders, the director of Campus Engagement, and I gathered in my office for a conference call with student leaders and colleagues from Miami Dade College. Eleven student leaders in Miami began to speak with eleven student leaders from Snead State about the devastating earthquake in Haiti. One student in Miami simply said, "I don't know why I even care about finishing school since 11 members of my family died in the earthquake." Another shared that his family had not been able to determine if his father and his uncle had survived. Immediately we were in tears with them and an undeniable bond formed.

As many students of Haitian descent depend on financial assistance from their families in Haiti, these Miami Dade students were in danger of leaving college because they had no way to pay for it. Snead State's student leaders decided to organize a fundraising campaign to raise money to help these students stay at Miami Dade. The effort was quickly named "Your Students = Our Students." Over the next few weeks, Snead State students raised over $8,000 to assist Miami Dade students impacted by the earthquake in Haiti.

Rather than mail a check, we decided to send all eleven student leaders, our chief academic officer, and our director of Nursing to Miami to personally deliver the check and to experience Miami Dade College and the South Florida community. A critical goal for this trip was to introduce Snead State students to a culture different from that which they know on Sand Mountain. Students participated in Miami Dade's well-established service-learning activities and experiences. One afternoon was spent working in an un-air-conditioned warehouse on the banks of the Miami River to sort, organize, and pack donated relief supplies headed for Haiti. Another experience involved time with mothers and their children at a shelter for abused women. Yet another involved traveling to the Florida Everglades to learn about its environment and the ongoing dangers to this unique habitat. As the Snead State and Miami Dade students worked side-by-side and documented and shared reflections via their journals, the community of "Your Students = Our Students" flourished. The week culminated in a formal presentation of the check to the president of Miami Dade's North Campus.

Shortly thereafter and in a similar spirit, eleven Miami Dade students, accompanied by staff and administrators, made a reciprocal journey to Snead State to learn about our culture and community. For five days the students from Miami experienced Northern Alabama and the culture of Sand Mountain. For many of them it was the first time they had traveled through mountains and hiked the trails of Little River Canyon. The students visited the Snead State campus, toured Cathedral Caverns and the Space and Rocket Center in Huntsville, attended City Council meetings, ate in local restaurants, and gathered at private homes. Students from both colleges spent one afternoon at the Albertville Recycling Center sorting plastics and paper items.

An ongoing dialogue regarding community and culture brought all participants to a much deeper understanding of both concepts, as well as a responsibility to care for one another. Students from these two colleges thousands of miles apart became one community and each gained much from this experience. All of the students acquired a deeper appreciation for different ways of living, different beliefs, and different nationalities. More importantly, each student learned more about life, about themselves, and about the importance of compassion. This compassion came full circle following the devastating tornados of April 27, 2011, which took the lives of hundreds in Alabama. Shortly after the storms, student leaders from Miami Dade contacted Snead State to say that they had raised nearly $5,000 for the Snead State Student Emergency assistance fund.

Lessons Learned

First, Snead State's students and faculty/staff learned that the definition and experience of community today is expansive (including individuals in another state or country). Service-learning and civic engagement, which are grounded in integrative education practices, have made it unacceptable to restrict the concept of community to a service area or a city limit or county line.

Second, we learned that the college, itself, can become a community service site and social service provider in the event of an emergency. Defining our service-learning and civic engagement efforts as actions and events off-campus with agencies in the local community is no longer sufficient. The campus can serve as the site of great service. Community is not what is "out there"; community is both of here and there.

Third, we learned that the most profound benefits of service-learning are often experienced at the level of awareness. Because of these two experiences, Snead State faculty and staff gained a different perspective on their work and Snead State students came to realize that the college experience is about far more than securing a degree to get a good job. Just as Palmer (Palmer and Zajonc 2010) postulates that ways of teaching and learning become our ethic for living, the impact of these events lives on at the college. For example, nursing faculty now require formal service-learning activities and experiences for the nursing students, and college employees are more aware of our heritage today. Likewise, service and civic engagement has become an expectation for our student organizations and our athletic teams. And, an increasing number of faculty members now utilize service-learning in various disciplines.

Fourth, we learned that service-learning is reciprocal and that its benefits are lifelong. Students at both Miami Dade and Snead State remain close friends today: Snead State students have traveled to the graduation of Miami Dade students and Miami Dade students have returned to Sand Mountain to visit. In addition, faculty members from our two institutions continue to share ideas and successes.

Fifth, we learned that service-learning is tied to our original institutional mission(s). Snead State Community College was founded to serve others, yet the college had become a bit estranged from its surrounding communities. Since instituting service-learning, this has changed significantly. Now it is not simply marketing when we say, "There is a reason for community being in our name."

Sixth, we learned how comprehensive service-learning projects/programs often draw on the community even as they serve the community. When I think of the scope of what we faced when responding to these two disasters, I remain amazed at how the community of Sand Mountain rallied to assist us. For instance, ten types of organizations or entities each played a very significant role in our operation of the hurricane shelter. The list includes the City of Boaz—Police, Fire, EMS and transportation, Marshall County Sheriff's Department, Marshall County Emergency Management, Marshall County Emergency Medical Services, Marshall Medical Center (south and north), Department of Human Resources, Department of Public Health, Community Emergency Response Team, numerous civic organizations and churches, the American Red Cross, and the Snead State Community College cafeteria. In addition, hundreds of local citizens volunteered in a variety of roles.

Conclusion

Returning to the original stated purpose of this chapter—reflecting on how my concept of community has evolved over the past several years within the context of service-learning and civic engagement—I am again struck by how gaining an understanding of integrative education explains the importance of engaging in service-learning.

For me, the ontological reality of community has moved from that of things and places to relationships and relational events. The Snead State community now includes relationships with people from New Orleans to Miami to Haiti and beyond. The epistemological necessity of community now requires that I immerse my whole being. I accept that my way of knowing must include subjective experience.

Likewise, I have no doubt that these two events significantly enhanced how we at Snead State now shape the teaching and learning experience. In many ways, they have reminded each of us that we do indeed create an ethic of living through how we perceive our work, how we know our work, and how we design our work in higher education. If community is "...the red thread...that runs through every level of integrative education" then I believe service-learning is the needle that pulls the thread (Palmer and Zajonc 2010, 43).

References

De Tocqueville, Alex. 1993. "Of the Use Which the Americans Make of Public Associations in Civil Life." In *Education for Democracy*, edited by Benjamin R. Barber and Richard M. Battistoni. Dubuque: Kendall/Hunt Publishing Company.

King, Jr., Martin Luther. 1993. "On Being a Good Neighbor." In *Education for Democracy*, edited by Benjamin R. Barber and Richard M. Battistoni. Dubuque: Kendall/Hunt Publishing Company.

Palmer, Parker, and Arthur Zajonc. 2010. *The Heart of Higher Education: A Call to Renewal. Introduction*. San Francisco, CA: Jossey-Bass, 2010.

CHAPTER 21

Expanding Faculty Participation and Research in Academic Service-Learning at a Community College

Diane B. Call

Queensborough Community College, the City university of New York, formally began implementing academic service learning in 2006–07 with three faculty, forty-two students, and six partner agencies. By 2012–13, 77 faculty with 38 community partners involved almost 1600 students in the high-impact practice of what is now formally designed and institutionalized as Academic Service Learning (ASL). The evolution of ASL and its expansion at our college has advanced through the work of faculty, staff, students, and our community and has been driven by research and assessment of ASL's impact on student learning and retention.

Our college has an established culture that values collaboration across divisions, interdisciplinary partnerships, and support for student-centered teaching and learning. In 2009, Queensborough launched the Freshman Academies, creating cohorts of first-time, full-time students arranged according to discipline clusters and intended to provide a sense of identity, community, and intellectual engagement in support of focused academic and career goals. The Freshman Academies provided early and ongoing outreach and academic advisement by "freshman coordinators" who worked with students throughout their first semester. There was no change in our curricula; however, our Freshman Academy model included the goal of engaging first-time, full time-students in two high-impact practices through courses in their degree program within their first year.

Initially, QCC faculty and staff selected five high-impact practices, modeled on those identified by George Kuh (2008) and promoted by the Association of American Colleges and Universities (AACU), and introduced them as pedagogical strategies. These faculty who, as individuals, explored high-impact practices, were brought together through several small grants from the university's central Office of Academic Affairs in support of a Coordinated Undergraduate Experience (CUE) aimed at improvements in student retention and academic performance. The small but positive outcomes reported by university and campus institutional research studies, as well as data from in-house satisfaction surveys of instructors using high-impact practices and the students experiencing, them prompted our Office of Academic Affairs to offer opportunities for peer-led faculty development and research to expand the cadre of faculty involved with high-impact practices, including ASL. The Office of Academic Affairs recruited faculty to lead this effort and supported their work to develop pedagogical frameworks and ongoing faculty development activities for other colleagues who volunteered to explore and apply high-impact practices in their courses on a voluntary basis.

Together, faculty and administrators leveraged the partnerships between academic affairs, student affairs (especially advisement), and our faculty to explore the concept of ASL, provide development opportunities for faculty to gain the confidence to incorporate ASL into their courses, fund its research and assessment, disseminate the outcomes to internal and external audiences, and expand the recruitment of faculty to adopt this pedagogical strategy in a variety of academic courses.

ASL caught the imagination of an increasing number of faculty. Beyond the common association with "volunteerism," ASL promoted the engagement of students in the learning process through an alignment of academic course objectives and their application in organized service activities. Given our diverse student body, our mission as a community college, and the existing and potential relationships with the communities of New York City, ASL was unique in its integration of service and academic learning and its use of continuous reflection to facilitate the development of knowledge, skills, and cognitive capacities necessary for students to deal effectively with the complex social issues that challenge New York City residents.

This integration of "mind" (theories), "heart" (values), and "hands" (contextual application) offered by ASL represented the ideal construct to achieve gains in student learning, by framing information as *pedagogical content knowledge*, as encouraged by Lee Shulman (2004), president emeritus of the Carnegie Foundation for the Advancement of Teaching. We began with our Strategic Plan, which launched our Freshman Academies and formalized our commitment to increase student retention and graduation through integrated academic and student support services, in and outside of the classroom. The adoption and assessment of ASL by several faculty early in our implementation of the academies allowed us to incorporate the pedagogy in our Strategic Plan objectives; its impact on student learning was reported annually by our campus Institutional Research Office, and it was presented in formal documents to the university, under performance management programs, as well as to grant sponsors such as AACU.

In addition to the satisfaction reported by individuals associated with an ASL experience, it was the data demonstrating improved outcomes on student learning and performance that persuaded more faculty, students, and community organizations to become supporters and participants. Faculty involvement in ASL, and, in particular, research activities related to its use and effectiveness as community college teaching pedagogy, was further encouraged through institutional support and recognition of those faculty involved in college publications, and at college-wide convocations, university events, and professional conferences.

Queensborough's formal Assessment Protocol, established in 2009 to evaluate the impact of the Freshman Academies, offered data to suggest that student participation in high-impact practices, especially ASL, had a positive effect on student course completion, grades, and progress toward degree. These data were encouraging. Our challenge was to expand and institutionalize the use and evaluation of ASL through a deliberate and organized approach that would serve our urban, commuter community college, with almost 16,000 students, 400 full-time faculty, and 500 adjunct faculty. The diversity of our student body, with equal percentages of Hispanic, Asian, African American, and Caucasian students from over 100 countries of origin, along with the extraordinary resources available in our New York City location, offered great potential for faculty interested in the research and implementation of innovative approaches to teaching and student learning. The diversity of our students was also reflected in learning styles. And data from our Academy Assessment Protocol supported anecdotal reports from instructors that ASL promoted student engagement regardless of their proficiency in the English language. Data on student retention and academic progress reflected a positive benefit for participants in ASL, especially for English language learners, as measured by course completion and pass rates.

In the last several years, beyond institutional data provided by the director of our Academy Assessment Protocol, it has been the research of faculty that continues to validate the effectiveness of ASL and encourage further participation and inquiry by their colleagues. Stimulating that research requires an intentional and directed effort to recognize pedagogical research as equal to that in academic disciplines. The effort to accomplish this goal paralleled the plan to implement any academic innovation. For the last 14 years, our institution has encouraged and supported faculty research in pedagogy. Although pedagogical research in community college teaching is not widely conducted by practitioner faculty, we were able to build on Queensborough's long-standing tradition of academic excellence, faculty participation in shared governance, and interdepartmental collaboration. These shared values of our collegium supported an openness to pedagogical research, recognition of its potential to improve student learning outcomes, and opportunities for and validation of faculty research and scholarship in the art and science of teaching. This environment was supported through a presidential philosophy introduced by my predecessor Eduardo J. Marti and continued under my presidency, which gave preeminence to pedagogical research and innovative teaching in the reappointment and promotion processes and provided significant financial support for faculty development and research activities in pedagogy. The resultant activity among the faculty capitalized on cross-disciplinary partnerships to advance research in the pedagogy of teaching at the community college, and in particular, the theories and practice of high-impact activities.

The degree of our success with ASL and growing interest in research on its effectiveness as a pedagogical strategy can be attributed to several factors that created the awareness of ASL on our campus: identification and recognition of faculty as early adopters and peer leaders of this strategy; the provision of resources for faculty, staff, student, and community engagement in ASL; and the expectation for and acknowledgment of formal assessment to encourage faculty research.

As president, I share with my immediate predecessor a strong belief in peer-led faculty experimentation and assessment of community college teaching pedagogies. As practice, there is a consistent articulation and demonstration of support for innovation and research in pedagogy by the president and senior leadership, including department chairpersons, evidenced in formal funding for faculty engagement in pedagogical initiatives and dissemination of their research, acknowledgment of their leadership and service at college convocations, in college publications and event programs, our website, and, most significantly, through recognition of faculty contributions to student-centered learning in the reappointment, tenure, and promotion process.

Institutionalization of faculty research on ASL is supported through our yearlong Strategic Planning process, led by our College Advisory Planning Committee (CAPC), comprising governance leaders, senior administrators, and students. The planning process includes a series of focus groups and open hearings to disseminate outcomes achieved the previous year as reflected in our Completion Report, as well as discussions led by our office for Strategic Planning, Assessment and Institutional Effectiveness, among the campus constituencies to establish our priorities for the plan under development. Since 2000, the Strategic Plan has formally committed the institution to provide faculty development opportunities, to engage in student learning outcomes assessment, and, since 2006, expand the exploration and assessment of high-impact practices, including ASL. Underscoring our commitment, Queensborough's annual Strategic Plan informs the resource allocation process that finances ASL and other initiatives included in the Strategic Plan through an all-funds budget, incorporating tax levy dollars, enterprise revenue, philanthropic contributions, and grants from the university central office, regional and national educational organizations such as AACU, federal and state educational agencies, as well as corporate and nonprofit foundations. The extent of our commitment to ASL and research on this pedagogical strategy is demonstrated in "line item funding" in our annual budget, Institutional Research support of faculty research projects on ASL, faculty incentives (time and/or stipends for participation in ASL, assistance from Sponsored Program staff to identify and secure external grant funding to expand ASL and research), and organized multimedia publicity through our Communications and Marketing Department.

To support institutional priority to stimulate faculty inquiry and research on community college teaching pedagogy, a significant investment was made to appoint over 100 new full-time faculty over the last six years, many of whom demonstrated interest in and experience with high-impact practices, and/or pedagogical research. The intent was to create an environment for faculty development opportunities led by *faculty for faculty* and to support the integration of new faculty into our college. An extended new faculty orientation program was designed that included formal and informal activities to build a cohort of peers, establish connections to the institution as well as their home departments, provide peer mentors who are veteran faculty, and introduce new faculty to pedagogical strategies for effective student learning, including ASL.

An advisory committee of department chairpersons, working with the president, created a formal structure to support and sustain faculty development and engagement in innovative pedagogical activities and research. A Center for Excellence in Teaching and Learning (CETL) was established to provide faculty-led development activities. CETL has grown in staff and funding to serve new and veteran faculty. Peer-led faculty teams have introduced and trained faculty in high-impact practices, as well as supported faculty who want to design and implement pedagogical research projects, including those examining ASL. Faculty participation in these research efforts is supported through college-funded pedagogical research challenge grants, competitively awarded each year to individuals or teams of faculty. Other incentives to encourage research include ongoing institutional assessment of student learning outcomes for continuous improvement of pedagogy, financial support for faculty (full time and adjunct) to present pedagogical research findings at regional, national, and international conferences, as well as to present, along with their students, their research findings along with their students, to our foundation Fund Board. With the growth of faculty interest in ASL and its impact, an Office for ASL, directed by our faculty and instructional support staff, was established several years ago. Today, Queensborough serves as a mentor institution in the AACU Roadmap Program.

Partnerships have contributed to the expansion of ASL and to research on this instructional strategy. A pilot program with our university's Graduate Center brought doctoral students studying academic disciplines to Queensborough as graduate teaching fellows. The experience of teaching at a community college, along with structured conversations with our faculty on pedagogy, enriched their discipline studies through exposure to strategies for effective instruction and student learning. Our partnership with Teachers College's Center for Community College Research focused on remediation, with our faculty participating in studies of various instructional strategies for active student learning, including ASL. And, our work with organizations such as New York State's Campus Compact and the AACU showcased our faculty and our institution as practitioners of ASL and investigators of its impact. That has resulted in a number of requests from sister institutions in the country to visit our college to meet with faculty and staff, or to host our representatives in preparation for their launch of ASL and our Queensborough Academies model.

While elements of ASL have been widely and consistently defined, institutionalization of this pedagogical strategy and research on its impact can take many paths, based upon educational philosophy, administrative leadership, style of governance, and resources. Over the last several years, ASL and the study of its outcomes have taken root at Queensborough Community College. Despite challenges ranging from faculty workload, funding pressures, contractual restrictions on faculty compensation, and the identification of faculty to lead pedagogical initiatives, ASL has grown in practice and its impact has increased on our students' academic performance and progress toward degree. A steady commitment by the institution's administration and faculty leadership to support and sustain the adoption of and research on ASL in small and significant ways created a path for ASL's growth on our campus. From the appointment of new faculty, possessing curiosity and a passion for innovation, to veteran faculty who share their philosophy of student-centered teaching for active learning, to institutionalized funding for faculty development, pedagogical research, and dissemination of outcomes, to the alignment of participation in ASL and other high-impact activities with formal recognition of faculty and career advancement, it is the consistent and widely held value and support of ASL by faculty, students, administrators, and community partners, based on assessment, that will encourage continued research and expanded application across disciplines and campuses.

References

Kuh, George D. 2008. *High Impact Practices: What Are They, Who Has Access to Them, and Why They Matter?* Washington, DC: AACU.

Shulman, Lee S. 2004. *The Wisdom of Practice: Essays on Teaching, Learning, and Learning to Teach.* San Francisco, CA: Jossey-Bass.

CHAPTER 22

Sustaining Momentum

Maria Hesse

Research offers compelling rationale and evidence for supporting service-learning in community colleges, but starting a service-learning program and sustaining one over the years is easier said than done. A number of premier community college service-learning programs, such as those at Brevard Community College (now Eastern Florida State College), Miami Dade College, and Middlesex Community College, have prospered for more than 20 years. Why is it that some programs take hold and flourish, while others fade away? What can be done to maintain positive momentum in long-standing service-learning programs?

My 25 years of experience in community colleges, and in particular my years as a faculty member, administrator, and college president at Chandler-Gilbert Community College (CGCC), are the source for the practical advice I offer here for helping a program survive and thrive. Although my comments are directed primarily at college faculty, I hope they will also be useful for a broader audience of administrators, researchers, graduate students, and other readers.

More than 20 years ago, in 1992, the service-learning program began at CGCC. It started with one teacher in one class section with 22 students and it has expanded over time to involve dozens of teachers and student services staff, hundreds of class sections, and thousands of students each year in both engaged learning and meaningful service to the community. At that time, CGCC was a relatively young college with a culture that encouraged innovation, a supportive administration, a heavy emphasis on faculty development for improved teaching and learning, and faculty members who had the conviction to take action and improve the learning environment for their students. Those conditions may or may not be in place at a college, but that does not mean that a service-learning program cannot be successfully implemented or improved.

Create True Partnerships with Community-Based Organizations

Faculty should start small and build from there. At CGCC we started our service-learning program with a handful of community organizations, such as a local youth support organization, a transitional housing program for homeless families, and a domestic violence shelter, with which the college already had connections. Twenty years later there was an active database of more than 200 organizations with which faculty and students had worked.

Community partners are often excited to have "volunteers" help their organization and their clients. It may take some discussion to have volunteer coordinators understand the nature of service-learning, and some organizations may require more than the usual amount of explanation. For example, we found that many local health care organizations required mandatory training before anyone could become a volunteer. While we applauded the notion of providing training and support for volunteers, it was not practical in a community college setting to insist that students attend 20 or more hours of training prior to engaging in a four-to-five hour or even 20–30 hour service-learning assignment. Faculty should not be afraid to suggest alternatives or pose possibilities. Could a lesser-trained helper assist a more extensively trained volunteer? In our case, it was determined that service-learning students could assist trained volunteers and staff, and as a result, our students, the trained volunteers and staff, the clients being served, and the health care organization benefitted.

A college can arrange orientations for community organizations to gain a better understanding of service-learning. Volunteer coordinators appreciate the opportunity to explore ideas with one another for how best to utilize students, and it provides a chance for the college to discuss appropriate student placements given the nature of specific service-learning assignments. During these community organization meetings, college faculty and staff might also discuss how to track student involvement, how periodic reporting and communication between the college and the community organization will work, how to reduce risks, and what to do if problems arise.

Allowing an organization's employees to hear or read student reflections is another wonderful way to provide benefit to community-based organizations. If faculty can find a way to recognize the contributions they are making to the college and raise their visibility in the community, nonprofit organizations are generally very grateful.

Serve with Your Students

Faculty should serve side by side with their students. They should read, write, reflect, and share with them. Faculty should not ask their students to do anything that they themselves are not willing to do. Serving together provides an occasion for faculty to connect with their students in a different way, and it often facilitates opportunities for faculty to learn more about students' hopes and dreams, curriculum, and college life. Through service-learning, faculty will get to know students as people, and having shared service experiences will make it easier for them to lead and participate in reflection sessions. As a result, faculty will understand their students better, realize what works and does not work in an assignment, and will grow in their knowledge of the community.

Structure Reflection Activities

Service-learning is not about mandatory service; it is about mandatory learning. One of the keys to learning is for students to be required to engage in reflective activities that ask them to think about the problems that face their communities, the nation, and the world. Most students want an opportunity to make a positive difference in the world, and to connect what they are learning to their lives.

Although reflection can take many forms, at CGCC we asked students to reflect in writing as a means of clarifying what they were thinking and what they had learned. Embedding time in each service-learning activity to think quietly afterward and begin writing, then to hear what others have learned, is critically important. Structured reflection allows students to ponder important questions such as whether one's perceptions changed as a result of participation, what was learned about a segment of the community, what the root causes are for a condition or situation, what can be done to improve conditions or address a community issue, and what was given and what was gained.

Invite Others into Your Classroom

When students are ready to read their reflections out loud to one another, faculty should consider whether it might be appropriate to invite into the classroom colleagues, administrators, or representatives from the community-based organizations where students served. Sometimes the work of a community college faculty member can be lonely and isolating; these efforts can help break down the walls of the classroom and create a celebration of learning.

Students will rise to the occasion when asked to prepare written reflections that demonstrate what they have learned to a real audience. Of course, faculty will want to make certain that their assignments have been constructed in a way that clearly connects course objectives to the service that was undertaken and that students have had a chance to think deeply about those connections and reflect on what they have learned as a result.

Students benefit from hearing the perspectives and learning "take-aways" of others. Representatives from community agencies often appreciate seeing how they helped contribute to important learning for students. Administrators are often inspired by what they hear from the students and they may become more committed to providing support. And it is personally and professionally very fulfilling for faculty to hear a chorus of student learning and be able to share it with others.

Compile Student Reflections

Written reflections can serve as good models for students to understand what they are supposed to be doing and learning, and to understand the expectations for assignment(s). Faculty should share appropriate writing with community partners, who are thrilled when student writing brings attention to their organization and community issues that need to be addressed. The writings can be used to help other faculty members understand how the service can connect to course curriculum, which may help inspire their own creativity. Administrators can see the benefits of providing a practical and relevant education for students and typically enjoy seeing the connections deepen between the college and the community.

At CGCC, many faculty asked their students to keep portfolios that contained a select subset of reflections and other writing. When faculty aggregate these materials and allow students to later reflect on the collection, students are able to see what they have learned and how they have grown over time. We also compiled select student reflections periodically into books or booklets. Most students are flattered when asked to contribute a piece toward such a book and many will provide permission to publish their writing when they believe it can be used to help other students or serve their community.

Find Others Who Can Help You

Not every college has support systems in place to help faculty incorporate service-learning into the curriculum, but that does not mean that faculty cannot be successful. Faculty must be resourceful. For example, when researching appropriate community placements, faculty might seek help from their community's coordinating organization for nonprofit organizations or a volunteers website.

There are multiple national resources that can also be helpful to faculty, including Campus Compact, the American Association of Community Colleges online service-learning resources, the Community College National Center for Community Engagement, and the Corporation for National and Community Service. There are listservs, websites, and books, all of which can help faculty better understand the rationale for service-learning, think about how to connect service to curriculum to improve student learning outcomes, and learn more about how to contribute to the community in which they live or work.

Faculty should also find colleagues with whom they can think through their ideas. If there are no faculty members at the college who are interested in these discussions, faculty should seek out colleagues at neighboring community colleges who might be interested. Faculty might consider checking with nonfaculty members as well. Individuals in student services departments may be glad to help.

At CGCC, we were fortunate to have colleagues in the student affairs unit who were steeped in student development philosophy. They were willing to think differently about the way in which student affairs professionals could partner with instructional faculty to provide expertise in planning events and activities, risk management, and leveraging student leadership to support the service-learning program. The Office of Student Life and Leadership provided coordination and support for the faculty such as finding appropriate community organizations that connected to faculty assignments, mitigating liability concerns and managing risk forms, scheduling bus transportation, helping to supervise students spread across different community sites, coordinating communications and orientations with community-based organizations, and more. Over time as the numbers of faculty involved in service-learning grew, the Office of Student Life and Leadership recruited, trained, placed, and supervised a cadre of student leaders who became service-learning assistants to support faculty members and their students.

It takes considerable time and effort to get a service-learning program running well. Faculty must be patient, build upon their successes, monitor and adjust, and find others who can help.

Stick with It

Whether trying to get a service-learning program started or reenergize an existing program, faculty must start with the people who show interest and enthusiasm, and try to ignore the nay-sayers. There will always be a faculty member who complains about not having enough time or not receiving a large enough salary to undertake time-consuming service-learning activities. There will always be a student who complains about not having the time or the inclination to participate. There will always be an administrator who is worried about liability issues or concerned about how faculty and students represent the college out in the community.

But just as often as there are naysayers, there are colleagues who are willing to support and work with faculty, there are administrators who appreciate the extra effort faculty put into making their classes meaningful and engaging, and there are students who appreciate having a relevant and interesting education that pertains to their lives and that of their family.

Good teaching takes considerable preparation; including service-learning components will require even more preparation. There will likely be some challenges along the way, but there are rarely insurmountable issues or "show stoppers" for committed faculty and staff. The key is having a passion for providing the best learning for students, being able to articulate what is being done and why, and being resourceful enough to get past the snags along the way.

Make It Mandatory and Meaningful

If the service-learning is well integrated into curriculum, there is no reason not to make it mandatory. At CGCC, making service-learning mandatory in core general education classes ensured that nearly every graduate had one or more service-learning experiences. Students would often refer to their service-learning experience as among the most significant moments of their academic careers.

Too often service-learning assignments are considered inconvenient for nontraditional students to complete because of their work schedules or other family obligations, so faculty may be inclined to make those assignments optional—but learning is not always convenient and easy. Adult students who have experienced some of life's challenges are often far more attuned to community issues and value the opportunity for a practical education that connects their learning to their lives. And students who have children are often very motivated to improve conditions in their community.

A key tenet of American life is that every citizen should take an active interest not just in their job or career, but in understanding issues in one's community, voting, and contributing to community life. One purpose of higher education in the United States is to help our students learn about life in a democracy and to become civically engaged. So why would we think that those assignments that are most likely to help that happen should be optional? There are numerous options for constructing service-learning assignments in a way that accommodates the population of students at a community college, while providing robust learning experiences.

Build Campus Community

Faculty should consider holding periodic gatherings where they can share what worked and what needs improvement in their service-learning assignments. Hearing about one another's successes and challenges helps put things into perspective for busy faculty, and helps build camaraderie. Faculty should consider bringing a student reflection or two to these gatherings to share with colleagues, and to write their own reflection about what they have learned about their students, about their community, and about themselves as educators. If there are staff who are central to supporting a service-learning program, they deserve to be invited too and to have their contributions acknowledged.

These are the moments when faculty and staff have an opportunity to reflect on their students and communities, to share best practices with one another, to celebrate one another's successes, to move ideas from concepts to action plans, to learn about or re-visit various resources, to cultivate friendships with colleagues, and to find renewal and inspiration to continue their important work. All of these efforts will help build a campus community of professional colleagues who respect one another and who are becoming increasingly knowledgeable about the communities being served by the college.

Allow the Program to Evolve over Time

As service-learning becomes a part of a college's culture, more and more faculty and staff will want to create experiences for their students. There will be additional areas of the curriculum involved and that may create the need for connection with a broader spectrum of community organizations and different models for serving and learning.

At CGCC, the service-learning program began in English but was quickly embraced by faculty in biology, teacher education, communication, and social sciences. Originally, there were two primary ways for a faculty member to involve students in service-learning. One option was to build a one-time four-to-five-hour service requirement into a course. For example, a biology course with a unit on developmental disabilities had students serve at an Alzheimer's unit at a local senior center or help at a Special Olympics event. Another option was to involve students for a greater length of time over a semester-long course. For example, the English curriculum required second-semester students to select a social issue related to their prospective career and then spend a more substantial number of hours serving during repeated visits to a nonprofit organization. That course required students to serve for 20 or more hours at an organization, while researching and writing about their careers and associated social issues.

Over time, the models of service-learning evolved. One teacher wanted to take her entire class to one organization each semester, connecting the service to a course theme that changed from time to time. Another wanted to work with one organization over a series of years. Another faculty member wanted to connect service-learning to the college's sustainability efforts. There was steady movement toward a more concerted focus on civic engagement, voting, and public policy issues. The service-learning program evolved to provide numerous options to fit various curricular needs, while still creating positive community impact.

Maintain Momentum

Sustaining a service-learning program over time, as programs tend to go through highs and lows, is difficult but it can be done, and I can vouch for the fact that it is professionally and personally very fulfilling.

Faculty and staff should visit another college or two to see how their program operates and attend national meetings to hear about others' work in this area. Faculty should also read books and articles about service-learning in community colleges. These exposures will provide ideas and inspiration. Faculty might also consider applying for a grant or an award for their service-learning work or program. When external organizations or state agencies acknowledge these efforts, it can sometimes cause internal people to sit up and take notice.

Faculty should try to get involved in research about service-learning. A college's institutional research office may be willing to offer support in constructing this research, or faculty might connect with colleagues from a research university to participate in broader studies. Likewise, faculty should present regularly at professional development opportunities, conferences, and professional organization meetings. The process of presenting about service-learning will encourage faculty to think about what they are doing and why, and to reflect on progress and improvements to be made.

Producing a videotape that provided a quick synopsis of the rationale for service-learning, with students explaining to other students what it meant to them, was helpful at CGCC. We made our first videotape, which in present day would be a YouTube video, to provide a short explanation to students about what we were asking them to do and why. The video included a statement from the college president, multiple faculty speaking enthusiastically about their assignments, diverse students discussing what they learned and what the experience meant to them, and representatives from community organizations explaining how the students addressed a community need. Although producing it was more time-consuming than anticipated, its use in classrooms as part of orientation for students, in faculty professional development sessions, in orientations about service-learning with community-based organizations, and in other venues was invaluable and allowed the perspectives of many different people to be heard.

Institutions should consider selecting a student commencement speaker who can articulate why service-learning was important to their educational experience. I was constantly amazed at students' insights and their passion for making a difference in the world. Having students explain the concept, and their learning as a result, in front of current students, alumni, faculty, staff, parents, and community leaders, can be a powerful way to advance understanding of service-learning.

A Word to Administrators

Most of my advice has been directed to faculty who use service-learning in their classes and to staff who coordinate service-learning programs, but college administrators have a special role to play in the success of service-learning programs. College leadership ought to be constantly asking the college community to reflect on the purpose of a higher education and the characteristics of an educated person. A natural next step in that discussion is to focus on how college contributes to the development of informed, engaged citizens. This is particularly germane in community colleges whose mission is to serve their communities.

Faculty and staff need to hear the college administration articulate a definition and rationale for service-learning and community engagement, and to identify and clear roadblocks. The community connections and linkages that a college administrator is apt to have can be tremendously helpful in starting or enhancing a service-learning program.

I'll share one specific example of what can happen over time. In 1989, the director of the local youth support organization connected with an administrator at CGCC. About a dozen employees and a handful of student leaders volunteered over several years at activities and events that supported the at-risk youth and families served by this organization. When the college's service-learning program began, several courses became intimately involved in service-learning experiences with the organization. Eventually college employees served on this nonprofit's board of directors. The organization posted position openings at the college and in time a number of their staff were alumni of the college. It was a mutually beneficial relationship on many levels. Our college undertook a campaign to involve other nearby community colleges with their local branch of this youth organization. Now ten local branches receive direct support from multiple community colleges, including service-learning and internship placements that support their functioning, scholarship programs for youth participants, and opportunities for young members to learn about the value of pursuing higher education.

Administrators can use their influence and their professional and community connections to advance service-learning programs in ways that complement and enhance the work of their faculty.

Looking to the Future

Over the last two decades, in the service-learning movement within community colleges, we have grown in our understanding of the problems our communities face, how students can apply their considerable energy and talents in the community, how we structure relevant and meaningful learning experiences, and how the community can be involved in the education of our students. We have worked to develop an ethic of service in both students and employees, while encouraging them to examine their capacity for community leadership.

Students enjoy service-learning because it helps them learn about themselves, their classmates, the course content, and their communities. Faculty, staff, and administrators find that service-learning helps them develop engaged citizens, learn about the communities the college serves, become knowledgeable about populations that need support, and connect with other organizations and resources within the community. Few programs are so intimately connected to the very nature and mission of community colleges. While there are challenges to developing, improving, and sustaining service-learning programs, the rewards are bountiful.

Contributors

Francisco Acoba has an MA in English with a specialization in literary studies from the University of Hawai'i at Mānoa. He teaches composition, professional writing, American literature, and contemporary fiction. His current research deals with the discourse of sustainability in business and technical writing. He organizes the service-learning learning outcomes assessment at Kapi'olani Community College, where he is an assistant professor.

Drew Allen is the director of Research and Evaluation for the Office of the Senior University Dean for Academic Affairs at the City University of New York (CUNY). He oversees the development and implementation of a comprehensive research and evaluation strategy for a variety of educational initiatives, with the aim of providing program leadership with data essential to program development and improvement. Since joining CUNY in 2008, he has helped shaped the evaluation agenda for the university's college readiness programs in New York City public schools by leading a variety of research and data management projects. He holds an MA in Quantitative Methods in the Social Sciences from Columbia University and is a PhD candidate in Higher and Postsecondary Education at New York University.

Mary Bandziukas is community outreach coordinator for the Queensborough Community College Office of Academic Service-Learning. She has a background in program management and specializes in the development and growth of new programs. At Queensborough, she identifies community organizations with the potential to develop interesting and sustained relationships with the office as well as with individual faculty members. She develops communication tools useful for faculty and partners in project planning, and she produces, maintains records on, and documents community-based service-learning projects. Prior to the service-learning program, she helped to pilot a career mentoring program at Queensborough. She has presented locally and nationally on the development and accomplishments of the mentoring and the service-learning programs.

Shana Berger is the Connect2Complete program director at Campus Compact. She also coordinates the teaching initiative of the Leading Change Network. She has over ten years of teaching and managerial experience working with adults and young people from diverse ethnic and linguistic backgrounds. Most recently, she taught Developmental English, ESL, and College Writing at Bunker Hill and Roxbury Community Colleges in Boston. She directed an alternative high school program in Lowell, MA, and has taught youth and adults with a union and several community organizations. She has a BA in anthropology from Colby College and a master's degree in adult education from Cornell University.

Michael Bradley currently works as an evaluation and research analyst for iMentor, a nonprofit organization that builds mentoring relationships to empower students from low-income communities to graduate high school, succeed in college, and achieve their ambitions. He earned his BA in psychology from Binghamton University. Bradley studied applied psychology, data analysis, and education while working on his MA in Human Development and Social Intervention at New York University. He worked with the coauthors during his studies. Bradley has also worked at The Graduate Center at the City University of New York and Achievement First charter schools.

Kristina Brezicha is a dual-title doctoral candidate at the Pennsylvania State University in Educational Theory and Policy and Comparative International Education program. Her research focuses on immigrant students' political socialization, student voice, and school reforms and improvement including leadership development and teacher quality. Prior to beginning her doctoral program, she taught elementary special education students in New York City. She holds a master's degree in Politics and Education from Teachers College, Columbia University, and another master's in Urban Education from Mercy College.

Robert G. Bringle is a Kulynych-Cline Visiting Distinguished Professor of Psychology, Appalachian State University; a professor emeritus of Psychology and Philanthropic Studies, Indiana University-Purdue University Indianapolis (IUPUI); and a senior scholar at the IUPUI Center for Service and Learning. Bringle has been an active administrator and scholar in the field of community engagement during the past two decades. He held the position of executive director of the IUPUI Center for Service and Learning from 1994 to 2012. He received the Ehrlich Faculty Award for Service-Learning and the Legacy of Service Award from Indiana Campus Compact. He was recognized at the International Service-Learning Research Conference for his outstanding contributions to the service-learning research field, which have included over a hundred journal articles, book chapters, and books.

Suzanne M. Buglione is dean of Teaching and Learning at Bristol Community College. Buglione has an EdD from University of Massachusetts Boston and is the founder of CommunityBuild, a consulting and training business. Her research interests are nontraditional students and their experiences of identity development, service-learning, and retention, as well as faculty development.

Diane B. Call has served as president of Queensborough Community College of the City University of New York since January 2013, having been the interim president for the previous three-and-a-half years. Call, whose career spans four decades at Queensborough, has held positions in virtually all of the major areas of administration and academics. Call holds an EdD in College and University Administration, an MA in Community College Administration, and an MA in Student Personnel Administration, all from Teachers College, Columbia University. Additionally, she holds a certificate in Curriculum Development from Harvard University. In her previous position as Queensborough's provost, Call led the Academic Affairs Division, in partnership with Student Affairs, in creating, implementing, and assessing the Freshman Academies.

Janelle Clay is the assistant director of the Office of Research, Evaluation, and Program Support, where she oversees the evaluation plans for workforce development and continuing education initiatives within the Office of the Senior University Dean for Academic Affairs at the City University of New York (CUNY). She is the lead evaluator for the CUNY CareerPATH program, an initiative funded by the US Department of Labor's TAACCCT Grant Program. Prior to joining CUNY, Clay was the deputy director for Research and Evaluation at the New York City Office of Financial Empowerment (OFE) where she was responsible for evaluating the division's financial services and asset-building initiatives. She holds a BA from Emory University and an MS in Urban Policy Studies from Georgia State University.

Patti H. Clayton is a practitioner-scholar and consultant (PHC Ventures), a senior scholar with the Center for Service and Learning at Indiana University-Purdue University Indianapolis (IUPUI) and with the Institute for Community and Economic Engagement at the University of North Carolina Greensboro, and a visiting fellow with the New England Resource Center for Higher Education. She codeveloped with students and faculty a research-grounded critical reflection and assessment model (the DEAL Model) and is coauthor of the service-learning tutorial *Learning through Critical Reflection*. She served as coeditor of *Research on Service Learning: Conceptual Frameworks and Assessment* and coauthored the *Democratic Engagement White Paper*. Her current work focuses on reciprocity, faculty learning, transformational institutionalization, and building capacity for service-learning and community engagement as scholarship.

Gloria Crisp is an associate professor in the Department of Educational Leadership and Policy Studies at the University of Texas at San Antonio (UTSA). Her work has been published in the *American Educational Research Journal, Teachers College Record, Research in Higher Education*, the *Review of Higher Education*, and the *Journal of College Student Development*. Crisp is an associate editor of the *Review of Higher Education*. Her survey instrument, the College Student Mentoring Scale (CSMS), is currently being used at institutions across the country and abroad to evaluate the effectiveness of mentoring relationships.

Paulette Dalpes is the deputy to the vice chancellor for Student Affairs at the City University of New York (CUNY), which serves over 270,000 degree-seeking students at 24 institutions in New York City—including seven community colleges. Dalpes has over 15 years of experience working at community colleges including in the role of the chief student affairs officer and currently serves as the director of the Community College Division for the National Association of Student Personnel Administrators (NASPA). She has also been faculty for several leadership institutes for NASPA. Dalpes is a coeditor of *The Handbook for Student Affairs in Community*

Colleges (2014). She holds an abiding respect for and commitment to community colleges and the mission of educational access.

Cristina Di Meo serves as the associate assessment analyst in the Queensborough Community College Office of Academic Service-Learning (OASL). She has over 15 years of experience conducting research and policy advocacy on economic security issues. Currently, she oversees the OASL assessment initiatives to evaluate the effectiveness of the service-learning pedagogy on student learning outcomes, workplace skills, and civic engagement. She has presented locally and nationally on Queensborough's efforts to institutionalize service-learning and the use of service-learning in career and technical disciplines.

Donna Duffy is professor of Psychology at Middlesex Community College in Bedford and Lowell, Massachusetts. She is the coauthor of *Teaching within the Rhythms of the Semester* and the coeditor of *With Service in Mind*, a monograph on service-learning and psychology. Duffy received the Thomas Ehrlich Faculty Award for Service-Learning in 1999 for her work connecting service in the community to student learning. She has worked as an Engaged Scholar with Campus Compact and is one of the authors of *The Community's College: Indicators of Engagement at Two-Year Institutions* and *Service-Learning Course Design for Community Colleges*.

Kathleen E. Edwards is a PhD student in Educational Leadership and Cultural Foundations at the University of North Carolina at Greensboro. Her scholarly interests attend to the cultural foundations of popular education and the democratic potential of community engagement as well as exploring and bringing non-Western and critical perspectives to bear on traditional conceptions and practices of service-learning and community engagement.

Sharon Ellerton is an associate professor in the Department of Biological Sciences and has served as Queensborough Community College's faculty liaison to service-learning since 2009. In that role, she leads service-learning faculty development workshops, assists faculty to incorporate service-learning into their classrooms, and researches the impact of service-learning on community college students. In addition, Ellerton is a practitioner of service-learning, leading an honors/service-learning program in Anatomy and Physiology and incorporating service-learning into her own coursework.

Scott Evenbeck was named Guttman Community College's founding president in 2011. Previously, Evenbeck served as professor of Psychology and founding dean of University College at Indiana University-Purdue University, Indianapolis. Long involved in designing, implementing, and assessing first-year experience programs, he has given more than 100 presentations at conferences and written many articles and chapters on academic achievement and persistence. He has served on the faculty for summer institutes for Association of American Colleges & Universities and other associations, and served on accreditation teams for three regional associations. Evenbeck was a task force advisor for the Foundations of Excellence in the First College Year and a board member of the American Conference of Academic Deans and other national associations.

Robert Exley serves as the president of Snead State Community College in Boaz, AL. He was the vice president for academic affairs at Iowa Western Community College. Prior to that he was the director of the Wellness Institute at Miami Dade College where he helped establish its nationally recognized service-learning program—winner of the Campus Compact National Center for Community Colleges 1998 Collaboration Award and in 1997 the National Council of Instructional Administrators' Exemplary Program in Student Learning Award. Exley holds the following degrees: an associate of Arts, a BA, MS, and a doctorate from the University of Texas at Austin. He is a Distinguished Graduate of the University of Texas at Austin's Community College Leadership Program.

Victor Fichera is the principal investigator for the Academy Assessment Protocol and has been employed at Queensborough Community College since 2001. From the City University of New York, he received a BA degree in Economics and Psychology and a PhD in Industrial/Organizational Psychology. For the past 17 years he has been employed in fields involving research and measurement within academic settings. He conducted and published psychophysiological research while at Baruch College, designed and validated licensure tests at the New York City Board of Education, and served as the testing director at Queensborough Community College. In his current position as an institutional researcher, he assesses the effectiveness of the Queensborough Academies, as well as other initiatives at the college.

Shannon S. Fleishman is a sociology instructor at Chesapeake College. Her research focuses on the emerging role and impact of the community-college sector on a broad array of education outcomes, especially for individuals from underrepresented populations. She earned her PhD in Sociology from Pennsylvania State University in 2013 and a master's of Public Policy from Georgetown University in 2005. She has previously held a variety of professional and research positions in the nonprofit, education, and government sectors.

Robert W. Franco is the director of the Office for Institutional Effectiveness at Kapi'olani Community College. He currently serves as the college's accreditation liaison to the ACCJC/WASC, Association of American Colleges & Universities, American Council on Education, Community College Survey of Student Engagement, Carnegie Foundation, and Campus Compact. He conducts training, technical assistance, and research dissemination at community colleges, universities, and other conference audiences in five states per year (38 states total) with research-based training designed to improve course success, semester to semester persistence, degree completion, and transfer rates through service-learning, community-based research, and authentic partnerships. Franco is also a recognized expert on contemporary Samoan, Polynesian, and Pacific Islander demographic, ecological, health, and cultural issues. He has extensive publications in these areas.

Maria Hesse serves as vice provost for Academic Partnerships at Arizona State University (ASU), helping to create and sustain productive working relationships with community colleges and other institutions on behalf of students who wish to complete their baccalaureate degrees. She has been at ASU since July 2009. Prior to that, Hesse served for seven years as president and chief executive officer for Chandler-Gilbert Community College, one of the ten Maricopa Community Colleges in the Phoenix metropolitan area. She worked in the Maricopa Community Colleges for 25 years serving in a variety of faculty and administrative positions at multiple institutions. Hesse is actively involved in the community and has served as a volunteer and on the boards of many nonprofit organizations.

Yao Zhang Hill is currently an assessment specialist in the University of Hawai'i at Mānoa Assessment Office, where she assists faculty with the development and use of student learning assessments and conducts research and evaluation studies into student learning outcomes for the purpose of program improvement. During her institutional research career at Kapi'olani Community College from 2008 to 2012, she was significantly engaged in the evaluation of academic and student affairs programs, particularly with service-learning, STEM, and faculty development. Her areas of research interest include: utilization-focused academic and co-curricular program evaluation; faculty development; culture change in learning outcome assessment; and psychometric measurement methods.

Krista Hiser is an associate professor of English, and teaches developmental and college-level writing with service-learning. She has an MA in English Composition from San Francisco State University and a PhD in Educational Administration from the University of Hawai'i at Mānoa, focusing on sustainability in the academic curriculum. As faculty service learning coordinator at Kapi'olani, she works with faculty to create curriculum and integrate service and sustainability learning across disciplines.

Zivah Perel Katz is an associate professor of English at Queensborough Community College of the City University of New York (CUNY). She is a graduate of Cornell University (AB, 1999) and the University of Delaware (MA, 2001 and PhD, 2005). Katz is interested in twentieth-century American war novels and film, primarily those from the two wars in Iraq. She has published in literature and film journals, as well as in volumes about teaching literature in the Modern Language Association's Teaching series. She is working on a critical volume about the literature and film of the Persian Gulf and Iraq wars, for which she received a fellowship from CUNY. Katz is also interested in community-college pedagogy, presenting both institutionally and at national conferences.

Arlene Kemmerer is a reading specialist who advocates incorporating high-impact strategies, such as service-learning into the developmental education curriculum. She is a member of SWIG, a student wiki interdisciplinary group, whereby students use e-Portfolio for a *Transformative Learning Experience* and she is a member of *Moving Ahead with ePortfolio* (MAeP) project. She has participated in three Pedagogical Research Challenge Awards given by Queensborough Community College to study effective methods of teaching and learning. She is also serving as project director of *Placing Effective High Impact Educational Activities and Academic Service-Learning into the Career and Technical Academies and Disciplines* grant at Queensborough Community College. She has presented locally and nationally on the use of high-impact practices with developmental students.

Adrianna Kezar is professor for Higher Education at the University of Southern California and codirector of the Pullias Center for Higher Education. Kezar is also director of the Delphi Project on the Changing Faculty and Student Success. She is a national expert on non-tenure track faculty, change, governance, and leadership in higher education. Her recent books include: *Embracing Non-Tenure Track Faculty* (2012) and *Understanding the New Majority of Non-Tenure Track Faculty* (2010).

Carrie Klein is a student affairs professional and PhD student at George Mason University. Her research interests include investigating the role of organizational privilege on change management in higher education institutions, the intersections of organizational structures, cultures, roles, and identity, and the impact of student affairs work in student retention, engagement, and completion. She has contributed to two books, has presented research papers at national conferences, and in the spring of 2014 was awarded the Gerald Saddlemire Masters Research Award from the American College Professionals Association (ACPA).

Jaime Lester is an associate professor of higher education at George Mason University. Lester's research agenda examines gender equity in higher education, retention and transfer of community college students, nonpositional leadership, and organizational change. She has published numerous articles, is editor of *Community College Review*, and has five books on gendered perspectives in community colleges, family-friendly policies in higher education, ways to promote collaboration in higher education, workplace bullying in higher education, and grassroots leadership and change in higher education.

Daniel Maxey is now a PhD candidate and dean's fellow in Urban Education Policy at the University of Southern California's Rossier School of Education and Pullias Center for Higher Education. He is also the coinvestigator for the Delphi Project on the Changing Faculty and Student Success, which has examined the causes and implications of growing reliance on non-tenure-track faculty in higher education, as well as working with wide-ranging stakeholder groups to advance strategies for positive change. His research focuses on non-tenure-track faculty, politics and policy in higher education, and governance.

Linda E. Merians joined Guttman Community College as chief of staff in September 2013. She came to the City University of New York (CUNY) in 2012, working for The Graduate Center and the Invest in CUNY campaign. Previously, she worked at State University of New York (SUNY)/Stony Brook as chief of staff for President Shirley Strum Kenny. Merians earned her PhD at the University of Maryland. She served in the English departments of Bucknell University and La Salle University, where she taught eighteenth-century British Literature, poetry, Shakespeare, composition, women's studies, and South African literature. She has presented papers at many academic conferences and published two books, several articles, and numerous book reviews. A passionate believer in public higher education, Merians is thrilled to be working at a community college at this propitious time for the sector.

Vanessa Smith Morest is interim dean of Academic Affairs at Norwalk Community College. She is an adjunct assistant professor for Higher and Postsecondary Education at Teachers College, Columbia University, and an affiliate of the Community College Research Center (CCRC). Morest holds a doctorate in Sociology of Education from Teachers College, Columbia University. Prior to her current position, she served as assistant director for Postsecondary Research at the CCRC, Teachers College, Columbia University. Morest has more than 12 years of experience conducting research on community colleges concerning a wide range of topics. Her research has focused on community college organization, leadership, and policy. Morest is the author of *Community College Student Success: From Boardrooms to Classrooms* and is coeditor of *Defending the Community College Equity Agenda*.

Josephine Pantaleo serves as the Queensborough Community College director of the Academic Literacy Learning Center, Academic Service-Learning, and e-Portfolio. She has over 40 years of experience in the education field with a specialization in developmental reading, composition, and experiential learning. She advocates for the use of service-learning pedagogy that promotes learning in a contextualized format. In her present role, she provides professional development support for faculty who wish to incorporate service-learning activities into their courses, and she coordinates service-learning efforts and events between and across faculty, college departments, and community organizations. She has presented both locally and nationally on Queensborough's efforts at institutionalizing service-learning.

Thomas Penniston earned his PhD studying Language, Literacy and Culture at the University of Maryland Baltimore County. His mixed-methods dissertation investigated the impacts of applied and service-learning participation on undergraduate students and found significant effects on diverse indicators of academic success as well as enhanced aspects of prosocial development.

Mary Prentice is academic department head and associate professor in the Educational Leadership and Administration department at New Mexico State University (NMSU). She began her career as a psychology instructor at Central New Mexico Community College (CNM) and developed her passion for service-learning through her involvement in the establishment of service-learning at the college. Prentice left CNM to earn her doctorate degree through the University of Texas-Austin's Community College Leadership Program. Her dissertation on service-learning institutionalization was the impetus for the collaboration with Gail Robinson at the American Association of Community Colleges in 2001. After graduating, Prentice was the dean of Social Sciences and Public Service at Illinois Valley Community College before joining the faculty in the community college administration program at NMSU.

Amy Pucino is an assistant professor of Sociology at the Community College of Baltimore County (CCBC). She incorporates service-learning into her courses and serves on the Service-Learning Committee at CCBC. Her research focus centers on understanding the extent to which pedagogical relationships can be a source of social capital for diverse student populations.

Tanya Renner is a professor of Psychology at Kapiʻolani Community College, where she recently developed a protocol for assessing general education student learning outcomes. She has a PhD in developmental psychology from the University of

California, Berkeley, and has, for many years, been a program evaluator and faculty trainer for service-learning. In 2009 and 2010, she was also a faculty mentor for assessment retreats held by the Western Association for Schools and Colleges. She was a member of the American Association of Colleges & Universities' team that wrote the VALUE rubric for critical thinking. She also recently published research on the process of developing an infrastructure for offering quality service-learning experiences in Mexico to students from around the world.

Gail Robinson is an education consultant who works with colleges, universities, and organizations to develop service-learning and community engagement programs. She was the director of service learning for the American Association of Community Colleges for 18 years, managing federal and nonfederal grant projects and administering more than 125 college grants. Robinson directed AACC's national data collection, evaluation, and research on community college service-learning initiatives and authored numerous reports and monographs. She served on the board of directors of the International Association for Research on Service-Learning and Community Engagement, is a senior advisor to the Community College National Center for Community Engagement, and is a member of the Carnegie Community Engagement Classification national advisory panel.

Regina A. Rochford is a professor of Developmental Reading and Writing and the chairperson of the Department of Academic Literacy at Queensborough Community College, the City University of New York. She earned a doctorate in Education from St. John's University, a master's of Science in TESOL, and a master's of Public Administration. She is the author of 13 published research articles and five developmental reading and writing textbooks.

Diana Strumbos is a research analyst in the Office of Research, Evaluation, and Program Support at the City University of New York (CUNY). She is responsible for leading the first year evaluation of the CUNY Service Corps and working closely with program staff to help understand and improve the program on an ongoing basis. Previously, Strumbos was the director of Evaluation at Single Stop USA, a nonprofit antipoverty organization. She has taught undergraduate courses in statistics, social science research methods, and the sociology of education at Queens College. Strumbos holds a BA from Washington University in St. Louis and is a PhD Candidate in Sociology at the CUNY Graduate Center.

Amanda Taggart is a graduate of The University of Texas at San Antonio's Educational Leadership and Policy Studies doctoral program. Her research interests focus on issues related to racial/ethnic minority student equity, access, and achievement throughout the P-20 educational pipeline, including the transition to college and the success of traditionally underrepresented groups in higher education. She has worked in the educational systems of Utah, Idaho, Nevada, Texas, and Mississippi. Her work has been published in the *American Educational Research Journal* and the *Hispanic Journal of Behavioral Sciences*.

Rebecca M. Townsend serves as associate professor of Communication and faculty coordinator of the Institute for Community Engagement and Outreach at Manchester Community College in Manchester, CT. Her research on the Federal

Transit Administration-funded "Partnership for Inclusive, Cost-Effective Public Participation," the work on which her chapter was based, was honored by the International Association of Public Participation's Core Values program and the White House Champions of Change for Transportation Innovation.

Amy E. Traver is an assistant professor of Sociology at Queensborough Community College of the City University of New York. Traver is interested in intersections of race/ethnicity, gender, and (dis)abilities in contemporary American families and educational institutions. She has published articles on these topics in such venues as *Qualitative Sociology, Sociological Focus, International Journal of Sociology of the Family,* and *The Journal of Education Policy.* Traver is also interested in community college pedagogies. In 2013, she published an article in *Internet and Higher Education* (with Volchok, Bidjerano, and Shea) on community college students' success in partially online courses. Traver has been active in the field of service-learning since 2004.

Amanda Wittman is the former director of Academic and Strategic Initiatives for Campus Compact, a national coalition of nearly 1,200 college and university presidents who are committed to the public purposes of higher education. She currently lectures in political science at Clark University in Worcester, MA. Wittman's PhD is from the University of Edinburgh and she is committed to research with practical uses for the field of civic and community engagement.

Heather B. Wylie is a tenured sociology faculty and area coordinator in the division of Arts, Communication, Social and Consumer Sciences at Shasta College, a two-year institution located in Northern California. Her areas of concentration include the sociology of professions, medicine, family, and marriage, and her teaching interests also include the sociology of minorities and gender. Beginning with her undergraduate degrees in cultural anthropology and women's studies, Wylie also developed an interest in civic and community engagement in higher education. As the founder and current coordinator of the College's Center for Community Engagement, she promotes cross-disciplinary efforts to institutionalize service-learning on campus.

Travis York is an assistant professor of Higher Education Leadership at Valdosta State University. York's research focuses on access and success in higher education for underrepresented groups. Most recently, York was honored by the International Association for Research in Service-Learning and Community Engagement, who awarded him their Dissertation of the Year Award for his research on low-income, first-generation college students and service-learning. York earned his PhD in Higher Education from the Pennsylvania State University in 2013 and his master's degree in Higher Education from Geneva College in 2007. Prior to earning his doctorate, York held several positions in Student Affairs and worked as an adjunct instructor.

Index

2 + 4 = Service on Common Ground, 16

Academic Service Learning (service-learning), 305–10. *See also* service-learning
Accreditation Board of Engineering and Technology (ABET), 213
Achieving the Dream, 40–1, 46, 242
Acoba, Francisco, 6, 9, 169
adjunct faculty. *See* part-time faculty
adult education, 8, 20, 82–4, 87–9, 145, 188, 211, 214, 259, 263–9, 315. *See also* nontraditional students
Alcantar, Cynthia M., 69, 98
Allen, Drew, 5, 95
Allen, Mike, 26, 157
Amel, Elise L., 172
American Association of Colleges of Nursing, 213
American Association of Community Colleges (AACC), 2, 6–7, 9n2, 15–16, 29, 45, 155, 187–9
  Broadening Horizons through Service Learning, 16, 24–5, 113, 144, 149, 160, 162, 165–6, 244, 274, 288
  Essential Learning Outcomes, 212–13
  Learn and Serve America, 9n2, 16, 155, 159–60, 162, 165, 188, 288
  Service-Learning Alumni Colleges, 288
American Association of Junior Colleges, 38
American Association of State Colleges and Universities (AASCU), 15, 288–9
Andolina, Molly, 188
andragogy, 84
Antonio, Anthony Lising, 244
applied learning, 43–4, 86, 159, 172, 176, 212, 215, 218–19, 306

assessment
  C2C, 126–35
  and career development, 214–22
  and civic engagement, 188–95
  CUNY Service Corps, 95, 105–8
  and developmental education, 114–21
  of e-portfolios, 294
  of faculty, 248, 250, 252–3
  Freshman Academies, 305–10
  KELA model, 169–81
  and mixed methods research, 276
  on nontraditional students, 281
  of online education, 289–90
  and research, 23–5, 28, 273–82
  and retention, 158, 164–5
  and social capital, 203–9
  student, 171, 222
  and theory, 280
  writing, 115–19, 121, 145
Astin, Alexander W., 26, 107, 145, 148, 157, 281
Astin, Helen S., 244

Badway, Norena, 258
Bahr, Peter Riley, 142–3
Bailey, Thomas, 119
Bandziukas, Mary, 7, 211
Barnett, Lynn, 2, 19, 144
Barr, Robert B., 19
Battistoni, Richard M., 20, 188
Bean, Martha S., 145, 148
Bell, Denise, 258
Bensimon, Estela M., 106–7
Benson, Lee, 17
Berg, Marlene, 228–9
Berger, Shana, 6, 125

Berry, Wendell, 298
Berson, Judith S., 24
Big Bend Community College, 128, 134
Bill and Melinda Gates Foundation, 46, 128, 289
Billig, Shelley H., 282
Bishop, Robin, 106
Black, Laura W., 230
Bouffard, Suzanne, 128
Bourdieu, Pierre, 200–2, 268
Bracken, Cheryl Campanella, 261
Bradley, Michael, 4, 7, 67, 211
Brandeis University, 129, 131–3
Brawer, Florence, 24
Bresciani, Marilee J., 214
Brevard Community College (Eastern Florida State College), 311
Brezicha, Kristina, 8, 257
Bringle, Robert G., 4, 13, 25–8, 158, 194
Broward College, 128
Brown, J. Stanley, 38
Buglione, Suzanne M., 5, 81
Bulot, James J., 267
Bush, Adam, 28–9
Butin, Dan W., 4, 54–5, 107

Call, Diane B., 8–9, 305
Campbell, Toni A., 130
Campus Compact, 15–16, 125–6, 158, 249–50, 274–5, 309, 314
  Connect2Complete (C2C), 6, 125–35, 250
capital
  social and cultural, 7, 54, 60, 127, 142–3, 150, 166, 199–209, 268
  students with varying forms of, 259, 264–5, 268–70
Carcasson, Martin, 230
career development, 28, 39, 47, 88, 100, 166, 172, 211–22, 257
Carnegie Foundation for the Advancement of Teaching, 16, 24, 289, 306
  Statway program, 43
Celio, Christine I., 172
Cepeda, Rita M., 142
Chandler-Gilbert Community College (CGCC), 9, 311–18
Chesbrough, Ronald D., 162
Chi, Winny YanFang, 142
Chickering, Arthur W., 22

Cho, Sung-Woo, 119
Choy, Susan, 257, 260, 262, 268, 270
citizenship, 20, 24–30, 45, 163, 172, 175–9. *See also* civic engagement; civil learning; democracy
City University of New York (CUNY), 72, 99–100, 115, 118
  Kingsborough Community College, 42, 70
  LaGuardia Community College, 42
  Queensborough Community College (QCC), 5, 7, 9, 68–78, 113–23, 213–22, 288, 305–10
  Service Corps, 5, 95, 99–108
  Stella and Charles Guttman Community College, 8, 293–4
civic engagement, 6–8, 14–16, 161–6, 185–96, 243–5, 249–53, 273–6, 294, 297–9, 303–4, 316
civic learning, 6, 13–16, 19–22, 25, 28, 30, 131, 289
classroom time, use of, 44
Clay, Janelle, 5, 95
Clayton, Patti H., 4, 13–14, 20–2, 25–8, 186
Cohen, Arthur, 24
Cohen, Geoffrey, 128
Coleman, James S., 201
collaborative learning, 22, 44, 134, 144–5, 173, 179, 221, 246
communication skills, 24, 26, 119, 134, 145, 163, 174, 207, 212–14, 221, 232–3
  and civic learning, 21, 193
  cross-cultural, 166, 217–18
  ethnography of, 229–30
  group, 227–30
  institutional, 47, 143, 147, 247–53
  oral, 58, 212, 214, 216, 219, 221, 226–9, 232–4
  written, 69–77, 89, 113–23, 122, 129, 133–4, 163, 212, 214, 216–17, 294, 312–14
Community College National Center for Community Engagement (CCNCCE), 16, 155, 314
Community College of Baltimore County (CCBC), 44
community college students
  challenges of, 41–2
  demographics, 1, 29, 37–40, 54–9, 62, 70–8, 81–3, 99–108, 113, 127–30, 142, 159, 263, 170–7, 266, 270, 306–7

diversity of, 40–1, 56–9, 69–72, 95–108, 113, 127, 130, 203, 214–15, 221, 265–6, 290–1, 300, 307
and life experience, 60, 85–6, 88–90, 121–2, 128, 148, 292
reasons for choosing community college, 40–2
Community College Survey of Student Engagement (CCSSE), 23, 37–8, 48n2, 171, 173, 179–80
community colleges
challenges of scale at, 45–7
compared with four-year institutions, 41, 45–6, 158–9, 187, 194–5, 200, 212, 243, 257, 273, 278, 281
cost of, 40
defined, 1–2
and degree completion, 40, 42, 130, 139–46, 151
as democracy's colleges, 1, 13–14, 30, 186
as global neighborhoods, 67–8
graduation rates, 40, 96, 100
history of, 2, 38–40
missions of, 2–4, 6–7, 13–30, 37–40, 47, 54, 140, 211–12, 243, 278, 287, 297, 306, 318
and noncredit development, 39, 100, 107, 129, 257–8, 270, 270n2
open door nature of, 38, 40, 47
and part-time faculty, 241–54
percentage that incorporate service-learning, 45, 140, 288
and student success movement, 42–4
and transfer, 6, 19, 39, 47, 81, 108, 118, 139–51, 178–9, 249, 300
See also *individual community colleges*; service-learning
Community Colleges Broadening Horizons through Service Learning, 16, 24, 113, 144, 149, 160, 162, 165–6, 244, 274, 288
community impact, 2, 23, 74, 140, 166, 234, 316
community partnerships, 58–9, 87–91, 150, 166, 170–1, 175, 180, 214–22, 279–80, 291–2, 311–13
community service, 25–6, 55, 99, 157, 161, 176–7, 188, 221, 234, 243–4, 259, 275, 277, 280–1, 293, 303
commuter students, 38, 41, 83, 141, 146

completion agenda, 6, 125, 141
Conley, Paige A., 57, 59–60
Connect2Complete (C2C), 6, 125–35, 250
Connell, Christopher, 67
contingent faculty. *See* part-time faculty
Conway, James M., 172
Cranton, Patricia, 20
creativity. *See* innovation, pedagogical
Cress, Christine M., 244
Crisp, Gloria, 3, 8–9, 23, 25, 159, 172–3, 258, 273
critical quantitative approach, 5, 95, 97–9, 103–4, 106–8
critical thinking, 14, 24, 26, 29, 47, 71, 75, 126, 145, 148, 159, 163, 166, 176–7, 179, 187, 212–14, 219, 222, 246, 282, 292
Crucible Moment: College Learning and Democracy's Future, A, 14–15
Cruz, Nadinne, 57
Cuban, Larry, 289
cultural and social capital, 7, 54, 60, 127, 142–3, 150, 166, 199–209, 268
cultural understanding, 26, 54–63, 67–78, 85, 105, 127–35, 170, 176, 212, 227–35, 291–2. *See also* global competencies
Cuyahoga Community College, 128

D'Agostino, Maria, 199–200
Dalpes, Paulette, 8, 287
Deans, Thomas, 69, 72, 77
deep learning, 22–3
degree completion, 40, 42, 130, 139–46, 151
Deil-Amen, Regina, 41
Delphi Project on the Changing Faculty and Student Success, 242, 246, 254n1
democracy, 1–2, 6, 13–22, 28–30, 44–5, 193, 230–4, 299–300, 315. *See also* citizenship
Democracy Commitment, 15
democracy's college, community college as, 1, 13–14, 30, 186
developmental education
community college and, 1, 3, 40–4, 46, 71, 107
Connect2Complete and, 6, 125–35
noncredit courses, 100, 107, 140
and retention, 113–23
and service-learning, 5, 24, 40–4, 113–23, 145, 178–80
and transfer students, 142

Developmental Education Initiative, 46
Dewey, John, 17–18, 74, 193, 200–2
Di Meo, Cristina, 7, 211
diversity, 28–9, 37–8, 54, 56–7
    ELL students, 67, 72, 74–7, 113, 115–23, 145, 148, 173, 260, 263, 278
    and ethnography of communication, 229
    faculty, 29, 142
    of learning styles, 307
    LGBTQ community, 61–2, 102
    low-income students, 27, 83, 101, 126–35, 158, 200, 211, 261, 263, 268, 290–1
    nontraditional students, 5, 8, 81–92, 113, 142, 203, 207, 257–70, 281, 315
    students of color, 40–1, 56–9, 69–72, 96–108, 113, 127, 203, 214–15, 265–6, 290–1, 300, 307
    understanding of, 72, 75–6, 174–5
    working students, 8, 41, 58, 188, 259, 264–5, 267–9
dual enrollment, 40
Duffy, Donna, 6, 18, 125
Duncan, Arne, 212
Durlak, Joseph, 172
Dymnicki, Allison, 172

Eastern Florida State College, 311
Eatman, Tim, 28–9
Eby, John W., 55
Edmonds Community College, 128, 132, 134
Edwards, Kathleen E., 4, 13
Ellerton, Sharon, 7, 211
Elwell, Marelene D., 145, 148
engagement, civic, 6–8, 14–16, 161–6, 185–96, 243–5, 249–53, 273–6, 294, 297–9, 303–4, 316
English Language Learners (ELL), 67, 72, 74–7, 113, 115–23, 145, 148, 173, 260, 263, 278. *See also* international students
environmental justice, 231
Estrella, Jeremy, 146
Evenbeck, Scott, 8, 287
Exley, Robert, 8, 297
experiential learning, 17, 19, 24–5, 27, 44, 84, 90, 213, 221, 293
Eyler, Janet, 23, 26–7, 107–8, 114, 157, 172

faculty
    assessment, 248, 250, 252–3
    faculty-student interaction, 22, 126, 143–4, 146–8, 158, 173, 179
    part-time, 7–8, 46, 81, 140, 143, 241–54
    professional development, 47, 149, 200, 214, 242, 244, 246–53, 317
    and service-learning, 305–10
Felten, Peter, 27
Fichera, Victor, 7, 211
first-generation students, 23, 53, 81, 83, 89, 96, 128, 142, 145–6, 158, 211, 221, 260–1, 263, 268
first-year seminars, 42–5, 145, 293, 305–7
Fitch, Peggy, 69
Fiume, Peter Francis, 188
Fleishman, Shannon S., 8, 257
four-year institutions
    community colleges compared with, 41, 45–6, 158–9, 187, 194–5, 200, 212, 243, 257, 273, 278, 281
    costs, 40
    nontraditional students in, 258–60, 263–70
    service-learning in, 15, 23–6, 156–7, 162, 187
    transfer to, 19, 25, 27, 39, 47, 139–51, 195
Franco, Robert W., 6, 9, 45, 169
Freire, Paulo, 18, 84
Frey, Christopher J., 215

Gallini, Sara M., 187
Gamson, Zelda F., 22
Garcia, Rudy M., 244–5
Gardner, Howard, 75–6
Gates, Bill, 289
Gerwien, Daniel P., 172
Giles, Dwight E., Jr., 23, 26, 107–8, 114, 157, 172
Glickman, Gena, 227
global competencies, 9, 14, 24, 163, 175–9, 289. *See also* cultural understanding
globalization, 67–78, 211, 289. *See also* immigration; international students
Goldstein, Don, 67–8
Gray, Charlene J., 26, 86, 172
Green, Ann E., 55–6
Green River Community College, 128, 134
group communication, 227–30
group learning, 22, 44, 134, 144–5, 173, 179, 221, 246

Grubb, W. Norton, 258
Gutheil, Irene A., 176

Hagedorn, Linda Serra, 142
Halttunen, Karen, 287
Hamlin, Maria L., 57, 60
Harkavay, Ira, 17
Harper, William Rainey, 38
Hartley, Matthew, 20, 186
Hartman, Eric, 193
Hatcher, Julia A., 22, 27, 158, 187
Heat-Moon, William Least, 287
Hesse, Maria, 9, 311
high-impact pedagogy, 23–5, 27, 71, 130, 157, 212, 221, 245–6, 258, 290, 305–10
   capstone projects, 171, 173, 176
   collaborative learning, 22, 44, 134, 144–5, 173, 179, 221, 246
   experiential learning, 17, 19, 24–5, 27, 44, 84, 90, 213, 221, 293
   first-year seminars, 42–5, 145, 293, 305–7
   global learning, 9, 14, 24, 67–78, 163, 175–9, 289
   internships, 25, 200, 221, 234, 318
   learning communities, 45–6, 68, 71–8, 145–6, 246, 292
   service-learning, 23–5, 27, 71, 130, 157, 212, 221, 245–6, 258, 290, 305–10
   student research, 43, 71–2, 75–8, 225–35
   writing-intensive, 69–77, 113–23, 129, 133–4, 216–17, 294, 312–14
Hill, Yao Zhang, 6, 9, 169
Hiser, Krista, 6, 9, 169
Hiss, Tony, 287–8
Hodge, Gary, 177
Holland, Barbara, 267
Hollis, Shirley A., 24
Holton, Elwood, 84
Holyoke Community College (HCC), 8, 290–2
Horinek, Jon B., 267
Horton, Myles, 18
Huguley, James P., 265–6
Hurricane Gustav, 300–1, 304

Ignash, Jan M., 143
Ikeda, Elaine K., 157
immigrant-origin students, 4–5, 41, 67–78, 104, 120, 123, 301–2
immigration, 57, 67–78, 81, 83, 96, 155, 177, 293. *See also* globalization
innovation, pedagogical, 1–2, 6, 19, 28, 46–7, 84, 86, 91, 135, 155, 169, 228, 245, 251, 290, 307–9, 313
Integrated Basic Education and Skills Training (I-BEST) program (Washington State), 43
international students, 67, 70, 170. *See also* English Language Learners (ELL)
internships, 25, 200, 221, 234, 318
interpersonal skills, 26, 68, 114, 128, 140, 157, 213, 218, 220. *See also* communication

Jaeger, Audrey J., 21
Jameson, Jessica, 21
Jay, Gregory, 77
Jeandron, Carol, 144–5, 147
Jefferson, Thomas, 193
Jenkins, Krista, 188
Jeong, Dong Wook, 119
job service. *See* career development
Johnson, Christopher J., 267
Joliet Junior College, 38

Kahne, Joseph, 20, 188
Kapi'olani Community College (KCC), 6, 169–81
Katz, Zivah Perel, 1, 4, 67
Kazin, Alfred, 294
Keeter, Scott, 188
Keith, Novella Zett, 68
Kemmerer, Arlene, 7, 211
Keup, Jennifer R., 158
Kezar, Adrianna, 7, 241
Kim, Karen A., 260, 262, 268
King, Martin Luther, Jr., 299
Kingsborough Community College (CUNY), 42
Kisker, Carrie, 24
Klein, Carrie, 6, 139
Knowles, Malcolm, 84
Kolb, David, 19
Koring, Heidi, 130
Kozeracki, Carol, 2–3
Kozma, Cara Lindsey, 69
Krippendorf, Klaus, 259, 261
Kuh, George D., 23, 130, 212, 290, 305. *See also* high-impact pedagogy

Laanan, Frankie Santos, 140–1
Ladson-Billings, Gloria, 74
LaGuardia Community College (CUNY), 42
Largent, Liz, 266–7
Larson-Keagy, Elizabeth, 57
Learn and Serve America, 9n2, 16, 155, 159–60, 162, 165, 188, 288
learning communities, 45–6, 68, 71–8, 145–6, 246, 292. *See also* high-impact pedagogy
lesbian, gay, bisexual, transgender, and queer (LGBTQ) community, 61–2, 102
Lester, Jaime, 6, 139
Levin, John S., 21, 259
Levinson, David L., 140
Lisman, C. David, 18, 29
Lockeman, Kelly S., 27
Logan, John R., 67
Lombard, Matthew, 261
Lorain County Community College, 128, 132
low-income students, 27, 83, 101, 126–35, 158, 200, 211, 261, 263, 268, 290–1
Lumina Foundation, 46

Mahon, Lisa, 291–2
Maldonado, David, 60
Manchester Community College (MCC), 225–35
Marchese, Theodore J., 22
Maricopa Community College Center for Civic Participation, 230
Markey, Vern, 26, 157
Marti, Eduardo J., 307
massive open online courses (MOOCs), 289–90. *See also* online education
Maxey, Daniel, 7, 241
McCarthy, Anne M., 280
McClenney, Kay, 172
McCourt, Frank, 294
McDowell, Cesar, 92
McGuire, Lisa, 25
McKay, Valerie C., 146
McKnight, John, 59
McLain, Melissa, 142
mentoring, 22–3, 58, 88, 126–31, 155, 164, 219, 232, 245–7, 250–1, 292, 308–9
Merians, Linda E., 8, 287
Merriam, Sharan B., 248–9
Miami Dade College, 128, 301–4, 311

Middaugh, Ellen, 199
Middlesex Community College, 311
Mills, C. Wright, 60
Mitchell, Tania D., 55–6
Moely, Barbara E., 187
moral development, 26, 128, 267, 282
Morest, Vanessa Smith, 4, 9, 37
multiculturalism, 67–8, 158. *See also* cultural understanding; globalization
Musoba, Glenda D., 108
Muthiah, Richard N., 27, 158
Myers-Lipton, Scott J., 127

National Center for Education Statistics (NCES), 82–92, 242
National Issues Forum Institute, 230
National Task Force on Civic Learning and Democratic Engagement, 14–15
neoliberalism, 14, 21–2, 28, 67
Neuendorf, Kimberly, 259
nontraditional students, 5, 8, 81–92, 113, 142, 203, 207, 257–70, 281, 315. *See also* adult education
Novak, Julie M., 26, 157–8
Novick, Sarah, 265–6

Obama, Barack, 125, 211, 214
Olivas, Alberto, 230
online education, 44, 268–9
    massive open online courses (MOOCs), 289–90
oral communication, 58, 212, 214, 216, 219, 221, 226–9, 232–4. *See also* communication
Owens Community College, 128

Palmer, Parker, 298–9, 303
Palmer, Robert T., 99
Pantaleo, Josephine, 7, 211
Parsons, Michael, 29
Partnership for Inclusive, Cost-Effective Public Participation (PICEP2) model, 225–35
part-time faculty, 7–8, 46, 81, 140, 143, 241–54
part-time students, 3, 29, 46, 82–3, 141, 146, 159, 186, 261, 263
Pascarella, Ernest T., 22
pedagogy
    capstone projects, 171, 173, 176

collaborative learning, 22, 44, 134, 144–5, 173, 179, 221, 246
experiential learning, 17, 19, 24–5, 27, 44, 84, 90, 213, 221, 293
first-year seminars, 42–5, 145, 293, 305–7
global learning, 9, 14, 24, 67–78, 163, 175–9, 289
high-impact, 23–5, 27, 71, 130, 157, 212, 221, 245–6, 258, 290, 305–10
internships, 25, 200, 221, 234, 318
KELA model, 169–80
learning communities, 45–6, 68, 71–8, 145–6, 246, 292
principles for effective, 170–2
service-learning, 23–5, 27, 71, 130, 157, 212, 221, 245–6, 258, 290, 305–10
student research, 43, 71–2, 75–8, 225–35
writing-intensive, 69–77, 113–23, 129, 133–4, 216–17, 294, 312–14
peer advocacy, 6, 126–35
peer mentoring, 128, 250, 380. *See also* mentoring
Pelco, Lynn E., 27
Penniston, Thomas, 7, 199
Perez, William, 69
Perna, Laura W., 98
person-culture match theory, 127
place, sense of, 287–94
Plater, William G., 14
Plato, 209n2
Port au-Prince Earthquake, 301–4
Prentice, Mary, 6–8, 24, 97, 114, 118–19, 144, 155, 175, 177, 185, 213
problem solving, 19, 21, 26, 97, 170, 212
public speaking, 219, 226–8, 232–4. *See also* oral communication
public transportation, 226, 231–3
Pucino, Amy, 7, 199
Puckett, John, 17
Putnam, Robert D., 202

reflection activities
community partner, 214–22
faculty, 215–22
group, 134
shared, 206, 312–14, 316
student, 20, 23, 58–63, 68, 72–6, 89–91, 129–30, 148–9, 170–6, 179, 214–22, 232, 251–2, 312–13
and transformative learning theory, 20

Renner, Tanya, 6, 9, 169
research
and assessment, 23–5, 28, 273–82
best practices for, 273–82
service-learning, 2–4, 16, 23–7, 273–82, 305–10, 317
student, 43, 71–2, 75–8, 225–35
retention, 5–6, 24, 40, 113–23, 126–35, 144–6, 156–60, 165–6, 171–2, 213–17, 220, 305–7
Robinson, Gail, 2, 6, 8, 19, 24, 97, 144–5, 147, 155, 175, 177, 187, 213, 244–5, 267
Rochford, Regina A., 5, 113–14, 145
Ronan, Bernie, 28
Ruiz, Ana, 187
Rush, Benjamin, 193
Russo, Pat, 119

Saddington, Tony, 84–6
Saltmarsh, John, 20–1, 28, 186
Savitz-Romer, Mandy, 128
Sax, Linda J., 26, 107
Schaffer, David F., 9n3
Schensul, Jean J., 228–9
science, technology, engineering, and mathematics (STEM), 99, 155, 170
Scobey, David, 293
Seider, Scott C., 265–6
self-efficacy, 26, 130, 144–6, 148–51, 268
sensitivity, 72, 75–6, 174–5. *See also* cultural understanding
service-learning
and achievement, 5–6, 73, 96, 121, 157, 169, 171–3, 177–80
and bridge building/border-crossing, 53, 55–6, 60, 63
and career development, 211–22
and civic mission, 15–17, 20–2
and community, 297–304
defined, 2, 24–5
and democracy, 15, 20–2
and disciplinary learning, 18–19
and diversity, 95–108
faculty, 7–8, 46–7, 81, 140, 143, 149, 200, 214, 241–54, 305–10, 317
and globalization, 67–71, 74–8
as high-impact practice, 23–5, 27, 71, 130, 157, 212, 221, 245–6, 258, 290, 305–10
history of, 17–20
and "ideal type" student, 53–6, 58–9, 62

service-learning—*Continued*
  and identity formation, 53–63, 69
  and immigrant-origin students, 4–5, 41, 67–78, 104, 120, 123, 301–2
  and learning communities, 45–6, 68, 71–8, 145–6, 246, 292
  mandatory, 71, 91, 315
  and meaning-marking, 87–9, 128
  and nontraditional learners, 81–92
  and part-time faculty, 241–54
  and place, 287–94
  prism effect of, 6, 8, 155–67
  research, 2–4, 16, 23–7, 273–82, 305–10, 317
  and retention, 5–6, 24, 113–23, 125–35, 145–6, 156–60, 165–6, 217, 220, 305–7
  and social capital, 199–209
  and social justice, 17–19, 47, 162, 166, 169, 174–5, 179
  student learning through, 22–7
  and student server/served binary, 4, 53–63
  and student-centered learning, 19–20, 22–3
  sustaining momentum for, 311–18
  See also assessment; community colleges
Service-Learning in the Disciplines (series), 19
Shasta College, 4, 53, 57–63
Shiarella, Ann Harris, 280
Shirky, Clay, 289
Shulman, Lee, 306
Sigmon, Robert, 15
Sink, Elizabeth S., 230
Smith, M. Cecil, 267
Snead State Community College (SSCC), 8, 297, 299–304
Snyder-Duch, Jennifer, 261
social and cultural capital, 7, 54, 60, 127, 142–3, 150, 166, 199–209, 268
social justice, 17–19, 47, 162, 166, 169, 174–5, 179
soft skills, 7, 212–14, 216–22
St. John, Edward P., 108
Stachowski, Laura L., 215
Stage, Frances K., 97–8
Stanton, Timothy, 16
Stavrianopoulos, Katherine, 114

Steinberg, Kathryn, 25, 194
Stella and Charles Guttman Community College (CUNY), 8, 293–4
Stenson, Christine M., 26, 172
stereotyping, 26, 87, 128, 176, 291–2
storytelling, 55, 91–2
Strauss, Valerie, 289
Strumbos, Diana, 5, 95
student as customer/consumer, 21
student success movement, 42–4
students. *See* community college students
students of color, 40–1, 56–9, 69–72, 96–108, 113, 127, 203, 214–15, 265–6, 290–1, 300, 307
Sturm, Susan, 28–9
Swanson, Richard, 84

Tagg, John, 19
Taggart, Amanda, 3, 8–9, 23, 25, 159, 172–3, 258, 273
Tallahassee Community College (TCC), 7–8, 128, 246, 248–54
technocratic approach to education, 18, 20–1
Teranishi, Robert, 98
Terenzini, Patrick T., 22
Tinto, Vincent, 22, 119, 126–7
Touqueville, Alexis De, 299–300
Townsend, Barbara K., 143, 145
Townsend, Rebecca M., 7–8, 225
transfer to four-year institutions, 6, 19, 39, 47, 81, 108, 118, 139–51, 178–9, 249, 300
transformative learning, 20, 85
Traver, Amy E., 1, 4, 67
Truman, Harry, 39
Tucker, Mary L., 280

University of Chicago, 38

Vaknin, Lauren Weiner, 214
vocational education, 1, 13, 39, 67, 211, 214, 243, 249, 267. *See also* workforce development
Vogelgesang, Lori J., 26, 157
volunteerism, 26, 44–5, 72–4, 101, 103, 107, 161, 185, 191–2, 194, 205, 207–8, 249, 278, 301, 304, 312, 318
Vygotsky, Lev, 170

Walton, Gregory, 128
Warchal, Judith, 187
Warren, Jami L., 158
Waterman, Alan, 282
Webster, Noah, 193
Wells, Ryan S., 97–8
Westheimer, Joel, 20, 188
Wiewel, Wim, 289
William Rainey Harper College, 246
Williams, Matthew J., 194
Wilson, Kristin B., 145
Wittman, Amanda, 5, 81
Wood, J. Luke, 99
workforce development, 28, 39, 47, 88, 100, 166, 172, 211–22, 257
working students, 8, 41, 58, 188, 259, 264–5, 267–9

written communication, 69–77, 89, 113–23, 122, 129, 133–4, 163, 212, 214, 216–17, 294, 312–14. *See also* communication
Wylie, Heather B., 4, 53

Ye, Feifei, 172
Yee, Jennifer A., 157
Yeh, Theresa Ling, 62, 127–8, 158, 268
Yorio, Patrick L., 172
York, Travis, 8, 257, 268
Younkin, William F., 24

Zajonc, Arthur, 298
Zhang, Wenquan, 67
Zlotkowski, Edward, 18–19
Zukin, Cliff, 188

GPSR Compliance
The European Union's (EU) General Product Safety Regulation (GPSR) is a set of rules that requires consumer products to be safe and our obligations to ensure this.

If you have any concerns about our products, you can contact us on

ProductSafety@springernature.com

In case Publisher is established outside the EU, the EU authorized representative is:

Springer Nature Customer Service Center GmbH
Europaplatz 3
69115 Heidelberg, Germany

www.ingramcontent.com/pod-product-compliance
Lightning Source LLC
LaVergne TN
LVHW051917060526
838200LV00004B/192